Hurricane
Squadron Ace

Hurricane Squadron Ace

The Story of Battle of Britain Ace

Air Commodore Peter 'Pete' Brothers, CBE, DSO, DFC and Bar

Nick Thomas

Pen & Sword
AVIATION

First published in Great Britain in 2014 by
Pen & Sword Aviation
an imprint of
Pen & Sword Books Ltd
47 Church Street
Barnsley
South Yorkshire
S70 2AS

ISBN 978 1 78159 311 0

A CIP catalogue record for this book is available from the British Library

Typeset in Ehrhardt by
Mac Style Ltd, Bridlington, East Yorkshire
Printed and bound in the UK by CPI Group (UK) Ltd,
Croydon, CRO 4YY

Pen & Sword Books Ltd incorporates the imprints of Pen & Sword
Archaeology, Atlas, Aviation, Battleground, Discovery, Family History,
History, Maritime, Military, Naval, Politics, Railways, Select, Transport,
True Crime, and Fiction, Frontline Books, Leo Cooper, Praetorian Press,
Seaforth Publishing and Wharncliffe.

For a complete list of Pen & Sword titles please contact
PEN & SWORD BOOKS LIMITED
47 Church Street, Barnsley, South Yorkshire, S70 2AS, England
E-mail: enquiries@pen-and-sword.co.uk
Website: www.pen-and-sword.co.uk

Contents

Introduction

Peter Malam 'Pete' Brothers CBE, DSO, DFC and Bar

Fascinated with flying from a very early age, Pete Brothers gained his pilot's license at the age of seventeen, by which time he was already an accomplished pilot, highly proficient at aerobatics and fighter combat techniques.

In 1936 Brothers enlisted into the RAF and following his flying training was posted to No. 32 Squadron, then heavily involved in the development of the Fighter Control system. Re-equipped with Hawker Hurricanes a little after the Munich Crisis, the squadron was to remain at the forefront of Home Defence.

Commanding 'B' Flight, operating out of Biggin Hill, Brothers played a pivotal role in No. 32 Squadron's campaign. His first 'kills' came on 18 and 23 May 1940, while the squadron was using French airfields by day, returning to the 'Bump' at nightfall. Pete later related how his initial combat had taught him to have his guns calibrated to converge at half the recommended distance, which meant that he would have to get in close to the enemy. More combats and victories came in July when the Luftwaffe turned their attention to the Channel Convoys and mainland Britain.

The Battle of Britain was intense, demanding much from No. 32 Squadron's pilots. Pete later related as to how he was kept going on a mixture of caffeine and Benzedrine; the downside of which was that when he did sleep it was so deep that on one occasion he did not even hear an air raid which had left a line of craters just outside the mess.

Leading from the front and often flying three or four sorties a day, Brothers continued to notch up claims and was awarded a much deserved DFC, which recognized his abilities not only as a combat pilot and flight commander, but also as a highly capable tactician.

When No. 32 Squadron was finally rested in late August, only a handful of the pre-war pilots remained, and most of these had been shot down, made forced-landings or had taken to their parachute at least once.

Brothers could not be afforded any rest and was immediately sent to take command of a flight of No. 257 Squadron's Hurricanes following the loss of both flight commanders in a single operation. With 'Bob' Tuck, he helped keep the squadron in the thick of the combat at a crucial time, striking decisive blows against the Luftwaffe on 15 September (Brothers adding two more victories to his score) and against the *Regia Aeronautica Italiana* on 15 November 1940.

With two back-to-back tours of operations under his belt, Brothers was briefly 'rested', becoming an instructor at No. 55 OTU. Promoted to Squadron Leader,

Brothers formed and led No. 457 (RAAF) Squadron, blooding them on Circuses, Ramrods and Rodeos over enemy occupied Europe, before their withdrawal to defend Northern Australia from the threat of Imperial Japan.

Taking over No. 602 Squadron from 'Paddy' Finucane, a hard act to follow, the charismatic Brothers quickly made his mark, demonstrating himself to be the equal of anyone in the air, whether it be leading a flight, squadron or wing. He led his squadron on four offensive sweeps during the ill-fated Dieppe Raid, once again demonstrating his supreme abilities as a tactician.

Marked down for one of the most demanding roles of any fighter pilot, Brothers was appointed as Wing Commander (Flying), Tangmere. Flying in the vapour trails of none other than his friend Group Captain Sir Douglas Robert Steuart Bader, CBE, DSO and Bar, DFC and Bar, FRAeS, DL, Pete excelled in the new role, even adding to his own personal tally. He was awarded a much deserved Bar to his DFC, gaining the admiration of his squadron commanders who included Squadron Leader Reginald Joseph Cowan 'Reg' Grant, DFC and Bar, DFM, and 'Johnnie' Johnson CB, CBE, DSO and two Bars, DFC and Bar, Légion d'Honneur (France), Officer of the Order of Leopold with Palms (Belgium), Legion of Merit (US), DFC (US), Air Medal (US).

There could be no rest for Brothers and following a taxing posting as Chief Flying Instructor at No. 52 OTU he was transferred to No. 61 OTU, before a brief spell directing operations at No. 10 Group.

Brothers' final combat role during the war was as Wing Commander (Flying) Culmhead Wing, making low-level strafes in support of the D-Day landings. Air-to-air combat became rare due to Fighter Command's dominance of the sky over Europe. Ground strikes were, however, every bit as dangerous, with pilots lost to ground fire and routinely flying at under 1,000ft over the combat zone, when there would be no opportunity to deploy a parachute if they got into trouble.

Brothers made his last claim, an Fw 190, on 7 August 1944. His role as a Wing Leader was rewarded with the award of the DSO, being credited with sixteen 'kills', one probably destroyed, one unconfirmed and three damaged.

Brothers' record was virtually unsurpassed. Having completed four tours, two as Wing Leader, he had flown 875 hours on operations and, despite a couple of forced-landings, never had to abandon an aircraft.

Following a brief spell in the Colonial Service, Brothers rejoined the RAF and commanded No. 57 Squadron during the Malayan Emergency, before attending Staff College and being taken on at the headquarters of Fighter Command, appointed as Wing Commander (Flying) Marham, flying the Valiant V-bomber. Further promotion took him to roles at the SHAPE headquarters in Paris. As Air Commodore, Brothers commanded the headquarters of the Military Air Traffic Operations, before being appointed as the RAF's Director of Public Relations during the height of the Cold War. Brothers' peacetime service was acknowledged when he was appointed as a Companion of the British Empire (CBE).

On retiring from the RAF, Brothers founded his own company, Peter Brothers Consultants.

Brothers became an advocate for former members of Fighter Command, in particular the men who won the Battle of Britain, many of whom had paid the ultimate price. Appointed deputy chairman of the Battle of Britain Association in 1993, he became chairman ten years later. These roles brought him into the company of Her Majesty the Queen Mother, and later with His Royal Highness Prince Charles, as Patrons of the Battle of Britain Fighter Association. But there was no side to Brothers and he was comfortable talking to anyone who had something sensible to say, no matter their status. He was always interested in what others were doing, or what their job entailed and chatted to all on an equal basis.

Brothers was a stalwart of the Battle of Britain Memorial Trust, campaigning for what became the Thames Embankment Monument and later he turned his attention to help save RAF Bentley Priory.

President of his local Air Crew Association in Hungerford, Berkshire, Brothers was also invited to act as patron of the Spitfire Association of Australia, a reflection of the esteem in which a 'Pom' was held by the Aussies, in remembrance of his service commanding No. 457 Squadron.

Brothers was described by friend and fellow aviator, Wing Commander Percy Belgrave 'Laddie' Lucas, CBE, DSO and Bar, DFC (DFC, *London Gazette*, 17 July 1942; DSO, *London Gazette*, 14 January 1944; Bar to the DSO, *London Gazette*, 2 October 1945; CBE 1981), as 'one of those distinctive Fighter Command characters, full of bonhomie, humour and decorations, who made light of the serious things, no matter what his innermost thoughts.'

Thus was the career of a dedicated, patriotic and charismatic officer. Brothers' courage and ability are a matter of record. What records can never reveal is the man himself; above all, family man, loving father, and the type of man whom, once met, became a friend. Those who knew him universally agreed how he could always lift the spirits of those around him with his charm and ready wit. As a friend he was fiercely loyal. He was a man with a zest for life and camaraderie, with a mischievous twinkle in his eye, whose chuckle would presage some prank or story, of which he had many.

In spite of his predilection to storytelling, his innate modesty prevented him from telling war stories unless they were humorous, or were against himself. His modesty is the most likely reason why his family could never persuade him to write his memoirs. His modesty, and the fact that he found many of the memories of lost friends too painful to revisit. On his own achievements he was always reticent. The telling of Pete's story is long overdue.

In life he had few equals, in death he has become an aviation legend.

Pete Brothers died on 18 December 2008.

Acknowledgements

I am very much indebted to Pete's daughters, Wendy Wallington and Hilary Cairns, for their interest and support throughout the writing of the late Air Commodore's biography. They have supplied not only background information but went to great effort to transcribe details from both Pete's civilian and RAF logbooks.

Thanks to Wendy and Hilary's kindness in making their late father's photographic archive available, few photographs have had to be sourced elsewhere, although a small number have been drawn from the author's collection.

Reference has been made to correspondence and informal interviews with the late Air Commodore, while further details have been drawn from correspondence with other Battle of Britain pilots including: Wing Commander D. H. Grice, MBE, DFC; Wing Commander T. F. Neil, DFC and Bar, AFC; Squadron Leader T. G. Pickering, AE and Wing Commander J. Rose, CMG, MBE, DFC.

The Operational Record Books and Combat Reports for all of the squadrons mentioned have been referred to on microfilm at the Public Record Office, Kew. Meanwhile, casualty details have been drawn from the Commonwealth War Grave's official web site.

Chapter 1

Born to Fly

Peter Malam 'Pete' Brothers was born at Prestwich, Lancashire, on 30 September 1917, the son of John Malam Brothers and his wife Maud. The younger of two children, Brothers lost his sister, Iris Elaine Brothers (born 31 March 1915), to meningitis ten days shy of his fifth birthday. Consequently, Brothers had few first-hand memories of his sibling. His parents treasured two large colour photographs of Iris, which hung in 'Westfield', their family home in Prestwich Park, which they shared with Pete's eccentric Aunty Matty, Maud's sister, who was to prove a source of many stories.

Brothers was educated at North Manchester School, a part of Manchester Grammar School, and despite never having been an enthusiastic pupil, he earned a good school's certificate, which would ordinarily have been the gateway to a white-collar job.

For the young Brothers there was, however, the opportunity to join the family business, Brothers Chemical Company Ltd. Their factory was situated in Trafford Park, regarded by many as the world's first industrial estate. By this date John, ably assisted by his brother, Thomas Edward Brothers, had taken over the mantle from their father, William. The company manufactured, among other things, precipitate of chalk, principally used in toothpaste and to slow the burning time of cigarettes. Their customers included the Players Cigarette Company, manufacturers of Navy Cut, No. 6, John Player Special and Gold Leaf. The Brothers Chemical Company Ltd. was bombed out in 1940 during the Blitz. With Pete needed in the RAF and his father not well enough to begin from scratch, the company ceased trading.

Brothers recalled that, 'The factory also produced bicarbonate of soda, which was a raising agent. We sold to people like Peek Frean the biscuit company, manufacturers of Garibaldi and Bourbon biscuits.'

The chemical processes used in the factory and research laboratory made them potentially dangerous places to work. Brothers explained that at around the time of his birth there had been an accident resulting in an explosion. Brothers' father was caught in the blast, 'It involved hydrochloric acid, some of which got in his eyes. He lost the sight in one and couldn't see a lot out of the other.'

As a result of his injuries Brothers' father had to use special binocular attachments designed by the German company Zeiss, which were fitted to his spectacles. When it came to more complex operations such as driving, these aids were insufficient, 'Father had a big lens which came down from the roof of the car. He could just about make out wider, horizontal light sources like another car or a building, but anything thin, like traffic lights or someone walking on foot, he just couldn't see them.'

This contraption helped him to keep driving for a while, but eventually Brothers' father was called for an eye test, which he inevitably failed. After this Brothers' mother chauffeured him about.

While it was desirable for the youngster to enter the family firm and maybe one day take over the helm, Brothers' father was aware that his real interest lay elsewhere, 'Since I was about five or six I had been mad about flying. To me train sets were boring, they just went backwards and forwards. I did nothing but play with model airplanes and, like many boys of my age, collected related news cuttings and [cigarette] cards.

'I used to have both British and enemy airplanes, and would imagine myself the pilot of one, getting onto the tail of the other, pretending to shoot it down in flames.'

Brothers' heroes were men such as Major Edward 'Mick' Mannock, VC, DSO and two Bars, MC and Bar, and Major John Thomas Byford McCudden, VC, DSO and Bar, MC and Bar, MM. 'I'd read all of the Biggles books: *The Camels Are Coming* [1932], *The Cruise of the Condor* [1933], *Biggles of the Camel Squadron* [1934] and *Biggles Flies Again* [1934]. I was absolutely enchanted by it. It was the only way to live.'

Perhaps half hoping that he would get the flying bug out of his system, or maybe pursue it as a hobby, John Brothers gave his son lessons as a sixteenth birthday present. And so the excited youngster was driven to the nearby Lancashire Aero Club, where he had his first close up view of the aircraft that had for so long been the object of his dreams.

The club was formed at Alexandra Park Aerodrome, just outside Manchester City Centre in around 1924 and was one of the first of its kind in the country. On the invitation of the Avro Aircraft Company, the club had moved to Woodford Aerodrome in the following year. It was here that Brothers made his first flight on 14 October 1933, when, under instruction from C.H. Wilson, he took off in G-EBQL, an Avro 594 Avian IIIA (powered by the Cirrus Mk III). Pete's civilian pilot's logbook recorded a twenty-five minute hop before landing back at the aerodrome.

Brothers was hooked and persuaded his parents to allow him to become a member and to take regular lessons, 'I learnt on Avro Avians and Cadets at Woodford.'

A 'natural' pilot, Brothers made steady progress and was soon highly proficient at the controls. On 4 November 1933, with 6 hours and 20 minutes on dual instruction, the time came when he was deemed ready to fly solo.

Sitting for the first time alone in his cockpit, Brothers opened the throttle, rapidly taking to the air, before climbing away and circling to the left. He remembered to widen the circuit a bit to allow for the shallower gliding angle, before throttling back, watching the speed, gliding towards touch down. Now at 200ft, he constantly checked his altitude; 100ft ... 75ft ... 50ft ... 10ft ... Levelling out and holding off, he gently eased back on the stick a second or two before feeling the wheels touch down. He was down safe.

Brothers had successfully cleared the first major hurdle and could continue his lessons with a growing confidence. Meanwhile, his father was already coming around to the idea that Brothers might make it as a pilot, 'After I had gone solo, I used to take my father flying.'

Shortly after his first solo his instructor put him into a competition, the aim of which was to test pilots agility by bursting balloons in flight with their propeller. Pete won and was always very proud of the tankard he was given as a prize.

The months that followed saw Brothers fly a number of different types of aircraft, including the Avro Cadet 7-cylinder, Avro 616 Avian IVM (powered by the Genet Major) and the Desoutter I (powered by the Cirrus Hermes II). He was, however, initially prevented from gaining his Civil Pilot's 'A' Licence due to the government unsportingly raising the threshold from sixteen to seventeen.

Meanwhile, Brothers studied the all-embracing Air Regulations, which had to be learnt from cover to cover if he was to pass the written exam, without which he would not be able to qualify for his licence.

In order to keep Brothers' interest going whilst waiting to take his test, one of his instructors, George Yuill, taught him advanced aerobatics. George and his wife Molly became lifelong family friends. Brothers would later credit Yuill's tutoring with saving his life during his early combats, 'I was taught some tricks that the Air Force never dreamed up. My instructor, George Yuill, was a Sopwith Camel pilot from the First World War ...'

Brothers' logbook reveals that another of his early instructors was V. H. 'Val' Baker, one half of the Martin Baker Company, which later developed a number of aviation products, most notably ejection seats.

The trainers were all open cockpit aircraft, which often meant enduring temperatures ranging from -20°F to -40°F when flying at higher altitudes, 'Often when we landed the oil had to be drained and heated to prevent it from solidifying.'

Finally, having attained his seventeenth birthday, Brothers was able to put in for his flying test, which he duly passed, receiving his Aviator's Certificate, Private Pilot's Licence No. 7189, dated 22 October 1934, granted by the Federation Aeronautique Internationale and issued by The Royal Aero Club.

With his pilot's licence safely under his belt, Brothers was still too young to apply for a short service commission in the RAF and took the opportunity to spend part of the spring of 1935 on the Continent. This was a time when political tensions were beginning to build in Europe due to the rise of the Nazi Party. Brothers took up the story, 'We had business in Germany, but Adolf Hitler's government put a stop to payments going overseas; we could only spend the money within the country's borders. My father decided that I should go over there and spend time with a Nuremburg family and their three sons.'

Over the previous few years the political situation in Germany had changed for the worse. The National Socialist German Worker's Party (NSDP) had risen from almost total obscurity and by January 1933 was the majority party in the German Parliament. But the Nazi Party's extreme policies meant that Hitler was unable to form a coalition. He immediately called a second General Election, on the eve of which the Reichstag, the home of Germany's Parliament, was destroyed by a fire supposedly started by a Dutchman called Marinus van der Lubbe, a Communist sympathizer. In reality the fire was part of a Nazi plot to implicate the Communist Party. Hitler ordered a raid on the Communist Party headquarters, his henchmen planting documents implicating its leaders in a coup. On the back of a wave of nationalism, Hitler gained sufficient seats in the second election. Consequently, the elderly Field Marshal Paul von Hindenburgh, the President of the Weimar Republic, was unable to prevent Hitler's appointment as Reich Chancellor. Meanwhile, on 7 March, the demilitarized zone of the Rhineland was reoccupied and twenty-one days later Hitler created a one party state – the 'Third Reich' had been born.

The leaders of the NSDP believed that the first step in the rise of the German-speaking people was the indoctrination of the masses. This would either be through exploiting patriotism and the fears of a defeated nation, or by brute force, 'When you went to the cinema there were news reels in the middle showing Germans marching up and down, and the "Seig Heil!" and all that.'

Despite these worrying developments it was still considered safe to travel, but when Brothers arrived in Germany he found that the three children of his host family were all involved in the national youth movements. Brothers recalled that Harald, the oldest, was, 'A big, burly chap. At 6 am you'd hear him outside in the street, marching along in his black [Waffen SS] uniform leading a bunch of chaps with shovels on their shoulders for rifles.'

The second eldest son, Kurt, was the same age as Brothers. Like Brothers, he had a passion for flying and it soon became apparent that Kurt was learning to fly powered aircraft; this at a time when, under the terms of the Treaty of Versailles, Germany was restricted to military glider schools and civil aircraft, 'As a pilot myself, I knew that Kurt did more than fly gliders. He would let things slip or would give me a knowing look when I was talking about my own experiences of pilot training.'

When pressed, Kurt would, of course, deny the existence of the Luftwaffe, saying, 'Oh yes, we haven't got an air force; ha ha!'

Brothers' suspicions were well founded and he later discovered that on completion of his pilot's training course Kurt went on to fly bombers, 'He died while flying on a raid over the Russian Front.'

At this time – officially – Germany had only a small air force called the Deutscher Luftsportverband (German Air Sports Union), also known as the DLV. The fliers were headed by the Great War fighter ace, Ernst Udet. The new Luftwaffe only officially came into being on 9 March 1935, and was commanded by Herman Goering, Hitler's great ally, and could boast a strength of over 1,875 aircraft and 20,000 officers and men, with conscription following a week later, accelerating its growth further.

The youngest of the siblings was Walther who was an imposing 6ft 8in, 'I remember asking him what he would do when the war came. He replied that he was going to be on U-boats and I recall that I said something about him banging his head a lot.'

Even as the guest of a German family, Brothers nevertheless found himself under pressure to acknowledge the Nazi regime. One incident occurred when he witnessed a group of uniformed youths on the march, 'As the soldiers paraded past, everyone seemed overtaken by a misguided loyalty toward Hitler and the Nazi Party, giving a highly vocal "Seig Heil!" and the outstretched arm salute.'

Amid the heavy rhythmic stomping of jackboots and the shouts of allegiance, Brothers suddenly became aware that he was being glared at. Standing out from the crowd in his flannels and a blazer, and with his hands firmly in his pockets, he had attracted the unwanted attention of two SS officers armed with Lugers and their 'ceremonial' daggers, 'They stood over me, rocking back on their heels, thumbs dug into their belts in a macho pose. I felt obliged to make the salute, otherwise I would have been beaten up by these thugs.'

Despite this unpleasant encounter, Brothers got on well with the family and Walther later travelled to England with him as a part of the exchange visit, staying for a fortnight at 'Westfield'. Not long afterwards events in Germany took a further ominous twist when the Nuremberg Laws released waves of pure hatred and heralded the open persecution of the Jews.

On 22 May 1935, in response to the advent of Germany's remilitarization, the British Government voted to treble the number of front-line military aircraft available to defend UK soil. This added up to an increase of 1,500 aircraft of all types, with the number of Home Defence squadrons being increased from fifty-two to seventy-five. The government's declared aim was to bring the RAF's total first-line strength to 128 squadrons within five years.

This rapid increase amongst all ranks, including pilots, meant a new approach to the process of pilot training. Previously, new pilots were given five months instruction on a basic aircraft before converting to an advanced type. Under the new syllabus, initial training was at a civilian run Elementary & Reserve Flying Training School (E&RFTS).

Brothers' time in Germany only stiffened his resolve to join the RAF. In reply to his exploratory note, Brothers received an 'enormous and rather complicated application form, along with a covering letter.' With the help of his parents, Brothers completed the paperwork, which he duly returned, 'My mother didn't object to my trying to join the Royal Air Force, because she reckoned I was a weakling boy who'd never pass the medical.' At length, with his headmaster's reference scrutinized, Brothers was invited to attend an Air Ministry selection board at Adastral House, Kingsway, London.

Reporting at the appointed hour, Brothers was directed to the third floor, Room 21. Here he underwent an initial medical, checking for any frailties that would have automatically precluded selection for pilot training.

The second stage of the process involved an interview board consisting of five inquisitors in civilian dress. Their job was to delve into Brothers' 'history', asking a number of direct and intimidating questions, searching for any flaws in his application, while at the same time assessing his character.

All seemed to go well and, after an anxious few weeks waiting on news, Brothers learned of his acceptance as a candidate for a short service commission in the General Duties Branch of the RAF – his journey had begun.

Chapter 2

The Road to War

Brothers reported for the two month long *ab initio* flying course at No. 4 E&RFTS, Brough, Hull, on 27 January 1936, 'My father's birthday – very appropriate!' Later the same day he made his first flight, under instruction from Flying Officer McNeill, in a Blackburn B2 (G-ACER). Brothers' logbook recorded the flight, which lasted twenty minutes. Against the entry he wrote the words 'local flying' and 'passenger flying'.

Brothers made two further flights in the side-by-side trainer on 30 January. These involved climbs, gliding and gentle turns, and quickly progressed to climbing turns. With around 110 flying hours as a civilian pilot Brothers was already an accomplished flier by any standard, '... they realized that I could fly already and could do aerobatics ...'

By 4 February Brothers had already moved on to practicing advanced forced landings, slow rolls and inverted flying, and was deemed ready to fly solo, which he did, staging not the usual simple circuit and landing, but ten minutes of authorized steep turns and spins.

Three weeks into the course and Brothers had completed 45 minutes on dual, 2 hours 5 minutes solo. As pilot, Brothers made two higher altitude flights on 11 and 12 February, reaching 10,000ft, without any adverse effects. Two days later, however, he experienced his first bit of bad luck when strong winds caused him to take out a wooden fence on landing. No blame was attached to Brothers and his training continued apace.

Brothers' logbook records that on 25 February he had a fifteen minute test flight at RAF Hendon, with No. 24 Squadron's Flight Lieutenant Hargroves. The next assessment came on the 7 March with Chief Flying Instructor, Flight Lieutenant Arthur Loton (Later Wing Commander A.G. Loton, AFC, *London Gazette*, 7 January 1938), when he performed loops, rolls, spins and stall turns. A further air test came a little under a fortnight later, when he flew in the company of Flight Lieutenant Rowe.

During his time at Brough, Brothers officially graduated to advanced forced landings, steep turns, spins, loops, vertical turns and various other aerobatics. Meanwhile, he had demonstrated his aptitude at navigation, with cross-country and instrument flying, as well as the usual circuits and landings.

By the time Brothers passed out of his course on 22 March, he had completed 15 hours 20 minutes dual and 25 hours 40 minutes solo, with a further 5 hours on instrument flying. His logbook was endorsed with an overall assessment of his proficiency as a pilot, which was noted as 'above average' with 'no areas of flying that gave concern'. But officially he remained, in the eyes of the RAF, a civilian 'pupil pilot' in uniform and on probation.

On the following day, however, Brothers was granted a short-service commission (*London Gazette*, 7 April 1936). This could be extended by mutual agreement for a further five years to a medium-service commission, or even converted to a permanent commission. At the end of his service he would be placed on the Reserve list, being liable to immediate call-up in the event of war, 'As a pilot officer, I earned the then princely sum of fourteen shillings a day, minus mess bills of six shillings, which covered food, laundry, accommodation and the provision of a batman – this excluded bar bills!'

Promotion to the rank of flying officer usually came after eighteen months service, while further advancement depended on passing promotion exams; a practice which was suspended in wartime.

Having passed through E&RFTS, Brothers began the mandatory two weeks disciplinary training, 'I reported to Uxbridge and was sent off to get fitted with a uniform and taught to march.'

Brothers was unimpressed at the RAF's insistence on its pilots learning basic drill, including 'square-bashing', 'I was an acting pilot officer, on probation, marching up and down with a rifle.'

Brothers recalled that he was not always the model student, his indiscipline having to be addressed by his warrant officer instructor, 'Will you stop talking Mr Brothers, Sir, when you are marching!'

During the many lectures, and on the drill ground, Brothers' thoughts were firmly fixed on his goal, 'I didn't join the Air Force to carry bloody rifles around; I joined to fly! What are we doing here wasting our time?'

Much as Brothers might have felt that his time at Uxbridge was an unnecessary diversion, he remembered the impact of an address by the Great War ace, Squadron Leader James Ira Thomas 'Taffy' Jones, DSO, MC, DFC and Bar, MM. Despite his thirty-seven victories and string of awards, the Welshman suffered from nerves and spoke with a stutter, 'There's g-g-g-g-going to be a f-f-f-f-f****ing war and you ch-ch-ch-chaps are going to be in it. Never f-f-f-f-forget that when you get into your f-f-f-f-first combat, you will find you're f-f-f-f****ing f-f-f-frightened! And never forget that the ch-ch-ch-chap in the other c-c-c-cockpit is twice as f-f-f-f****ing frightened as you!'

It was with fondness that Brothers recalled, 'Taffy later became a Group Captain and was station commander up in Cheshire somewhere on a Spitfire conversion unit [No. 57 OTU at Hawarden in 1941]. He decided he'd fly a Spitfire ... he took off and pulled the wheels up too soon and slid along his belly halfway down the runway. He got out and said, "This f-f-f-f****ing machine is b-b-b-broken! Get me another one!" Dear old Taffy.'

On 4 April, Brothers was posted to RAF Thornaby-on-Tees as a part of No. 9 Flying Training School's first intake. Here he was to undergo a six-month course of intermediate and advanced flying training. On arrival each pupil was handed twenty-plus textbooks covering navigation, meteorology and aircraft armament, along with the practical workings of the aero-engine and the cockpit controls, 'There were written exams all along the way, and we were required to achieve an aggregate of sixty per cent for a pass.'

There was a reissue of flying kit, with a new flying helmet, gauntlets, overalls and a Sidcot flying suit and flying boots, and, perhaps most importantly of all, a parachute.

Brothers' initial flights were on Bristol Bulldogs, which he described as, 'great big powerful monsters by comparison with what you were used to.'

While at Thornaby, Brothers saw an announcement posted on the Duty Board: 'Flying Officer Grandy has been promoted to flight lieutenant and awarded a permanent commission in the air force.' Brothers attended a party in the mess marking the occasion, 'I'd never had a glass of beer [before] and I got well and truly pie-eyed.' Grandy would later become Marshal of the Royal Air Force and Brothers would often tease him for introducing him to alcohol.

Not unnaturally, Pete sailed through the flying practical, suitably impressing the visiting Central Flying School instructor and qualifying for his Certificate 'B' Licence on 26 June 1936. Then in mid-July, Brothers heard the news that he was most waiting for, he had been selected for fighter-pilot training and transferred onto flying the Gloster Gauntlet. This was at a time when many operational squadrons were still only equipped with the Bristol Bulldog, as Pete later explained, 'They were saying, "We're the operational squadron and yet these chaps have got the new ones!" Then that was changed. Those [training units] that had Gauntlets lost them pretty smartly and the squadrons got them.'

Returning from a brief period of leave, Brothers and his fellow pupils began the next phase of their course, which included cross-country, blind flying, cloud and formation flying, night flying, altitude tests, gunnery practice, battle manoeuvres, interceptions and target practice. While not in the air, Brothers continued his studies, striving to maintain a good pass rate.

All fighter pilots had to demonstrate proficiency at air-to-ground firing before being allowed to fire live rounds at a drogue: 'Air-to-air firing involved firing at a drogue towed through the sky at a steady and constant speed and was designed to give the pilots their first experience of firing at a moving target and was an introduction to the rudiments of deflection firing.'

By the time Brothers passed out of Thornaby he had completed 39 hours 40 mins dual and 79 hours and 50 minutes solo flying on the Hawker Hart, Audax, Tutor and Gauntlet. Much to his delight, he was assessed as having an 'above average' rating on Gauntlets, then the fastest fighter in service with the RAF.

At the end of the course, Pete Brothers was back drilling on the parade ground in preparation for the all-important passing out ceremony.

On 11 October 1936, Pilot Officer Brothers was posted to No. 32 Squadron, recently re-equipped with the Gloster Gauntlet II and flying out of Biggin Hill. Sitting on a plateau in the rolling Kentish hills and affectionately known as 'Biggin on the Bump', the station had, since January 1933, been commanded by Wing Commander E.O. Grenfell, MC, DFC, AFC, a First World War ace with eight 'kills'. The airfield was slightly higher than its neighbours and often remained open when they were declared 'fogbound'.

The station had purpose-built barrack blocks and married quarters, along with officer's and NCO's messes, while there were even squash and tennis courts. Brothers' first impressions were all good, 'It was a nice little airfield, well known for its *joie de vivre* – when not flying we pilots enjoyed a "jolly" in the mess bar or the White Hart [at Brasted], and visits to the London night clubs. Among our favourite haunts were the Shepherd's pub [in Shepherd's Market], or the Bag of Nails. If we had a pound for the entrance fee, then it was the Four Hundred.'

In the pre-war years dining-in nights were held every week. These were compulsory and allowed junior NCOs to mix with their seniors, also bringing the officers who lived in the married quarters into the fold.

At Biggin Hill, meals in the officer's mess ranked with those served in some of the finest London restaurants. They consisted of four or five courses; the first of either mock turtle or brown Windsor soup was followed by a fish dish. The main course was usually a roast dish, and then came pudding and, at dinner, a savoury, while at lunch, cheese. There was a strict dress code. The officers wore black ties and blue waistcoats, while the mess stewards were equally resplendent in their white jackets and gloves.

With dinner over, fruit bowls were introduced to the table, while those gathered stood to drink the Loyal Toast. Drinks were brought to the officer's table and were signed for and added to the mess bill, the bar was not opened until later. Meanwhile, the officers would retire to the anteroom where, 'suitably jollified by alcohol', they would push the furniture to the edge of the room and the traditional mess games began, 'we really used to amuse ourselves. Biggin was the finest flying club in the world; it really was.'

Thursdays were guest nights, when white ties and No. 1 mess dress were worn, and in the style of the best restaurants of the day, the station band played throughout the meal.

In many ways the services were still an extension of public schools; everyone knew their place, 'When you arrived on the squadron, you were the new boy; the bog rat, just a pilot officer, lowest of the low. None of the more senior officers spoke to you, other than to tell you to press the bell to summon a waiter to get them a drink, or some similar trivial reason.'

The squadron's 'A' Flight was composed of Red and Yellow Sections, while Blue and Green Sections made up 'B' Flight. All newly qualified pilots were initially assigned to the Training Flight, only being permitted to take part in squadron manoeuvres once they were deemed ready. Naturally, Brothers was the first of the new influx to make the transition.

Among the replacement pilots with Brothers were 'Little' Guy Harris and 'Humph' Russell, with whom he had trained at No. 9 FTS, 'The three of us went to the same squadron. So we could talk to each other.'

Brothers recalled the pattern of daily life during those pre-war years, 'You were on parade at 0800 hours, colour hoisting; inspection of the chaps by the station commander and you marched off to your hangar.'

With the formalities of the morning parade over the pilots made their way to their duties, 'you went to the pilot's room and had a cup of coffee and then at 1000 hours the flight commander told you to go off and do a reconnaissance of your sector and for us that was Kent and Sussex.

'The pilots were given a map and sent off on navigation exercises and instructed, "You have got to find a church at this map reference and draw a picture of it on your knee pad" … or you'd be doing formation practice.'

While Brothers was still undergoing training the RAF's Home Defence Force had begun a major reorganization. On 14 July 1936 it was reformed into four commands: Bomber, Fighter, Coastal and Training. Fighter Command, whose headquarters were at Bentley Priory, Stanmore, was under Air Chief Marshal Sir Hugh Caswell Tremenheere 'Stuffy' Dowding (later 1st Baron Dowding, GCB, GCVO, CMG), and was divided into a number of groups, each protecting the airspace over a different part of the UK. No.10 Group covered south-west England and only became operational in July 1940, No. 11 Group controlled south-east England and London, No. 12 Group defended the industrial Midlands and East Anglia, while No. 13 Group covered the North of England and Scotland.

Biggin Hill was a part of No. 11 Group, whose headquarters was Hillingdon House, RAF Uxbridge. Here, the Group Operations Room was in an underground bunker. Commands were passed to the Group's Sector Stations, each of which was in charge of several airfields and their fighter squadrons. The Sector airfields were: RAF Tangmere (A Sector), RAF Kenley (B Sector), RAF Biggin Hill (C Sector), RAF Hornchurch (D Sector), RAF North Weald (E Sector), RAF Debden (F Sector), RAF Middle Wallop (Y Sector) and RAF Northolt (Z Sector).

When Brothers arrived, No. 32 Squadron was still participating in experimental air operations, as Pete put it, 'doing practice interceptions on civil aircraft.'

Throughout 1936 the Air Ministry's establishment at the Bawdsey Research Station near Felixstowe, Suffolk, was experimenting with radar equipment. No. 32 Squadron's role was in the refining of the detection and interception systems, including those identifying the plots of 'friendly' aircraft using direction-finding apparatus. It was important for the controllers to know where 'friendly' aircraft were located if they were to direct them from the ground to intercept enemy formations. This was achieved by the use of a transponder, which automatically replied to 'interrogation' from the ground with an identification signal. This system was later known as Identification Friend or Foe (IFF): 'Three of you would be launched off. I was the junior so I carried the stopwatch and every two minutes I gave a fifteen second radio transmission.'

This was picked up by a series of monitoring stations, 'Once they had your signal they knew your direction, using the plots from any two monitoring stations gave your position.'

The routine was well rehearsed: 'Radar would plot incoming aircraft to Croydon, for example, and we'd go off to intercept them somewhere over the Channel or East Kent.'

The station commander, acting as controller, gave a vector (or course) on which to steer, 'and off you went. We'd just fly past and report how close we'd been and when we first sighted them.'

The controller would follow visual reports on the target's position against those of the fighter. At the moment his own data indicated that the fighters should have made a successful interception, he gave the command 'Fire!' upon which the lead fighter dropped a flare. Ground observations recorded the relative distances between hunter and prey at that particular moment in time.

The early days of using the system could be frustrating, but were not without their amusing moments, especially when the controller accidentally left his microphone open as he followed the plot, which had to be updated every few minutes: 'Then you'd hear him over the radio, saying, "Vector: How the hell can I see the blackboard with your fat bottom in the way?"'

A new series of experiments began in December 1937. These included the 'interception' of RAF Ansons and foreign airliners. It was important that the pilots of the latter didn't become suspicious of the encounters: 'We weren't allowed to fly close to them [the airliners]. We had to fly straight past and pretend we just happened to be in the air at the same time. But as early as 1937, we were "intercepting" KLM and Lufthansa airliners.'

The 'targets' frequently began their descent soon after crossing the coast, making it difficult for the Canewdon Chain radar station, near Biggin Hill, to maintain a fix. This, and the plots of aircraft not involved in the experiments, led to fifteen failures out of twenty-nine attempts. On 31 March 1938, however, Sir Henry Tizard, Chairman of the Aeronautical Research Committee, wrote to Sir Wilfred Freeman, Air Member for Research and Development (later Air Chief Marshal Sir Wilfred Rhodes Freeman, 1st Baronet, GCB, DSO, MC.) regarding one of these experiments, conducted during a lull in general flying activity. An Avro Anson was plotted making an approach from the Belgium coast: 'It was detected with great regularity and accuracy by Dover and was intercepted by Biggin Hill right on the coast. The whole experiment was very satisfactory, particularly, as although it was a fine day, there were a good many clouds about and I should not have thought it was a very easy day as far as visibility was concerned.'

As a result of taking part in these experimental interceptions Biggin Hill was, as Brothers explained, 'the first station to have an Operations Room'. In the early developmental days, the equipment and plotting methods remained fairly rudimentary: 'In those days, all the plotting in the Operations Room was done in chalk on a blackboard.'

While the use of a blackboard was low tech for such a crucial system upon which the nation's defence depended, it was used successfully under wartime conditions. When the Biggin Hill Operations Room was hit, it was able to transfer its operations, reverting to the pre-war methods.

Brothers explained that each of the squadron's pilots spent time chalking-up the 'enemy', something which gave them a greater insight when called into action, 'When we weren't flying, we acted as plotters in the Operations Room, so we watched the system develop, which meant that we understood more fully what the controllers were doing.'

It was during these flights that new code words were created, which became a part of the fighter pilot's vocabulary, including 'angels' for altitude, 'orbit' for circling while searching out the enemy, or 'bandits, 'tally-ho!' was used for attack, and 'pancake' was used as the order to land.

A series of radar masts along the south and east coasts formed what was known as Home Chain Low. Information from the radar stations (which could only look out to sea) was relayed to Headquarters Fighter Command's Filter and Operations Room, along with details of visual sightings from shipping and then from Observer Corps posts (once the 'enemy' was over land). Updated every five minutes, the strength, speed, altitude, location and direction of each enemy raid was plotted on the operation room table. The counters were colour-coded in synchrony with the coloured zones on the Sector Station clock. If the plots were old, a shout would go up, 'Three colours of the table!'

It was intended that as the raid developed, HQ Fighter Command, Stanmore, would forward details to the appropriate Group Headquarters where the state of operational readiness of each squadron was displayed. The Group Controller would feed details down to their Sector Stations. The Sector Controllers in turn scrambled the appropriate fighter response. It was not possible to scramble overwhelming numbers into the air for fear of missing the raiders, or leaving the way clear for the enemy once the fighters landed to rearm and refuel at the same time.

A Red Letter Day for the squadron had come on 19 January 1937, when, following His Majesty King George VI's approval of their Crest, a 'Hunting Horn, stringed', with the motto, 'ADESTE COMITES' (Rally round, comrades), it was formerly presented to the squadron by Air Vice-Marshal F.L. Gossage, DSO, MC, acting AOC in Chief, Fighter Command: 'We wasted no time in getting the crest painted onto the tails of our Gauntlets.' Eight days later Brothers reached a personal landmark when his commission was confirmed (*London Gazette*, 20 February 1937).

Changes were on the horizon, when on 22 March, as a part of the expansion of Home Defence, the squadron lost 'B' Flight, which became the nucleus of the newly reformed No. 79 Squadron, also flying the Gloster Gauntlet II and based at Biggin Hill; the two squadrons continued to have close links, sharing both pilots and ground crews well into 1940. The inter-squadron rivalry, however, was keen, as Brothers later recalled, 'We decided we'd have a contest to see who could do the shortest landing. We had to pack it up when some chap hit the hedge and turned his aircraft over and smashed it up.'

On 12 April, Squadron Leader A.W.B. McDonald, who had been detached to help form No. 79 Squadron, returned to command No. 32 Squadron upon which, 'Our former CO, Wing Commander G.T. Richardson, assumed command of No. 97 (B) Squadron on promotion.'

On Empire Air Day, 24 May 1937, an audience of 20,000 gathered at Biggin Hill to enjoy the annual airshow. Nos. 32 and 79 Squadrons took part in a Wing Formation. This preceded team competitions, both units fighting hard for superiority in a number of challenges, including the battle-climb. 'As a sideshow, spectators were able to pay sixpence to speak to us at 5,000ft. There was a set menu of aerobatic manoeuvres and they could make a request and we'd put our Gauntlets through the manoeuvre you saw.'

More public relations work followed on 26 June, when the squadron took part in the 'Mass Flight', of twenty-five squadrons as a part of the eighteenth and final RAF Display at Hendon.

July saw a fortnight of Combined Operation and Coast Defence exercises, while between 9 and 12 August, nineteen squadrons took part in the annual Home Defence exercise. It was officially reported that, 'most day and night raiders were intercepted and attacked'. Analysis of the exercise, however, demonstrated that the control and display system still lacked the speed and precision to provide effective interceptions; there was a fine line between success and failure.

In late September and early October, the squadron's pilots gained further gunnery practice in readiness for the Sir Philip Sassoon Flight Attack Competition, which was held on 7 October. Brothers' logbook recorded that the squadron came a creditable second.

There were further changes when, on 15 January 1938, Squadron Leader R. Pyne, DFC, arrived at Biggin Hill as supernumerary squadron leader. He assumed command nine days later, on Squadron Leader McDonald's posting to RAF Staff College.

Meanwhile, on the international scene, on 15 March, Hitler's troops marched into Austria, which was absorbed into the Reich. This marked a further increase in the pace of squadron training. The Empire Day flying demonstrations of 23/24 May 1938 took on a more warlike form than in previous years, perhaps being aimed at an international audience. One of the set pieces was an attack on a 'torpedo boat' and on a bridge, while anti-aircraft batteries successfully peppered a drogue.

The RAF's new fighter, the Supermarine Spitfire, treated the spectators to a breathtaking demonstration, while a heavily guarded Hawker Hurricane provided a static display. Famously, a month earlier, a Hurricane had made a high-profile flight from Edinburgh to Northolt, achieving an average speed of 408 mph. Little did the audience and the nation realize that at the time, the aircraft on which liberty would soon depend were equipped with guns that didn't work over 15,000ft.

Meanwhile, the Luftwaffe had 500 bombers, including Heinkel He 111s, Dornier Do 17s and Junkers Ju 87s, which, along with the Messerschmitt Bf 109A, had already seen service in the Spanish Civil War.

It would be another three months before No. 32 Squadron was modernized. On 1 June, still flying the Gauntlet II biplane, Brothers was assessed as 'above average' as a pilot and in air gunnery.

July 1938 saw Fighter Command take part in its second major air defence exercise. With four more radar stations in operation, the system's coverage was greatly increased. Operationally, however, the detection, information filtering and control of interception aircraft often fell short. Consequently, investigations began looking into how to refine the operation of the defence system.

Britain's Shield, an air defence exercise, was held between 5 and 7 August 1938, using the five stations: Bawdsey, Dover, Canewdon, Great Bromley and Dunkirk. Meanwhile, members of the Observer Corps forwarded details of overland sightings. Brothers' logbook records that he participated in the first two days of the trials.

Rumours that the squadron was about to be re-equipped with the Hawker Hurricane were confirmed on 11 August 1938, when they received their first dual control Miles Magister. Over the following few weeks all of the squadron's pilots were given training on the type: 'Compared to the Hurricane Mk I the Magister was heavier and 25 mph slower. Its handling characteristics were very similar, even to the extent that it could "get away" from a less experienced pilot, especially in a dive.'

One of the many differences in the Hurricane from anything the pilots had flown before was the cockpit layout. Unlike earlier aircraft the instruments were ordered, something which was soon adopted in most future designs: 'The standardization of the instrument layout greatly assisted "blind flying". It also made picking up new types easier.'

In a sign of the growing threat of war, orders were received on 23 August for the squadron's Gauntlets to lose their silver dope finish for a camouflaged scheme of dark green and dark brown, with the belly and underside of the wings and tailplane being painted black.

Politically, the situation remained tense. Prime Minister Neville Chamberlain flew to Germany twice between 15 and 29 September, during what was to be coined the 'Munich Crisis'. Chamberlain famously returned, having secured an agreement signed by Great Britain, France, Germany and Italy, by which Hitler annexed the majority German-speaking industrialized Sudetenland, but guaranteed the sovereignty of the remainder of Czechoslovakia. Arriving back at Heston airport on 30 September, Chamberlain held aloft the signed document in triumph, announcing, 'I believe it is peace in our time'.

Churchill's prophetic response was, 'you were given the choice between war and dishonour. You chose dishonour and you will have war.'

During the crisis the government had ordered 'the emergency deployment of a greater part of the home defences.' The station was under a state of 'immediate readiness for war' following the issuing of the code word 'Diabolo'. While the squadron's heightened state of Readiness was in time downgraded, the events in Munich signalled a further increase in flying time for all of the squadron's pilots. Meanwhile, the squadron had taken delivery of the first batch of Hurricanes, Brothers making his first flights in L1655 on 24 and 30 September, '...we got Hurricanes, which was a great change ... Oh yes; great fun ... You read the book and then you were off ... we converted to Hurricanes, and carried on doing the same sort of thing, plus gunnery practice.'

On 24 November and again a fortnight later, Brothers was able to practice air-to-ground firing in the Hurricane. The deafening noise and the recoil of the eight rapid-fire Browning machine guns came as a surprise compared to the two Vickers machine guns of the Gloster Gauntlet. Meanwhile, the difference in airspeed meant quicker reactions were vital, but Brothers soon felt at home with all aspects of the new type, 'I'd flown a Hawker aircraft at training school: Hawker Harts and so on. Interesting thing about Sydney Camm's designs …all the Hawker aircraft I flew, on the stall they always dropped the left wing; notorious. Something in the design I suppose …'

During the weeks and months that followed, the squadron spent more time on interception exercises and mock combats: 'We trained flying in the "vic" formation, using the RAF's standard air attacks, which were designed to take on unescorted bomber formations.'

The RAF's Fighter Attack Nos. 1–6 were drilled into fighter pilots during their advanced training and were the cornerstone of squadron exercises. Aerial combat had, however, moved on, with new techniques having been used during the Spanish Civil War. The Bf 109 pilots flew in pairs (the Rotte), or in two pairs (Schwarme), which allowed them to search the sky for their prey. The RAF's tight 'vic' meant that only the leader was able to concentrate on looking out for the enemy, the rest of the formation was too busy avoiding collisions. For the time being, at least, Brothers continued flying the RAF's prescribed attacks, but explained that once real combat came this would all change, 'we'd throw away the idea of Fighter Command Attack No. 1, No. 2, No. 3, different formations and so on, because they didn't fit in with what the enemy was doing.'

Wing Commander Richard 'Dickie' Grice, DFC (later Air Commodore Grice, DFC, OBE), assumed command of Biggin Hill on 15 November 1938. Grice, a First World War fighter ace with No. 8 Squadron, had, along with Freddie West (Captain F.M.F. West, VC, MC), witnessed the final air battle of Manfred von Richthofen. Another former squadron member was Leigh-Mallory (later Air Chief Marshal Sir Trafford Leigh-Mallory, KCB, DSO and Bar).

Biggin Hill was on the flight path of Lufthansa aircraft bound for Croydon airport and its preparations for war were closely monitored. On one occasion a Lufthansa aircraft, a Junkers transport, flew so low that a signal mortar was discharged in its direction, causing it to veer off. Lufthansa reconnaissance photographs were discovered in German archives following the end of the war, confirming that during 1939 some of the civilian flights were being used for spying purposes.

The modifications included the excavation of slit trenches and construction of sandbag emplacements, and the planting of trees and shrubs to help break up the linear outlines of the station's ground-plan. The white concrete aprons and the parade ground had been disguised by covering them with bitumen and granite chip. Meanwhile, the 90th AA Regiment was posted to provide a defence against enemy raiders seeing their first 'action' on 3 September 1939, when they opened fire on No. 601 Squadron's Blenheims returning from a false alarm raised by a listening station.

On 2 November 1938, Wing Commander R. Pyne, DFC, left the squadron on attachment to the Air Ministry, Squadron Leader Thomas Bain 'Mexican Pete' Prickman, being appointed to command. 'Why "Mexican Pete"? Well, everyone in the RAF had a nickname, Prickman's came from his wearing a non-regulation moustache.'

It was at about this time that the station began receiving visits from a VIP:

'During 1938 Winston Churchill occasionally used to come into the mess at Biggin Hill … The door would open just before six o'clock and he'd say,

"Would you mind turning on the radio, so that I can hear the six o'clock news?"'
Evidently aircraft recognition was not Churchill's forte as, 'he'd ask us about
our Supermarine Spitfires, whether we were content with them, and that sort
of thing. He'd spend a few minutes with us, then he'd get on his way home, we
never told him that we were actually flying Hawker Hurricanes.'

By November 1938 both Nos. 32 and 79 Squadrons were flying Hurricanes, No. 79
Squadron from early December, then under the command of Squadron Leader G.D.
Emms.

Meanwhile, Brothers' promotion to the rank of flying officer was announced in the
London Gazette on 27 October 1938. Pete was by now an old hand on the squadron,
'...and, as senior pilots departed to newly-formed squadrons, I became a Flight
Commander that December.'

Now in a position to lead rather than be led, Brothers felt able to pass on some
of the tricks that he had learnt from George Yuill. These included how to avoid
blacking out in a tight turn, or when pulling out of a dive: 'By putting your head on
your shoulder you don't get such a direct flow of draining blood from the head, like
putting a kink in a pipe.'

Brothers had found that, with practice, the technique could allow him to pull
another couple of 'G' before his vision greyed out, 'I used to tell the chaps in the
squadron; it's a good trick and it worked. I bought myself an accelerometer which I
hung in my Hurricane, showing the "G" Force.'

Brothers tested his purchase by putting his aircraft into a steep dive, pulling out
hard, 'and [I was] just about blacking out at about 6 and a half "G" or so. And then
tried the same thing with my head on one side and found I was doing about 8 G, so
it worked all right.'

The New Year saw Brothers steadily building up his hours on the Hurricane,
while further opportunities to hone his gunnery skills came with seven visits to the
ranges, made between February and late April. The results of these test firings would
convince Brothers that to have the best chance of bringing an enemy aircraft down
his guns needed realigning, 'Our machine guns were arranged to fire a pattern at 250
yards, although some of us decided to have our guns turned in to concentrate at a
point. Usually, we tried to get much closer than 250 yards.'

The importance of the squadron's tight training programme was brought into
greater focus when on 15 March 1939, Hitler seized the remainder of Czechoslovakia
(Bohemia and Moravia), tearing to shreds the Munich 'agreement' on which
Chamberlain had placed so much store. In response to the deepening world crisis
the station was put on alert and the aircraft were dispersed around the airfield. In the
event, Europe once again stepped back from the abyss.

Brothers, meanwhile, had plans of his own. One of the haunts of the young officers
was Pitt's Cottage, a restaurant and tea shop in nearby Westerham, owned and run
by Elsie Wilson. Here Brothers met a young woman, Annette Wilson, Elsie's niece,
'I happened to meet her and that was it'. Following a brief courtship he proposed,
much to his future father-in-law's dismay: 'My wife's father was not very much in
favour of this, "Fly boys – all they do is get killed – not a good idea."'

Marriage in the Armed Forces was not exactly frowned upon, but like everything else, there were accepted protocols to be observed: 'You had to be a squadron leader or aged twenty-eight to be able to get married and we were both twenty-one'.

Brothers decided he would go to Wing Commander Grice and ask for his permission. Grice replied, 'You are a bit bloody young aren't you? What if I said no?'

Brothers confessed that this was not exactly the reply he had anticipated, 'And being a stupid Lancastrian who can't resist saying his piece I said, "It would be a bit difficult to send you an invitation to the wedding Sir!"'

Fortunately Grice was not without a sense of humour, as Brothers recalled, 'He roared with laughter, fortunately, and allowed it'.

The couple married on 22 March 1939, Pete's great friend and fellow pilot John 'Millie the Mooch' Milner acting as best man. Originally, Pete had intended that the couple should travel to Germany, revisiting some of the places he had toured in his teens. Due to the prevailing international tension, however, Wing Commander Grice strongly advised against such a plan, instructing Brothers, 'You can't leave the country', adding that he was to remain 'near a telephone at all times.' Consequently the couple honeymooned in Cornwall.

The days passed quickly and the newly-weds' thoughts soon turned to married life back at Biggin Hill, 'I got a telegram the day before we were due to come back, it was from my deputy who was running my flight in my absence to say, "Congratulations! You are promoted to flight lieutenant"'.

Brothers' pay was now twenty shillings and two pence a day, a big jump from fourteen shillings, and, as Pete joked, very necessary, as he now had responsibilities, 'I had to keep the bull terrier (Merlin) after all, and he only ate steak!'

Accommodation was something of a bugbear. Despite having gone through the appropriate channels, the couple were not able to move into the married quarters, which remained the preserve of those who conformed to tradition: 'you were entirely on your own. Well, you were living in sin, officially, you weren't supposed to be married. We rented a little bungalow on the edge of Biggin Hill for twenty-five bob a week. My father, bless him, bought us some carpets and furniture.'

Back at Biggin Hill, with the display season fast approaching, Brothers was involved in rehearsals on 16, 17 & 19 April, before putting his training into practice the following day when a record crowd of 25,000 spectators enjoyed the station's Empire Air Day airshow. Biggin Hill had changed significantly since the previous year's open day. Their aircraft were no longer set out in neat rows but dispersed across the aerodrome, while the hangars had been camouflaged.

Two days later the situation in Europe took another ominous twist when Adolf Hitler and Benito Mussolini signed the military alliance known as the 'Pact of Steel'. The Fascist alliance was a real threat to France and Britain, as Italy, with its colonial interests in North Africa, had a very strong Mediterranean Fleet, while its air force was developing monoplanes which would rival the RAF's Hawker Hurricane.

Over 8 and 9 July, the squadron undertook No. 11 Group's Preliminary Air Exercises, made in conjunction with aircraft of Bomber Command.

Air Defence warning and control systems had greatly improved over the previous months and senior officers from No. 11 Group were able to report sixty per cent interception rates. None of the squadrons, however, gained any experience of attacking large formations of bombers, as Air Chief Marshal Edgar Ludlow-Hewitt, KCB, CMG, DSO, MC, Commander-in-Chief of Bomber Command, still refused to make sufficient aircraft available. Meanwhile, the controllers were under less pressure to hold fighter aircraft in reserve to meet second and third waves of bombers, and thus were able to deploy every available fighter, something which could never have been done under real combat conditions.

At the time, Brothers was off the flying rota. Meanwhile, No. 32 Squadron was deployed in the night fighter role during the annual Home Defence air exercise held between 8-11 August 1939.

Winston Churchill and Sir Kingsley Wood, Secretary of State for Air, observed the daylight operations from Biggin Hill during 10 August. A review of the exercise left both confident that daylight raids would eventually prove too costly to the Luftwaffe, Sir Kingsley Wood suggesting up to twenty per cent enemy casualty rates, which would reduce the enemy to less accurate night raids.

No. 11 Group was able to report: 'RDF information and plotting throughout the exercise was consistently first-rate and enabled interceptions to be effected on the coast.'

Fighter Command's night fighter defence capabilities, however, were rudimentary. The Hawker Hurricane lacked any form of on-board system to locate a target at night, relying on visual contacts and ground based radar, which could only plot a raid as it approached the coast. The aircraft's short exhaust stubs reduced forward visibility, the flames dazzling the pilot, particularly when throttling back on landing. Their pilots were, however, some of the most experienced when it came to controller-led interceptions.

Simulated raids involving 500 aircraft were made against London and other targets during the night of the 10/11 August. Early in the proceedings, Flying Officer Harold Stewart Olding was ordered up to observe the blackout, but after circling, his engine cut out. Grice ordered the fire tender off in the direction of the crash, while Flying Officer Arthur Robin 'Woolly' Buchanan-Wollaston took off to illuminate the wreckage with a locating flare. Tragically, his Hurricane crashed into the top of Tatsfield Hill, only a few hundred feet away from the first Hurricane – both pilots were killed outright. It was a tragic blow for everyone on the squadron, and a poignant reminder of the ever-present dangers.

But there was little time to morn, as events abroad continued to move at a fast pace and the very real threat of a world war lay on the near horizon. Churchill had always warned that German expansionism would not end at Czechoslovakia's borders. Growing tension now lay around the question of the port of Danzig (Gdansk), ceded to Poland under the terms of the Treaty of Versailles. The port's land corridor cut East Prussia off from the Fatherland.

Herr Hitler favoured an uprising by armed pro-Nazi sympathizers from within the predominantly Germanic population, allowing Danzig to be reabsorbed. On 13 August the Polish Government issued an ultimatum demanding the reinstatement of border controls. Meanwhile, on 23 August, it was announced that Germany and Russia had signed the 'non-aggression' treaty known to history as the 'Molotov-

Ribbentrop Pact'. In response, Great Britain and Poland signed a mutual assistance treaty two days later. Hitler was not deterred by what he considered to be a hollow display of unity.

On 27 August work began at Biggin Hill on sandbagging the fighter pens, while a dummy airfield was under construction to the east of Lullingstone. Training was once again stepped up a gear. Brothers recalled that, 'We flew interception practice up to 30,000ft, made fighter attacks according to the book, and that sort of thing.'

The RAFs three main Fighter Air Attacks, as practiced can be summarized thus:

No. 1 Attack: A succession of fighter aircraft – usually three or six – attacking from astern, against a single bomber.

No. 2 Attack: Two or more fighter aircraft attacking in line abreast against a single bomber aircraft.

No. 3 Attack: Three fighter aircraft attacking a single bomber simultaneously from the rear, beam and rear quarter.

While these worked well against the single bomber which Bomber Command supplied for exercises, they would soon prove to be near useless against mass formations protected by fighter escorts.

The ground crews became well practiced in refuelling and rearming the aircraft and scrambling their pilots off in good time: 'You were a well-grounded team because you all knew each other intimately, they were a good bunch of characters and you were all after the same thing.'

With Europe looking to be edging towards war, the British Ambassador to Berlin, Sir Nevile Henderson, met with Hitler. The German Dictator refused to give up his demands. With German forces massing on the border, Poland began a general mobilization on 30 August.

On the following day Adolf Hitler issued his Directive No. 1 for the Conduct of the War. The document outlined Hitler's plans for the invasion of Poland and the initial phase of the campaign against France and Britain, stating that:

'If Britain and France open hostilities against Germany, it will be the duty of the Wehrmacht formations operating in the west to conserve their forces as much as possible and thus maintain the conditions for a victorious conclusion of the operations against Poland. The right to order offensive operations is reserved absolutely to me.

'The Navy will carry on warfare against merchant shipping, directed mainly at England.

'The Air Force is, in the first place, to prevent the French and British Air Forces from attacking the German Army and German territory.

'In conducting the war against England, preparations are to be made for the use of the Luftwaffe in disrupting British supplies by sea, the armaments industry, and the transport of troops to France. A favourable opportunity is to be taken for an effective attack on massed British naval units, especially against battleships and aircraft carriers. The decision regarding attacks on London is reserved to me.'

At dawn on 1 September, Wehrmacht forces invaded Poland, closely supported by the Luftwaffe. Meanwhile, Danzig came under naval bombardment.

At 0540 hours Adolf Hitler's message to his Armed Forces was broadcast:

'Poland has refused my offer for a friendly settlement of our relation as neighbours. Instead she has taken up arms.

'I am left with no other means than from now on opposing force with force.'

As the full enormity of the morning's events sank in, hurried meetings were held in Whitehall and at the Ministry of Defence. Orders were issued to Biggin Hill, bringing it to a state of Readiness and all personnel were recalled with immediate effect.

Later that day a sombre Neville Chamberlain addressed Parliament stating that if His Majesty's Government did not receive assurances of the withdrawal of Germany's armed forces: 'His Majesty's Government in the United Kingdom will without hesitation fulfil its obligations to Poland.'

In a last-ditch hope of averting war, the Prime Minister made an appeal to right-thinking Germans: 'We have no quarrel with the German people, except that they allow themselves to be governed by a Nazi Government. As long as that Government exists and pursues the methods it has so persistently followed during the last two years, there will be no peace in Europe.'

At 2000 hours on 1 September 1939, in line with the other Services, orders were issued for the general mobilization of the Royal Air Force, calling up members of the RAF Reserve and RAF Volunteer Reserve.

Meanwhile, the RAF had already begun secretly taking its first positive actions and deployed ten light bomber squadrons and two squadrons of Hurricanes in France. These units were to form part of the Advanced Air Striking Force (AASF), with their HQ at Rheims; the RAF squadrons were mainly based to the east and north-east. The fighter unit's role was to protect the Maginot Line, while the Fairey Battle and Blenheim bombers proved a woefully inadequate strike force. Also operating out of France during this early phase would be the Air Component.

Hitler gambled that a swift conclusion to the Polish campaign would lead to a weakening of British and French resolve. He ordered his forces to continue their merciless onslaught.

Early the following evening, Churchill visited Biggin Hill on his way to his nearby home of Chartwell and had his customary glass of sherry in the officer's mess, saying to those assembled, 'Well, I've no doubt all you young men here will be as brave and eager to defend your country as were your forefathers.'

Voice from the back of the crowd, 'Cheer up, Sir. It won't be as bad as all that!'

The British Government was, however, already preparing an ultimatum which would be delivered at 0900 hours on 3 September.

Chapter 3

The So-Called Phoney War

The morning of Sunday, 3 September 1939, saw the dying throws of diplomacy being played out in Berlin, as, for the second time in a generation, Britain stood on the brink of war with Germany.

In their respective messes, the pilots gathered to listen to what the BBC had advised would be, 'an important announcement.' At 1115 hours, fifteen minutes after the British ultimatum had expired, Neville Chamberlain broadcast to the nation:

> 'This morning the British Ambassador in Berlin handed the German Government a final note stating that, unless we heard from them by eleven o'clock that they were prepared at once to withdraw their troops from Poland, a state of war would exist between us. I have to tell you now that no such undertaking has been received and that consequently this country is at war with Germany. Now may God bless you all.'

Meanwhile, a defiant 'erk' cycled past No. 32 Squadron's temporary dispersal tents singing a popular refrain, 'Pack up your Goebbels in your old kit-bag and Heil! Heil!'

Moments later the tannoys crackled into life, the Station Commander announcing, 'As you will all have heard, we are now at war with the Hun'. His words were drowned out by the whine of air raid sirens, which were sounded in response to an incoming radar plot.

The station's defences swung into action, as across Kent and the capital, civilians headed for their nearest air raid shelter. All along the aircraft's anticipated flight path anti-aircraft gunners scoured the skies, while London's balloon barrage was deployed.

Brothers' Blue Section was at Readiness when the telephone at dispersal rang. At the other end of the line was Biggin Hill's controller (codenamed Sapper control). The shout went out, 'Blue Section. Patrol Gravesend 5,000ft. Scramble!'

Springing into action, Brothers and the rest of his section raced to their Hurricanes where the 'erks' were already waiting to strap them in, leaping off the wings to remove the chocks as soon as the Merlin engines burst into life. A few minutes into the patrol the aircraft was identified as a French transport, which Brothers escorted to Croydon. This would be the first of many X-raids: 'some plot that turned out to be nothing.'

That evening Winston Churchill, mindful of the need for political unity, spoke in Parliament, 'We must not underrate the gravity of the task which lies before us, or the temerity of the ordeal, to which we shall not be found unequal'.

Understanding that Hitler's goals lay beyond Poland, Churchill emphasized, 'This is not a question of fighting for Danzig or fighting for Poland. We are fighting to save the whole world from the pestilence of Nazi tyranny and in defence of all that is most sacred to man'.

Churchill's address was statesmanlike, demonstrating to many that he had the energy, self-belief, charisma and the political and military know-how, to unite the nation and bring it through to victory.

Closely monitoring Great Britain's response, along with that of her ally France, the Reich-Führer issued his Directive No. 2:

'The declaration of war by England and France has the following consequences:
   'Attacks upon English naval forces at naval bases or on the high seas will only be made in the event of English air attacks on similar targets and where there are particularly good prospects of success.
   'I reserve to myself the decision about attacks on the English homeland.'

The Luftwaffe, however, could defend against attacks on the Reich: 'In general the employment of the air force in the west is governed by the need to preserve its fighting strength after the defeat of Poland for decisive actions against the Western Powers.'

The first few days of hostilities saw one flight or the other at a state of Readiness from before dawn until well after dusk, while a number of patrols and scrambles were flown, the plots turning out to be 'friendly'. But the false alarms kept the pilots on their mettle. Brothers explained that there were two telephones at dispersals, 'You quickly learnt to tell the difference between the bell on the 'ops' room telephone against that of the 'admin' line'.

Fighter Command had various states of readiness: Standby – sitting in cockpit ready to take-off; Readiness – to be able to take-off in three minutes; Available – able to take-off at a set amount of time denoted by a prefix i.e. 15 minutes Available; Release – stood down until a given time.

The restrictions on non-operational flying were partially lifted on 11 September with Nos. 32 and 79 Squadrons taking the opportunity to fly interceptions and mock combats. Everyone was eager to put their training into practice. Meanwhile, on Continental Europe, events escalated. Poland's fate had already been sealed under the terms of the secret 'Ribbentrop-Molotov Pact'. Before dawn on 17 September, Russian forces invaded eastern Poland. It was claimed that as the Polish government no longer existed, Russia's earlier promise to respect Polish sovereign territory was null and void. Ten days later, at 2010 hours Berlin time, German radio announced: 'Warsaw has unconditionally capitulated.'

On 9 October, Adolf Hitler turned his attention towards the West when he issued his sixth War Directive, ordering preparations for: '… an attacking operation on the northern wing of the Western Front, through the areas of Luxembourg, Belgium and Holland. This attack must be carried out with as much strength and at as early a date as possible …'

Meanwhile, Brothers had had the opportunity to test his gunnery skills in air-to-air firing, when, on 29 September, he was scrambled to bring down a barrage balloon which had broken free from its moorings. Brothers followed the controller's directions and, taking the prevailing wind into account, soon had the balloon in his sights, unleashing his eight Browning machine guns and raking it with 0.303 rounds. A similar sortie would be flown nearly a month later with the same result.

An entry in the squadron's Operational Record Book (ORB) on 30 September throws more light on the initial weeks of Biggin Hill's war: 'No. 32 Squadron has been operating from a dispersal point on the east side of the aerodrome. A temporary camp of tents has been erected there to enable pilots and crews to sleep near their machines.'

Brothers recalled that the dispersals were, 'made a bit more homely with an old wind-up gramophone and some Lloyd Loom chairs'.

Meanwhile, the flying facilities were being upgraded with the construction of concrete runways and taxiing tracks. It was also recorded that: 'A new dispersal point on the south side of the aerodrome was allotted to No. 32 Squadron and plans for the semi-permanent dispersal point have been made out by Squadron Leader T. B. Prickman.'

With the onset of winter fast approaching, there were plans to supplement the tents with wooden huts. Meanwhile, following the lifting of the ban on non-operational flying, the ORB recorded: 'Both 'A' and 'B' Flights have been engaged in training their new pilots, this is progressing well. During the month the squadron carried out Night Flying, Squadron Formation attacks, as well as individual training.'

Meanwhile, during the afternoon of 16 October, radar detected the Luftwaffe's first major air offensive against British targets, when fifteen Junkers Ju 88s of I./KG 30 attacked Royal Naval vessels in the Firth of Forth. Successfully vectored onto the enemy, the Spitfires of Nos. 602 and 603 Squadrons claimed two Ju 88s destroyed, damaging a third. The combat victories were a vindication, both of Dowding's support of radar and Fighter Command's Air Defence System.

If the Air Ministry was to gauge the offensive capability of the enemy it was vital to maintain an accurate record of their losses. During a dogfight an enemy aircraft might be fired upon by two or three pilots from the same or different squadrons, particularly one which was already damaged and posed an easy target.

The Air Ministry's strict guidelines when assessing combat victories were:

Destroyed:
a) Aircraft must be seen on the ground or in the air destroyed by a member of the crew or formation, or confirmed from other sources, e.g. ships at sea, local authorities etc.
b) Aircraft must be seen to descend with flames issuing. It is not sufficient if only smoke is seen.
c) Aircraft must be seen to break up in the air.

Probables:
a) When the pilot of a single-engined aircraft is seen to bail out.
b) The aircraft must be seen to break off the combat in circumstances which lead our pilots to believe it will be a loss.

Damaged:
Aircraft must be seen to be considerably damaged as the result of attack, e.g.
undercarriage dropped, engine dropped, aircraft parts shot away, or volumes of
smoke issuing.

Poor local weather meant there was no flying on 19 October and so the pilots were stood
down. J.B. Priestly joined Brothers and the other officers in the Pilot's Room where he
'gave a short address'. A gift for expressing the sentiments of a nation, from the early
summer of 1940, Priestly would make weekly evening broadcasts on the BBC.

The 30 October was a sad day for Brothers and the other pilots as they said 'goodbye'
to Squadron Leader Tom Prickman, who was replaced by Squadron Leader Robert
Alexander Chignell. The latter had served at Sector HQ, Biggin Hill, since 10 July
1938 and was already well known and respected on the base.

Tom Prickman was posted away to command RAF Stradishall, being promoted to
Wing Commander on 1 January 1940. A month later he was posted to HQ, No. 11
Group. He was appointed to command RAF Kenley on 20 April. Prickman was then
posted to RAF West Malling on 28 July before returning to command RAF Kenley
on 18 August. In recognition of his vital role as Sector Controller, he was awarded the
OBE on 17 March 1941. Prickman retired holding the rank of Air Commodore, CBE
(*London Gazette*, 14 June 1945), CB (*London Gazette*, 1 June 1953).

As the daily scrambles continued, life inevitably became stressful for the pilot's
families, especially the wives living on or close to the base. At the time Annette was
still living on the approach, overlooking the aerodrome, '... she used to count us in.
Every time I came back from a sortie, I had to do a whiz over the house to reassure
her I was still around.'

Their Bull terrier called 'Merlin', for obvious reasons, could tell which aircraft was
Pete's when they came back into land from a mission, which was very reassuring for
Annette.

Aware that Biggin Hill, the location and significance of which were well known to
German aviators, would very likely become a target for Luftwaffe bombers, Brothers
decided that it was time for Annette to relocate, 'when war was declared I said, "I've
got to move you because this is not a good place to be." So she went and lived with
her aunt in Westerham. I could commute there when I was stood down, as it was only
six miles [from Biggin Hill].'

The first big shake-up at Biggin Hill came on 11 November, when No. 79 Squadron
was transferred to RAF Manston, No. 32 Squadron taking over their dispersal point
hut. A few days later, news of their sister squadron's first victory was greeted with
a sense of relief and no little envy. Flying out of Manston on 21 November, Flying
Officer 'Jimmy' Davies and Flight Sergeant Brown shared in the destruction of a
Dornier Do 17 over the Straits of Dover. The Dornier spun down with one engine
alight, crashing into the sea, exploding on impact (the first enemy aircraft to be
destroyed over the Channel).

Meanwhile, No. 32 Squadron, like most of Fighter Command, was yet to sight an enemy aircraft. Their luck was typified by the following day's events. Up and at dispersals since before dawn, Flight Lieutenant Brothers led 'B' Flight on a scramble at 0935 hours with orders to patrol Biggin Hill. After an hour and a half of stooging around the patrol landed.

False alarms caused by flocks of birds, thunderstorms and training flights that got lost became commonplace, causing the pilots of No. 32 Squadron to compose a little ditty which, according to Flying Officer 'Grubby' Grice, went something like this:

'The plots that appear on the screen, tra la,
 Have nothing to do with the Hun.
 The AOC's having a dream, tra la,
 And won't send us off in a stream, tra la,
 To fight the Hun in the sun.
 And that's what I mean when I say and I scream.
 Oh bother the plots that appear on the screen!'

Hitler's plans to dominate North-Western Europe depended on sidelining Great Britain. On 29 November Hitler issued Directive No. 9 for the Conduct of the War, its aims being to cripple Britain's economy. Prime targets included merchant shipping and their escorts, oil, cold food and grain storage facilities, industrial plants and troop transport. Meanwhile, ports and shipping lanes were to be mined.

During the day Biggin Hill's No. 601 Squadron made a rare offensive patrol when they escorted No. 25 Squadron's Blenheims on a daring raid to destroy the Luftwaffe's seaplanes at their base at Borkum in the Friesian Islands.

For No. 32 Squadron much of December was taken up with occasional scrambles and fighter patrols, along with convoy escorts. On 9 December, Flight Lieutenant Michael 'Red Knight' Crossley led a section to Manston where they relieved one section from No. 79 Squadron, flying regular patrols and scrambles. The posting lasted until 23 December, but proved notable only for an escort made for King George VI on 13 December. While stationed at Manston the squadron's pilots were able to use the house at Port Lympne formerly belonging to the late Sir Philip Sassoon as their billet.

Crossley, Brothers recalled, 'was an Old Etonian. He'd studied aeronautical engineering before taking a job at the Elstree Film Studios as an assistant director, then making a career change and joining De Havilland as an apprentice'.

An amateur musician of some ability, Crossley was proficient at a number of instruments, including the trumpet, guitar and ukulele, 'His signature tune was *It's Only a Paper Moon* made famous by Ella Fitzgerald. I remember, someone wrote a song about the squadron, adding verses on each of the pilots. It went something like, "High rank, low rank, everybody come, join us in the pilot's room and make yourself at home. Take off your gloves and overalls and light your pipe and let us introduce you to the fighting 32."

'And then came a verse on each of the pilots and key staff.'

During the festive season, Sir Howard Kingsley Wood, Secretary of State for Air (March 1938–May 1940), visited the sergeant's and airmen's messes in the company of Wing Commander Grice, wishing all ranks a 'Very Happy Christmas!' Following the time honoured service tradition, the officers and senior NCOs took care of all of the Christmas Dinner arrangements, serving the junior NCOs and men. In the evening all ranks were invited to join the officers for a drink and to toast the King's health. Details of the celebrations were later related by Sergeants J.W. 'Chalky' White and J. Proctor in a BBC broadcast entitled 'Christmas Day at a Fighter Squadron'.

At 2359 hours on 31 December the officers broke off their own party to join all ranks on the station to wish them a 'Happy New Year!' None could have known just how momentous the months ahead would be.

The New Year began with a change of scene. On 1 January 1940, orders were received for No. 32 Squadron to transfer to Gravesend, from where they also had brief postings to Manston, finally returning to Biggin Hill on 1 April: 'The move was to allow for the construction of deep air raid shelters, while a short concrete runway was also laid.'

The squadron's first operational sortie from their new base was made on 4 January, with many more scrambles and patrols to follow.

Flight Lieutenant Crossley recorded in the unofficial Squadron Diary: 'Gravesend in peacetime was an excellent little private flying club with quite a large aerodrome, a useful sized hangar and a very nice little club house. It was not, however, designed to accommodate about 250 whole-time boarders.'

Sleeping arrangements for all but the lucky ones was on palliasses laid on the floor, while catering was from a mobile unit.

But no one minded the lack of facilities if it meant the possibility of combat. This looked to be on the cards on 12 January, when Green Section was vectored onto a formation of Do 17s making an attacking approach on Manston. The pilots went through their drill, lowering their seat to gain better protection from enemy rounds, or fire from the engine, and taking the safety catch off the gun button. As they positioned themselves for the attack they were thwarted by heavy and accurate anti-aircraft fire which dispersed the bombers but prevented the Hurricanes from getting in close enough to engage.

Brothers led Blue Section on a convoy escort between 1115 – 1300 hours on 25 January. Two oil tankers sailing off North Foreland were reported to be under attack and Red Section was scrambled to provide support, but no contact was made.

The squadron took delivery of twenty improved Hawker Hurricanes with variable-pitch propellers on the following day, with more arriving between 10 – 14 February, their old aircraft being handed over to Nos. 242 and 253 Squadrons: '… we got some de Havilland variable-pitch metal things which were terrible. They hadn't a great pitch range, they chucked oil all over the windscreen, and then we got Rotol wooden-bladed jobs, and they had a great pitch range …'

The wooden blades shattered if someone had a rough landing and touched the propeller on the ground, while a metal one might suddenly stop, stripping the reduction gear on the engine. Pete explained, 'The wood just broke up, you did a check of the reduction gear, and put a new propeller on.'

Training continued, now with a greater focus on battle climbs, the RAF's Nos. 1 to 6 Attacks and mock combats. There was a definite sense that what they were doing was for real. This couldn't have been more true than when Brothers flew mock combats using cine camera guns for the first time on 10 January, 'Three of the new Hurricanes were fitted with cine camera guns to help improve our gunnery skills. We operated in pairs and with the gun cameras, flew mock dogfights. The film was exposed by pressing the gun button. Back on the ground the film was analyzed; it helped us master deflection shooting.'

The Hurricanes were fitted with a reflector gunsight, so called because of the red dot on the underside of the angled sight. The target's wing dimension was fixed on the scale at the base of the gunsight against which the pilots could set a rotating marker. This latter feature helped pilots to correctly judge their distance, which ideally should be 250 yards, although many pilots preferred to get closer. Later in the war the gyroscopic gunsight was introduced – in time for the campaign in Northern Europe.

When firing at a moving target the pilots had to take into account that the enemy aircraft would have moved its position by the time the bullets reached their target. The relative speeds and flight path of the gun platform and target had to be taken into consideration; it needed to fly into the stream of the bullets, this was the essence of deflection shooting.

There was a ground covering of snow for much of January and February 1940, severely limiting flying time. Everyone lent a hand to clear the dispersal points and runway once the temperature began to rise and there was the threat of enemy air activity. The Hurricane's Merlin engine had to be run every half-hour or so in order to keep it warm enough for an immediate scramble.

During 10 February a number of fighter patrols were made, Brothers taking part in an uneventful convoy escort, 'We relished the possibility of getting to grips with the enemy, but would soon tire of the monotony of the seemingly endless defensive, convoy, and escort patrols.'

When approaching a convoy, Brothers would bring his formation in on a wide arc, to let the spotters identify his silhouette, 'The Navy gunners had a reputation of being trigger-happy and would throw up flak at anything that approached them'.

In the hope of combating this problem, from November 1939, Royal Navy vessels had carried an RAF officer to assist with identifications, while patrols would use coloured flares to identify themselves as 'friendly', but this did not prevent further incidents occurring.

March began as February had ended, with the patrols stepping back up between the second and twenty-seventh: 'We operated out of our forward base at Manston, returning to Gravesend between dusk and dawn'.

Manston was the RAF's closest base to enemy occupied Europe and No. 32 Squadron was just one of many units to use the airfield as an advanced base. Here, they landed, refuelled and took off on convoy escorts or Channel patrols. Scrambled from Manston, however, the squadron's Hurricanes would have little time to gain altitude before engaging the enemy, making them particularly vulnerable to being 'bounced' by the enemy fighters. Even with the use of long-range radar, the RAF only had twenty minutes advanced warning, while it took three minutes to scramble and a further twelve to attain operational altitude. There was little room for error.

On 7 March, No. 32 Squadron temporarily transferred to RAF Manston to relieve No. 79 Squadron, which flew to Biggin Hill two days later. Back flying out of Gravesend,

No. 32 Squadron lost Flying Officer Bowler (flying N2531) while on patrol two miles off Folkestone on 23 March. Although not due to combat, this was nevertheless the squadron's first wartime casualty and brought the realities of the conflict home to the pilots and ground staff alike. Flying Officer (39431) Lancelot Gordon Bowler, RAF, was the son of Ernest and Sarah Bowler, of Wavertree, Liverpool. He was 22-years-old. Bowler is remembered on the Runnymede Memorial, Panel 5.

Pete's 'B' Flight returned to Biggin Hill on 1 April, to be joined a week later by 'A' Flight, which had spent the week flying out of Manston. There would be further changes over the next few weeks and months. On 8 April No. 79 Squadron's 'B' Flight, which had been flying out of Biggin Hill, returned to Manston until 15 April, from when they operated out of Biggin Hill again. Meanwhile, 'A' Flight proceeded to Manston on 22 April. Between 1 – 10 May, No. 79 Squadron continued to operate out of Biggin Hill and Manston. On 6 May, No. 32 Squadron's 'A' Flight returned from Manston, being relieved by No. 79 Squadron.

Meanwhile, Hitler was preparing to strike again, to secure Norway and the port of Narvik through which Germany imported Swedish iron ore for its war machine. On 9 April, Hitler's forces launched Operation Weserübung, initially targeting the airfields and ports. Both France and Great Britain dispatched expeditionary forces, which were doomed from the start, the campaign ending in defeat on 10 June.

The House of Commons began debating the Norway campaign on 7 May, Lloyd George summing up the House's feelings when he said, 'I say solemnly that the Prime Minister should give an example of sacrifice, because there is nothing which can contribute more to victory in this war than that he should sacrifice the seal of office.'

Chamberlain's majority was cut from 213 to eighty-one and privately he admitted to Churchill that he could no longer continue in office.

Meanwhile, back at Biggin Hill, Squadron Leader R.A. Chignell was posted away on 6 May. Chignell flew at least one operational sortie with No. 145 Squadron to qualify for the Battle of Britain clasp, although not serving with them. He was posted to the Far East and killed at Kallang on 14 February 1942 when the Japanese strafed the boat in which he was escaping following the fall of Singapore. By then he was a Wing Commander. Chignell is remembered on the Singapore Memorial. He was posthumously Mentioned in Despatches on 1 October 1946.

Squadron Leader John 'The Baron' Worrall, formerly Senior Controller at Biggin Hill, took over command. Worrall would need to get flying time under his belt if he was to become as accomplished on Hurricanes as most of the pilots under his command. In the meantime he relied on his flight commanders, Brothers and Crossley, who would bear the brunt of the combat in the air – neither would be found wanting.

Worrall joined the RAF in 1930, flying with No. 1 Squadron before transferring to No. 208 Squadron on 28 February 1933. Commanding No. 32 Squadron during the Battle of France and the early phases of the Battle of Britain, Worrall was awarded the DFC (*London Gazette*, 6 August 1940). Soon afterwards he returned to his role as Fighter Controller at Biggin Hill, finally retiring at the rank of Air Vice-Marshal on 1 January 1963.

Chapter 4

Blitzkrieg to Dunkirk

The war entered a new and dramatic phase on 10 May when Hitler launched his Blitzkrieg against the Low Countries.

The German plan anticipated the Allies' advance to counter their invasion of neutral Belgium. German armour would then spring the trap, bypassing the Maginot Line via the supposedly impenetrable Ardenne Forest, swinging northwards to the Channel and cutting off the Allies in their advanced positions.

At around 0400 hours German land forces began the assault, coordinating with air raids on road and railway junctions and other infrastructure. Half of the Belgian Air Force was destroyed on the ground, while many French airfields were badly hit.

Much now rested on the small RAF contingent operating in France. During the afternoon, thirty-two Battle light bombers of the Advanced Air Strike Force (AASF) made their first major raid, attacking German columns in an attempt to slow their advance through Luxembourg. Thirteen were lost and the remainder damaged. Outnumbered ten to one, the one hundred strong fighter force of the AASF and Air Component accounted for fifty enemy aircraft, losing fewer than ten of their own machines, with three pilots wounded.

Throughout what would become known as the Battle of France, it was the Hurricane squadrons that bore the brunt of the action rather than those operating with Spitfires. With a wider and more forward set undercarriage, the Hurricane would cope better with the rough airstrips, while their largely fabric-covered fuselage could be repaired on squadron. Added to this, Dowding was reluctant to deploy his Spitfires and would later threaten to resign if ordered to deplete Home Defence in this way.

During the morning No. 32 Squadron made patrols over Middlekirk and Zeebrugge, before returning to base at 0945 hours. There was little further activity until the early evening when Squadron Leader Worrall led a fighter patrol. Brothers recalled, 'we pursued two suspected enemy aircraft over the Channel, but they dived into thick haze as we tried to overhaul them.'

Meanwhile, No. 79 Squadron, operating out of Biggin Hill and Manston, received orders to 'proceed to aerodrome in France', setting up a temporary base at Merville. Their role at Biggin Hill was taken by No. 610 Squadron's Spitfires, which flew down from Prestwick, operating in No. 11 Group until the end of August.

At dawn the following day, No. 32 Squadron flew to Manston, refuelling before taking off at 1640 hours to strafe the recently captured Ypenburg aerodrome, near The Hague.

Looking over to starboard as he crossed the Scheldt and Maas estuaries, Brothers caught sight of a red haze, '[which] as we drew closer, I realized was Rotterdam'.

Just as the lead Hurricanes reached The Hague the recall order was issued, but the fighters were by then beyond wireless range and the mission continued.

Brothers, who in later years added the words, 'fired guns "in anger" for the first time' in his logbook against the flight, recalled the raid:

'I was leading the squadron because the commanding officer was new, and flying No. 2 to me. We left 'A' Flight up above to protect us whilst we went down to ground strafe.

'There were a large number [sixteen] of Ju 52 troop transport aircraft on the ground. We dived down to find they were already all burned out; only the wing tips and tails remained intact.

'Coming around again we spotted a single transporter parked between two hangars, so we set that on fire and climbed back up again.'

Only later did Brothers learn of the consequences of the breakdown in communication, 'the Dutch had recaptured the airfield about two hours before we arrived and burnt out these German aircraft: one had been kept for them to escape to England in'.

In Parliament it had long been clear that Chamberlain was on borrowed time. The Norwegian campaign was on the point of collapse, while the Allies' defensive lines in North-Western Europe would soon be swept away. Luxembourg fell by the end of the day. While the House of Commons favoured Lord Halifax, British Foreign Secretary, as Prime Minister, it was Churchill who was summoned to Buckingham Palace. By midnight he had formed his Coalition Government, serving as both Prime Minister and the Minister for War.

In his maiden speech in the House of Commons as Prime Minister, Churchill gave his rallying call:

'We have before us an ordeal of the most grievous kind. We have before us many, many months of struggle and suffering.

'You ask, what is our aim? I can answer in one word. It is victory. Victory at all costs – Victory in spite of all terrors – Victory, however long and hard the road may be, for without victory there is no survival.

'Let that be realized. No survival for the British Empire, no survival for all that the British Empire has stood for.'

At 0420 hours on 12 May, No. 32 Squadron took off for Manston from where they patrolled the Dutch Coast, escorting Blenheims seen near Flushing-Zeebrugge. The pilots remained at Readiness until after dusk, returning to Biggin Hill at 1805 hours.

Four additional squadrons of Hurricanes had already been sent to France, with a further thirty-two aircraft crossing the Channel the following day. The equivalent of another four squadrons, including No. 32 Squadron, would soon be operating over France: 'We took off from Biggin Hill at around 0400 hours, flew ops throughout the day and often didn't return until after 2200 hours.'

Meanwhile, the land campaign suffered a further disaster when the retreating Belgian Army failed to destroy a vital bridge along the river between Givet and Sedan. The way was thus open for the Germans to roll on through to the French border. Elsewhere, the Dutch had been pushed back to Rotterdam.

Mounting losses amongst the Hurricane squadrons based in France led to the secondment of a number of pilots and, on 14 May, the squadron lost Flying Officer Jones, Pilot Officers Gardner and Rose, along with Sergeant Ware, who were posted to No. 3 Squadron at Merville. Two days later, Pilot Officer Smith and Sergeant Bayley, were sent on temporary postings, both returning on 24 May.

Pilot Officer Jack Rose recalled that there were a number of failings in the rushed secondment, 'We had no armour plate but all the chaps there did have. Our radios didn't have the right frequencies so we couldn't communicate with anybody'.

With the situation in France continuing to deteriorate the French premier, Paul Reynaud, telephoned Winston Churchill on 15 May, conceding, 'We are beaten: We have lost the battle.'

By that evening the Allies had retired to the River Senne, in Belgium, reaching the Dendre the following day, and the Escaut and the area around the Sedan by 17 May. The situation was grave and Churchill wrote to Roosevelt: 'We expect to be attacked here ourselves, both from the air and parachute and airborne troops in the near future, and we are getting ready for them.'

During the morning of 16 May, Brothers led 'B' Flight on a fighter patrol, landing back at Manston before being scrambled at 1230 hours to intercept a raid off the French coast. But the enemy turned back and Brothers was ordered down to conserve fuel.

Air Chief Marshal Hugh Dowding, who had already reported growing losses to the Cabinet on the previous day, wrote a letter in which he expressed his views on sending more fighters across the Channel at the expense of fatally damaging Home Defence. He was duly summoned to No. 10 Downing Street. Churchill explained the predicament and that he had promised to provide more fighters to support the campaign in France. Dowding, however, remained adamant; Home Defence had already been reduced from fifty-two squadrons, the accepted minimum, and could not be further depleted, 'I am well aware of the situation Prime Minister, but my task at hand is for the air defence of this country and it is my belief that I cannot achieve this if half my aircraft are in France. We are losing aircraft at a far quicker rate than we can produce them,' adding that his thirty-six remaining squadrons were nowhere near enough for a successful defence of Britain, concluding, 'We need more aircraft, and more pilots to fly them.'

Churchill flew to Paris for further talks, during which Reynaud stated that France would fall far sooner than he had anticipated. Churchill immediately telephoned the War Cabinet asking for six Hurricane squadrons; they would operate from French bases close to the Channel, from where they could be rapidly withdrawn.

And so, on 17 May, the squadron was up at 0315 hours in preparation to fly over to France from where they would operate that day: 'we were getting up at about three o'clock in the morning, having breakfast, getting off an hour before first light.'

Taking off at 0825 hours Brothers landed at Abbeville a little under an hour later, where his aircraft was refuelled while the squadron awaited orders, 'we had no ground crew. We refuelled from tins, and then we had no contact with anybody, the headquarters was on the move somewhere, retreating fast; everything was chaotic and so we'd just go off and patrol around to see what we could find.

'If you were lucky, you bumped into some Germans. Otherwise you just flew about the sky looking at what was going on down on the ground.'

Occupied by No. 615 Squadron, the airfield and adjacent road, which was already lined by large numbers of refugees, was under artillery fire: '615 were pretty jumpy. One of their sergeant pilots hadn't turned up for breakfast, and when they went to his billet he was lying in bed with a knife stuck in his chest. They didn't know if it was a Nazi sympathizer or someone trying to rob him or what.'

During a squadron patrol made in the vicinity of Amiens, Peronne, Lacapelle, Mons and Lille, Brothers sighted an He 111. This would be his first taste of action. Setting his gun sight to the enemy's wingspan, Brothers closed to within range and switched the gun button to 'Fire'. As the Heinkel filled his sight Brothers depressed the gun button, but nothing happened. His guns hadn't been cocked and failed to fire, 'I pressed the gun button and nothing happened at all, because the guns hadn't been reloaded. On landing back, I had the armourer in the office, drew my pistol, and said, "I'll shoot you if you ever do that again."'

The weeks of pressure building up to the French campaign had taken its toll on both pilots and ground staff. Brothers recalled that everyone was tired and his actions were out of character.

Meanwhile, an incident which occurred while the squadron was on the ground awaiting orders cemented Brothers' thoughts on the general predicament: 'we were refuelling when suddenly a lone Do 17, possibly on a reconnaissance mission, flew across the airfield at about 4,000ft. A French pilot, who was doing aerobatics in a Morane fighter at about the same height, had failed to see the enemy bomber.

'I thought. Oh Christ, we're going to be caught on the ground, but he flew straight past us. The French Station Commander was there. I raced to the control tower and shouted, "Tell him about the Dornier and he can shoot it down!"'

'It is not possible, mon Capitaine,' was the reply.

'Not possible?' shouted Pete, adding: 'There's the Dornier,' gesticulating with his outstretched arm.

'Not possible, mon Capitaine. You see today he is only authorized for aerobatics, not combat!'

Brothers turned away in dismay, thinking: 'what have we got for Allies?'

The squadron operated out of Morseele aerodrome, Belgium, on 18 May. Still with no direction on the ground their first real action didn't come until 1600 hours when they were scrambled to provide an escort to a Blenheim raid. During the patrol two Heinkels 111s were observed below the clouds. Pilot Officer Flinders claimed one aircraft destroyed 'unconfirmed'.

Meanwhile, Pilot Officer Grice had become detached and formed up with another squadron, destroying a Bf 110 'unconfirmed':

'I had been with the squadron (253 Squadron) about ten seconds when between six and nine Me 110s appeared and a general dogfight ensued. I fired two short bursts [firing 1,067 rounds] at one Me 110 and the last I saw of it, it was diving straight for the ground. I noticed bits flying from the enemy but I was unable to follow it down below 1,500ft as I had another Me 110 on my tail following me down.'
(signed) Grice.
'My personal opinion is that the Me 110 is not as manoeuvrable as a Hurricane.'

After spending all day in France, the squadron returned from operations, Brothers recalling the routine, how they: 'then came out at Le Havre and back across the Channel, reaching Biggin Hill at 2130 or 2200 hours, having a meal and falling into bed. Then being called up in the morning and then you'd be off again. Very wearing.'

Unlike most of the other pilots Brothers didn't turn-in straight away. He'd sit and discuss the day's patrols with his ground crew. This became a fairly regular thing with him, 'We wouldn't have got off the ground but for them. They were all superb. And of course, their aircraft had to be the best in the squadron, naturally.'

Although draining, operating out of France did have its plus points, as Brothers explained, 'I came back from France one evening and the flight sergeant said, "oh you've got this bloody French 90 Octane stuff [the RAF used 100 Octane]. Chuck it in the ditch." I said, "Hang on, stick it in our cars."'

In their cockpits well before dawn on 19 May, the squadron took off for Merville, France, at 0745 hours, landing for refuelling forty-five minutes later. Following an uneventful patrol between Lille and Valenciennes at noon, Brothers led the squadron into the air with orders to patrol Cambrai, Le Cateau, Baval and Bailnciennes. While flying over the Foret de Mormal, five miles east of Le Cateau, a formation of twenty-three Bf 109s and a number of higher flying Bf 110s was spotted escorting enemy bombers.

Leading the fighters into the attack, Brothers (flying N2588) engaged the Bf 109s at 14,000ft over Le Cateau, claiming one Bf 109 destroyed:

'I saw Green Section engage Me 109s astern of me, so I turned and flew towards them. Three 109s flew over me in line astern, so I turned sharp left as they dived on my tail. They turned away [and] as I was turning a 109 flew across my sights. I gave him a short burst and he slowly turned on his back and dived, inverted, at about 45 degrees. I followed him down, but he gained speed and remained inverted. I looked round and saw another 109 on my tail. I turned steeply to the left and he opened fire with tracer ammunition. His shooting was hopeless and I saw his tracer pass behind me. I turned onto his tail, but as I was firing he dived into cloud and I lost him. I circled round, but all a/c appeared to have gone home, so after a few minutes I returned to Merville. The N W part of Cambrai was burning furiously.'
(signed) P.M. Brothers F/Lt.

Many years later Brothers remembered this, his first combat, 'I thought, "Oh, those bloody de Havilland propeller oil specks all over the windscreen" but they grew bigger very rapidly. The Bf 109s were flying in the opposite direction and the formations were drawing close.' The formations crossed, apparently without either firing. The Bf 109's cannon had a greater range than the Hurricane's 0.303 machine guns and so should have been able to open up earlier and at least get a short burst in even if caught off guard. Having missed their initial opportunity and lost the advantage, the Bf 109s turned and came down on the Hurricanes. 'Our reactions were very slow, I remember seeing this thing whizz over my head, I could see the oil streaks on the fuselage. I thought, Good Lord, it's the bloody enemy! I looked round to see where they'd gone and they were turning around to attack us. He dived on me, and I got on his tail. Shot him down.'

Searching the sky for another Bf 109 that might be out for revenge, Brothers found he was quite alone. He quickly got his bearings and headed for a friendly airfield.

And so Brothers had claimed his first victory, the Bf 109 flown by Feldwebel Heinz Pohland of I.(J)/LG 2. Unknown to Brothers his victim had bailed out and was taken as a PoW: 'Taking on the enemy was a game to start off with, you didn't wish to hurt anybody. You wanted to shoot an aircraft down.'

Brothers wasn't the only victor in this encounter with the enemy. Flight Lieutenant Crossley (flying N2461) claimed one Bf 109 destroyed, firing only 100 rounds:

'Fired a full deflection shot as Me 109 flew across my bows from right to left. I followed him round and saw him turn slowly on his back and dive to earth.'
(signed) M. Crossley 'A' Flight.

Red 2, Pilot Officer 'Polly' Flinders (flying N2463), claimed one Bf 109 destroyed, firing 400 rounds at 200 yards:

'I turned immediately to starboard and climbed and saw an Me 109 on my starboard side. I positioned myself on his tail and, as he came out of the turn, opened fire. After about three seconds he turned slowly onto his back and dived inverted at an angle of about 60 degrees. I saw one machine which I believed to be a Hurricane in flames and the pilot descending by parachute.'
(signed) P/O Flinders.

Pilot Officer Grice (flying N2459) attacked the same formation, claiming two Bf 109s (one unconfirmed):

'I fired two bursts of about two seconds at the first 109 using from full to three-quarters deflection. The machine burst into flames. The second Me 109 [was] attacked from dead astern on a steep climb at range of approximately 300 yards. On opening fire, streams of white vapour appeared from the enemy – petrol possibly. At the end of the burst (six seconds) the 109 flick-rolled upwards and then started spinning. I watched it spinning for 5 to 6,000ft but did not see it go in.'
(signed) D. Hamilton Grice P/O.

Blue 2, Sergeant Turner (flying N2657), claimed one Bf 109 as destroyed east of Forest de Marmal, firing eighty rounds during a three second burst at 100 yards, making a, 'Dead astern attack after 109 had overshot. Enemy used tracer. Black smoke seen and pieces seen flying off. No parachute seen. Impression gathered the Me 109 was faster, but shooting poor.'

Meanwhile, Green Leader, Sergeant J.W. White (flying N2582), engaged a lone Do 17 which he destroyed, firing all fifteen seconds of ammunition at 200 yards. He noted that there was:

'No rearguard action from enemy, which had presumably just bombed Cambrai or town below on fire. Tail unit of E/A broke off and it went down in smoking spiral.'
(signed) Sgt White.

'B' Flight's Sergeant G.L. North was credited with probably destroying the Bf 109 which was lining-up to shoot at Pilot Officer Milner, who had taken to his parachute:

'The Me 109 approached from astern. I turned and attacked, firing three times [at 350 yards]. When last seen E/A was travelling eastwards vertically at an estimated speed of 400 mph and it did not apparently pull out.'
(signed) Sgt G.L. North.

Pilot Officer Daw (flying N2527) destroyed a Bf 110, his combat report having since been lost.

Meanwhile, 'B' Flight's Pilot Officer Eckford (flying N2409) engaged a formation of twelve Bf 109s and Do 215s, claiming one Bf 109 as doubtful. He also saw a Hurricane go down: 'We were attacked from behind and above by a Hurricane diving vertically in flames and a parachute above it. An Me 109 turned towards me and I fired for three or four seconds head on. His tracer missed up to the right. He passed on my starboard side and continued diving.

'I had to shake off another Me 109 which was on my tail and spun out of a turn, losing the other aircraft.'

Alan Francis 'Shag' Eckford and Victor George 'Jack' Daw joined the RAF on short service commissions in November 1938 and on completion of their flying training at No. 9 FTS, Hullavington, followed by a period at Air Observer School, Manby, were posted to No. 32 Squadron on 5 September 1939. Both would become fighter aces.

Short of fuel following the combat, the Hurricanes landed at various aerodromes in France. Once on the ground Brothers and the other pilots discovered that there was no one available to help with the refuelling process or take-offs, 'the only way to get the Hurricanes started was to have a chap each side winding the handles, so I'd get into mine and we'd get mine started and then leave it ticking over. Then I'd jump out and wind somebody else's until we'd got them all going. It was pretty ghastly and the French, I'm afraid, were totally demoralized by this time.'

Once back at Biggin Hill the pilots reported to their Intelligence Officer, Flying Officer Leighton. Piecing together the narrative of the air battle it quickly became apparent that Flying Officer J.C. 'Millie the Moocher' Milner (flying N2462) had been shot down in flames during combat with Bf 109s of I./JG 2 near Le Cateau, but had made his escape by parachute.

Brothers recalled: 'The first chap we lost was my great chum, Johnny Milner. (Milner was to remain a friend of the family until his death in 1968/9 and is remembered by Pete's daughter Wendy as 'a delightful man.') He bailed out and became a PoW.

'Nobody saw what happened [sic] and we just hoped for the best. It took about two months ... we got a card from a Kriegsgefangenenlager, which read, "Sorry I left you the other day; I wasn't looking! Wonder if you are still at the Bump. Do drop in and see me any time you're round these parts – love to everybody and good luck. Millie."

'He was locked up for the rest of the war. He got out a couple of times.'

Recaptured, Milner was transferred to Stalag Luft III, from where he made further escape attempts, although he was not one of those who took part in the Great Escape: 'He got out much earlier. He got himself to a German airfield and lay and watched it for a couple of days to check out the routine. He chose an aircraft but he couldn't get it started – it was awaiting an engine change! I think he got out twice.'

Despite the loss of one Hurricane, the squadron's haul led to a message from HQ No. 11 Group: 'Air Officer Commanding sends hearty congratulations to No. 32 Squadron on their very good shooting yesterday and today.'

To which Squadron Leader Worrall replied, '32 Squadron thanks the AOC 11 Group for his very kind message. Our tails are up and will remain so.'

During the day Churchill had made a broadcast to the nation which set the tone of his leadership during the war years:

'I speak to you for the first time as Prime Minister in a solemn hour for the life of our Country, of our Empire, of our Allies, and, above all, of the cause of Freedom.

'A tremendous battle is raging in France and Flanders. The Germans, by a remarkable combination of air bombing and heavily armoured tanks, have broken through the French defences north of the Maginot Line, and strong columns of their armoured vehicles are ravaging the open country.'

Churchill extolled the role of Fighter Command and their successes:

'In the air – often at serious odds, often at odds hitherto thought overwhelming – we have been clawing down three, or four to one, of our enemies; and the relative balance of the British and German Air Forces is now considerably more favourable to us than at the beginning of the battle. In cutting down the German bombers, we are fighting our own battle as well as that of France. My confidence in our ability to fight it out to the finish with the German Air Force has been strengthened by the fierce encounters which have taken place and are taking place.'

But not hiding from the possibility that France might fall, leaving Great Britain and her Empire to fight alone, Churchill added:

> 'Our task is not only to win the battle – but to win the war. After this battle in France abates its force, there will come the battle for our Island – for all that Britain is, and all that Britain means. That will be the struggle.'

During a meeting of the War Office that day, a number of subjects were discussed. These included the appointment of Vice Admiral Bertram Ramsey, Flag Officer Commanding Dover (later Admiral Sir Bertram Home Ramsay, KCB, KBE, MVO), who was to oversee the 'possible but unlikely evacuation of a very large force in hazardous circumstances, via Boulogne, Calais and Dunkirk'. The collapse of the Front would be so rapid that the plan came into almost immediate effect.

The squadron spent the following day at Manston, taking off at 1745 hours on a wing-strength bomber escort to Blenheims targeting Arras and Cambrai. Pilot Officer Daw destroyed a Bf 109, while Flight Lieutenant Humpherson damaged a Bf 109, Pilot Officer Grice claiming another. Meanwhile, Squadron Leader Worrall and his No. 2, Sergeant North, attacked a Henschel Hs 126 spotter aircraft of 3(H)/41 (8 Panzer Division) over Arras, killing the pilot, Oberleutnant Seppell.

'B' Flight's Sergeant North (flying N2583) claimed the Hs 126 probably destroyed at 1825 hours:

> 'Green One (Squadron Leader Worrall) dived to attack [firing 1,689 rounds but losing the enemy while trying to gain a better position]. After a few minutes Green One broke away and I engaged the E/A at an estimated height of 100ft. I fired and the enemy adopted evasive tactics, climbing and turning, displaying exceptional manoeuvrability. I engaged the enemy again at a height of about 50ft and from 100 yards got in a long burst. The rear gunner appeared then to have been silenced (he had been firing tracer), but then there was a loud explosion coming from the direction of the port tank [of Sgt North's Hurricane]. The aircraft caught fire [hit by return fire from the Hs 126 of 3 (H)/41], my cockpit filling with acrid smoke. I put it down with the wheels in the up position in a ploughed field approximately ten miles S.E. of Arras, near Pelves.'

North evaded capture and made it back to England via Vimy, Merville and Calais, reporting for duty on 23 May.

Meanwhile, on 21 May, the squadron took off for Hawkinge at 0835 hours, refuelling before making two patrols of Abbeville, Fervent, Montreuil, Etaples, Lille, Seclin and Merville. A total of fifty-two sorties were flown, during which Pilot Officer Daw was credited with a Bf 109 destroyed.

Back at Biggin Hill, it was almost as if normality had resumed. Of their time flying out of French airfields Brothers said, 'It all seemed rather pointless too, because we didn't feel we were achieving very much. We had several engagements in France but not enough, I would have said, to justify our presence there. Occasionally you did bump into some Germans, whereas you wouldn't have done if you'd been sitting at Biggin Hill, there'd been so much disorder and chaos beforehand, now we're settled, we're back at home and everything is organized here and we can just get on with it'.

On the following day Nos. 32 and 601 Squadrons flew a joint patrol at 1900 hours, attacking eight Bf 109s encountered over St Pol in two formations.

'A' Flight's Flight Lieutenant M. Crossley claimed one Bf 109 destroyed, his combat report taking up the narrative:

'I was leading a patrol of sixteen Hurricanes, bound for the Bethune – Arras patrol line, and had crossed the French coast at Calais. On approaching St. Omer I saw what I thought was a Spitfire high up to starboard, and said so. Almost immediately after, I saw five single engine a/c go past to port and below. I told Blue Section to go and investigate, but they didn't hear, and the a/c appeared to become mixed up with our rear Flight (601). I then saw four larger a/c in echelon go past down to the right and turned to follow them, but lost sight of them on seeing a melee going on behind. I turned round preparing to join in, but immediately decided first to ascertain whether a further supply was coming up. I saw three more to the south flying around. I approached the back one who was doing a step L.H. turn, and opened fire. After a while he caught fire and blew up. The other two Me 109s were about to dive on me from the front, and I, not knowing how much ammunition was left, dived steeply and escaped.'
(signed) Flt Lt M. Crossley.

Also flying with Red Section was Pilot Officer Daw, who destroyed one Bf 109:

'I sighted six enemy a/c which turned as if to attack us from behind, one section of the squadron turned and engaged these – a few minutes later another nine appeared out of the sun; which Red Section turned and attacked. I managed to get on the tail of one, I gave three long bursts. Parts of the tail unit came off and he dived earthwards in large circles.'
(signed) P/O Daw.

Yellow Section's Pilot Officer D. Hamilton Grice claimed one Bf 109 destroyed:

'An Me 109 got on my tail and fired a burst of about one second which passed under my port wing. I turned and the enemy dived vertically, pulling out at ground level. Having followed it down I fired at 250 yards dead astern. The 109 immediately emitted white vapour from the wings and dense black smoke from the engine. I continued firing in short bursts until my ammunition was expended. The machine continued flying for a further minute and finally flew into the ground.'
(signed) D. Hamilton Grice.

While flying ten miles east of St Omer, 'A' Flight's Sergeant Nowell witnessed the destruction of one of the Bf 109s, which had been previously damaged by the squadron:

> '…he just dived straight into the ground. I had not fired and presumed the enemy to have already been attacked.'
> (signed) Sgt Nowell.

'B' Flight's Pilot Officer Humpherson claimed one Bf 109 'inconclusive':

> 'In the general dogfight that ensued I attacked an Me 109 at a range of about 250 yards. After a burst of about ten seconds the enemy a/c rolled over onto its side, smoke coming from the starboard side. I was unable to watch the machine crash as I was forced to take violent evasive tactics.'
> (signed) P/O Humpherson.

Flight Lieutenant R.V. Jeff (flying P2755) claimed one Bf 109 destroyed twenty miles north-west of St Pol:

> 'Enemy aircraft sighted behind and above us, broke section away and engaged a/c attacking a Hurricane. The enemy a/c turned on his back and dived vertically to the ground, a stream of petrol pouring out of his burst tank. I had no difficulty in keeping up during the dive or the climb that followed. After a further dive and chasing among tree tops, I fired from dead astern until black smoke poured out of the machine and the engine stopped so suddenly I nearly collided. I left the machine gliding down to force land.'

A further Bf 109 was claimed by Pilot Officer Eckford.

Meanwhile, 'B' Flight's Sergeant Guy Turner was reported as missing, shot down over St Omer at 2000 hours, making a forced landing. He later made his way back to the squadron and filed a combat report:

> 'The squadron was engaged by six enemy Me 109s, nine more Me 109s approaching from the east. I left my squadron to attack the latter, but was shot in the engine by cannon fire at a range of approximately 800 yds. The cannon firing appeared similar to a green Very light emerging from the starboard wing close to the fuselage. Evasive action after I was hit was a vertical dive, with engine stopped for 9,000ft. I landed with undercarriage up near to Tourneham, about twenty miles east of Calais.
>
> 'It appears very noticeable in France that all enemy a/c keep away while our fighters patrol, but immediately the latter return to refuel, enemy bombers take advantage of this to come over and bomb.'
> (signed) Sgt Turner.

Meanwhile, the news from the ground forces was all bad and on 23 May the British were pushed back from Arras and, in a further setback, the French withdrew as the right flank was turned. By the evening the British too were in full retreat along the Douai road out of Arras.

During the early morning Brothers flew on what turned out to be an uneventful squadron patrol between Arras–Cambrai–Dover. Brothers' second patrol of the day came when 'B' Flight provided a fighter escort for a Blenheim reconnaissance mission.

At about 1310 hours eighteen Bf 110s were encountered while flying in the neighbourhood of Ypres. Climbing to attack, the squadron was bounced by fourteen Bf 109s. During the ensuing dogfight Flight Lieutenant Crossley claimed two Bf 109s and Flight Lieutenant Brothers destroyed one Bf 110. The squadron suffered the loss of Sergeant Nowell, who was shot down in flames, while Pilot Officer Flinders was reported as missing.

'A' Flight's Flight Lieutenant M. Crossley wrote in his combat report:

'I saw about twelve 109s just south of us, chose one and took a full deflection shot at him. Something large blew off his tail and he wobbled and turning on his back dived vertically. I was about to follow him when I saw another above to the left, about to dive at my left flank. I had no time for evasive tactics so I swung head on to him and fired. He opened fire too and his tracer went above to starboard. When I turned round I saw black smoke mingled with white and he was diving steeply.'
(signed) M. Crossley F/Lt.

Meanwhile, Brothers' combat report read:

'I was escorting a Blenheim a/c carrying out a recon. As the weather was bad (low cloud, rain and occasional clear patches) I was not certain of my position, but I was somewhere east of Ypres, when I saw about eighteen Me 110s and fourteen Me 109s behind them. I turned and climbed up behind the rear 110 (they were in line astern) intending to pick them off, when they vanished into a cloud. I circled and saw below me a fight between 109s and Hurricanes. I waited until one pulled clear of the fight, then dropped on his tail, closed to 100yds and opened fire. Petrol, oil and smoke poured out, and some pieces broke off. He went into a steep dive and I followed until he hit the ground. As all the other a/c had vanished, I returned home. My engine was running very badly so I climbed high and crossed the Channel, after having to return to the French coast until my engine ran a little better.'
(signed) P.M. Brothers F/Lt.

Post-war research undertaken by Brothers led him to the conclusion that his victim had been Leutnant Hans-Wedige von Weither.

Before being shot down, Sergeant Nowell (flying P3550) claimed one Bf 109 destroyed near Lille, firing four second and one second bursts at 300-200 yards:

'I notified leader that there were nineteen a/c above and to our right. Everyone made a right turn with the obvious intention of attacking, which left me wide out and well behind, there were six Me 109s coming up in our rear, I notified Leader and turned to attack. The foremost 109 went well above me and turned on his back. I put my nose up and gave him a good burst of fire as he passed me. He continued on his way upside down with smoke pouring out of him.

'I stall turned off my attack and on levelling out I saw four Me 109s diving at me from the front. I saw no means of avoiding their attack so lifted my nose and got in a short burst on the leader before I was hit by cannon in the right arm. My machine burst into flames [Nowell suffering burns] and I succeeded in landing by parachute.

'I was fired at and hit in the right ankle by the French before they realized their mistake and packed me off to hospital.'
(signed) Sgt G.L. Nowell

Sergeant Nowell bailed out near Arras. He made his way back via Calais and by 1 June was in Pinderfields Casualty Hospital, Wakefield, Yorkshire. While Nowell was still officially posted as missing, news reached the squadron that he had been awarded the DFM for his service with No. 87 Squadron, a Bar following less than a week later.

Sergeant Nowell's, DFM was announced in the *London Gazette*, 28 May 1940.
'740099 Sergeant Garet Leofric Nowell

'This pilot shot down four, and possibly seven, German aircraft. He has displayed a high standard of courage and devotion to duty. One morning [10 May] he attacked two enemy aircraft [Hs 126s] and brought both down. His own aircraft received many hits but he successfully brought it back to the aerodrome. On the afternoon of the next day, with six other aircraft of the squadron, he engaged more than forty enemy aircraft [Do 17s and Bf 109s]. He showed conspicuous gallantry and dash in driving off the enemy single-seaters and shot down two enemy aircraft. His own engine was hit and he was forced down. Showing great coolness, he landed carefully and avoided injuries to personnel.'

Sergeant Nowell's Bar to the DFM was announced in the *London Gazette*, 4 June 1940.
'740099 Sergeant Garet Leofric Nowell, DFM.

'Sgt Nowell has continued to shoot down enemy aircraft with excellent initiative and leadership. He brought down twelve enemy aircraft in one week. This is the highest individual total of which there is a record in the Group.'

Nowell, one of the forgotten heroes of the Battle of France, didn't fly operationally again until late 1942.

A signal was sent by HQ No. 11 Group to No. 32 Squadron at Biggin Hill on 24 May:

> 'As a result of engagement over the Continent on Thursday, 23 May, squadrons in No. 11 Group accounted for forty-three German aircraft at the cost of eight casualties, thus providing support to the British Army and the Navy at a very critical time. The Air Officer Commanding congratulates the pilots, also the personnel at stations whose hard work has maintained a high serviceability of aircraft and supported the flying personnel. Squadrons will be relieved for short periods of rest whenever humanly possible to spare them from supporting their comrades fighting on the ground.'

During the day (23 May) No. 79 Squadron returned from France on the SS *Biarritz*, remaining at Biggin Hill until 27 May, before transferring to RAF Digby. In the meantime, Squadron Leader Alexander was posted away and Flying Officer G.D.L. Haysom took temporary command, as well as leading 'B' Flight, while Flying Officer Davies was appointed to command 'A' Flight.

On 24 May, Brothers led a flight strength fighter patrol targeting Stuka dive-bombers reported in the Dunkirk-St Omer-Boulogne area, making a second uneventful patrol in the afternoon.

Following the BEF's withdrawal, twelve Blenheims of No. 82 Squadron were dispatched to bomb the southern end of the Arras road. Acting as their escort, No. 32 Squadron successfully fended off a concerted attack by thirty Bf 109s and 110s, claiming three Bf 109s without loss.

Meanwhile, with the campaign going better than even Hitler could have imagined, he issued his Directive No. 13, ordering the destruction of the Belgian, English and French forces in what would become the Dunkirk 'pocket'. Meanwhile, the Luftwaffe was ordered to prevent their evacuation.

Next day 'A' Flight flew two operations against Stuka dive-bombers. At Biggin Hill, reports of an attack by German paratroopers led to the station being stood-to, gun pits were manned and the perimeters patrolled with parties dispatched to secure key buildings against possible attack. Brothers later recalled how for some time afterwards, 'some of the pilots carried their Webley 0.38, even when they went to the pub.'

During the day Calais fell, while Bolougne was to be overrun within twenty-four hours. Dunkirk would remain as the only escape route for nearly 400,000 Allied troops.

Since the beginning of the campaign the RAF had lost a quarter of its fighter strength. The battle-weary pilots were now called upon to cover the BEF's retreat and evacuation from the beaches as Vice Admiral Ramsay received orders to put Operation Dynamo into action. The evacuation was planned 'with a view to lifting up to 45,000 of the BEF within two days, at the end of which it was probable that evacuation would be terminated by enemy action.' Keith Park was placed in control of the air defence of the English Channel, Dunkirk and its hinterland.

The situation looked desperate and when Viscount Gort spoke candidly to the Secretary of State for War he said, 'I must not conceal from you that a great part of the BEF and its equipment will inevitably be lost, even in the best circumstances.'

At 0630 hours on 26 May, a flight strength formation escorted eighteen Blenheims bombing targets at Menin. During the early afternoon Brothers took part in a fighter patrol of the Calais-Dunkirk area made in the company of No. 605 Squadron.

Whilst returning over the Channel at about 1400 hours, Crossley, who was leading, spotted a Ju 88 approaching from the east. Uncertain as to whether it was a Blenheim, he held his fire until it was too late and the German bomber escaped, with Brothers in hot pursuit, but unable to get within effective range. A second Ju 88 flew from Crossley's right, heading for home. Breaking away from the formation, he began the chase, closing to within firing range and hitting both engines, which left a telltale trail of smoke:

'I gave "line astern" and fell in behind it, and opened fire at about 500 yards thinking he might disappear before I got within easy range. White and black smoke was pouring from each engine and the port wing was rather down. I had to break away as a machine from 605 [possibly Pilot Officer T.P.M. Cooper-Slipper] cut in on me and nearly collided. My No. 3, who was following, saw him gently lose height, still smoking hard, and go right down to sea level and disappear.'

As Crossley suspected, No. 605 Squadron was independently in pursuit of the same enemy aircraft, which dived into the sea, one of a formation of four or five seen bombing, using the smoke for cover, Pilot Officer T.P.M. Cooper-Slipper making a claim. The squadron damaged two more Ju 88s. Meanwhile, Pilot Officer Muirhead (flying N2346) fired on what he believed to have been a Bf 110, but what could have been another Ju 88. He silenced the rear gunner, but not before receiving damage to his own aircraft's glycol system. He bailed out and was rescued by a naval vessel.

Temporarily relieved by No. 213 Squadron's 'A' Flight, No. 32 Squadron's pilots flew their aircraft to Wittering, where they were to be 'rested'.

Monday, 27 May, was the first full day of the Dunkirk evacuation, the naval operations being covered by the RAF. The general situation worsened when at midnight the Belgium government surrendered, opening the north-east area of the BEF's defensive perimeter. Disaster was, however, averted and the gap plugged.

No. 79 Squadron made two patrols over France and Dunkirk. During the second of these, flown in the company of Nos. 19, 145 and 601 Squadrons, the formation came up against some Bf 110s. Flying Officer J.W.E. Davies claiming one destroyed and one damaged, Pilot Officer D.W.A. Stones claiming one confirmed and a second unconfirmed, while Sergeant Cartwright got one unconfirmed. Meanwhile, Flying Officer Duus and Pilot Officers D.G. Clift and Stevens all destroyed a Bf 110. Landing at Biggin Hill, the squadron began its move to RAF Digby, Lincolnshire.

A number of squadrons operated from Biggin Hill during May and early June, also spending time in France and elsewhere. The squadron claims, losses and gallantry awards are included here to help complete the Biggin Hill story:

No. 79 Squadron

No. 79 Squadron's victories and casualties while operating in France may be summarized:

11 May	Pilot Officer L.L. Appleton – He 111
	Pilot Officer J.E.R. Wood – He 111
12 May	Flight Lieutenant C.L.C. Roberts – He 111 (shared), Do 17 (shared)
	Flying Officer R. Herrick – Bf 109 probable, He 111 (shared)
	Pilot Officer T.C. Parker – He 111 (shared), Do 17
	Sergeant H. Cartwright – He 111 (shared)
	Flying Officer Davies – He 111, He 111 unconfirmed
	Sergeant A.W. Whitby – Do 17, Do 17 (shared)
14 May	Flying Officer Davies – Hs 126, Bf 110
	Pilot Officer L.L. Appleton – Hs 126 (shared)
	Pilot Officer D.W.A. Stones – Ju 88, Ju 88 (shared)
	Sergeant H. Cartwright – Ju 88, Ju 88 (shared)
	Sergeant L.H.B. Pearce – Hs 126 (shared)
	Sergeant A.W. Whitby – Do 17 unconfirmed
16 May	Pilot Officer T.C. Parker – Fw 198
	Pilot Officer D.G. Clift – Fw 198
	Sergeant H. Cartwright – Fw 198
17 May	Sergeant A.W. Whitby – Bf 109 unconfirmed
	Pilot Officer L.R. Dorrien-Smith – Bf 109
18 May	Flying Officer Davies – Do 17
	Flying Officer F.J.L. Duus – Do 17
	Pilot Officer L.R. Dorrien-Smith – Do 17 damaged
	Pilot Officer T.C. Parker – two Do 17s damaged
	Pilot Officer D.W.A. Stones – Bf 110, Bf 110 damaged
19 May	Pilot Officer D.W.A. Stones – Hs 126
	Sergeant H. Cartwright – Do 17
	Pilot Officer D.W.A. Stones – Hs 126
20 May	Flying Officer F.J.L. Duus – He 111 probable
	Pilot Officer D.W.A. Stones – Hs 126 (shared with below)
	Sergeant H. Cartwright – Hs 126 (shared), Do 17 damaged
	Sergeant L.H.B. Pearce – Hs 126 (shared), Do 17 damaged
	Sergeant R.R. McQueen – Bf 110 damaged
	Sergeant A.W. Whitby – Do 17, Do 17 (shared with No. 213 Squadron)

11 May   Flying out of Merville, the squadron lost two Hurricanes while attacking an He 111 of KG1. Flight Lieutenant R. Edwards (flying L2068) suffered burns before he was able to bail out near Mons. Pilot Officer L.L. Appleton (flying L2049) force-landed.

12 May   Pilot Officer C.T. Parker bailed out when his Hurricane (L2065) was damaged in combat with a Do 17 of KG 77. He evaded capture and made it back to British lines (for which he was later mentioned in despatches *London Gazette*, 13 March 1942).

14 May   At 1530 hours Pilot Officer L.L. Appleton (flying P2689) was shot down and killed by a Bf 109 near Sean.

Pilot Officer (40497) Llewellyn Lister Appleton, RAF, was the son of Charles and Mary Appleton, of Hartley, Kent. He was 23-years-old and is remembered on the Runnymede Memorial, Panel 71.

Pilot Officer J.E.R Wood (flying N2490) bailed out injured following combat with a Ju 88 north of Leuze.

Flight Lieutenant R. Roberts, 'B' Flight Commander, was wounded in combat.

16 May   Sergeant Cartwright was shot down in combat but managed to make a forced-landing.

17 May   Flying Officer R. Herrick (flying L2140) became a PoW after being shot down by a Bf 109 of 6./JG 52, bailing out near Valenciennes. He spent much of the remainder of the war in Stalag Luft III.

Sergeant Valentine force-landed following combat.

18 May   Pilot Officer D.W.A. 'Dimsie' Stones (flying P3451) forced-landed following combat with a Bf 110 of II./ZG 76, near Vitry, at 1830 hours.

20 May   Sergeant Valentine was wounded during operations.

Pilot Officer T.C. Parker, flying P2624, was shot down at 1400 hours by ground fire while strafing a troop column in the St Quentin area. He bailed out safely. A second victim of the ground fire was Pilot Officer L.R. Dorrien-Smith, hc was shot down and killed (flying L2142).

Pilot Officer (72501) Lionel Roger Dorrien-Smith, RAFVR, was the son of Major Arthur Algernon Dorrien-Smith, DSO, DL, JP, and Eleanor Salvin Dorrien-Smith, of Tresco, Isles of Scilly. His brothers Algernon and Francis also died in service. Dorrien-Smith (whose uncle was the general by the same name) was 21-years-old and is remembered on the Runnymede Memorial, Panel 8.

23 May   Pilot Officer W.D.W. Stones descended through fog at Biggin Hill and landed off the runway, colliding with a gun emplacement. His aircraft (P2698) was written off.

No. 213 Squadron

From 17 May 1939, No. 213 Squadron's 'B' Flight operated out of Merville in France. Meanwhile, their 'A' Flight, based at Biggin Hill until 23 May, made the daily flight to Merville from where they too operated during daylight hours.

Their combat details may be summarized:

19 May	Pilot Officer L.G.B. Stone – Bf 109
	Flying Officer W.N. 'Bill' Gray – He 111, He 111 (shared)
	Pilot Officer P.M. Gardner – He 111 (shared)
20 May	Flying Officer W.N. Gray – Hs 126 (shared)
26 May	Nos. 213 and 242 Squadrons flew a joint patrol over Gravelines where they encountered ten Bf 109s, shooting down two without loss.
27 May	The squadron was heavily outnumbered when taking on a formation of Ju 88s and He 111s escorted by Bf 109s. During an air battle which lasted some five minutes, seven enemy aircraft were destroyed.

No. 213 Squadron's 'A' Flight lost two pilots during this phase:

28 May	Pilot Officer L.G.B. Stone (flying P2792) killed-in-action. Pilot Officer (43695) Laurence George Beauchamp Stone, RAF, is remembered on the Runnymede Memorial, Panel 10.
31 May	Flying Officer W.N. Gray killed-in-action. Flying Officer (40108) William Napier Gray, RAF, was the son of William N. and Jane MacLaurin Gray, of Pollockshield, Glasgow. He was 22-years-old and was buried in The Hague (Westduin) General Cemetery, Allied Plot, Row 3, Grave 51.

No. 229 Squadron

No. 229 Squadron operated out of Biggin Hill between 25 May and 7 June, making patrols in defence of the Dunkirk beaches and the retreating BEF. The following is a summary of their casualties and combat victories over France and the Channel:

28 May	Sergeant J.C. Harris – Bf 109
	Squadron Leader H.J. Maguire – Do 17 damaged
29 May	Pilot Officer R.R. Smith – Bf 109
	Pilot Officer V.M. Bright – Bf 109
31 May	Pilot Officer V.M. Bright – Bf 110 destroyed and Bf 110 damaged
	Pilot Officer B.S. Verity – Bf 110
	Sergeant D.F. Edgehill – Bf 109
I June	Pilot Officer R.E. Bary – Ju 87 unconfirmed
	Pilot Officer E. Smith – Ju 87 and another unconfirmed

28 May   Sergeant S.A. Hillman (flying N2551) was killed-in-action.

Sergeant (565993) Stanley Albert Hillman, RAF, was the son of Tom and Lily Louisa Hillman, of Exmouth, Devon.

29 May   Flight Lieutenant F.N. Clouston (flying P3489) shot down by a Bf 109 and was killed-in-action.

Flight Lieutenant (40990) Falcon Nelson Clouston, RAF, was the son of Robert Edmund and Ruby Alexandra Clouston, of Upper Montere, Nelson, New Zealand. Clouston was 27-years-old and was buried in Sage Cemetery, S. F. 14.

Flight Lieutenant P.E.S.F.M. Browne (flying P2636) shot down by a Bf 109 and killed-in-action.

Flight Lieutenant (33222) Patrick Edgar Sempill F.M. Browne, RAF, was the son of Patrick Edgar and Osran Browne. Husband of Ann Eileen Browne. He was 28-years-old and is remembered on the Runnymede Memorial, Panel 4.

Sergeant J.C. Harrison (flying P2876) was shot down by a Bf 109 and killed-in-action.

Sergeant (519293) James Charles Harrison, RAF, was buried in Sage War Cemetery, 8. A. 5.

Flying Officer W.G. New (flying N2473) bailed out safe.

Pilot Officer A.S. Linney (flying N2521) bailed out safe.

31 May   Pilot Officer V.B.S. Verity (flying P3492) bailed out following combat with a Bf 110.

Sergeant D.F. Edgehill (flying P3553) was wounded in combat with a Bf 110.

Pilot Officer J.E.M. Collins (flying L1982) was killed-in-action.

Pilot Officer (41830) John Edward Martin Collins, RAF, is remembered on the Runnymede Memorial, Panel 7.

No. 242 Squadron

No. 242 Squadron flew out of Biggin Hill between 21 May and 8 June (when it became the last squadron posted to France, setting up base initially at Chateaudun. It was forced to change base twice in the next eight days (to Ancenis and then Chateau Bougon), before, in mid-June, helping to cover the evacuation from St Nazaire and Nantes.

The following is a summary of their casualties and combat victories over France and the Channel while operating out of Biggin Hill:

22 May   Flight Lieutenant D.R. Miller – Hs 126
Pilot Officer N.K. Stansfeld – Hs 126 (shared)
Pilot Officer D.G. MacQueen – Hs 126 (shared with above)
Flying Officer J.W. Graafstra – Hs 126 (shared)
Flying Officer G.A. Madore – Hs 126 (shared with above)

23 May	Unknown pilot(s) – two Bf 109s unconfirmed
25 May	Squadron Leader Gobell – Bf 109
	Pilot Officer R.D. Grassick – Bf 109 destroyed, Bf 109 damaged
	Pilot Officer P.S. Turner – two Bf 109s, one Bf 109 unconfirmed
28 May	Flight Lieutenant D.R. Miller – Bf 109 unconfirmed
	Pilot Officer W.L. McKnight – Bf 109
	Pilot Officer P.S. Turner – Bf 109
29 May	Flight Lieutenant J.H. Plinston – Bf 109
	Pilot Officer R.D. Grassick – Bf 109
	Pilot Officer W.L. McKnight – Bf 109, unconfirmed Bf 109, Do 17
	Pilot Officer P.S. Turner – Bf 109 unconfirmed, Bf 109 damaged
	Pilot Officer D.G. MacQueen – Bf 109
	Pilot Officer J.B. Latta – Bf 109
	Unknown pilots – four Bf 109s
31 May	Flight Lieutenant G.H. Plinston – Ju 88, Bf 109
	Pilot Officer D.G. MacQueen – Do 17
	Pilot Officer N.K. Stansfeld – Bf 110
	Pilot Officer W.L. McKnight – two Bf 110s, Bf 109
	Pilot Officer P.S. Turner – Bf 109
	Pilot Officer J.B. Latta – Bf 109
	Pilot Officer R.D. Grassick – Bf 109
1 June	Pilot Officer N.K. Stansfield – Ju 87 destroyed
	Pilot Officer P.S. Turner – Bf 110, Bf 109 unconfirmed
	Pilot Officer W.L. McKnight – two Ju 87s, one unconfirmed Ju 87, Ju 87 damaged
	Flight Lieutenant D.R. Miller – two Bf 109s unconfirmed
8 June	Pilot Officer P.S. Turner – two Bf 109s

23 May	Flying Officer J.W. Graafstra (flying P2809) was shot down by Bf 109s and killed.
	Flying Officer (39381) John William Graafstra, RAF, was the son of Thomas and Sarah Bingham Graafstra, of Souris, Manatoba, Canada. Graafstra was 27-years-old and was buried at Wancourt Communal Cemetery, Grave 2.
28 May	Pilot Officer A.H. Deacon (flying N2651) was shot down by a Bf 109 and made a PoW.
	Pilot Officer D.F. Jones (flying L1746) was killed-in-action by a Bf 109. Pilot Officer (42131) Dale Frederick Jones, RAF, was the son of Luther E. and Vera Hope Jones, of Dinsmore, Saskatchewan, Canada. He was 26-years-old and was buried at Oostduinkerke Communal Cemetery.
30 May	Pilot Officer J.F. Howitt (flying L1756) was injured.
31 May	Pilot Officer G.M. Stewart (flying P2732) was killed-in-action in combat with a Bf 109.
	Pilot Officer (41625) Gordon McKenzie Stewart, RAF, is remembered on the Runnymede Memorial, Panel 10.
	Flight Lieutenant G.M. Plinston (flying P2884) was shot down, safe.

The following pilots received gallantry awards for operations during this period:

Pilot Officer 'Willie' McKnight, was awarded the DFC (for service with No. 242 Squadron and while on secondment to Nos. 607 and 615 Squadrons), *London Gazette*, 14 June 1940:
'Pilot Officer William Lidstone McKNIGHT (41937).

'One day in May 1940, this officer destroyed a Messerschmitt 109 and on the following day, whilst on patrol with his squadron, he shot down three more enemy aircraft. The destruction of the last one of the three aircraft occasioned a long chase over enemy territory. On his return flight he used his remaining ammunition, and caused many casualties, in a low flying attack on a railway along which the enemy was bringing up heavy guns. Pilot Officer McKnight has shown exceptional skill and courage as a fighter pilot.'
(Awarded a Bar to the DFC, *London Gazette*, 8 October 1940.)

Flight Lieutenant Grassick, was awarded the DFC (for service with No. 242 Squadron and while on secondment to Nos. 607 and 615 Squadrons), *London Gazette*, 15 July 1941:
'Acting Flight Lieutenant Robert Davidson GRASSICK (41579), No. 242 Squadron.

'This officer has been a member of the squadron since its formation. He has displayed an indomitable spirit and has proved himself to be a first-class section leader. Flight Lieutenant Grassick has destroyed at least six enemy aircraft.'

Percival Stanley 'Stan' Turner, was awarded the DFC, *London Gazette*, 8 October 1940:
'Acting Flight Lieutenant Percival Stanley TURNER (41631).

'On 15 September 1940, Pilot Officer P.S. Turner succeeded in shooting down one enemy aircraft, when his own aircraft was hit by a cannon shell which put it temporarily out of control. On recovery, he saw and attacked a further enemy aircraft which he destroyed, afterwards bringing his own damaged aircraft safely back to its base. This officer has personally destroyed a total of ten hostile aircraft during engagements over Dunkirk and England. He has proved himself a most courageous and capable leader, displaying coolness and initiative in the face of the enemy.'
Awarded a Bar to the DFC, *London Gazette*, 5 August 1941. Awarded the DSO, *London Gazette*, 23 May 1944.

No. 610 Squadron

No. 610 Squadron was moved to Gravesend on 27 May, continuing to fly operations during the battle for France. Their combat victories and losses for this period may be summarized:

27 May	Squadron Leader A.L. Franks – two Bf 109s
	Squadron Leader E.B.B. Smith – He 111
	Flight Lieutenant J. Ellis – Bf 110
	Flight Lieutenant A.T. Smith – Bf 110 probable
	Flying Officer G.M.T. Kerr – Bf 109 destroyed
	Flying Officer P.G. Lamb – He 111 damaged
	Flying Officer W.H.C. Warner – He 111 damaged
	Pilot Officer P. Litchfield – Bf 110
29 May	Squadron Leader A.L. Franks – Bf 109
	Flight Lieutenant J. Ellis – Bf 109
	Flying Officer G.L. Chambers – Bf 109
	Flying Officer W.H.C. Warner – Bf 109
	Pilot Officer P. Litchfield – Bf 109
	Pilot Officer S.C. Norris – Bf 109
31 May	Flight Lieutenant J. Ellis – Bf 110, Do 215
	Pilot Officer P. Litchfield – Do 215

27 May   Flying Officer A.R.J. Medcalf (flying L1016) – killed-in-action.
Flying Officer (90339) Albert Rupert John Medcalf, AAF, was the son of Rupert Medcalf, OBE, FRIBA, and Florence Mabel Medcalf, of Cheshire, B. Arch (Liverpool) ARIBA. Medcalf was 26-years-old and is remembered on the Runnymede Memorial, Panel 6.
Sergeant W.T. Medway (flying L1003) – killed-in-action.
Sergeant (740320) William Thomas Medway, RAFVR, was buried in Oostduinkerke Communal Cemetery, Row E, Grave 111.

29 May   Squadron Leader A.L. Franks (flying N3177 'T') – killed-in-action. Squadron Leader (26053) Alexander Lumsden 'Bonzo' Franks, AFC, RAF, was the son of James Gordon Franks and of Margaret Franks (née Fitzgibbon). Husband of Kirsten Franks, he was 32-years-old and was buried in Sage War Cemetery, Grave 7. F. 15.
Flying Officer J. Kerr-Wilson (flying N3289) – killed-in-action.
Flying Officer (90338) John Kerr-Wilson, AAF, was the son of Henry Kerr-Wilson and Lucy Gladys Kerr-Wilson, MA, BSc, of Heswall, Cheshire. He was 32-years-old and is remembered on the Runnymede Memorial, Panel 6.
Flying Officer G.M.T. Kerr (flying L1006 'R') – killed-in-action.
Flying Officer (90336) Gerald Malcolm Theodore Kerr, AAF, was the son of Frederick Bernard and Margaret Kerr; husband of Barbara Morton

Kerr, BA, BSc (Oxon), of Frodsham, Cheshire. Kerr was 30-years-old and is remembered on the Runnymede Memorial, Panel 6.

Sergeant P.D. Jenkins (flying DW 'K') – killed-in-action.

Sergeant (740830) Peter Douglas Jenkins, RAFVR, was the son of Frederick Seymour Jenkins, and of Dorothy Marian Jenkins, of Breage, Cornwall. Jenkins was 20-years-old and is remembered on the Runnymede Memorial, Panel 16.

31 May   Flying Officer G.L. Chambers (flying N3274) – killed-in-action.

Flying Officer (90343) Graham Lambert Chambers, AAF, is remembered on the Runnymede Memorial, Panel 5.

Pilot Officer G. Keighley (flying L1013 'E') – bailed out safe.

13 June   Sergeant P.I. Watson-Parker – killed-in-action.

Sergeant (741433) Patrick Ian Watson-Parker, RAFVR. He was buried at Cudham (SS Peter and Paul) Churchyard, Orpington, Section NN, Grave 24.

Chapter 5

The Fight Goes On

With their forces continuing to close in on Dunkirk during 1 June, the German High Command issued a communiqué which summed up the day's events from their force's perspective:

'In hard fighting, the strip of coast on both sides of Dunkirk, which yesterday also was stubbornly defended by the British, was further narrowed.

'Altogether, four warships and eleven transports with a total tonnage of 54,000 tons were sunk by our bombers. Fourteen warships, including two cruisers, two light cruisers, an anti-aircraft cruiser, six destroyers and two torpedo boats, as well as thirty-eight transports with a total tonnage of 160,000 were damaged by bombs.'

During the early hours of 2 June, Operation Dynamo drew to a conclusion, the Royal Navy (RN) rescuing many of the men who had held the Dunkirk perimeter, their places having been taken overnight by French soldiers.

At Readiness before dawn, No. 32 Squadron flew to Martlesham, refuelling in preparation for the day's operations. Ordered to patrol Dunkirk at 0745 hours, they provided air cover for the final phase of the withdrawal. The Hurricanes quickly entered into combat with a force of three Ju 88s, six He 111s, and their escort of twenty-one Bf 109s and Bf 110s. During the brief air battle Pilot Officer Smyth (Yellow 3) claimed one Ju 88 destroyed and a Bf 109 probably destroyed:

'Saw [a] Ju 88 underneath. I told Yellow 1 [but R/T was u/s] then broke away and followed it down to 4,000ft. It was on its back and probably crashed after two bursts from my guns [firing at 250-100 yards at 12,000ft]; climbed up and ran into six Me 109s. I attacked one of these and got in several short bursts [at 8,000ft] and [it] went down, but do not know whether he crashed or not.'
(signed) P/O Smyth.

As the squadron reformed it became apparent that Sergeant D. Flynn (flying P2727) was missing, shot down in combat with Bf 109s and Bf 110s. He spent the remainder of the war as a PoW in Stalag 357, Kopernikus, Poland.

Meanwhile, a letter was received from Headquarters, No. 11 Group, dated 2 June: 'Air Officer Commanding sends following message to pilots and all personnel of the Fighter Stations, Sector Stations and Forward Airfields:

'During the last two weeks our Fighter Squadrons operating over France have shot down a total of 527 German bombers and fighters, 371 of which have been confirmed as destroyed, for the loss of eighty of our pilots [with many more wounded or as PoWs]. By their successes in air combat our squadrons have protected the Army during [the] retreat, have enabled the Navy to embark the Army from Dunkirk and the beaches. The Air Officer Commanding congratulates the pilots on their magnificent fighting and highly commends the technical and administrative personnel whose work made it possible.'

The squadron's pilots flew back from their temporary base at Wittering to Biggin Hill on 4 June. During the day, in a speech made in Parliament, Churchill announced, 'All our types – the Hurricane, the Spitfire, and the new Defiant – and all our pilots have been vindicated as superior to what they have at present to face.'

While the evacuation of Dunkirk had concluded, members of the BEF and French forces were still in action in western France, the RAF continuing to fly operations: 'It is hoped that we shall be given a short respite in which to organize, refit and train new pilots in order to inflict yet heavier casualties on the German fighters and bombers when they attack this country and coastwise shipping.'

On 5 June, No. 79 Squadron flew down from Digby, joining No. 32 Squadron on an escort to Blenheims raiding Abbeville. In his debriefing, a naturally frustrated Brothers reported that two Ju 88s were observed over the Channel but at a great distance and could not be pursued, 'The reconnaissance Ju 88 had a top speed of about 300 mph, so if they had the jump on us, it was difficult to overhaul them before they reached the [French] coast.'

With the bulk of the BEF now safe, King George VI sent a message to Winston Churchill:

'I wish to express my admiration of the outstanding skill and bravery shown by the three Services and the Merchant Navy in the evacuation of the British Expeditionary Force from Northern France.

'The measure of its success – greater than we had dared to hope – was due to the unfailing support of the Royal Air Force, and, in the final stages, the tireless efforts of naval units of every kind.

'We think with heartfelt sympathy of the losses and suffering of those brave men, whose self-sacrifice has turned disaster into triumph.'
'George R.I.'

Winston Churchill remained bullish when he spoke in the House of Commons later that day:

'We must be very careful not to assign to this deliverance the attributes of a victory. Wars are not won by evacuations.

'I have, myself, full confidence that if all do their duty, if nothing is neglected, and if the best arrangements are made, as they are being made, we shall prove ourselves once again able to defend our Island home, to ride out the storm of war, and to outlive the menace of tyranny, if necessary for years, if necessary alone.

'We shall go on to the end; we shall fight with growing confidence and growing strength in the air; we shall defend our Island, whatever the cost may be. We shall fight in the fields and in the streets, we shall fight in the hills; we shall never surrender.'

In private, Churchill acknowledged that Dunkirk, despite the rescuing of 338,000 Allied troops, represented 'the greatest military defeat for many centuries.' Over 68,000 soldiers were listed as killed or missing, or had been taken as PoWs, while virtually all of the BEF's equipment was lost. As the German forces advanced, however, they freed four hundred Luftwaffe pilots and aircrew, most notable among their number was the fighter ace Mölders.

The squadron flew a number of offensive operations during 6 June, but without making any claims.

Although the fighting around Dunkirk was over, elsewhere the battle for France continued. Scottish and Canadian troops had been landed in France to provide support to the 51st Highland Division, whose line fell between Abbeville and Dieppe. On 7 June, Brothers took off from Manston on a squadron patrol in the company of No. 79 Squadron, flying as escort to eighteen Blenheims bombing targets in the Abbeville area. No. 32 Squadron's role was to stick closely to the bombers. When a formation of forty-plus Bf 109s was sighted over Abbeville at 1400 hours, No. 79 Squadron's Hurricanes were ordered to peel off and engage them. Pilot Officer T.C. Parker claimed two Bf 109s, while Flying Officer 'Jimmy' Davies destroyed one and a second unconfirmed, and Sergeant R.R. McQueen got another confirmed. Flight Lieutenant Roberts and Pilot Officer D.W.A. Stones both shot down a Bf 109 (unconfirmed). Sergeant A.W. Whitby sighted an Hs 126 which he destroyed.

With their primary mission accomplished, No. 32 Squadron was able to go on the offensive. Having sighted a formation of twelve He IIIs and ten Bf 110s, they were given the order to attack.

Pilot Officer Smythe and Flight Lieutenant Crossley shared in the destruction of an He 111, while Pilot Officer Grice destroyed an He 111. Engaging a formation of six Bf 109s, Sergeant Pearce claimed one destroyed. Meanwhile, to the east of Abbeville a lone Bf 109 was engaged and shot down, as was a second near Curey.

Returning to Manston, Brothers and the rest of the squadron refuelled and awaited the next operation. This came at 1715 hours with a repeat of the earlier escort, resulting in the destruction of a further He 111.

Taking off from Manston at 0820 hours the following day, a flight of No. 32 Squadron's Hurricanes joined No. 79 Squadron on a patrol to Le Treport. Grice recalled, 'Our role was to provide air support for troops embarking from the harbour.'

An hour into the patrol a formation of twenty He 111s of I./KG 1 was sighted flying 3,000ft below. Crossley scoured the skies for their Bf 109 escort, but they were too far behind the bombers – they would make their presence felt soon enough.

Ordering the squadron line astern, Crossley took the Hurricanes in for a No. 6 attack with instructions, 'Going down to starboard; Leader taking port machine; Echelon starboard; Go!'

With each of Red Section's pilots lining up an He 111, they dived down, closing to firing range before letting loose a salvo. Veering off to port, they completed their pass, leaving the way clear for Yellow Section's attack, during which Pilot Officer Daw sent two bombers down in flames. Crossley, flying on a parallel course to the bombers, saw his first victim crash-land, before he engaged a second which plummeted into the ground. Daw then spotted a Bf 109 attacking a Hurricane, successfully picking the enemy fighter off.

Meanwhile, Pilot Officer Grice (flying P3530) lined up on the lead bomber of a section, getting close before firing a short burst. But his own aircraft was badly hit by the crossfire from the defending air gunners and later by Bf 109s of III./JG 26.

Fearing his ruptured fuel tanks might ignite, Grice turned the engine off and glided fifteen miles before crash-landing near a small village between Rouen and Neufchâtel-en-Bray at 0925 hours, his Hurricane turning on its back. With another RAF officer in tow, Grice searched for an open aerodrome. Finally, at Dreux, he found an aircraft and flew back via Jersey, rejoining the squadron on the following day.

The bomber's Bf 109 escort arrived on the scene and were engaged by No. 79 Squadron, with Squadron Leader Joslin and Pilot Officer Haysom both claiming a Bf 109. Meanwhile, Flying Officer Davies, Pilot Officers Stones and Wood shared an He 111 over Abbeville. Flying Officer Mitchell was wounded and Joslin made an emergency landing at Hawkinge.

Also drawn into the general dogfight were those pilots from No. 32 Squadron with ammunition, the remainder heading for Rouen-Boos landing-ground to refuel and rearm. Here they found that there was no means of siphoning fuel and so they made the hop to Drex, where they refuelled. No. 32 Squadron's wider claims were listed in the ORB, although not all were remarked upon in the general commentary:

'Pilot Officer Daw engaged twenty Me 110s, ten Bf 109s – destroying two He 111s. [The squadron's Operational Record book also credits Daw with one Bf 109 as destroyed].

Flying Officer Humpherson engaged twenty He 111s, destroying one He 111.

Pilot Officer Flinders engaged twenty He 111s, destroying one He 111.

Sergeant Pearce engaged three Me 109s, claiming one Me 109 unconfirmed.

Sergeant Bayley engaged three Me 109s, claiming one Me 109 unconfirmed possible.

Flight Lieutenant Crossley attacked seventeen He 111s, claiming two He 111s.

Pilot Officer Grice engaged ten He 111s and six Me 109s, claiming one Me 109 destroyed and one He 111 destroyed'.

During debriefing it was learned that one Hurricane had been seen to crash in flames, while another was observed close to the ground and under heavy attack from Bf 109s. These later proved to be the aircraft flown by Pilot Officer Cherrington and Pilot Officer Kirkcaldie. Cherrington was shot down by Bf 109s of III./JG 26, during an attack on He111s of I./KG 1 over Rouen. His aircraft crashed at Fief-Thoubert, St-Saëns. Meanwhile, Kirkcaldie was shot down by Bf 109s of III./JG 26, during an attack on He111s of I./KG 1 south-east of Rouen, his Hurricane (N2406) crashing near Houville-en-Vexin. Pilot Officer (42589) Geoffrey Inglesby Cherrington, RAF, was originally buried alongside the crash site as an 'unknown' RAF airman and re-interred on 4 June 1941 in Ste Marie Cemetery, Le Havre, Division 67, Row T, Grave 20. His identity was not confirmed until 1947 when the original crash site was investigated and the identification of Hawker Hurricane No. N2582 confirmed from serial numbers on the engine and airframe. Pilot Officer (72526) Kenneth Kirkcaldie, RAFVR, was the son of Herbert and Kathlen Kirkcaldie, of Wellington City, New Zealand; husband of Esma Mae Kirkcaldie, of Lagos, Nigeria. He was 28-years-old. Kirkcaldie was buried in Houville-en-Vexin Churchyard, collective grave.

During the day No. 213 Squadron returned to Biggin Hill, their Hurricanes operating out of the 'Bump' until 18 June. Making only routine patrols the squadron were unable to make any claims, although a number of 'B' Flight's pilots had already become aces while flying out of French airfields during the Battle of France. These included Flight Lieutenant R.D.G Wight, DFC (*London Gazette*, 3 June 1940) and Sergeant S.L. Butterfield, DFM (*London Gazette*, 14 June 1940).

The squadron flew a flight strength patrol of the area Le Treport-Dieppe-Fecamp during the late morning of 10 June, but otherwise remained at Available.

Helping to pass the time while awaiting the scramble, some of the pilots would play chess, cards, or even cricket, or kick a football about with the 'erks'. The games could, however, sometimes get a little out of hand. Brothers recalled that one involved the discharging of a Very pistol, 'You blindfolded a chap and then you all stood around him in a circle. Then someone – and he had to be bloody brave – spun him round until he became disorientated. Everyone ran like hell as he counted to ten before raising the Very pistol and firing.'

The game was as dangerous as it sounded and on one occasion a young sergeant pilot was blasted in the backside, 'The incident caused a bit of a stir down at the stores as they wanted to know how he had burnt a hole in the seat of his pants and needed a new issue; we had to give it up after that.'

On the political scene, expecting that Britain would soon sue for peace, Benito Mussolini declared war on Great Britain, her Empire and Dominions. In honouring the terms of the 'Pact of Steel', he extended the conflict into the Mediterranean and North Africa, where the Italians had territorial interests.

Meanwhile, Brothers flew two operational sorties during 11 June, the first a squadron fighter sweep made between 0930 and 1120 hours, when Nos. 32 and 79 Squadrons were ordered to patrol the Le-Treport-Fecamp area. The squadron landed and refuelled, repeating the patrol an hour later, extending the line to Dieppe. Three He 126s were encountered, with Pilot Officer Daw claiming one destroyed and

Pilot Officer Smyth bagging a second. A third was damaged by Sergeant Jones (flying N2533 GZ 'X'), who was shot down by return fire and reported as missing, believed taken as a PoW.

Brothers flew on a joint dawn patrol between 0505 and 0650 hours on 12 June, 'Our job was to patrol St. Valery, giving some protection for the embarking troops, with 79 giving us top cover.'

No enemy aircraft were encountered, which gave some relief for the Royal Navy below. The operation was repeated on the following morning with the same result.

Brothers' second sortie on 13 June saw him joining the squadron on a fighter patrol between 1920 and 2115 hours, providing top cover for Nos. 79 and 213 Squadrons. The operation proved to be an uneventful sweep of the French coast between Le Havre – Dieppe. Meanwhile, Brothers flew on two joint patrols in the area of Dieppe – Le Havre – Abbeville – Boulogne on 14 June.

It was probably during one of these operations that Brothers found himself under-fire. He later recalled the incident, 'Operating over France as a flight commander, I naturally took our last "new boy" under my wing to fly as my No. 2. Glancing up and immediately behind me [I saw] an Me 109 filling my mirror!' Brothers immediately took evasive action just as the enemy opened fire, 'I pulled away very violently and he shot away upwards; as I was doing a tight turn, looking for my No. 2, cutting the corner to get back into position, as I thought, until he opened fire – at me!' Brothers snapped over the radio for him to ceasefire. He was mad, not only because his No. 2 had failed to warn him of the attack, but that when he had tried to shoot Brothers down with an easy shot, he'd missed, 'I took him off operations for two days for intensive gunnery training'.

Brothers recalled, 'I also used to warn them that, if we were jumped by escorting fighters and you saw tracer passing on your left, turn into it, not away. Instinctively you want to turn away, but the enemy, having seen he was firing to the left of you, was then correcting his aim to fire to the right. Well, if you turned left you threw his aim completely; you went through some of his fire, and took your chance on that.'

Sadly, Brothers' advice and the extra training didn't help his wingman, as he added that he was killed later in the battle.

During the day German forces took Paris, which had been declared an open city. The French government established a temporary HQ at Bordeaux, the Great War hero, Marshal Philippe Petain assuming the premiership from Reynaud.

Events were gathering pace in France and on 18 June Marshal Petain spoke to the nation, 'People of France, it is with grief in my heart that I have to tell you to stop fighting'.

Meanwhile, Ramsay, who was not fully aware of the part played by the RAF's fighter pilots and the tactics they had been forced to adopt, wrote of the earlier evacuation: 'For hours on end the ships off shore were subjected to a murderous hail of bombs and machine-gun bullets. In their reports the COs of many ships, while giving credit to the RAF personnel for gallantry in such combats as were observed from the ships, at the same time express their sense of disappointment and surprise at the seemingly puny efforts made to provide air protection during the height of this operation.'

What Ramsey was not to know was that the real air battles were taking place high above France and that only the enemy aircraft that got through were seen over the beaches and the Channel.

In a speech made initially in the House of Commons and later broadcast to the nation, Churchill reflected on the events surrounding the extrication of the larger part of the BEF from France and the realities of the struggle that lay ahead:

'During the last few days we have successfully brought off the great majority of the troops, that is to say, about 350,000 out of 400,000 men. We have, therefore, in this island today a very large and powerful military force.'

Wing Commander Grice had Churchill's speech copied and posted around the station as a source of inspiration:

'What General Weygand called the Battle of France is over. I expect that the Battle of Britain is about to begin. Upon this battle depends the survival of Christian civilization, our own British life, and the long continuity of our institutions and our Empire. The whole fury and might of the enemy must very soon be turned on us.

'Hitler knows that he will have to break us on this island or lose the war. If we can stand up to him, all Europe may be free.

'Let us therefore brace ourselves to our duties, and so bear ourselves that if the British Empire and its Commonwealth last for a thousand years, men will still say, "This was their finest hour".'

The previous few days had seen little air activity for the squadron, while on the following day, the 19 June, Brothers led two section strength fighter patrols against X-raids, but without making contact with the enemy. The air defence system relied on regular updates as the enemy could change speed, altitude, or heading at any moment, leaving the intercepting fighters way off course; 'They tried their best but their information wasn't always as good as it should have been.'

During a section strength bomber escort to Amien Aerodrome, No. 32 Squadron flew in the company of No. 79 Squadron, whose Sergeant McQueen attacked three He 111s south-west of Amiens, shooting one down and claiming a second unconfirmed. McQueen had given a warning, unaware that his radio transmitter was faulty and no one in the formation could hear him.

Meanwhile, Churchill, aware of the crucial role that Fighter Command would play in the defence of these shores, gave great emphases to the RAF's role in the previous week's fighting and the struggle ahead, announced to the Commons on 20 June:

'I am happy to inform the House that our fighter strength is stronger, at the present time, relatively to the Germans, who have suffered terrible losses, than it has ever been; and consequently we believe ourselves possessed of the capacity to continue the war in the air under better conditions than we have ever experienced before. I look forward confidently to the exploits of our fighter pilots – these splendid men, this brilliant youth – who will have the glory of saving their native land, their island home, and all they love, from the most deadly of all attacks.'

There would be a brief respite while the Luftwaffe established themselves in their new bases from Norway down to Northern France. When they renewed their campaign they would, however, have Great Britain as their target.

It was evident that the civilian population would be targeted every bit as much as military infrastructure; 'There remains, of course, the danger of bombing attacks. I do not at all underrate the severity of the ordeal which lies before us; but I believe our countrymen will show themselves capable of standing up to it.'

Across the country Civil Defence and Air Raid Precautions personnel had been mobilized at the outbreak of the war. They would be joined by an army of other volunteer war workers, including firemen, ambulance crews, rescue workers and hospital staff, to name but a few.

More than most, Brothers knew that the onslaught that had overwhelmed the French army, then considered the strongest in Europe, would soon be directed on these shores, 'If the Luftwaffe gained air superiority then, of course, the whole country was open to them'.

Brothers expected that the enemy would soon attack in growing numbers and the RAF, particularly Biggin Hill, would be in their sights, 'You were worrying about your own chaps, your own aircraft, and your own ground crew. It was day-to-day, minute-to-minute and one was tired, inevitably.'

Earlier there had been rare welcome news at Biggin Hill when a message came through from Group; Michael Crossley had been awarded the DFC. The award was promulgated in the *London Gazette*, 21 June 1940. The citation referred in particular to the events of 8 June:

'Acting Flight Lieutenant Michael Nicholson CROSSLEY (37554).
'In June 1940, this officer was the leader of two squadrons of fighters which were carrying out an offensive patrol in the Le Treport area. Flight Lieutenant Crossley sighted seventeen Heinkel 111s, and displayed outstanding initiative and courage in his method of attack. As a result of the engagement seven enemy bombers were destroyed. Flight Lieutenant Crossley himself destroyed two, and had to break off a further fight as his ammunition was expended. He had his first combat in May 1940, when he succeeded in destroying a Messerschmitt 109. He has displayed exceptional skill and leadership and, since the middle of May 1940, has destroyed seven enemy aircraft.'

During the early afternoon of 22 June, Brothers and the rest of the squadron took off to accompany No. 79 Squadron on an escort for a formation of eighteen Blenheims on a raid to Merville, their one-time base. The operation passed off without incident.

More good news reached the squadron when it was learnt that two gallantry medals had been confirmed. The awards of the DFC to Pilot Officers Victor George Daw and Douglas Hamilton Grice were announced in the *London Gazette* of 25 June 1940. Both citations include references to the squadron's combat on 8 June:

'In June 1940, when seventeen Heinkel 111s were sighted, Pilot Officer Daw succeeded in destroying two and, immediately afterwards, shot down a Messerschmitt 109, which was attacking one of his fellow pilots. Previously, in May 1940, he carried out a head-on attack on three enemy aircraft and destroyed the leader, and a few days later he destroyed another Messerschmitt 109. By his tenacity, skill and courage, this officer has succeeded in destroying a total of six enemy aircraft.'

The award to Grice also alluded to his being shot down over France and making his own way back to the squadron:

'Pilot Officer Grice has displayed great courage and determination in attacks on enemy aircraft and has destroyed at least six in various combats. On one occasion he was himself shot down but, after overcoming many difficulties, he succeeded in making his escape and returned to his unit.'

Brothers flew on a squadron strength escort made from Manston. Landing back at their advanced airfield at 1215 hours, the pilots waited in their cockpits while the ground crews descended on their Hurricanes. Refuelled, the squadron was back in the air fifteen minutes later, flying with Nos. 79, 111 and 615 Squadrons on an escort to a flight of Blenheims making a photographic reconnaissance to St Valery and Berk-sur-Mer.

On the return leg, just as the Hurricanes crossed the French Coast, No. 79 Squadron, flying as top cover at 10,000ft, was attacked by three Bf 109s. Pilot Officer Parker, who was acting as Tail-end-Charlie, called out a warning, but his radio had developed a fault and no one heard him. In a pursuit which went down to 20ft, Parker, who's Hurricane was hit by an early burst of fire, shook off three Bf 109s. Caught off guard, Sergeant McQueen (flying P3401) and acting Flight Lieutenant Davies (flying P3591), were sent into the Channel. McQueen bailed out. He was circled in the water while the Rye Lifeboat headed to the scene, hauling his unconscious body out of the water. Transferred to a RN launch, he died before reaching shore.

Sergeant (993914) Ronald Revan McQueen, RAFVR, was 24-years-old. He was buried in Glasgow Western Necropolis, Section R, Grave 2288. Flight Lieutenant (37796) James William Elias Davies, DFC, RAF, was the son of David Ashley Davies and Catherine J. Davies, of Carmarthen. He is remembered on the Runnymede Memorial, Panel 4. He was 26-years-old.

At 1515 hours the King held an award ceremony at Biggin Hill, having that morning presented the DSO to Squadron Leader James Anthony Leathart and

DFCs to Flight Lieutenants Adolf Gysbert 'Sailor' Malan, Robert Roland Stanford Tuck, 'Al' Deere, and Pilot Officer John Lawrence 'Johnny' Allen.

The King stood a little to the front of Group Captain Grice, who was beside a small table on which sat a small cushion bearing five DFCs and two DFMs. On parade, outside of one of the hangars, were as many of the station's personnel as could be spared from duty. Lined up directly in front of the King and ready to march forward to receive their awards were six recipients. To be awarded the DFC were No. 32 Squadron's Crossley, Daw and Grice, along with No. 79 Squadron's Stones, while Sergeants Cartwright and Whitby were to be awarded the DFM. Cartwright was killed-in-action only a few days later, on 4 July.

Pilot Officer Stones' award was promulgated in the *London Gazette*, 4 June 1940:

'Pilot Officer Donald William Alfred STONES (42276), RAF.
'This officer shot down five enemy aircraft during recent operations. He was indefatigable during his search for enemy aircraft, and during one day he was in the air for eight hours.'

Pilot Officer Stones, who had formerly flown with No. 32 Squadron, was still only nineteen when he was awarded the DFC. Remarkably, he would earn a Bar to the DFC and become a Squadron Leader by the age of twenty-one.

Both Sergeants Cartwright and Whitley's awards were announced in the *London Gazette*, 28 June 1940:

'741466 Sergeant Henry CARTWRIGHT.
'This airman shot down four enemy aircraft and throughout the recent operations was a most effective fighter who displayed an excellent offensive spirit.'

'580256, Sergeant Alfred WHITBY.
'This airman has exhibited great courage and determination as a fighter pilot. During only a few days in France he destroyed five enemy aircraft and since his return to England has destroyed another. He has given valuable assistance as a navigator.'

In turn the recipient's names were called out and they marched up to the King and saluted as their award and citation were read aloud. The King then plucked their medal from the cushion before reaching forward to place it on a small hook sewn above the left breast pocket. As he did so His Majesty congratulated each man, his brief words conveying the gratitude of a nation.

At the conclusion of the ceremony, Flight Lieutenant Davies' DFC remained unclaimed. It was a poignant moment for all present.

Acting Flight Lieutenant Davies' award was announced in the *London Gazette*, 28 June 1940:

> 'Acting Flight Lieutenant James William Elias DAVIES (37796).
> 'This officer has shown ability as leader of his squadron on many offensive patrols. On one occasion, while attacking a Messerschmitt 109, he was himself attacked by six Heinkel 113s. He at once turned on the Heinkels, destroying one and badly damaging a second before being compelled to break off the engagement owing to shortage of ammunition. The following day while leading a section of his squadron he sighted a large formation of Heinkel 111s and shot one down in flames.'

With the formalities over No. 32 Squadron's pilots were presented to His Majesty. The King had asked about that day's combat and so His Majesty was joined by No. 79 Squadron's Pilot Officer Parker in the Royal Car as they drove to the hangar where a group of 'erks' were working on his battle damage Hurricane. The King was later driven to No. 79 Squadron's Dispersal Point where he spoke with Squadron Leader J.D.C. Joslin (later killed-in-action on 7 July) and the other pilots at Readiness.

Back on the daily grind of operations, the end of the month saw the squadron flying patrols and scrambles, but without making any claims.

Chapter 6

Target Britain

On the 1 July 1940, the process began of upgrading No. 32 Squadron's Hurricanes with the constant speed propeller. The de Havilland Company had been quick to respond to the Air Ministry's order and the converter kits arrived with two technicians who soon trained up the fitters.

During the day, No. 79 Squadron moved from Biggin Hill to Hawkinge, transferring to Acklington, Northumberland, on 13 July (having spent two days at RAF Sealand). They would return to Biggin Hill on 27 August.

There was little 'business' for No. 32 Squadron on 2 July, the day that saw the return to Biggin Hill of No. 610 Squadron, which was to share the base until 12 September. The Spitfires encountered the enemy during the course of two section strength patrols, claiming a Do 17 and a Do 215 destroyed.

Meanwhile, the war was about to enter a new phase, when on the Continent, Goering issued the first Luftwaffe operational orders for the campaign against England and the RAF. Poor weather conditions, however, meant they could not be properly implemented until 10 July, the date later designated by the Air Ministry as the beginning of the Battle of Britain.

Brothers (flying N2524) led 'B' Flight on a scramble on 3 July. Airborne a little after 1600 hours, the Hurricanes were vectored onto Enemy Raid 21, a lone Do 17. This was successfully intercepted by No. 610 Squadron. Meanwhile, at 1627 hours, Brothers was given a new course onto Enemy Raid 34, another Do 17. At 1643 hours bombs were reported landing on Kenley. Closing in on the bomber, Brothers gave the 'Tally-Ho!' over Tonbridge and the Hurricanes went in, 'We were often compelled to attack from the stern, because we were usually scrambled late in the day'.

The Do 17 was shared by Pilot Officer Gardner, along with Sergeants Bayley and Higgins.

Flying as Blue 2, Pilot Officer Gardner's combat report read:

'Saw the E/A flying west, I chased him amongst the clouds firing intermittently. He finally emerged from the cloud bank and when I saw him he was pursued by two other Hurricanes. I joined in and we all attacked several times, the gunner having been killed in my first burst, but the gun was taken up by another member of the crew, who fired throughout the action. Sergeant Bayley, who was firing after me, finally put the last burst into it. No outstanding damage was done, the engines were not stopped, being protected by armour plating, only being slowed down by having the propellers riddled. Two of the crew were

killed and two taken prisoner. I opened fire [five-second burst] at 200 yards closing to 50 yards.'
(signed) PO P.M. Gardner.

Gardner later examined the wreckage, which crashed in Paddock Wood, adding, 'I would like to suggest that a beam attack is more effective than the stern, as in this instance looking at the a/c afterwards, the beam attack avoids the armour plating.' Pilot Officer Peter Melvill Gardner, who had been seconded to No. 3 Squadron since May, had only recently returned to the squadron, having claimed a Do 17 destroyed on 15 May, an He 111 on 19 May and a Do 17 on the following day.

Sergeant Higgins of Blue Section placed the encounter 'east of Redhill'. His combat report read:

'After a running chase, I was able to position myself in a clearing for a stern attack at 250 yards range. I maintained a long burst of fire at the enemy [eight-second burst], at the same time receiving considerable fire from the rear machine guns. I pushed home the second attack [three-second burst], following this with two further attacks [three-seconds and two-seconds, firing a total of 2,250 rounds]. A second Hurricane assisting in the destruction after my second burst. The enemy continued to lose height down to the ground level. Finally crashing in a large hop field.'
(signed) Sgt W.B. Higgins.

Sergeant E.A. Bayley adding to the commentary:

'One Hurricane was just starting to attack and I followed it in, in a stern attack, with a long burst, and closing to 50 yards. The rear gun had stopped firing when I broke away. I made a second stern attack by which time the EA was losing height rapidly with both engines stopped. I followed it down.'
(signed) Sgt E.A. Bayley.

Brothers later led a section strength scramble to make an interception over Tonbridge, but with the danger passed they were recalled after only twenty minutes in the air, such aborted operations would become commonplace as the campaign developed.

During 4 July, Brothers (flying N2524) flew on an offensive patrol to Le Havre, but on this occasion the enemy declined combat. Meanwhile, in the early afternoon the Luftwaffe made their first major shipping raid in British home waters, when a convoy passing through the Straits, just east of Dover, was targeted by Do 17s. Scrambled from Hawkinge, No. 79 Squadron's Hurricanes were bounced by the bomber's Bf 109 escort. A dogfight then developed during which Sergeant Cartwright's Hurricane was seen to dive vertically into the Channel near St Margaret's Bay, Dover. Sergeant (741466) Henry Cartwright, DFM, RAFVR, was the son of Peter and Elizabeth Cartwright, of Droylsden, Lancashire. He was 25-years-old and is remembered on the Runnymede Memorial, Panel 12.

Later that day, No. 32 Squadron's 'A' Flight was scrambled with orders to join No. 79 Squadron in the interception of Enemy Raid 20. At 1850 hours, they were bounced over Dungeness by six Bf 109s of JG 26, with two Hurricanes downed.

Pilot Officer Grice was shot down over Deal and tried to make for Manston in a straight glide, but 'finished up in a field at Cliffsend'. Meanwhile, Pilot Officer Gillman (flying N2724) made a forced-landing at Hawkinge, not far from his parent's house. He made the most of the opportunity to pay them an impromptu visit.

Pilot Officer Grice (Yellow 1) reported:

'I observed six Me 109s appear from a cloud in line astern about 2,000ft above us to the right and proceeding in the opposite direction. I warned the rest of the squadron by R/T and climbed to meet them.

'The first Me 109 opened fire at me from at least 600 yards, and as I could see the cannon shells approaching, it wasn't very difficult to avoid his fire. I selected a victim and started to manoeuvre for position. Unfortunately, before I could open fire, I was attacked from below and astern, machine-gun fire severing my rudder control and a shell through the port wing root severing my aileron control.'
(signed) P/O D. Hamilton Grice.

Pilot Officer Smythe (Yellow 3) sent one Bf 109 into the Channel, damaging a second which made a force-landing in France:

'I saw one attacking P/O Grice so attacked it myself. I fired two short bursts [250, closing to 100 yards] and saw glycol starting to stream from the engine. The E/A turned on its side and dived towards the sea. As I was then being attacked by another E/A I could not follow it down. After a few turns the second a/c broke off the attack and dived to sea level in an attempt to escape. I caught him up about eight miles off the coast and after four bursts [second burst at 300 yards, three bursts closing to 50 yards] he crashed into the sea, the tail unit breaking away.'

Smythe added a cautionary note:

'As has happened several times before, the last section was suddenly attacked by 109s coming out of cloud. It would appear that if fighter pilots are to devote their whole attention to looking for bombers, they must have an escort of Defiants to cover their tail.'
(signed) PO Smythe.

An often repeated request, this tactic does not appear to have been used, despite the outline of the Defiant strongly resembling the Hurricane. The idea behind its conception was to have an aircraft that lured the enemy into an astern attack and whose armament was designed to pick off any enemy fighters attacking from above and out of the sun – the classic fighter approach. With no forward firing guns, the Defiant relied on its rear turret for its defence. Even used sparingly in mixed formation, the Defiant might have forced the enemy to momentarily hesitate before bouncing Hurricane squadrons – drawing a few hundred feet closer before opening fire would have given the RAF pilots longer to spot any attackers.

Commanded by Squadron Leader W.A. Richardson, No.141 Squadron was posted to Biggin Hill on 12 July. While its HQ was based on the 'Bump', their Defiants operated out of West Malling. They were not, however, to enjoy the same successes as No. 264 Squadron, which had claimed thirty-seven enemy aircraft on 29 May.

On 5 July, concerned at the previous day's convoy losses, which had been inflicted despite the RAF's concerted efforts, Winston Churchill sent a memo to the Vice Chief of the Naval Staff marked 'Action this day'. It read, 'Could you let me know on one sheet of paper what arrangements you are making about the Channel convoys now that the Germans are all along the French coast? The attacks on the convoys yesterday, both from the air and by E-boats, were very serious, and I should like to be assured this morning that the situation is in hand and that the Air is contributing effectively.'

Brothers (flying N2524) made two scrambles on 7 July, but no enemy aircraft were engaged despite following hopeful vectors which turned for home before the fighters got within striking range. The Luftwaffe were flying probing sorties to test the RAF's capabilities in preparation for the all-out assault which would come later.

No. 79 Squadron suffered a grievous loss during an evening patrol, when in the half-light Squadron Leader J.D.C. Joslin (flying P2756) was shot down by a Spitfire while over Chilverton Elms, near Dover, in a case of 'friendly fire.' Squadron Leader (34158) John Davies Clement Joslin, RAF, was the son of Davies Clement and Elizabeth Joslin; husband of Louisa Margot Joslin of Buckden. Born in Russell, Manitoba, he was 24-years-old.

During 8 July, Nos. 32 and 610 Squadrons were assigned to maintain section strength convoy escorts. While attacking a formation of nine Do 215s some ten miles off Dover, Pilot Officer Arthur Lionel Boultbee Raven's Hurricane (R6806 'T') was hit and set on fire. Raven managed to ditch his aircraft and was seen in the water. With no dingy and wearing a sea-green Mae West, it was nigh-on impossible to spot a man in the choppy waters of the Channel. Pilot Officer (91089) Arthur Lionel Boultbee Raven, RAF, is remembered on the Runnymede Memorial, Panel 9.

In a later flight strength patrol, No. 610 Squadron was flying five miles south of Hythe when they sighted seven Do 215s and their escort of Bf 109s. The enemy were engaged but without results. Peeling away after the combat, Pilot Officer C.O.J. Pegge encountered three Bf 109s, sending one down in a vertical dive emitting black smoke.

During the afternoon, No. 32 Squadron's Yellow and Red Sections flew alternate patrols over a convoy sailing west off Dungeness. While on their second patrol, Yellow Section was bounced by six Bf 109s.

Pilot Officer Grice (Yellow 1) claimed one Bf 109 as probably destroyed:

'At approximately 1550 hours I saw three enemy a/c approaching, so we turned towards them and made a head-on attack. I turned round to make a further attack when three more E/A arrived and made a pass at me; I therefore concentrated on these three and left P/O Smythe [Yellow 2] to deal with the others.

I managed to split them up and attack an individual one from astern. I followed it down [from 3,000ft] to sea level firing occasional short bursts [all deflection shots], one of which must have hit it in the glycol tank as the E/A was streaming white smoke.'
(signed) D. Hamilton Grice.

Pilot Officer Smythe's Hurricane (N2400) was shot up during the initial attack and made an emergency landing at Hawkinge.

No. 32 Squadron made four scrambles and fighter patrols in the Hawkinge area on 9 July. During one of these operations Flight Lieutenant R.F.H. Clerke shared in the destruction of an He 111. Educated at Eton, he had flown with No. 32 Squadron since June 1938.

Meanwhile, Flight Lieutenant 'Big Bill' Smith led a flight of No. 610 Squadron's Spitfires on a patrol between Dungeness and Cap Griz Nez, during which all of the pilots fired their guns in an inclusive battle, claiming one Do 215 damaged. Flight Lieutenant Smith had assumed command of No. 610 Squadron following the death of Squadron Leader Franks while on a patrol over Dunkirk.

The battle of the convoys continued and at around 1000 hours on 10 July, Convoy Bread was sighted by a Do 17 reconnaissance aircraft as it sailed out of the Thames estuary and rounded North Foreland. This was one of eight convoys sailing down the east coast or through the Channel, Fighter Command being forced to fly standing patrols between Wick and Exeter.

Six Spitfires of No. 74 Squadron were scrambled, engaging a formation of twenty-plus Bf 109s of I./JG 51, flying as escort to the reconnaissance aircraft, but still managing to kill two of the crew. One Bf 109 was damaged, but the Spitfires flown by Pilot Officer Freeborn and Sergeant Mould made force-landings when hit by return fire.

A little after, a *staffel* of Bf 109s was plotted in the area of Dover, with nine of No. 610 Squadron's Spitfires closing in fast. Flight Lieutenant A.T. Smith's aircraft suffered damage to his port wing and crash-landed at Hawkinge, but the enemy were forced to retire.

Following a long period at Readiness, No. 32 Squadron's 'A' Flight was scrambled and took up station over the convoy off Dungeness by 1315 hours, anticipating a raid picked up by radar. Not long into their patrol, twenty-six Do 17s of I./KG 2, escorted by around three *Staffeln* of Bf 110s of I./ZG 26 and two *Staffeln* of I./JG 3's Bf 109s were sighted. Radioing for reinforcements, No. 32 Squadron's Flying Officer Humpherson led the Hurricanes into the attack, where they were joined by fighters from Nos. 56, 74 and 111 Squadrons, bringing their number up to thirty-eight. The Spitfires immediately tackled the Bf 109s, No. 74 Squadron finding they had 1,000ft advantage.

During the confusion of the air battle, which involved over a hundred aircraft, No. 111 Squadron's Flying Officer Higgs was killed when his Hurricane lost a wing in a collision with a Do 17 during a head-on attack (then a tactic almost solely used by No. 111 Squadron, but later adopted by other squadrons on Park's insistence). He was forced to bail out but his parachute failed to open properly. Flying Officer (36165) Thomas Peter Kingsland Higgs, RAF, was the son of Arthur Hilton and Alice Higgs. Higgs was buried at Noordwijk General Cemetery, Plot 1, Joint Grave 8. Thomas Higgs was 23-years-old and held a BA (Oxon) Merton College.

No. 32 Squadron's Flying Officer Humpherson led Green Section in an attack on a Do 17, which was hit and the rear turret silenced, Sergeant Pearce following the bomber to mid-Channel, by which time the Dornier had descended to 3,000ft. Having expended their ammunition the fighters returned to Biggin Hill.

Flying Officer J.B.W. Humpherson claimed a Do 215 (actually a Do 17) destroyed, two miles east of Dungeness:

'I saw a formation of about fifty Do 215s approaching the convoy from SE. Blue Section had now become separated from my section as we had just passed through a heavy rain cloud.

'I put Green Section into line astern and carried out a No. 1 attack on a single E/A that had become separated from the rest of the formation. I opened fire at about 250 yards and then closed to about 50 yards, firing two bursts of about ten seconds duration. I encountered heavy fire from the rear gunners of the Dornier, but this ceased about three-quarters of the way through my attack.'
(signed) Flg Off J. B. W. Humpherson.

Sergeant Pearce (Green 3) followed up the initial attack:

'Followed in No. 1 on attack on single bomber of section, so closed in again and expended ammunition in short bursts over period of two minutes [firing a three-second burst at 250 and 200 yards and three, three-second bursts at 150 yards; two guns experienced stoppages]. Rear fire encountered after first two bursts. E/A last seen over mid-channel at 3,000ft, gliding at 105-110 mph.

'One bullet removed from the tip of my airscrew blade (wood – Rotol).'
(signed) Sgt L Pearce.

Meanwhile, No. 79 Squadron was also scrambled to defend the convoy, but was bounced by Bf 109s, with the loss of Pilot Officer J.E.R. Wood and Flying Officer E.W. Mitchell flying P3461.

No. 64 Squadron's Spitfires now pursued the Bf 110s back to France, destroying one near Calais. With their escort dispersed the bombers became easier to pick off, with three destroyed and more damaged.

As a result of the engagement No. 56 Squadron's Sergeant Whitehead claimed a Bf 110. One of their Hurricanes crash-landed at Manston, while another, from No. 32 Squadron, crash-landed at Lympne, a second at Hawkinge.

The convoy escort continued with another flight strength patrol made between 1445 and 1610 hours, but no further enemy aircraft were encountered. Meanwhile, Pilot Officer W.H.C. Warner, of No. 610 Squadron, claimed a Bf 109 destroyed 'doubtful', during a flight strength patrol.

During the day's attacks some 150 bombs were dropped, but the fighters did their job and made the enemy rush their aim. Consequently, only one 700 ton vessel (the steamer *Bill S)* was lost.

Operating out of Hawkinge, Brothers flew on the second of two scrambles made during the afternoon and early evening of 13 July, investigating an approaching raid which turned back. Ordered to pancake, he waited out the rest of the day until released.

Throughout the battle many of the pilots went to the local pubs as soon as they were allowed off the station. They would try to wind-down with a drink and a game of darts, or a sing-song. The NCOs tended to frequent the Old Jail in Biggin Hill, while the officers drove further afield to the White Hart, run by Teddy and Cathy Preston: 'Often we weren't stood down until 2200 hours, which only gave us fifteen minutes to get to the pub for a quick pint. The Station CO [Group Captain Grice] rigged-up a tannoy on his car and as he approached the pub, one of his passengers would order six pints and a large gin. They served Page & Overton bitter straight from the barrel.'

While Pete recalled the tannoy as being attached to Grice's car, other accounts mention the tannoy as being on the 'station bus'. It was Group Captain Grice who established the White Hart as the station's pub, the second mess for his pilots during the height of the Battle of Britain. He was the first to chalk his name on the blackboard, the signing of which was thereafter reserved for special occasions. Among those who later added their names were: Pete Brothers, Tony Bartley, Mike Crossley, 'Al' Deere, 'Grubby' Grice, Colin Gray, 'Shag' Eckford, 'Sailor' Malan, 'Dickie' Milne, 'Jonnie' Johnson, 'Jamie' Rankin and Jack 'Bunny' Rose.

Meanwhile, during the day, No. 610 Squadron lost Sergeant (741433) Patrick Ian Watson-Parker, RAFVR, who failed to return from a routine patrol. Watson-Parker was buried in Cudham (SS Peter and Paul) Churchyard, Orpington, Section NN, Grave 24.

The Air Ministry had decided that it was important that the RAF should fly offensive patrols over the French coast; they were to prove costly in terms of both pilots and aircraft, as Brothers explained:

'After Dunkirk we were flying these utterly stupid patrols in wing strength to demonstrate air superiority. We would be detailed to fly down the French coast, cross in at Calais and then fly down to Amiens, before turning around and coming back.'

Given sufficient warning of the RAF's flight path, the Luftwaffe at Merville and Abbeville would take off in readiness for their return leg, knowing that they would have the advantages of height, sun and fuel:

'We were losing people unnecessarily, the Germans would just wait and watch you fly past and wait for you to come back. By then you were coming north and you had got the sun behind you, which was just how they wanted it. They would then simply climb up and jump us. This happened time and time again, and we were getting hammered for no reason at all.'

Brothers recalled that in mid-July he and his fellow No. 32 Squadron pilots were sitting on the grass at Hawkinge awaiting the order to scramble when 'Stuffy' Dowding joined them, 'By then I was getting rather tired and I duly told him what I thought of those bloody silly patrols. We did one the next day and then they were stopped.'

At their dispersal point at Manston since dawn on 14 July, Brothers (flying 2921) led two section scrambles in the Dover area in quick succession. Despite following updated vectors based on data supplied by the Observer Corps spotters, they were unable to locate the enemy – another opportunity for combat gone begging. Tired and frustrated, Brothers gave the order to make for base. Between 1450 and 1615 hours Nos. 32 and 610 Squadrons were scrambled to defend a convoy under attack from Ju 87s between Eastborne and Dover. During the melee Pilot Officer P. Litchfield engaged a formation of three Bf 109s, destroying one and damaging a second.

The action was witnessed by the BBC's Charles Gardner, who gave a running commentary, following the Hurricanes and Spitfires in their dogged defence of the convoy against a concerted Stuka attack.

The broadcast received a mixed response, accused of being reminiscent of an account of the Grand National or a Cup Final by a former pilot, the Reverend R.H. Hawkins (*The Times*, 17 July), while Mr C. Fisher's views were perhaps more in tune with the nation, 'To me it was inspiring, for I almost felt that I was sharing in it, and I rejoiced unfeignedly that so many of the enemy were shot down, and that the rest were put to ignominious flight.' (*The Times*, 19 July.)

During the day the Prime Minister spoke in the House of Commons weighing up recent developments in the early stages of the battle:

'This has been a great week for the Royal Air Force, and for Fighter Command. They have shot down more than five to one of the German aircraft which have tried to molest our convoys in the Channel, or have ventured to cross the British coast line. These are, of course, only the preliminary encounters to the great air battles which lie ahead, we hope to improve upon them as the fighting becomes more widespread and comes more inland.'

Despite Churchill's optimism, Fighter Command was already under pressure, committed to the draining tactic of mounting standing patrols over the Channel Convoys.

Meanwhile, No.141 Squadron's HQ staff arrived at Biggin Hill, their Boulton Paul Defiants operating out of the satellite at West Malling. The squadron had their first contact with the enemy over the Channel on 19 July, when they lost six aircraft with four pilots and five air-gunners dead. Withdrawn to Prestwick, Scotland, they converted onto night-fighter duties.

Brothers flew on a forty minute scramble on 15 July, taking off from Manston in the half-light, later joining an uneventful squadron strength fighter patrol of the Dover area, made between 0505 and 0640 hours – nothing was seen.

But the battle was soon to intensify as, on 16 July 1940, Adolf Hitler issued his Directive for the Conduct of the War No. 16, for the invasion of England. The initial phases, which included the destruction of Fighter Command as an effective force, were to be completed by the middle of August. The invasion was codenamed *Unternehmen Seelöwe* (Operation Sealion).

The document was intended only to be seen by his Commanders-in-Chief, but was forwarded by Reichsmarschall Goering to his Air Fleet Commanders, via the Enigma coding machines. The message was intercepted and later decoded at Bletchley Park:

'As England, in spite of her hopeless military position, has so far shown herself unwilling to come to any compromise, I have decided to begin preparations for, and if necessary, to carry out the invasion of England.

'This operation is dictated by the necessity to eliminate Great Britain as a base from which the war against Germany can be fought. If necessary the island will be occupied.

'The English Air Force must be eliminated to such an extent that it will be incapable of putting up any substantial opposition to the invasion troops.'

Meanwhile, Germany prepared twenty divisions across the Channel in readiness for the invasion of Britain. But all was dependent on the destruction of Fighter Command.

At 1625 hours on 17 July Brothers led 'B' Flight on a scramble from Manston, following a vector onto Enemy Raid 54. On seeing the Hurricane's approach the enemy aircraft dived for cloud cover, the fighters in hot pursuit. With no further trade, the controller issued the recall.

At Readiness since dawn, Brothers (flying N2921 'L') led an uneventful flight strength patrol of the Hawkinge area between 0735 and 0805 hours on 18 July; once again the raid turned away.

It was during the morning that Biggin Hill lost its first pilot due to enemy action since the beginning of the battle. Scrambled to take on another plot which turned back, No. 610 Squadron's Spitfires fell into the trap and were bounced by Bf 109s waiting high above in the sun. Green Leader, Pilot Officer (76461) Peter Litchfield, RAF (flying P9452 'T'), was shot down over the Channel by Hauptmannn Tietzen of II./JG 51. There was no parachute. Litchfield is remembered on the Runnymede Memorial, Panel 9. He was 25-years-old. In a few hectic weeks Litchfield damaged or destroyed at least three enemy aircraft. With little time between ops, he had scratched his sortie times down on the inside of his silver cigarette case, which serves as a poignant reminder of an aspiring fighter ace.

From mid-July Brothers largely flew N2921 which carried the letter code GZ – L. It was on this Hurricane that he had the Blue Peter flag painted on the port side of the cockpit. This aircraft was one of three Hurricanes which were delivered from No. 15 MU on 11 June to replace the same number of fighters lost on an operation to Le Treport three days earlier.

Brothers didn't waste any opportunity to increase his aircraft's performance and fighting capability, making his own modifications, 'I took the mirror off the top and bought myself a car [rear-view] mirror that was curved, and had that mounted inside the windscreen'. The mirror, which Brothers purchased over the counter at Halfords, not only gave him a better overall view, but by putting it inside the cockpit, he reduced the aircraft's drag. Brothers had another trick up his sleeve, as he explained, '... and then when we were sitting on the ground, my rigger and I used to sit on the wing with some sandpaper. The Spitfire was all flush riveted and the Hurricane was pock riveted, so we'd file some of the pock off the top.' They had to be careful not to weaken the rivet, just to flatten it a bit. Brothers said, 'I reckon we got an extra seven miles an hour out of the aircraft. No one else bothered, but I thought it was worth doing and it gave me something to do on the ground.'

On 19 July, Brothers (flying N2921) was ordered off and made a fifty minute patrol before landing at Manston to await further instructions. With the destruction of No. 141 Squadron over the Channel at the hands of a *staffel* of around ten Bf 109s of II./ JG 2 (the *Richthofen Geschwader*), No. 32 Squadron was brought from Release to a state of Readiness.

During the afternoon a large enemy formation was plotted heading for Dover. At 1530 hours No. 32 Squadron was scrambled to intercept Ju 87s dive-bombing the harbour. As they made their approach the pilots kept an eye out for the fighter escort, which they knew would be lurking somewhere above, ready to pounce. While making an adjustment to avoid flak, however, they were attacked by twelve Bf 109s.

A total of thirty-five Spitfires and Hurricanes had met the raid, with Brothers destroying a Bf 109, his combat report having since been lost. Brothers later spoke of a raid on Dover and the events surrounding his debriefing between sorties, 'After we returned from an operation, the intelligence officer would want all the details. We weren't all that interested, it was over, finished. We could be scrambled in the middle of telling him something.'

It was under these operational conditions during a raid on Dover that Brothers landed at the squadron's forward base, 'I'd shot down a Stuka and then gone into the airfield at Hawkinge to refuel and rearm. I didn't even get out of the aircraft. They were rearming the aircraft and there was a chap standing on the wing in front of me, pumping fuel into the tank.

'The battle was still going on up above and, as we watched, a Spitfire shot down a 109, and the pilot bailed out.'

The airman, who was refuelling Brothers' Hurricane had his eyes fixed skywards and was ecstatic, 'Got him!' But as the parachute was seen, the 'erk' was none too pleased and turned to Brothers, 'Oh jammy bastard!'

As soon as the ground crew gave the signal, Brothers fired up the Merlin. The starter leads were already plugged in, the engine still hot from his last sortie. It burst into life, the exhausts spitting out flames. Brothers taxied before racing down the grass runway, lifting off, and back into the fray. Brothers adding, 'I got a 109 on that day.' It should be noted that this narrative could equally relate to 29 July 1940, as Brothers claimed a Bf 109 over Dover on both days. No written claim survives for a Ju 87, which would allow a positive dating of the events Brothers recalled.

The possibility that Brothers did in fact destroy a Ju 87, not included in any of his tallies, may be inferred by his later explanation of the tactics often used to take on the Ju 87 dive-bomber:

'Stukas were pretty easy meat because you could shoot straight into the top of them as they pulled out of their dive and they were slower than we were. That awful screaming sound they made had been built into them to terrify people. Once they had started the dive, you could follow them down, and hit them if you were lucky. If you were too close, of course, you'd overtake.'

Meanwhile, other members of the squadron who engaged the same raid had been able to make claims. Squadron Leader J. Worrall (flying P3112), Green 1, destroyed one Bf 109 unconfirmed at 1605 hours:

'We intercepted about five Ju 87s [flying at 6,000ft] and about twelve 109s escorting. Just as Green Section were about to attack the 87s, Red Section was attacked by a section of 109s, which were followed by some more, and a general dogfight ensued. I found two 109s about 2,000 feet above me and climbed up after them. I got onto the tail of one and fired a one second burst [at 200 yards] and holed his port tank, a few bits flew off the wing near the port tank. I was still closing and about to reopen fire [one-second burst at 125 to 150 yards, firing a total of 400 rounds], when a Spitfire appeared from underneath and to one side and the Spitfire followed him down.'
(signed) Sqn Ldr J. Worrall.

Weaver Sections Yellow 1, Pilot Officer Smythe (flying P3522), claimed one Bf 109 probably destroyed while defending Red Section:

'A section of 109s passed over me to attack Red Section. I pulled the nose up and fired a quick burst [two bursts, one short and one about 320 rounds at 250 yards; total of 400 rounds fired] at one as it passed over me. I then climbed and attacked the leader of the formation; he turned sharply and I saw my bullets entering his wings; and [his] engine cowling blew off, but I was unable to follow him down as I was being attacked by another 109.'
(signed) PO Smythe.

Also flying with Yellow Section, Pilot Officer B. Henson (flying P3677), claimed one Ju 87 destroyed:

> 'I turned towards [Dover] harbour when a machine came from above and got on my leader's tail. I gave him a short burst [two-seconds] in his side at about 40 feet range, but I could not turn fast enough to follow him.
>
> 'I saw a Ju 87 dive towards the harbour. I dived after him keeping above him, and as he pulled up in front of me I opened fire at 300 yards (one burst of about eight-seconds), he turned to port and dived. I throttled back, turning inside his turn, and gave him a fifteen second burst. Clouds of smoke came from his engine; he then slowly glided towards the French coast.
>
> 'I closed in to about 50 yards and was giving him another burst when bullets coming from behind me passed my starboard wing. I tightly turned, completing a circle to port, and noticed a machine climbing away from me. I then looked for my victim and saw a terrific splash in the sea about eight miles from the French coast.'

Flying as Yellow 2, Pilot Officer K.R. Gillman (flying P3146) destroyed one Bf 109 on the Folkestone side of Dover:

> 'Three Me 109s dived in front of the section to attack Red Section, and I followed No. 2 of the enemy formation, who dived gently to port, and fired three bursts of approximately fifty rounds per gun [firing three-second burst at 250 yards closing to 150 yards, 1,200 rounds fired], part of the aircraft was shot away, and it dived vertically towards the sea.
>
> 'It was obviously out of control, but I had no time to follow it down, as I was attacked by another Me 109.'
>
> (signed) Plt Off K.R. Gillman.

During the engagement Flight Sergeant Turner (flying P3144) was shot down in flames, his aircraft crashed and burnt out at Church Hougham at 1625 hours. He managed to bail out despite being badly burnt. Turner was admitted to Union Road Hospital, Dover. He was placed on the danger list, being transferred to Orpington Hospital. Here he made great improvement. Turner was later admitted to Queen Victoria Hospital, East Grinstead, for plastic surgery, where he became one of Sir Archie McIndoe's guinea pigs.

Meanwhile, Adolf Hitler made a speech before the *Reichstag*, blaming the war on England and France. He played to the pacifists on both sides of the Channel when he claimed to reason for peace:

> 'In this hour I feel it to be my duty before my own conscience to appeal once more to reason and common sense – in Great Britain as much as elsewhere. I can see no more reason why this war must go on.

'I am grieved to think of the sacrifices which it will claim. I should like to avert them, also for my own people.'

Lord Halifax gave Great Britain's reply to what he coined a 'summons to capitulate', in a broadcast made on 22 July, when he declared bluntly that, 'We shall not stop fighting until freedom is secure.'

Brothers' second sortie of the day on 20 July was a flight strength offensive patrol. Red Section attacked three Bf 110s dive-bombing Dover Harbour from 8,000ft, before releasing their bombs at 2,000ft and diving to sea level and making their escape. Flight Lieutenant Crossley (flying N2461) and Pilot Officer John Ernest Proctor (flying N2458), shot down a Bf 110. He had earlier served with No. 501 Squadron in France, destroying a Bf 110 and Bf 109 on 12 May, two He 111s on 14 May, and a Bf 110 on 15 May. He was awarded the DFC, *London Gazette*, 18 March 1941.

'A' Flight's Flight Lieutenant Crossley's combat report was timed at 1330 hours:

'Red Section gave chase and overtook him about twelve miles out [south-east of Dover]. When within about 800 yards he started to zig-zag slightly, increasing in intensity as I approached. At about 400-500 yards he tried a burst of tracer, to which I replied with a short burst. I then closed to about 250 and opened fire properly, getting some deflection shots as well as astern [five or six bursts, closing to 100 yards], as he continued zig-zagging he suddenly pulled sharply up to starboard for about fifty degrees. I swung away to port for the dual purpose of getting in a beam attack, and avoiding the attentions of another Jaguar [Bf 110] which was lining up on me from above. I pulled round to starboard in front of both E/A and as I did so I saw the first a/c go into the sea.'
(signed) Fl Lt M. Crossley.

Meanwhile, ten miles off Dover, Convoy Bosom was sailing eastward through the Kenley and Biggin Hill Sectors of the Channel, its location identified by the enemy. Two Spitfire and two Hurricane squadrons were ordered to maintain a standing patrol. No. 32 Squadron's Green Section took up station at around 1700 hours. Not long into the patrol they spotted a formation of Stuka dive-bombers of II./St 1 approaching the convoy, escorted by fifty-plus Bf 109s and Bf 110s.

Blue Section was scrambled from Hawkinge, while No. 615 Squadron's Hurricanes also pitched in, along with nine Spitfires from No. 610 Squadron which had been patrolling at altitude to the west of the convoy. Having the advantage of altitude, the defending fighters came from out of the glare of the evening sun, penetrating the JG 51s Bf 109s, destroying one. Getting in amongst the Ju 87s and Bf 110s, they claimed two Ju87s, two making forced-landings at Lannion, France, with two damaged. Flying Officer A. Eyre and Flight Lieutenant L.M. Gaunce, both shot down Bf 109s. During the same engagement the Spitfires of No. 615 Squadron destroyed a Bf 109 of I./JG 27 and three of I./JG 51, including in their haul the aircraft flown by Gruppenkommandereur Hauptmann Helmut Riegel.

Green 1, Squadron Leader Worrall (flying N 2532 'H'), led his Hurricanes straight through the Bf 109s and into the bombers, damaging two Ju 87s before fire from one of the Bf 110 escorts forced him to disengage. Worrall soon lost the fighter-bomber and was attacking another Stuka, when a Bf 109 of JG 51 raked his Hurricane with machine-gun and cannon fire, slightly wounding him:

'At 1740 hours Sapper told me Blue Section was joining me, also E/A between 10,000 and 20,000 feet were approaching the convoy. Almost at once I spotted them and, ordering Green Section line astern, attacked the first Ju 87 just as he was starting his dive. Despite the fact that I had throttled right back I overtook him after a two second burst. I turned and took on another, but had to break off as I was attacked by a 110. I then lost the 110 and saw the Ju 87s bombing a destroyer, I attacked the nearest who started smoking. I had to break off as I was attacked by a 109. I could not find the 109 so attacked another 87 which was near. He started to smoke and again I was attacked by a 109. I broke away, I attacked a third 87 which also started to smoke. I was just about to fire another burst when I saw tracer going over my port wing. I immediately broke away and felt bullets entering the a/c from behind, which were stopped by armour-plating. Then two cannon shells hit, one in the engine and one in the gravity tank. I had to make a crash-landing in a small field half a mile to the east of the 'drome. Almost immediately she went up in a slow fire, giving me half a minute to get out.'
(signed) S/L Worrall.

Flying as Red 1, Flight Lieutenant Crossley (flying N2461) claimed one Bf 109 destroyed (unconfirmed):

'I took off with Red Section and joined Green and Blue at 10,000ft and immediately sighted about twelve 109s to the south, but my attention was diverted by a string of Ju 87s in the act of bombing. I turned towards them and fired a burst at one at close range as he went past, but did not observe the result as I saw an Me 109 coming round in front of me. I tacked one and got a deflection burst at close range [4-500 rounds fired in a three-second burst at 100 yards], at about 1,000ft up. He went straight down into the sea about one mile south of Dover Harbour.

'During the engagement I observed a Ju 87 crash into the sea about two miles S.E. of Dover.'
(signed) Flight Lieutenant M. Crossley.

Red 2, Pilot Officer Proctor (flying N2458), was unable to make a claim, although he saved Crossley from a concerted attack, firing 1,200 rounds, with a one-second burst at 400 yards and a four-second burst at 150 yards:

'Enemy sighted 8,000 feet, dived to floor and I gave chase behind Red 1. After ten miles got within range and gave one burst, E/A swung from side-to-side and suddenly rose to about 50 yards when I gave a further burst. I broke off

attack to engage another Jaguar which was about to attack Red 1. I fired a short burst of three seconds but was overtaking so quickly I had to disengage.'
(signed) Plt Off Proctor.

A second, undated, combat report by Pilot Officer Proctor (flying N2458) records that he destroyed a Bf 109:

'On sighting E/A approaching convoy, Red Section circled to gain height into the sun. Red 1 dived down to attack Ju 87s and I followed close astern. At about 4,000ft I spotted five Jaguars approaching convoy from the SE about 500ft below me. I rolled over and attacked the nearest one at 100 yards [five-second burst, firing remaining rounds at 200 yards], the E/A turned over onto its back and went straight into the sea. I followed it down, but could see no trace of survivors or wreckage.'
(signed) J.E. Proctor.

Flying as Red 3, Sergeant Bayley (flying P3481) followed his leader down towards the bombers and got onto the tail of a Bf 110 as it dived away from its attack, claiming one Bf 110 destroyed (unconfirmed):

'I opened fire at 250 yds and closed to 100 yds, by which time we were about ten miles offshore and the Jaguar's port engine was on fire. I then observed tracer coming past my port wing and attempted to get into position behind a second Me Jaguar which was on my tail, but he dived away.'
(signed) E.A. Bayley.

Flight Lieutenant Brothers (flying N2921) led Blue Section into the fray, destroying one Bf 109 of I./JG 51 ten miles off Dover:

'At 1805 hours I was leading Blue Section when I saw a number of enemy bombers start to attack a convoy off Folkestone. I saw about thirty Me 109s doing guard, so I climbed to attack one Me 109 and set him on fire. As I got on the tail of a second, two, in line astern, attacked me head-on, a third was on my tail and a fourth firing a full deflection shot at me from my right. I attacked the first two head-on and as they went over my head, I turned steeply to the right and fired at the one on my right, afterwards trying to get on the tail of the one behind me. Unfortunately, I lost him and as I had finished all but about twenty rounds of my ammunition [in five-second bursts at 150 yards and closing], I circled round trying to get my section together. As I could neither find nor get in touch with them, I landed to refuel and rearm.'
(signed) Fl Lt P.M. Brothers.

Brothers would later tell his junior pilots the details of this encounter as a warning, 'I looked around and saw five 109s in a 'V' formation, heading for home all on their own'.

Brothers hoped to form up at the rear of the 'vic', where he would pick the Bf 109s off, one by one. But the pilot on the right of the formation spotted him and veered off. Brothers pursued him, 'An almost fatal mistake. As I was about to open fire, he opened the throttle wide and started climbing rapidly. I pulled the stick back to follow him, and at that moment all hell broke loose.'

Brothers had fallen for the oldest trick in the book, 'the other four came in behind and they all had a go at me. I shot off fairly quickly and they all whizzed past, firing at me, and then they were gone. I didn't get anything other than a severe fright, but I never did that again, I used to warn chaps about it.'

Flying as Blue 2, Sergeant Pearce (flying N2524) claimed one Bf 109 as damaged:

'I followed Blue 1 [Brothers] climbing to intercept Me 109 escort to bomber formation. After Blue 1 turned left to engage E/A, which appeared directly in front of and above me crossing left to right in steep climb. Opened fire [with a three-second burst at 200 yards] on which E/A turned sharply away and dived steeply. I followed him, firing two more bursts [of two and three-seconds at 200 yards] and while trail of petrol or glycol came from E/A.'
(signed) L. Pearce.

Green 3, Sergeant Higgins (flying P3679) claimed one Bf 110 destroyed (unconfirmed):

'I singled out a Jaguar which had already commenced a dive attack on a destroyer. Approaching and overtaking in an astern attack I opened fire from about 300 yds, continuing to fire for fully seven seconds [firing 1,000 rounds] during which time smoke poured from the enemy machine. At approximately 1000ft from sea level I broke from the attack, the bomber crashing near the destroyer and sinking almost instantaneously.'
(signed) Sgt W.B. Higgins.

Flying Officer J.B.W. Humpherson (flying P3122) claimed one Ju 87 confirmed:

'I eventually closed with a Ju 87. The enemy a/c was apparently returning to France and it was flying just above the surface of the water at about 30ft. I approached from behind and at the same height as the E/A. I closed to about 200 yds and opened fire. After a very short burst [130 rounds] the E/A dived straight into the sea and disappeared below the surface.'

During the melee, Sub-Lieutenant Bulmer's aircraft (N2670) was hit by a Bf 109 of JG 51, flown by Oberleutnant Priller while in combat over Dover. He was reported to have bailed out near North Foreland, but drowned. Sub-Lieutenant (A) Geoffrey Gordon Robson Bulmer, FAA, was the son of Leslie Thomas and Mabel Ada Bulmer, of Bradford, Yorkshire. Bulmer, 20-years-old, served with HMS *Daedalus* and had been seconded to No. 32 Squadron on 1 July. He is remembered on the Fleet Air Arm Memorial at Lee-on-Solent Memorial, Bay 1, Panel 3.

Meanwhile, Sergeant Higgins was slightly wounded in the face by splinters from bullets which hit the seat armour, but managed to limp back to Hawkinge. His Hurricane had been hit by *Staffel Kaptain*, Hauptman Horst Tietzen while destroying a Bf 110. Hauptman Tietzen, who had twenty victories, was shot down and killed on 18 August off Whitstable.

Despite the squadron's successes, a number of bombers had already got through and one destroyer was hit and sank the following day. Overall, the defence of the convoy cost eight fighters, with seven pilots killed. Four more fighters were damaged.

Of the operation, Crossley recorded in the Squadron Diary:

'The following tipped stuff into the drink: Hector, Pete B, Higgins, Humph and Red Knight. The Mandarin [Squadron Leader Worrall] converted three non-smoking Ju 87s into smoking 87s but earned the attention of at least four squadrons of 109s to such an extent that he just couldn't make the 'drome (fan stopped). He force-landed in a field, 2532 caught fire and burnt out. Mandarin jumped out with cuts and a string of language which did justice to his position.'

Meanwhile, No. 610 Squadron's haul was one Bf 109 damaged. They later intercepted a second formation between Ashford and Folkestone. Pilot Officer G. Keighley was wounded when his Spitfire (N3201 'S') was shot down during combat with JG 51. He successfully bailed out and landed at Lydden, near Canterbury.

During the defence of the convoy the RAF claimed a total of fifteen enemy aircraft of which thirteen are confirmed by German records.

The following few days saw operational patrols and scrambles between dawn and dusk, but No. 32 Squadron's pilots were unable to make any claims.

By 24 July the Luftwaffe was being aided by radar operating from the cliffs at Wissant, opposite Folkestone. This meant that they were better able to monitor the progress of the convoys and to direct their own bomber and fighter forces, looking to outmanoeuvre the RAF's response.

With shipping still active in the Channel, a flight of Hurricanes took off at 0530 hours with orders to patrol off Dungeness. Landing at 0705 hours the pilots remained in their cockpits while their aircraft were refuelled. Fifteen minutes later they were airborne and back on patrol. Later that morning No. 610 Squadron patrolled Dover, claiming three Bf 109s destroyed.

Despite the RAF's best efforts, that day's raids accounted for 17,000 tons of shipping.

An uneventful flight strength patrol was made of Hawkinge between 0615 and 0645 hours the following morning. Brothers (flying N2921) took off at noon on a squadron patrol, with orders to escort Convoy CW8, its progress closely monitored by the enemy. Forty-five minutes into their patrol, and while flying over Dover in the company of Kenley's No. 615 Squadron, eight Bf 109s were encountered providing cover for a formation of Ju 87s bombing the merchant vessels below.

During the ensuing combat Flight Lieutenant Crossley (flying P3146), who was leading, claimed one Bf 109 probably destroyed:

'We observed eight 109s approaching from the south on a level with us, ie 22,000ft [two miles south of Dover], we wheeled round to the left to engage them, their leader turned and opened fire with cannon at me, out of machine gun range, head on. I waited until I could fire and did so at about 300 yds [firing 800 rounds] pulling sharply up as he went over my head. I observed white plumes of petrol or glycol pouring from the wings, near the fuselage. This was confirmed by Yellow 3, P/O Gillman, who saw the E/A yaw away to starboard and go down fairly steeply.'
(signed) Fl Lt M. Crossley.

Meanwhile, Pilot Officer Daw became separated from the rest of his flight in the general melee and ran into six Bf 109s which he attacked. Daw's Hurricane (P3567) was hit before the Bf 109s disengaged. Short of fuel he made for base but crashed a few miles north-east of Dover. Having received a slight leg wound, he was admitted to the Royal Masonic Hospital, Hammersmith.

Despite their successes against the Bf 109s, Nos. 32 and 615 Squadrons were unable to penetrate the dive-bomber's fighter cover and the Ju 87s were able to bomb their targets.

At 1458 hours, No. 610 Squadron's Red, Blue and Green Sections were scrambled. Now sailing between Dover and Folkestone, the convoy was being targeted by twenty Stuka dive-bombers, with fifteen Bf 109s flying as top cover. These were attacked, with four 109s claimed as destroyed, only one confirmed. Pilot Officer F. T. Gardiner (flying R6595 'O') was wounded in the arm.

Half an hour after the engagement with the Bf 109s, Squadron Leader Smith's Spitfire (R6693 'A') was seen limping back towards Hawkinge, smoking and obviously in difficulties. While making his approach his aircraft seemed to stall and crashed into a disused engine testing shed, and caught fire. Smith was killed as his aircraft burned out. Squadron Leader (90337) Andrew Thomas Smith, AAF, was the son of Andrew Thomas and Marie Emily Gabrielle Smith; husband of Dorothy Smith, of Manley. He was buried at Delamere (St Peter) Churchyard, South part. He was 34-years-old.

Following the loss, Flight Lieutenant Ellis was promoted to the rank of squadron leader and took command. A brave pilot and fine tactician, by the end of October he would have ten enemy aircraft to his tally.

That afternoon Flight Lieutenant Ellis led No. 610 Squadron on another patrol when they sighted about fifteen bombers attacking a destroyer in mid-Channel, two dozen Bf 109s providing escort. During the engagement five Bf 109s were confirmed as destroyed, while three more remained unconfirmed. Ellis, who had destroyed a Bf 109 that morning, destroyed two, closing to ten yards in each attack:

'The E/A were flying in fours in line astern and the last a/c presented a very easy target. I must have taken the section by surprise as they did not break; this E/A rolled over and plunged towards the sea out of control.

'I sighted another section of four Me 109s in line astern, carried out a climbing attack again on the last a/c, it fell out of the sky burning furiously and hit the sea.'

Brothers was scrambled at 1620 hours, with orders to intercept a raid near Folkestone, before being redirected onto a second raid. Both were either dispersed or forced to turn back, for a brief while those on-board the convoy were safe.

The Luftwaffe's raids on the convoy continued, while Brothers' last sortie of the day proved to be an uneventful squadron patrol of the convoy off Dover. His recollections of this phase of the battle were that, 'you were doing convoy patrols in the Channel [then] they started attacking convoys. The excitement grew slowly and progressively.'

Despite the RAF's and RN's valiant defence of convoy WC8, only two of the original twenty-one vessels were left undamaged. Seven RAF fighters had been lost during its frantic defence. These combined losses brought an end to daylight Channel convoys and signalled the completion of the first stage of Adolf Hitler's plan – he had won the battle for the English Channel.

There was low cloud, accompanied by heavy rain, for much of 26 July, with Brothers (flying 2921) making a single operational sortie in the afternoon lasting only twenty minutes: 'We were stood down at 1100 hours one day because it was low cloud and pissing with rain. We filled the bar and got pissed and at 1400 hours the sun came out and we were called to Readiness and scrambled. I remember taking off and – switch on gun sights; gun sights!! We were all absolutely tanked up.'

The squadron flew a number of uneventful patrols during 27 July. Meanwhile, three pilots, Sergeants Whitehouse, Gent and Pickering, arrived straight from No. 5 FTS, Sealand. On inspecting their logbooks, Worrall sent them straight on to No. 6 OTU at Sutton Bridge, where they converted onto Hurricanes. All three returned on 25 August.

Brothers (flying N2921) flew three fighter sorties during 28 July. Sitting out the day and making aborted scrambles was both frustrating and draining. Most pilots agreed with that: the hours of stressful waiting could be as tiring as any physical work, while the lack of restful sleep meant that both the pilots and ground crews were suffering from the effects of fatigue: 'Very often you just slept between scrambles.'

The following day Brothers' 'B' Flight operated out of Hawkinge. The pilots were at Readiness when a Fox Film Unit arrived to make an instructional film for the Air Ministry. A stills photographer captured Brothers and the rest of the flight between sorties – the photographs have since become iconic images of the Battle of Britain.

Scrambled, Brothers (flying N2921) led a patrol off the Kent Coast at about 1800 hours, shooting down a Bf 109, which was seen to plunge into the sea. There was no parachute. Brothers' combat report has since been lost, but his logbook records: 'Patrol & to Hawkinge 1 hr 10 mins, shot down Me109 into sea confirmed'.

Brothers made a second sortie, this time in Hurricane P3147, patrolling for forty minutes before being ordered to pancake.

Meanwhile, No. 610 Squadron's 'A' Flight damaged a Do 215 during the interception of Enemy Raid 49 off Dungeness at 1245 hours.

At Readiness since before dawn the following day, Brothers (flying P3112) made three patrols from Hawkinge, but without sighting the enemy. Brothers' three patrols probably represented raids that never materialized, either because the enemy changed course and passed through another sector, or they were ordered down as the enemy turned back. The close proximity of their forward base to the coast meant that the enemy might easily make sneak raids and catch them with too little time to scramble and gain operational altitude. At times this necessitated the need for tiring standing patrols, of which Brothers and No. 32 Squadron flew on many.

Brothers was scrambled at 1730 hours on 31 July, his third patrol of the day. Once airborne, he was ordered to intercept six He 111s and their fighter escort sighted heading over the Channel. The enemy aircraft at once made off in the direction of Le Touquet. For Brothers it was a frustrating end to the month.

Nos. 79 and 610 Squadrons operated out of Biggin Hill alongside Pete's No. 32 Squadron. While some of their sorties are referred to in the main body of the text, their contribution to the battle is expanded upon here:

No. 79 Squadron

No. 79 Squadron's operations, victories and casualties for July/August may be summarized:

4 July	Pilot Officer D.W.A. Stones – Bf 109 damaged
	Flight Sergeant F.S. Brown – Do 17 damaged
9 July	Pilot Officer W.H. Millington – Bf 109
	Pilot Officer D.W.A. Stones – Bf 109 unconfirmed
	Midshipman M.A. Birrell – Bf 109 damaged
9 August	Flight Lieutenant R.F.H. Clerke – He 111 (shared)
	Pilot Officer G.H. Nelson-Edwards – He 111 (shared)
	Sergeant J. Wright – He 111 (shared)
15 August	Flight Lieutenant R.F.H. Clerke – Bf 110, Do 17 unconfirmed (shared)
	Flight Lieutenant G.D.L. Haysom – Bf 110
	Flying Officer G.C.B. Peters – Bf 110
	Pilot Officer D.G. Clift – Bf 110
	Pilot Officer W.H. Millington – three He 111s
	Pilot Officer G.H. Nelson-Edwards – Bf 110 probable
	Pilot Officer T.C. Parker – Bf 110 and Do 17 (shared)
	Pilot Officer O.V. Tracey – He 111
4 July	Sergeant H. Cartwright, DFM – killed-in-action.

7 July	Squadron Leader J.D.C. Joslin – killed-in-action (friendly-fire).
8 July	Flying Officer E.W. Mitchell (P3461) – killed-in-action.

7 July   Squadron Leader J.D.C. Joslin – killed-in-action (friendly-fire).
8 July   Flying Officer E.W. Mitchell (P3461) – killed-in-action.
Flying Officer (37820) Edward William Mitchell, RAF, was buried in Hawkinge Cemetery, Plot O, Row 1, Grave 8.
Pilot Officer Wood – bailed out badly burnt (DoW).
Pilot Officer (33448) John Edward Randell Wood, RAF, was buried in Hawkinge Cemetery, Plot O, Row 1, Grave 7.

No. 610 Squadron

No. 610 Squadron's combat victories and casualties for the months June/July may be summarized:

7 June   Flight Lieutenant J. Ellis – Bf 109
12 June   Flight Lieutenant J. Ellis – He 111 (shared)
Sergeant N.S.J. Arnfield – He 111 (shared)
Sergeant P. Else – unknown type (shared)
3 July   Flight Lieutenant J. Ellis – Do 17 (shared)
Flight Lieutenant E.B.B. Smith – Do 17 (shared with below)
Flying Officer P.G. Lamb – Do 17 (shared)
Pilot Officer P. Litchfield – Do 17
Sergeant P. Else – Do 17 (shared)
Sergeant R.F. Hamlyn – Do 17 (shared)
Sergeant N.H.D. Ramsay – Do 17 (shared)
8 July   Pilot Officer C.O.J. Pegge – Bf 109
Sergeant P. Else – Do 215 damaged
9 July   Squadron Leader A.T. Smith – Do 215 (shared)
Flight Lieutenant E.B.B. Smith – He 111, Do 17 damaged
Sergeant C.A. Parsons – Do 215 (shared)
10 July   Flying Officer W.H.C. Warner – Bf 109 unconfirmed
14 July   Pilot Officer P. Litchfield – Bf 109, Bf 109 unconfirmed
20 July   'Green 2' – Bf 109 unconfirmed
24 July   Flight Lieutenant J. Ellis – two Bf 109s
Flight Lieutenant E.B.B. Smith – Bf 109, Bf 109 unconfirmed, Bf 109 damaged
Flight Lieutenant D.S. Wilson – Bf 109
Pilot Officer S.C. Norris – Bf 109
Sergeant H.H. Chandler – Bf 109
Sergeant P. Else – Bf 109
Sergeant C.A. Parsons – Do 17 (shared), Bf 109 unconfirmed
25 July   Squadron Leader E.B.B. Smith – Bf 109
Flight Lieutenant J. Ellis – three Bf 109s
Flight Lieutenant D.S. Wilson – Bf 109

Flying Officer F.T. Gardiner – Bf 109 damaged
Flying Officer D.S. Wilson – Bf 109
Pilot Officer S.C. Norris – two Bf 109s
Sergeant H.H. Chandler – Bf 109
Sergeant P. Else – Bf 109, one Bf 109 unconfirmed
Sergeant C.A. Parsons – Bf 109

27 July	Squadron Leader E.B.B. Smith – Bf 109 damaged
29 July	Squadron Leader E.B.B. Smith – Do 17 damaged (shared)
	Pilot Officer S.C. Norris – Do 17 damaged (shared)
	Sergeant R.F. Hamlyn – Do 17 damaged (shared)

29 June   Sergeant R.W. Haines was involved in an air accident when he attempted to take off in P9498 with his propeller in course pitch. He crashed into a pillbox and was killed. Sergeant (742106) Ronald William Haines, RAFVR, was the son of Ernest W. and Alice Haines of Gillingham. Haines was 20-years-old and was buried at Gillingham (Woodlands) Cemetery, Kent, Section B, Grave 431.

2 July   Sergeant (745103) Sydney Ireland, RAFVR, was buried at Knockbreda Cemetery, Section E, Grave 78.

8 July   Pilot Officer A.L.B. Raven – shot down and killed over the Channel.
Pilot Officer (91089) Arthur Lionel Boultbee Raven, RAFVR, was 51-years-old. He is remembered on the Runnymede Memorial, Panel 9.

10 July   Squadron Leader A.T. Smith (L1000 'D') – crash-landed Hawkinge

12 July   Sergeant S. Ireland is believed to have been killed during dogfight practice with Sgt H.H. Chandler. His Spitfire (P9502) failed to pull out of a dive and crashed at Titsey Park, four miles south of Biggin Hill. Sergeant (745103) Sydney Ireland, RAFVR, was buried at Knockbreda Cemetery, Section E, Grave 78.

18 July   Pilot Officer P. Litchfield (P9452 'T') – killed-in-action.
Pilot Officer (76461) Peter Litchfield, RAF, is remembered on the Runnymede Memorial, Panel 9.

20 July   Pilot Officer G. Keighley (R6621 'S') – bailed out wounded in leg.

25 July   Squadron Leader A.T. Smith (R6693 'A') – crashed at Hawkinge following combat.
Squadron Leader (90337) Andrew Thomas 'Big Bill' Smith, AAF, was the son of Andrew Thomas Smith and Marie Emily Gabrielle Smith, husband of Dorothy Smith, of Manley. Smith was 34-years-old and was buried in Delamere (St Peter) Churchyard.
Flying Officer F.T. Gardiner (R6595 'O') – wounded.

26 July   Sergeant P. Else – shot down and wounded in left forearm, bailed out.

Chapter 7

The Battle Heightens

August 1940 saw the squadron in a regular routine of being at Readiness before dawn, the pilots flying daily scrambles, patrols and occasionally flying convoy escorts. The squadron's pilots were under constant pressure with the ever-present possibility of engaging the enemy and all that combat might bring. Three or four times a day they raced to their fighters, took off and made a battle climb before patrolling behind their leader. Familiarity reducing what had begun as exciting, adrenaline-pumping action to almost something approaching routine, but nonetheless draining, 'If you weren't airborne, then you were in the bar or trying to catch some sleep. We were just ordinary chaps doing what we had to do.'

On 1 August Hitler issued his Directive No. 17 for the Conduct of Air and Sea Warfare Against England and with it heralded a new phase in the battle, with Fighter Command's airfields becoming the primary targets:

'In order to establish the necessary conditions for the final conquest of England I intend to intensify the air and sea warfare against the English homeland. I therefore order as follows:

'The German Air Force is to overpower the English Air Force with all the forces at its command, in the shortest time possible. The attacks are to be directed primarily against flying units, their ground installations and their supply organizations, but also against the aircraft industry, including that manufacturing anti-aircraft equipment.

'Attacks on the south coast ports will be made on the smallest possible scale, in view of our own forthcoming operations.

'I reserve to myself the right to decide on terror attacks as measures of reprisal.

'The intensification of the air war may begin on, or after, 5 August. The exact time is to be decided by the Air Force.'
(signed) Adolf Hitler.

Three Polish pilots, Pilot Officers Pfeiffer, Wlasnowalski and Pniak arrived from No. 6 OTU, Sutton Bridge, on 4 August. The men would quickly settle into the squadron, and as 'adopted' RAF pilots they had to have nicknames, and were affectionately known as 'Fifi', 'Vodka' and 'Cognac'.

The squadron made a number of patrols during 6 August, but without making any claims. Meanwhile, there was welcome news when Squadron Leader John Worrall's DFC was announced in the *London Gazette*:

'This officer's splendid leadership has been reflected in the work of the squadron, which has now destroyed forty-three enemy aircraft and possibly a further twenty-two. In July he led his squadron in a successful attack against a superior number of enemy aircraft and assisted in destroying three of the enemy force. Squadron Leader Worrall has displayed great skill, courage and leadership.'

Meanwhile in Berlin, Hermann Goering was still confident that the Luftwaffe, who had already won the battle for the Channel, would crush the RAF; 'I have told the Führer that the RAF will be destroyed in time for Operation Sea Lion to be launched on 15 September, when our German soldiers will land on British soil.'

Operating out of their forward base at Manston on 9 August, Brothers led 'B' Flight during a squadron scramble at 1655 hours. Vectored onto two Bf 109s reported to be over Dover, the pilots searched the sky for signs of the enemy but the fighters had evaded them, 'you were very often scrambled so late you couldn't get the height you wanted. People used to complain like hell, saying, "God, the bloody controllers". It was one thing to launch us off because a raid was coming across the Channel, and then as soon as we were well and truly airborne, the raid would turn round and go home, and we would land. Then the real raid would arrive whilst we were refuelling. So, we were inevitably cautious, which gave us problems.'

Sitting in their cockpits at Readiness since before dawn on 11 August, No. 32 Squadron was scrambled at 0740 hours and immediately vectored to the Dover area. While flying between Deal and Dover, Flight Lieutenant Crossley (flying P3146) spotted nine Bf 109s, engaging one, but without observing any results. Meanwhile, Pilot Officer Barton (flying N2596) damaged another. Brothers, leading 'B' Flight was unable to make a claim.

Pilot Officer Barton's combat report read:

'Three 109s appeared diving from behind us, to the left and slightly below, going in the same direction. I gave the last one three short bursts [one to two second bursts at 300 yards, firing 480 rounds per gun] – pieces flew off. I then took a quick look behind as I had heard there were eight of them about. I lost sight of the damaged 109.'
(signed) Plt Off Barton Red 3, A Flight.

The squadron was scrambled from Biggin Hill at 1005 hours and again vectored onto a raid reported in the Dover area. Brothers' engine was running rough and so he was forced to return early.

Meanwhile, Green 1, Flying Officer Gardner (flying P3679), who had become separated from the rest of the squadron, engaged a formation of Bf 109s, damaging one:

'I saw five aircraft flying in line astern [flying at 4,000ft over Dungeness]. They were flying just above the cloud level so I went up astern of them to within 75 yards and fired a short burst [three-second burst at 250 yards] at the last one, several pieces fell off it, and he seemed to stagger and then fell into the clouds. I followed but all I could see was three streaking for France.'

Also flying out of Biggin Hill, No. 610 Squadron claimed one – described as an Me 59 – as destroyed mid-Channel. The squadron lost two Spitfires, shot down off Calais at around 1130 hours, with both pilots killed. Flight Sergeant (565125) John Henry Tanner, RAF (flying 6918 'D'), was the son of John William and Eva Tanner, of Enfield, Middlesex; husband of Helen Maria Tanner. Tanner was buried in Calais Southern Cemetery, Plot P, Grave 17. He was 25-years-old. Sergeant (741783) William John Neville, RAFVR (flying R6630), was the son of William James and Julia Kathleen Neville, of Shepperton, Middlesex. He is remembered on the Runnymede Memorial, Panel 17. Neville was 26-years-old.

Brothers' logbook records two further patrols of forty-five and twenty-five minutes duration, during which he may have destroyed a Bf 110, a swastika and '110' appearing in red biro as later annotations.

During the following day, radar covering much of the Biggin Hill sector was down due to air strikes and so the controller was forced to maintain elements of Nos. 32 and 610 Squadrons on standing patrols. This was the day that Goering issued his infamous message, which heralded the next phase of the battle: 'From Reichsmarschall Goering to all units of Air Fleets 2, 3 and 5. Operation Eagle: within a short period you will wipe the British Air Force from the sky. Heil Hitler.'

At 0810 hours No. 610 Squadron was scrambled to intercept an enemy raid approaching Dungeness, engaging nine enemy aircraft over New Romney. Pilot Officer E.B.B. Smith's aircraft was hit by a Bf 109, two cannon shells exploding in the cockpit, wounding him in the face and neck. Smith bailed out of the burning Spitfire (K9818 'H') over New Romney and was picked up by a motor boat and landed at Dover. Meanwhile, Flying Officer F.T. Gardiner (flying R6891 'Q') had a lucky escape when his petrol tank was ruptured by a cannon shell, a second bursting in his cockpit causing only a slight leg wound. Two further aircraft (P9495 'K' and R6621) were severely damaged. During the dogfight No. 610 Squadron claimed two Bf 109s destroyed, six Bf 109s unconfirmed, two Bf 109s 'probables' and one Bf 109 damaged.

Among those making claims were Sergeant B.G.D. Gardner of 610 Squadron, who claimed three Bf 109s, while Pilot Officer Cox claimed one Bf 109 destroyed (confirmed by Pilot Officer Rees) and a second unconfirmed over Dungeness.

At 1650 hours No. 32 Squadron was scrambled and vectored onto a formation of thirty to forty Do 215s, with an escort of fifteen Bf 109s, flying at 12,000ft halfway between Dover and Manston. After the initial engagement the squadron became dispersed and a number of individual battles took place ranging from Dover to north of Whitstable.

Commanding the squadron and at the head of 'A' Flight, Flight Lieutenant Crossley (flying P3146) claimed one Bf 109 destroyed, firing all of his ammunition:

'We sighted a large formation of Do 215s, with Me 109s escorting, coming from the SE towards us. We climbed up and attacked almost head on, and were

almost at once mixed up with the Me 109s. I did not see what damage I did to a 215 I was attacking as a 109 crossed above me and I fired up at it, from about 100 yards, a burst of about three seconds. Yellow 1 saw a large red flash from it and a stream of black smoke, and saw it go down steeply with thick black smoke pouring from it, on fire.'
(signed) Flt Lt M. Crossley.

Red 2, Pilot Officer Proctor (flying N2458), fired all his ammunition, claiming one Bf 109 probably destroyed:

'We carried out a combined quarter attack on the Do 215s on the starboard side with no result. I was engaged by several Me 109s, but after a short encounter they drew away. I then followed the enemy formation northwards from Whitstable when I managed to get up sun behind several Me 109s. I dived down with a quarter attack on a straggler and opened fire about 350 yds closing to 50 yds. A large piece (about 5ft long) of his starboard main plane broke off and the E/A flicked on to its back. I was immediately engaged by some more 109s, but as I had no ammunition left – I evaded them and returned to base.'

Flying Officer Humpherson (flying P3112) probably destroyed another Bf 109:

'As we turned to attack the bombers we were engaged by the escort. A general dogfight ensued and I attacked one Me 109, after a very short burst a piece flew off the tail unit of the machine and it went into a spin.'
(signed) Flg Off J.B.W Humpherson.

Sergeant Higgins (flying N2524) claimed one Bf 109 destroyed (unconfirmed), a second escaping with damage:

'I attacked one Me [firing eight bursts from 300–100 yards] remaining on his tail for several minutes until, in my final burst, the aircraft was seen descending in a flat spin, finally crashing in the sea just off Manston.
    'I sighted a second Me 109 which immediately went into a dive almost to ground level. I was able to put in several bursts of fire [firing four bursts from 500 – 300 yards] but the Me gradually drew away from me well across the Channel.'
(signed) Sgt W.B. Higgins.

Green 1, Pilot Officer Gardner (flying P3147), claimed two Bf 109s destroyed, (unconfirmed), having expended all of his ammunition:

'Saw three Me 109s below me over Deal. I gave the last one a five-second burst [at 100ft] and he dived straight into the sea. Then looking round for something else, I

saw four Me 109s north of Ashford. I chased them to just by Whistable, destroying one either in the sea or on the land [firing a three-second burst at 100ft].'
(signed) Plt Off P.M. Gardner.

Flying as Yellow 2, Pilot Officer Smythe (flying P3522) destroyed a Do 215, having fired 2,400 rounds:

'I fired a short burst [of two-seconds at 250 yards] from the starboard quarter, but was then attacked by a 109 and had to break off.
   'The AA Guns started firing and separated one 215 from the formation, this I attacked [firing a four-second burst at 250 yards, closing to 50 yards] and set the port engine on fire, the 215 started to sideslip violently towards the sea.'
(signed) Plt Off R.F. Smythe.

The Do 215 was seen to fall into the sea two or three miles off Dover by the AA gunners.
   Yellow 3, Sergeant Bayley (flying P3481), claimed one Do 215 destroyed, firing a total of 2,000 rounds:

'We followed Red 1 in to attack the bombers (Do 215s) and got mixed up with the escorting fighters (Me 109s). This raid, consisting of about thirty bombers and twenty fighters, then turned out over the coast. I saw two more raids of approximately the same size in the distance and above me. I continued to climb, and about five minutes later saw a fourth raid, again of about the same number, coming in just below me, I made a beam attack on the bomber formation on the last three aircraft. The centre one dropped behind slightly and I broke away and came up beneath him in an astern attack [two to five second burst]. I was then forced to break away by an Me 109 on my tail.'
(signed) Sgt E.A. Bayley.

Pilot Officer Pniak (flying R4106) claimed one Bf 109 destroyed (unconfirmed):

'I attacked a Do 215 and got in a few short bursts at 100 yards one quarter deflection, I then broke away, a dogfight with an Me 109 then ensued and I was attacked from above by an Me 109. I turned inside him and got on his tail, he spiraled down and [I] got in two or three, one to two second bursts [firing two bursts at 100 yards] in a short time. I followed him down to 3,000ft and last saw him in a very tight vertical spiral, still smoking hard.'
(signed) PO K. Pniak.

Flying Officer Grice (flying N2524), claimed one Do 215 damaged, firing three, three second bursts during two head-on attacks and expending 1,200 rounds. The combat took place at 10-15,000ft in the Canterbury-Deal-Hawkinge-Ashford area, otherwise the details are lost.

Forming up with what he initially thought were two Hurricanes, Flight Lieutenant Crossley claimed one Bf 109 destroyed, unconfirmed, ten miles south of Dover:

'As they'd not seen me I joined on behind and chased them until within range and opened fire at the rear one [firing a six-second burst at 250 yards]. After about three seconds there was a red flash and it caught fire behind the pilot and dived steeply, burning well.'
(signed) Flt Lt M. Crossley.

Pilot Officer A.R.H. 'Tony' Barton (flying N2596) was shot down and bailed out uninjured while over Dover at 1700 hours, his Hurricane crashing two miles west of Hawkinge. He made his own way back to Biggin Hill and was next seen sinking a pint in the mess – such was the spirit of Dowding's Fighter Boys.

While No. 32 Squadron was airborne, Hawkinge had been heavily bombed, two hangars receiving direct hits, the landing-ground being peppered with craters and unexploded bombs. Elsewhere, both Manston and Lympne were temporarily out of action. There was no choice but to land at their advanced base at Hawkinge, despite the damage. Five Hurricanes, including Crossley's, picked their way through the craters. Miraculously, all landed without damage. As they rolled to a halt another raid arrived overhead. Although caught on the ground the Hurricanes were well dispersed and none were damaged. During the day the Biggin Hill squadrons flew a total of 100 operational sorties.

It was at about this time that the war got too close for comfort to the Brothers family home: 'When things began to hot up, she [Annette] was sitting at her dressing table putting on her lipstick at about 5 pm, hoping I was going to go down that evening; and some clumsy Hun dropped a bomb fairly near, and a piece of shrapnel whizzed in through her open window and smashed her mirror. I said: "That's it; you're moving. You must go and stay with my parents in Lancashire." So that's what she did, which got her away from the worst of it anyway and when I got a week's leave I'd go up and spend it there.'

On 13 August 1940, 'Adler Tag' or 'Eagle Day', the Luftwaffe launched their new offensive. The first raid arrived over the coast, on a line between Dungeness and North Foreland, at about 0530 hours. Some aircraft peeled off and headed for a convoy in the Thames estuary. Forty-five minutes later, four raids totalling two hundred and fifty enemy aircraft headed for Portsmouth. Fighter squadrons from Nos. 10 and 11 Groups were already in the air to meet the bombers, which suffered heavy casualties with only small losses to Fighter Command.

The attacks continued with two minor raids around noon. A large formation crossed the coast between Portland and the Thames estuary at 1525 hours. Half-an-hour later six formations totalling 150 aircraft closed in on their targets; largely along the south-west coast as far west as Bristol.

Meanwhile, 150 aircraft headed for Ramsgate, Deal and Dover, with Eastchurch Aerodrome also being hit. Other targets in East Kent included Detling airfield, which was bombed by Ju 88s. The latter attack demonstrated the enemy's poor intelligence gathering.

Despite making five scrambles and patrols between 0840 and 1320 hours, No. 32 Squadron was unable to make contact with the enemy, which evaded them. Other squadrons had better luck and the RAF's tally for the day was forty-five destroyed for the loss of fourteen fighters, with seven pilots reported as safe.

Brothers did not fly on 14 August, although the squadron was once more engaged. At around 1150 hours radar plotted eighty-plus Ju 87s of II./St G 1 and IV./LG 1 flying towards the coast near Dover, closely escorted by Bf 109s of I. and III./JG 26; the fighters of II./JG 26 flying in a roving role.

The controller scrambled No. 32 Squadron's 'A' Flight at 1230 hours, joining fighters from Nos. 65, 610 and 615 Squadrons, bringing the defending force up to forty-two aircraft. Thirty minutes into the patrol, Pilot Officer Smythe, leading Yellow Section, spotted nine Bf 109s circling above at 16,000ft, north-west of Hawkinge.

During the engagement, Pilot Officer Barton's Hurricane (P3146) was hit by Bf 109s and force-landed at Hawkinge, while Pilot Officer Wlasnowalski's stricken Hurricane force-landed north of Dover.

Pilot Officer Smythe (flying P3171), claimed the Bf 109 flown by Feldwebel Gerhard Kemen of I./JG 26 as destroyed, before making an emergency landing at Hawkinge:

'I was leading Yellow Section and sighted about nine 109s above us on the port quarter circling to attack. I called the squadron leader and turned in towards them. Some more 109s appeared behind and my section split up. However, two 109s were still in front of me, so I chased them and caught up just behind Dover. The one I fired at started to break up, turned on its back, and went down vertically, the pilot bailed out [over the Channel, badly wounded].

'Then some more 109s attacked me and got my glycol.'
(signed) R.F. Smythe, P/O.

The fighters of No. 610 Squadron intercepted the enemy in the area of Folkestone at around 1230 hours.

Sergeant B.G.D. Gardner (Green 2) attacked a formation of twenty Bf 109s at 8,000ft over Dungeness at 1230 hours, destroying one Bf 109 before being shot down by Leutnant Joseph Bürschgens:

'I saw an enemy aircraft coming head on and firing, I immediately took evasive action and chased it to the sea, where I gave it one long burst, smoke came pouring out from it and I saw it crash into the sea. I then went to attack ten a/c and received a tracer bullet in the left arm. I forced landed in a field at Wye and was taken to Ashford Hospital.'
(signed) B.G.D. Gardner.

Sergeant N.H.D Ramsay (Green 3) destroyed one Bf 110 at 8,000ft between Folkestone and Dover:

'I climbed up and found myself below and behind an Me 110, coming up astern of him, I fired a short burst at about 150 yds. He immediately started to climb to the left with smoke coming from his engines. I fired again and the E/A seemed to drop out of the sky turning on its back and going down with smoke pouring from it.'
(signed) Sgt N.H.D Ramsay.

Pilot Officer B.V. Rees (Blue 2) engaged elements of a formation totalling some 400–450 enemy aircraft, which included Ju 87s and their Bf 110 and Bf 109 escort, flying over Hawkinge. He claimed one Ju 87 probably destroyed:

'I remained in the cloud until I saw some Ju 87s diving down about to attack a ground objective. I picked an enemy a/c on the left side of the vic and delivered a long burst from about 300–200 yards. The E/A turned round (almost like a spin) and disappeared into the low cloud. It seemed definitely out of control.'
(signed) P/O B.V. Rees.

Sergeant D.F. Corfe (Blue 3) claimed one Bf 109 destroyed and another damaged, firing a total of 1,600 rounds:

'Three Me 109s detached themselves from the formation and attacked me. I went into a steep right-hand turn through 360 degrees and saw one Me 109 ahead at same level. I closed to 300 yards and fired five, one second bursts, closing range. Flames came from his engine and a piece flew off his starboard wing. He rolled on its back and went down flaming. I dived into cloud and came out again. About half a minute later, right on top of another Me 109, I fired three, two second bursts at him [at 150 yards]. Smoke came intermittently from his exhausts giving the impression that his engine was missing.'
(signed) Sgt D.F. Corfe.

No. 610 Squadron overall claims were:

Three Bf 109s confirmed destroyed – Sergeants Corfe, Chandler and Gardner
Two Ju 87s confirmed destroyed – Pilot Officer Norris
One Bf 110 confirmed destroyed – Sergeant Ramsey
Four Bf 109s probably destroyed – Sergeants Corfe, Else, Hamlyn, 'a/n other'
Three Ju 87s probably destroyed – Pilot Officers Norris and Rees, and Sergeant Parsons

While the air battle had raged on, a further raid hit Manston, destroying three of No. 600 Squadron's Blenheims in their hangars.

Both Nos. 32 and 610 Squadrons were at fifteen minutes Available from before dawn on 15 August, the pilots having slept under their aircraft's wings from 0300 hours. In the early afternoon No. 32 Squadron was ordered to their forward base at Hawkinge, which along with Lympne and Manston, had been bombed at noon.

Meanwhile, at 1243 hours, No. 610 Squadron was scrambled, Acting Flight Lieutenant W.H.C. Warner leading eight Spitfires in intercepting twenty-five Do 17s and their Bf 109 escort ten miles south-east of Biggin Hill.

The squadron claimed:

One Bf 109 probably destroyed – Pilot Officer Cox, Flight Lieutenant Warner
Two Bf 109s damaged – Sergeants Arnfield and Corfe

At 1500 hours Stuka dive-bombers attacked Martlesham Heath. The Hurricanes of No. 17 Squadron had been scrambled, but were unable to locate the enemy. By this time two separate raids had developed, the first, estimated at 100-plus was monitored by radar as it headed for the Kent coast, a second attack of 150-plus following thirty minutes later. Nos. 1, 32, 64, 111, 151 and 501 Squadrons were scrambled to make interceptions.

At 1525 hours Pilot Officer 'Grubby' Grice (flying N2459 'C') was shot down in flames by Bf 109s, about fifteen miles off Harwich. One of the rounds had pierced the fuel tank behind the instrument panel and, 'the cockpit filled with vapours and acrid smoke.' Pulling the pin to release his aircraft's canopy, Grice turned the Hurricane onto its back and was free, 'I remembered my parachute drill and waited a second or two before pulling the rip cord. I was relieved to see land, but an offshore breeze carried me out over the sea.' It wasn't until he had hit the water, some two miles out, that Grice realized that he had been badly burnt on the face and wrist. He was picked up after ten minutes by a rescue launch and taken to the Royal Naval Hospital at Shotley. His Hurricane was seen to crash into the sea at Pye Sands, Pennyhole Bay, south of Harwich. The remainder of the squadron returned to Biggin Hill.

Grice had been with the squadron since 1938 and had destroyed eight enemy aircraft, earning the DFC. Having recovered from his injuries, he became Controller at Biggin Hill and was Senior Controller at Northolt from June 1941 until February 1942, and at North Weald until December 1943, He was then Senior Controller at Tangmere until August 1945. Grice was awarded the MBE (*London Gazette*, 1 January 1946), and retired from the Service as a Wing Commander in April 1947.

His fiancée, Cypher Officer Pam Beecroft, worked in the Operations Room at Biggin Hill; she was ferrying the pilots to dispersals when the news came through.

Meanwhile, at about 1600 hours, Pilot Officer Wlasnowalski (flying N2671) set a Bf 109 on fire:

'I was flying No. 3 of Red Section, when I saw nine Me 109s above me in vic formation [flying off Harwich at 11,000ft]. I climbed up and attacked one of the Me 109s from astern; we circled round each other, then the Me 109 dived away.

I got in a good [five second] burst [firing 800 rounds at 200 yards] and the Me 109 burst into flames and dived down towards the sea.'
(signed) Plt Off Wlasnowalski.

Another raid was launched in the early evening, this time targeting Kenley and Biggin Hill. No. 501 Squadron was the first to engage, splitting the formation and forcing many of the bombers to make for their secondary target at West Malling.

Scrambled at 1720 hours, No. 32 Squadron made contact with several formations of Ju 88s and Do 215s, and their escort of Bf 109 and 110s, off Selsey Bill.

'A' Flight's Flight Lieutenant Crossley (flying P3481) destroyed two Ju 88s:

'We sighted about thirty Ju 88s, accompanied by several Me 110s, crossing the coast near Portsmouth [flying at 13,000ft]. One section of three 88s was a little way behind and I led Red Section at it, and fastened onto the port a/c and fired approximately half my rounds at him [at 200 yards] when he broke out of formation and headed off SE in a slight dive with his port engine smoking. On being engaged from above I left him.

'I then climbed up and attacked a straggler in a beam attack [firing the remainder of his ammunition at 200 yards]. His port engine caught fire and he also headed off in a SE direction, the port motor ticking over.'
(signed) Fl Lt Crossley.

'B' Flight's Flying Officer J.B.W. Humpherson (flying P3112) claimed one Ju 88 destroyed (shared):

'One 88 appeared to detach itself from the main formation. I went in to attack. I put in a short burst [firing 800 rounds in five seconds at 200 yards], but after I had fired the enemy machine caught fire in the starboard wing. It eventually crashed about five miles W of Chichester.'
(signed) Flg Off J.B.W. Humpherson.

The Hurricanes were quickly turned around and the pilots awaited their next sortie, which wasn't long in coming. At 1850 hours the controller scrambled No. 32 Squadron to intercept the last enemy raid of the day. Orbiting Biggin Hill, the pilots could clearly see the smoke rising from Croydon as it came under attack, the enemy having mistaken it for their intended target, Kenley. The raid composed of fifteen to twenty Ju 88s and Do 17s, escorted by Bf 110s and Bf 109s.

The Squadron Diary recorded:

'We turned and beat it for Croydon as fast as we could. Sure enough when we approached, we saw a large party in progress. Masses of Me 110s were dive-bombing the place. As they did not appear to notice our approach, we steered straight past them with the object of getting between them and the sun.

'No. 111 had also been scrambled to engage the same formation and Squadron Leader J.M. Thompson placed his [nine] Hurricanes ahead of the bombers, which were hit from the flank by No. 32 Squadron's Red, Green and Blue Sections. Moments later, No. 111 Squadron made a head-on attack, claiming five Bf 110s.'

Meanwhile, the Dorniers hit the still non-operational West Malling, their attack causing minimal damage. Reading through the squadron's combat reports a fuller picture of the air battle, which raged down to treetop level, emerges. At 1900 hours Red 1, Flight Lieutenant Crossley (flying N2461), destroyed a Do 17:

'I attacked a Do 17 from astern and opened fire at 200 yards, setting the port engine on fire.
    'I broke away and Red 2 closed in and knocked some pieces off it. He then gave way to Red 3, who also hit it. We followed, and the fire appeared to go out, giving place to two streams of white smoke. Red 2 and 3 then went in and knocked it about so badly that it crashed east of Sevenoaks, the pilot escaping by parachute '
(signed) M. Crossley.

This was shared with Red 2, Squadron Leader Worrall (flying P3205), who fired two bursts of three to four seconds at 100 yards, closing to 25 yards:

'We intercepted a number [fifteen to twenty] of Do 17 and 110s [and Bf 109s] over Canterbury.
    'Red 1 led attack onto a Do 17. Just as he broke away the port engine started to burn. I closed and fired a short burst only, as a mass of flames appeared from the same engine. Red 3 then closed. I fired another short burst which restarted the fire, and bits flew off the tail. Red 3 closed again and delivered the *coup de grace*. One of the crew bailed out. Enemy aircraft crashed somewhere near Plaxtol (south of Borough Green) in a wood.'

Red 3, Sergeant Henson (flying P3522), claimed a Do 215 as probably destroyed over Selsey Bill, firing 2,000 rounds in five bursts from 300 yards, closing to 100 yards. His combat report read:

'I closed in on the nearest section of nine Do 215s. I attacked the starboard machine which turned sharply to starboard leaving the rest of the formation, firing a five second burst in his broadside. (The rear gunner started firing at me at about 500 yds before the Do 215 broke formation), but after my second burst the rear gunner stopped. I fired another burst, and then saw bits falling off; bombs were released over the sea. Also, white smoke poured from the starboard engine, he then went into a steep dive. I followed him down firing until I ran

out of ammunition. I was then attacked by an Me 109. I landed at Tangmere for more ammunition but it was found that a bullet had pierced my crankcase.'
(signed) Sgt B. Henson.

Green and Blue Sections followed Red Section and in ten minutes of furious combat claimed three Do 17s, two Ju 88s and four Bf 109s destroyed, each of the pilots getting one.
Flying Officer Humpherson (flying P3112) claimed a Bf 109 probably destroyed:

'I saw about six Me 109's flying in line astern. I went into the attack on the rearmost enemy machine, as I did so another 109 appeared on the scene and tried a beam attack on me. He broke away in front of me and sat right in my sights about 100 yards away. I immediately opened fire [twelve second burst at 250 yards] and shot away a large piece of the radiator of the E/A, glycol streamed out and the E/A lost speed rapidly.'
(signed) F/O J.B.W. Humpherson.

Pilot Officer Pain (flying R4106) engaged the same formation, claiming one Bf 109 probably destroyed:

'Six Me 109s dived from about 1,500ft about me and opened fire, and then [pulled] up in a climbing turn. I turned and opened fire on the last machine [three, two second bursts at 200 yards]. Saw smoke coming from the enemy. Gave him another short burst [two, three second bursts at 150 yards] and the smoke increased.'
(signed) P/O J. Pain.

'B' Flight's Sergeant Pearce (flying N2755) claimed one Do 17 destroyed:

'I selected a Do 17 flying south from Croydon district and, when about 600 yards from it, saw another Hurricane level with me. I dived and came up below it, firing into front fuselage mainly [firing 600 rounds in a five second burst from 300 closing to 75 yards], while the other Hurricane attacked from astern. Port engine caught on fire and aircraft dived on fire probably at Redhill.'
(signed) Sgt L. Pearce.

Green 1, Pilot Officer Gardner (flying P3679), destroyed a Ju 88:

'I saw some Me 110s coming in to attack us, so I broke up my section and headed them off, and then dived away from them. Climbing back I attacked a Ju 88 [with a five second burst of 400 rounds at 200 yards] and started him downwards minus several bits and one engine. He must have come down somewhere SE of Croydon, but I was attacked by a 109.'
(signed) P.M. Gardner.

Pilot Officer Pniak (flying N2524) claimed one Do 17 and one Bf 109 probably destroyed, firing all of his ammunition in one to two second bursts from 200 to 100 yards:

> 'I attacked a Do 17 at 11,000ft which turned over Croydon. I opened fire from 200 yards, I fired several short bursts from astern and the Do 17 began to smoke. I saw him glide down with much thick black smoke coming from him. When I climbed up, I saw an Me 109, which was attacking another Hurricane; I attacked him from astern opening fire at 250 yards. I fired several short bursts, he planed down zigzagging with thick black smoke coming from him. I was attacked by another Me 109 from head-on, I pressed my trigger but found I had run out of ammunition.'
> (signed) Pniak.

During the same engagement Pilot Officer Russell destroyed a Bf 110, but his combat report is now lost.

In the pre-war years most operational squadrons had a Training Flight, some retaining the facility during the early phase of the war before the role was taken over by the Operational Training Units (OTUs). On No. 32 Squadron the flight was maintained well into August/September. Crossley recorded that, '"Polly" Flinders had taken the Training Flight up and that he and "Humph" slapped down one each. Day's bag twelve.'

Pilot Officer J. Flinders (flying N2062) and Flight Lieutenant Russell, who had been posted as 'A' Flight Commander on 14 August, had taken off and headed towards Croydon, engaging the enemy over Caterham, Flinders claiming one Bf 109 probably destroyed:

> 'Saw two Ju 88s on my right and 3,000ft above me flying in a SE direction about four miles away. I gave chase and was catching them up when an Me 109 came towards me from the starboard side. I throttled back completely and he passed in front of me and into my sight. I fired for about two seconds [at 100 yards] and a stream of white smoke came from his engine. The aircraft dived towards the ground. A minute later I saw a parachute open at about 6,000ft south of Sevenoaks.'
> (signed) PO Flinders.

Also defending Biggin Hill were the pilots of No. 610 Squadron. Sergeant D.F. Corfe attacked a Do 215 before damaging a Bf 109 over Maidstone: 'Several Me 109s came down on us. I engaged one Me 109 and fired four, three second bursts at him [at 250 yards]. My tracer appeared to hit him about the rear of the fuselage and wings.'

During the same engagement, Pilot Officer K.H. Cox claimed one Bf 109 probably destroyed, firing a three second burst at 250 yards: 'We were about to attack from the sun when I saw an Me 109 on my port side, apparently about to make a beam attack.

'I turned and engaged, got on his tail and after three short bursts he went into a vertical dive with engine on fire.'

Much of the combat had been played out within full view of those below, although none witnessed more than a single scene of the overall battle. A report in the *Daily Express* recorded some of the events of the day's fourth air raid: 'To see these fighters diving through great masses of enemy planes, to see them tear, one after the other, out of the sky and rise again to dive back, is the most heroic and inspiring thing I have ever seen in my life. There are no words to express their fury and their bravery.'

Churchill had observed the events as they unfolded at Bentley Priory, on his return he was heard to say of the air-battle: 'It is one of the greatest days in history.'

Later Brothers too was able to reflect: 'The hardest day was 15 August. That was a very big raid. There was a change of tactics and it took us by surprise. Quite a few aircraft were caught on the ground. They were bombing Biggin Hill from high-level, a raid against which I was involved, but they also ran a low-level raid at Kenley, which was next door to Biggin Hill.

'We'd see the damaged buildings and craters when we got back to the aerodrome after it had been bombed while we were elsewhere, intercepting other raids, the little flags stuck in the ground to mark off unexploded bombs. We'd either land on the perimeter path or make a path of our own through them all.'

Thursday, 15 August 1940, would be christened 'Black Thursday' by the Luftwaffe, the Biggin Hill squadrons once again flying a total of 100 sorties, contributing in no small measure to the enemy's losses (reckoned at seventy-five enemy aircraft destroyed for the loss of thirty RAF aircraft, with seventeen pilots killed).

On 16 August, Squadron Leader Worrall was posted to resume his role as Senior Sector Controller at Biggin Hill, with Brothers' friend, now acting Squadron Leader Michael Crossley, assuming command.

A little before noon radar located several formations totaling 150 enemy aircraft which crossed the coast near Dover before dispersing to hit various targets. No. 32 Squadron was scrambled at 1215 hours and vectored onto fifteen-plus Bf 109s approaching Dover, engaging the enemy fighters around forty-five minutes later.

Red 1, acting Squadron Leader M. Crossley (flying N2461), destroyed a Bf 109:

'I was over Dover at 10,000ft with Red 2 and 3, when I saw a battle between about five machines in progress about six miles NW of us. As we approached, two 109s broke away to starboard and headed for home. I selected the port machine and did a quarter attack [firing 260 rounds each gun at 200 yards], and suddenly a thick puff of black smoke came from him and he wobbled and went on his back and dived for about 1,000ft vertically and then recovered; he turned slowly on his back and went vertically into the sea about two miles off Folkestone.'
(signed) Sqn Ldr M. Crossley.

Red 2, Pilot Officer Comte Rudolphe Ghislain Charles de Hemricourt de Gunne (flying P3481), claimed one Bf 109 destroyed:

'When we saw two Me 109s slightly below. I saw F/Lt Crossley attack the last one, so I attacked the other. I saw the E/A attacked by F/Lt Crossley dive into the sea. The Me 109 turned sharply but I was able to get in two bursts of approximately two seconds [firing 320 rounds] from astern, at 40 yds range. I passed the E/A and saw the pilot slumped forward in the seat. I turned and fired another burst into him from astern. A lot of smoke came from his engine. F/Lt Crossley saw the E/A dive into the sea.'
(signed) P/O De Grunne.

The Belgian, Pilot Officer De Grunne, had arrived from No. 7 OTU on 9 August. Flying Messerschmitts for Franco during the Spanish Civil War, he claimed to have been credited with fourteen 'kills'.

Green 1, Pilot Officer Gardner (flying P3679), claimed one Bf 109 destroyed, firing 450 rounds in a five second burst at 100 yards: 'I saw twelve Me 109s coming down to attack us [at 12,000ft some three miles north of Folkestone]. I shouted over the R/T and turned to attack them. Three set on us but I managed to get away from them with a damaged tail wheel.'

Gardner heard over the radio that the enemy was approaching Ramsgate and flew to make an interception: 'I went there but saw nothing except one Me 109, 6,000ft above me running for home. I went underneath him until he reached my level of about 200ft and then tipped him into the sea, just east of the Goodwins.'

Brothers took part in a squadron strength scramble, made at 1640 hours, with orders to intercept a raid in the Biggin Hill area. A formation of fifty-plus Ju 88s and Bf 110s, and their escort of Bf 109s, were encountered. The main body was attacked head-on at 1730 hours.

The fighter's targets were of course the enemy bombers; the destruction of their escort was a means to an end. Park advocated head-on attacks on the bombers to break up their tight formations, 'Attack the ones in front. If you shoot them down, the formation will break up in confusion. Then you can take your pick.'

With closing speeds in excess of 500 mph there was little chance of destroying an enemy aircraft with machine-gun fire, while the tactic had high risks attached. Head-on collisions were not uncommon, enemy aircraft breaking in the same direction as the fighter, or neither breaking in time. Meanwhile, the rear gunners got a clear shot as the fighters wheeled by. The enemy's fighter cover generally placed themselves above and to the rear of the bombers, ready to catch the attacking fighters in a crossfire, or to dive down onto them as they exited the cone of fire provided by the enemy air-gunners.

Brothers recalled how ominous the sight of larger formations could be. It wasn't unusual for the Hurricanes to be facing odds of six, seven, eight, or even ten to one, 'The German planes blackened the sky, all stacking up with fighters on top and below a vast bomber formation. You thought, where do we start on this lot?'

During the engagement Squadron Leader Crossley (flying N2461) claimed one Ju 88 destroyed, with a Bf 110 probably destroyed over Sevenoaks:

'While being vectored back to base from Dover we met about eighty Ju 88s and Me 110s heading towards us. We attacked the main body almost head-on, and then I singled out a straggling formation of three 88s just behind and took the starboard one from in front and below [firing half his ammunition]. It immediately caught fire and started to spin. This was seen by P/O Pain in Blue Section. A moment later I opened fire [at 250 yards, using the remainder of his ammunition] from behind and below at a 110 who came across my front. After a fairly long burst his port engine caught ablaze, and a stream of white smoke, possible petrol or coolant, poured from behind the starboard engine. He went down steeply in a SE direction.'
(signed) S/Ldr M Crossley.

His Wingman, Red 2, Pilot Officer Barton (flying P3900), claimed two Bf 109s probably destroyed:

'As I was chasing a Ju 88 southwards from Base at about 15,000ft, several 109s appeared just overhead going northward. I saw them turn, so I left the bomber and started to turn round quickly to the right. A 109 appeared to make a half-hearted dive at me and shot round in front of me in a climbing turn to the right. I fired bursts at him, turning inside him and firing at one quarter deflection. Bits flew off and white smoke came from his engine. He wobbled and turned over. Another 109 did exactly the same thing and I dealt with him in exactly the same way. White smoke came from his engine and from his starboard wing root. He went down.'
(signed) Barton.

Sergeant Bayley (Red 3) damaged a Bf 109, firing 1,200 rounds:

'I followed Red 1 into a full frontal attack on a formation of twenty Ju 88s and after a burst of two or three seconds [at 250 yards] broke away behind the formation. Red 1 turned round to make astern attack, and I made a head-on attack from underneath on two Me 110s which were escorting the Ju 88s. I was only able to hold this burst for about two seconds [at 200 yards]. I came down on the formation which immediately formed a defensive circle. I fired a short burst at the nearest E/A and climbed away again. I repeated this twice [each burst at 150 yards] and finally got a long burst in from behind the rear E/A, I saw my tracer hitting and he dived vertically for the clouds.'
(signed) E.A. Bayley Sgt.

Meanwhile, Pete Brothers (flying N2921 'L') led 'B' Flight into the engagement over Westerham, personally claiming one Bf 110 destroyed:

'I was leading Blue Section, in company with Red Section, when I sighted approximately eighty Ju 88s escorted by twenty Bf 110s. I dived through the

formation of Ju 88s and fired a short burst at two, with no apparent success. I was in a poor position when I broke away and I had to give chase. I eventually caught up [with] an Me 110 cruising behind the Ju 88s and fired all my rounds into him from below and behind. His port engine was smoking badly and he slowly turned to port and dived through the clouds. I followed him down and he hit the sea about twelve miles due south of Brighton.'
(signed) Peter M. Brothers F/Lt.

Brothers noted in his logbook, 'Raid on B.H. one hr. (confirmed) one Do 17', adding later in pencil, 'actually it was a Ju 88 of II./KG 76'.

The Ju 88 was notoriously difficult to bring down, as Brothers explained, 'the best way was to make a head-on attack, killing the crew'.

Pilot Officer Pain (flying P3147) claimed one Ju 88 probably destroyed:

'I attacked a Ju 88 in the rear of the formation [150 yards with about four, two second bursts] and saw bits fall off the port engine and tail assembly. He jettisoned his bombs almost immediately. I pulled away as there were several more E/A behind and above, and I exhausted my ammunition on them.'
(signed) Plt Off J. Pain B Flight.

Sergeant Pearce (flying R4106) claimed one Bf 109 destroyed over Heathfield, firing all of his ammunition with a five second burst at 350-100 yards, with three, three second bursts at 200-150 yards and a five second burst at 100 yards:

'Acting as rear guard to the squadron I followed them in beam attack from above on large formation of Do 17s [forty Do 17s at 14,000ft] without visible result or return fire. Me 110s above [twenty Bf 110s at 20,000ft] and behind climbed to avoid action. Saw five Me 109s [at 15,000ft] below and picked one which half rolled and dived away, after several bursts from about 150 yards using the remainder of ammunition. One hexagonal panel about eighteen inch across and two smaller fragments fell off E/A, and transparent honeycombed pieces about two foot square struck starboard mainplane, knocking off [my] inner gun panel. glycol came from E/A which dived into 10/10 cloud. My own aircraft was almost uncontrollable without panel.'
(signed) Sgt L. Pearce.

No. 610 Squadron was also scrambled and made an interception over Dungeness, where they engaged a force of fifty Ju 88s and their escort of twelve Bf 109s at 25,000ft. During the course of the dogfight they claimed one Bf 109 and one Ju 88 destroyed for the loss of Acting Flight Lieutenant (90344) William Henry Cromwell Warner, AAF (flying R6802 'Z'), one of their most experienced pilots and flight commanders. He is remembered on the Runnymede Memorial, Panel 5. Warner was 21-years-old.

Also involved in the same combat were Nos. 56 and 501 Squadrons.

As a result of the day's combat, two enemy aircrew were in the cells at Biggin Hill awaiting collection for interrogation. One, an air-gunner, was entertained by the pilots of No. 610 Squadron, the other, a hauptman, was 'claimed' by No. 32 Squadron, 'We shot a 109 chap down near Biggin. He bailed out and was picked up by the police and put in the guardroom at Biggin. We found out and we got him out and took him over to our dispersal.

'We had the wing of a 109 propped up against the wall of the hut, which Flying Officer Rupert Smythe had shot down [sic]. He'd come back to Biggin Hill with it on the roof of his car. We said to the German, "One of your 109s!" All he said was "maybe"; he spoke very good English, but he wasn't going to commit himself.

'We took him inside and gave him a drink. We had some booze illegally in the dispersal hut.'

Brothers adding, 'Another of the squadron's trophies was a machine gun from a Ju 88 and the tail fin from an He 111, onto which Pniak had chalked "Made in Germany, finished in England!"'

Brothers continued: 'The Luftwaffe officer was taken for a drink in the officer's mess. In good English he said, "May I have paper and pencil?"'

We said, "Why?"

He said, "Tomorrow, when the Luftwaffe blackens the sky and you lose the war, I want to write all your names down to make sure you are well-treated." And we laughed and laughed. He couldn't understand it.

"Why are you laughing?"

"Oh you poor fellow! You are going to lose!"'

Brothers' personal opinion of the Luftwaffe pilots he came up against in the air was quite favourable, 'They [German pilots] were bloody good! Most of them had fought in Poland and they were so experienced, and they were arrogant to the extent that they were all-conquering.'

Brothers explained that not everyone was able to view the German pilot simply as a fellow aviator. Sat stoney-faced in the corner were the three Poles, 'if we hadn't have kept an eye on them, they might have attacked him – but I guess I would have wanted to do the same if I had had to leave my homeland to the will of the Nazis'.

That night the traitor, William Joyce, known as Lord Haw Haw, made his regular radio broadcast, threatening, 'This is Germany calling, Germany calling; yesterday our mighty Luftwaffe bombed Croydon from the map, soon it will be your turn, Kenley and Biggin Hill'.

Meanwhile, in a bizarre incident, a local councilor from Sevenoaks telephoned Group Captain Grice, complaining that his squadrons were making interceptions over the town which led to the Luftwaffe bomber crews jettisoning their bombs on his constituency. The councilor requested that the Station Commander tell his pilots to intercept the enemy elsewhere! The Group Captain's reply was no doubt brief and to the point.

On the following day Luftwaffe activity was minimal, with only a handful of enemy reconnaissance aircraft crossing the Channel, causing Crossley to note in the squadron's unofficial diary: 'Not a single sausage, scare, flap or diversion of any description today. Amazing. Heavenly day too.'

Sometimes a lack of activity was a bad thing, as Brothers explained: 'The worst part was being on the ground, waiting, because your mind could then stray to your chum who you'd just been to see in hospital who'd been badly burnt, and start thinking "Oh Christ that could be me one of these days!"'

Brothers was probably referring to 'Grubby' Grice, who only a few days earlier had suffered hand and facial burns. Grice's burns healed relatively quickly, aided by the fact that he was almost immediately immersed in salt water.

Chapter 8

One Day's Battle: 18 August

Continuing their assault on the RAF's airfields and infrastructure, the Luftwaffe launched further mass attacks during 18 August, hitting Fighter Command's airfields at Biggin Hill, Kenley, North Weald and Hornchurch, along with RAF Gosport and RAF Thorney Island.

The first large-scale raid of the day, postponed from 0900 hours due to bad weather, had started to form up on the other side of the Channel by about 1230 hours. A force of 300 enemy aircraft was approaching the coast, heading for Hornchurch, sixty He 111s of I./KG 1 making for the Sector Station at Biggin Hill.

Meanwhile, low-flying Do 17s from 9./KG 76, twenty-seven Do 17s of I. and III./KG 76 (the latter escorted by Bf 109s from JG 51), and twenty-one Ju 88s of II./KG 76 (escorted by twenty Bf 110s III./JG 51 led by Hannes Trautloft) were approaching Kenley. Fighter cover and diversions were provided by Bf 109s of JGs 3, 26, 51, 52 and 54 and Bf 110s of ZG 26 targeting Kenley and Croydon. It should be noted that 9./KG 76 was a specialist low-level attack squadron commanded by Hauptman Joachim Roth, who was lost during the raid. They would reach landfall at Beachy Head, following the Brighton to London railway towards their target, where they dropped their twenty 110lb bombs at 50 – 100ft.

In answer to the possible threats to Kenley and Biggin Hill, the controller scrambled Nos. 64 and 615 Squadrons (based at Kenley), along with Nos. 32 and 610 Squadrons. Also entering the fray were No. 111 Squadron; six of their Hurricanes were lost in defence of Kenley airfield, with Flight Lieutenant Connors killed-in-action. Flight Lieutenant (40349) Stanley Dudley Pierce Connors, RAF, was the son of Pierce Frederick John Patrick and Norah Muriel Connors; husband of Marjorie Violet Connors, of North Berwick. He was 28-years-old and was buried in North Berwick Cemetery, Section B, Grave 123.

No. 615 Squadron's Hurricanes climbed to operational altitude, almost immediately taking on the Bf 109s providing an escort for the Ju 88s of II./KG 76. They suffered a mauling, with Pilot Officer Petrus Hugo wounded for the second time in as many days, making a forced-landing. The South African born Petrus Hendrik Hugo would soon become one of the most highly decorated pilots of Fighter Command. Hugo was awarded the DFC (*London Gazette,* 23 August 1940), Bar to the DFC (*London Gazette*, 25 November 1941), the DSO (*London Gazette*, 29 May 1942), Second Bar to the DFC (*London Gazette*, 16 February 1943), the CdeG (France), and the DFC (US) (*London Gazette*, 14 November 1944).

Sergeant Walley was killed at the controls of his Hurricane, while Flight Lieutenant 'Elmer' Gaunce bailed out with a slight eye injury. Sergeant (819018) Peter Kenneth

Walley, AAF, was buried at Whyteleafe (St Luke) Churchyard, Row F, Grave 32A. Pilot Officer D. Looker landed his damaged Hurricane at Croydon, through a hail of anti-aircraft fire. The 'kills' were claimed by JG 3's Oberleutnant Lother Keller and Leutnants Helmut Meckel and Landry. By drawing off the Bf 109s, however, No. 615 Squadron opened the way for other fighters – including No. 32 Squadron – to get at the bombers.

No. 32 Squadron had been scrambled at 1255 hours, quickly followed by No. 610 Squadron. Once airborne they were vectored onto a large formation, then reported to be near Tonbridge Wells. The raid would hit Kenley first, nine Do 17s of 9./KG 76 coming in low.

Next, about thirty Ju 88s of II./KG 76 came in to bomb, cratering the airfield. Around ten minutes after the Kenley and Croydon raids struck, Biggin Hill's satellite at West Malling was also hit.

Flying in a wide climbing turn, the Hurricanes met the enemy, approximately sixty Do 215s, Do 17s and Ju 88s, with their escort of forty Bf 110s and Bf 109s (stepped) in the rear, over Sevenoaks.

As the two formations closed, Crossley placed the squadron in position for a head-on attack, as he later recalled: 'We sighted them as we were coming from Biggin, and swung round in front of them. We didn't have to work very hard to do it. We had plenty of time to line up.'

In a series of strikes, Squadron Leader Crossley (flying V6535) claimed one Ju 88 destroyed, one Bf 110 probably destroyed and one Do 215 damaged, firing 1,600 rounds at 250 yards:

'Having carried out a head-on attack on the main formation of Do 215s. I climbed and saw a single 88 [piloted by Rudolf Ahrens] about 2,000ft below. I did a quarter attack on it and after about five seconds there appeared to be an internal explosion [an oxygen bottle, which injured the flight engineer], and masses of bits flew off all round. I pulled away sharply to avoid them and flew alongside to observe the result [including damage to the right engine]. He jettisoned about ten small bombs and his undercarriage came down, and he glided down and crashed near Ashford [at Romney Marsh].

'While carrying out the head-on attack, I took the starboard machine [a Do 215] and Red 3 said that it turned sharply up out of line, but could not confirm that it crashed.

'I carried out another head-on attack on a 110 and caused its port engine to issue a stream of white smoke, but owing to my attention being taken elsewhere, I did not follow it up.'
(signed) S/Ldr Crossley.

Yellow 2, Henson (flying V6536), claimed one Do 215 destroyed, firing 800 rounds in six bursts at 200 yards:

'One machine was out of formation so I chose it as my target. I closed in to 200 yards (my machine was hit several times by rear gunfire from another machine at about 500 yds or more). I gave one good burst of fire into the starboard side of the Dornier, the underneath part of the starboard engine burst into flames, then my own centre tank burst and I had a lap full of petrol. I was struck in the face by a piece of bullet, so I broke off the attack, switched off my engine and petrol. I forced landed in a field at Shoreham. An army officer watched the bomber dive down in flames about eight miles SW from where I landed.'
(signed) Henson.

Yellow 3, Sergeant E.A. Bayley (flying P3481), claimed one Do 215 destroyed, with a Bf 110 damaged, firing 2,500 rounds:

'We made a quarter frontal attack [firing a two second burst] on the formation of twenty-four Do 215s, broke away, and came up behind and below in an astern attack; after a five second burst I broke away to engage the Me 110s [twenty to thirty in the formation] which were closing in and as I climbed up I saw the Do 215 burst into flames and dive away. I made a front attack on an Me 110 and we exchanged fire for about three seconds. I broke away and chased the bombers, which were now running for home, I caught up with the rear one and gave him a long burst [five seconds]. His port engine started to smoke but he kept going.'
(signed) Sgt E.A. Bayley.

Red 3, Pilot Officer Barton (flying P3900), claimed one Ju 88 destroyed, firing half of his ammunition in several two to three second bursts at 300 yards:

'I noticed a long line of bombers in threes reforming to go home (88s and 215s). I went in behind a section of Ju 88s and attacked the right hand one. After one burst bits flew off the fuselage – I put another burst into his starboard engine – smoke and flames came from it. He wobbled and lost his position in the section; it is extremely unlikely that he could have got home.'
(signed) Barton.

Squadron Leader Donald McDonald's No. 64 Squadron now intervened to take on the Bf 110s and damaged the Messerschmitt flown by Ruediger. Meanwhile No. 32 Squadron's 'A' Flight commander, Flight Lieutenant "Humph" Russell (flying V7363), claimed one of the Bf 110s which came to the bomber's aid as destroyed over Edenbridge, firing one burst of six seconds at 300 yards:

'I broke away upwards and to the left. I then saw about thirty Me 110s which had been following the bombers circling. I did a diving attack on one and opened fire with a quarter deflection shot. I had given him a six second burst and had seen my incendiary enter his cockpit, when I heard a very large explosion behind me [cannon shell burst in cockpit] and my machine went out of control. I then took to my parachute.

'I am in Edenbridge Hospital suffering from wounds [left foot and elbow], and the local authorities state that the Me 110 at which I was firing caught fire.' (signed) F/Lt Russell.

'Humph' Russell, who had been with the squadron since 1936, had only returned the previous day from secondment to the Biggin Hill ops room. He had to apply a tourniquet on the way down from 10,000ft. His Hurricane (V7363) crashed at Skeynes Park Farm, Edenbridge, following combat over Biggin Hill at 1345 hours. Russell returned in April 1941, commanding No. 32 Squadron until January 1942. He was awarded the DFC (*London Gazette*, 19 May 1944), having become a PoW in the same month.

Leading 'B' Flight into the attack, Brothers (flying N2921) could see the enemy's cannon and machine-gun fire as the Bf 110s drew ever closer: 'In head-on attacks the question was whether you went over the top of the aircraft or underneath it after the firing. I always used to go down, because I thought the bomber would pull up instinctively.'

Easing the throttle back too far Brothers accidentally put his nose past the vertical and gravity closed the needle valve in the float carburetor. With his Merlin engine starved of fuel, Brothers' Hurricane stalled out of the attack.

Recovering from his spin, Brothers latched onto a Do 215 [actually a Ju 88], which he shared:

'It was on 18 August 1940 when I shot down Wilhelm Raab in his Dornier 17. He was leading the formation, and I thought "You've got to take the leader out." It was a bit stupid, because I was trapped in the crossfire. But I got his port engine nicely burning.

'Bringing down a bomber was really satisfying, particularly if you got it before it dropped its bombs. Getting them when they were on their way home was better than nothing, but if you'd caught them before they'd made their drop, it was a real success.

'You envied them their cannon. You also broke the Fighter Command rules that your guns were supposed to be towed in to 200 yards *[sic]* range, where the rounds are gathered together in shot, but you weren't going to get very far like that; the odds were that you towed them in considerably and you got up jolly close – 50 yards if you could – as close as you could get and then you really did hammer it.'

The cannon shell had a greater weight and velocity than the 0.303 bullet. The cannon shell detonated on impact, delivering a deadly explosion which sent fragments into the target area. While the rate of fire of the cannon was slower, the enemy only had to hit his target with one or two shells and there was a good chance of delivering the fatal blow. As had been seen from German bombers brought down as early as 1939, literally hundreds of rounds could strike them from astern (where the engines and pilot had the protection of armour-plating) before a vital component was hit.

Pilot Officer Boleslaw Wlasnowolski (flying P3679) claimed a Do 215, which is believed to have been the same Ju 88 that was claimed by a number of other pilots, including Brothers, who saw his victim crash at Ide Hill, eight miles south of Biggin Hill. The pilots consequently awarded a 'half kill' included Flight Lieutenant James Sanders of No. 615 Squadron and 'a/n other' of the same squadron, Flying Officer James O'Meara, Flight Sergeant Adrian Laws and Sergeant Ernest Gilbert, all of No. 64 Squadron.

Meanwhile, Pilot Office J. 'Polly' Flinders had taken off in one of the squadron's trainers and caught up with the bombers as they headed for the coast, claiming a Do 17 and a Do 215 destroyed, expending all of his ammunition:

'At 1320 hours about thirty enemy aircraft [Do 17s and 215s] were seen 3,000ft above us approaching from the SE while we immediately engaged and broke up. I got on to the tail of a Do 17 and fired four bursts [of three seconds at 200 yards], clouds of black smoke and flames poured from the machine and it went into an almost vertical dive. The engagement took place in the vicinity of Godstone.

'I then sighted another enemy aircraft, believed to be a Do 215 at 12,000ft flying east about two miles away and gave chase. He immediately dived towards the ground. A running fight then ensued, the Do pilot doing barrel rolls and half rolls in an attempt to get rid of me. We were now down to 300ft and as I knew I had very little ammunition left I refrained from firing until I had a certain target.'

The pursuit moved towards Canterbury, where they came within range of the guns of 12th Light Anti-Aircraft Regiment which opened fire, damaging the German fighter.

Flinders' combat report continued:

'The Do 215 pulled up out of a dive: and as he lost speed I closed to 150 yards and got in a good burst [four seconds]. The starboard engine caught fire and the machine dived to the ground and exploded [at Harbledown, north-west of Canterbury, both crewmen dying in the wreckage].'
(signed) P/O Flinders.

Flinders had earlier flown Spitfires with No. 74 Squadron on 20 November 1939, claiming an He 111 (shared). Now with No. 32 Squadron, he probably destroyed an He 111 on 18 May, claiming a Bf 109 the following day. He destroyed an He 111 on 8 June and a Bf 109 on 15 August.

Another member of the Training Flight, Pilot Officer K.R. Aldridge, claimed one Do 215 damaged, firing fifty rounds at 200 yards:

'Fifty E/A sighted at 10,000ft above me over Biggin Hill. Intercepted one Do 215 between Maidstone and Sevenoaks. Delivered an astern attack from

slightly above. A burst of four seconds hit the starboard engine dislodging part of the cowling and leaving the engine smoking.'
(signed) Plt Off K.R. Aldridge.

The Squadron ORB recorded the following additional victories for which the combat reports are now lost: 'P/O Eckford (flying P3936) one Do 215 damaged, P/O De Grunne (flying R4081) one Me 110 probably destroyed, one Do 215 probably destroyed.'

Not listed was Pilot Officer Pain's Do 17, as he was shot down in flames and slightly wounded, landing by parachute at Horsmonden. Pain's Hurricane (P3147) crashed near Herne Bay. He was admitted to hospital in Tonbridge Wells.

Sergeant Henson (flying V6536) forced landed at Otford with a slight face wound and was discharged from the Royal Herbert Hospital, Woolwich. The remainder of the squadron landed at 1345 hours; rearmed and refuelled, ready to take on the next attack.

Meanwhile, fifteen Spitfires of No. 610 Squadron were also engaged, reporting a force of about fifty enemy bombers and a similar number of escorting fighters, flying five miles south-east of Biggin Hill. They succeeded in destroying five Bf 109s, 'A' Flight attacking the bombers, claiming one He 111, three Do 215s, a Bf 110 and a Do 17, which landed virtually intact at Romney Marsh and was 'captured' by a local parson. Their guns also damaged three Do 215s and one He 111; all without loss.

Among those claiming 'kills' was Pilot Officer K.H. Cox, who destroyed one Bf 109, probably destroying a second, firing several two second bursts and one five second burst:

'We intercepted Me 109s at 31,000ft. I engaged two, firing short bursts at each. I then got one long burst and one went down in flames. After a short while I saw an Me 109 about to attack me from behind. I was over anxious and blacked out, stalled and spun. On recovering I found I was immediately underneath the Bf 109, so I finished off my remaining ammunition in a climbing attack and broke away, as I looked back I saw a large smoke trail but could not see a machine.'
(signed) Pilot Officer K.H. Cox.

Meanwhile, Pilot Officer B.V. Rees claimed one Do 217 and a Bf 109 destroyed, firing three long bursts at 300 to 200 yards:

'I chased a Dornier which was separated from the rest and delivered two long bursts, his port engine went on fire, smoking very badly, following it down when I was attacked from behind [by a Bf 109]. I put my propeller in fine pitch and throttled back. My attacker shot past me and I gave it a very long burst at very short range (at about 150 yds). It suddenly turned over and crashed into a wood about ten miles from the aerodrome.'
(signed) P/O B.V. Rees.

With the majority of No. 11 Group's fighters either in the air or refuelling, the third wave of bombers were more successful, leaving Kenley extensively damaged with only one hangar remaining unscathed. Critically, the Operations Room sustained direct hits and had to be transferred to a butcher's shop in Caterham. Unable to see the airfield for thick black smoke, the Ju 87 dive-bombers had to divert to West Malling. Here they were targeted by the Hurricanes of No. 501 Squadron.

Another element of the same raid, including a formation of He 111s, made for Biggin Hill, which they had hit at around 1330 hours. The bombers were over the airfield for barely ten minutes, hounded by sporadic attacks by Hurricanes and Spitfires, aided by gunners from the 58th Heavy AA Regiment firing from their positions around the perimeter. Added to this was light-arms fire of the men of the 4th Platoon of the Kent Home Guard.

The enemy did not escape unscathed. Sergeant Harry Newton damaged the Do 17 flown by Günter Unger before being hit by return fire and bailing-out. Meanwhile, four Do 17s were destroyed, including that flown by Feldwebel Johannes Peterson, which was entangled by the rocket-fired cable defences launched by Aircraftsman D. Roberts, who also hit the aircraft piloted by Wilhelm Raab, but he managed to free the cable before its parachute could deploy. The remainder of the Do 17s were damaged.

One Dornier of KG 76, which had earlier bombed Kenley as a part of the second wave and been hit by the airfield's anti-aircraft gunners, was subsequently attacked by the Hurricane of No. 111 Squadron's Sergeant Dymond. Flying low, it was set alight by withering fire from the Home Guard, rolling on its back it crashed on the far side of Biggin Hill, to the cheers of the gunners. The crew survived. Sergeant William Lawrence Dymond was one of the many unsung heroes of 1940. He destroyed an He 111 (shared) on 10 April, Do 17s on 13, 18 and 19 May, damaging an He 111 on 31 May, destroying a Bf 109 on 11 June, a Do 17 (shared) on 13 August, a Bf 110 and a Do 17 on 15 August, before damaging a Do 17 on 17 August and destroying another the following day. Further 'kills' came when he destroyed an He 111 on 24 August and damaged a Bf 110 on 30 August. Sadly, Dymond was killed in action on 2 September (flying P3875), following combat over the Thames estuary.

The airfield suffered considerable damage to the landing strip, with a number of station buildings also being hit, along with one of the Bofors 40mm gun emplacements. One gunner was killed; the remainder of the wounded crew were taken to Decontam. In a shameful scene that followed, a young leutnant from the Do 17 crew, apparently spat in one of their faces.

Some 500 bombs were dropped, ninety of which were delayed action. As the explosions died down, telephonist WAAF Sergeant Joan Eugene 'Elizabeth' Mortimer, whose lines were by then dead, grabbed handfuls of red flags and began marking the bomb craters and unexploded bombs. She knew that the station's fighters, including among which was her boyfriend, might be returning at any moment from their combat. One bomb detonated close by, throwing her to the ground. Staggering to her feet Mortimer continued her efforts, ignoring orders.

For her courage and coolness, Sergeant Mortimer was awarded the Military Medal, which was announced in the *London Gazette* of 5 November 1940: 'During an intensive enemy raid on an aerodrome, Sergeant Mortimer displayed courage and example of a high order.'

Mortimer's gallantry award was one of three made to WAAFs at Biggin Hill that summer.

Meanwhile, as the raiders withdrew, they were met by fresh Hurricane and Spitfire fighters, Nos. 46, 54, 56, 151 and 266 Squadrons all making claims.

The RAF's airfields had taken a pounding, but the day's raids were not yet over and by about 1700 hours another raid, estimated at 250 aircraft from *Luftflotte* 2, had been plotted crossing the French coast. The formation included fifty-eight Do 17s and their escort, which were heading for Hornchurch. A second formation of fifty-two He 111s targeted North Weald. Both bomber formations were escorted by Bf 110s and Bf 109s.

At around 1730 hours, fifteen Hurricanes of Nos. 32 and 501 Squadrons were scrambled to intercept the Hornchurch raid, which they encountered fifteen minutes later at 12,000ft coming in from the Thames estuary north of Herne Bay. Squadron Leader Crossley led No 32 Squadron into the attack, but the Hurricanes were bounced by the escorting Bf 109s of II./JG 51.

Pilot Officer De Grunne (flying V6535) was shot down in flames over Gillingham and bailed out with burns and slight wounds, being admitted to Willesborough Hospital. He did not return to the squadron and, after a spying mission over Brussels, was shot down and killed on 25 May 1942, over the Channel while on a bomber escort mission. Sergeant Pearce (flying R4106), was forced to bail out near Canterbury, his Hurricane crashing at Rose Garden Cottage, Chartham Hatch. Pearce was posted to No. 249 Squadron on 18 September 1940, on recovering from his wounds.

But the combat was not all one-sided. The squadron claimed six Bf 109s destroyed and a Bf 110 probably destroyed.

'A' Flight's Crossley (flying N2461 'F') claimed one Bf 109 destroyed, firing a five second burst:

'While climbing to intercept about fifty bombers away to our left, we ran into a dozen 109s. One flew across in front of me so I joined in behind and opened fire at 100 yds. He swerved, turned on his back and went straight down in flames. I watched him crash. The pilot did not get out.'
(signed) M. Crossley.

Crossley later claimed one Bf 110 destroyed and another as probably destroyed. On his way back to base he tackled eight Bf 110s in line astern, but got shot up. Undoing his straps he rolled over and bailed out uninjured, landing in an allotment at Gillingham at 1730 hours. He was picked up by members of the Home Guard who took him to the Queen's Arms, 'where they got me plastered'. His Hurricane crashed near Wigmore.

The Bf 109 of II./JG 51 flown by Oberleutnant Walter Blume was shot down by a combination of attacks by Crossley, Eckford and Pniak, the badly wounded pilot being made a PoW.

Crossley shot at a Do 17, seeing it rear up. Meanwhile, Pilot Officer Eckford (flying P3936) claimed a Do 215: 'The bombers were stepped up in close formation. I remember thinking, as I was approaching the formation, that if I opened fire at the first one and then gradually lifted my nose and kept the button pressed, several would have to pass through my fire.'

Due to their closing speeds, Eckford only hit the lead aircraft before he had to push hard on the stick to avoid a collision. Looking back he saw the Do 215, piloted by Oberleutnant Werner Stoldt, spin down near Canterbury.

Blue 2, Pilot Officer Pniak (flying N2524), claimed two Bf 110s destroyed north of Canterbury, firing 2,000 rounds:

> 'I saw on the same height two Me 109s. I attacked the one which was nearer me, from a distance of 250 yards, I gave him first short burst [one to two seconds]. He was quite surprised. I drew nearer and gave him two, two second bursts.
>
> 'Just after I saw an Me 109 in black smoke and flames. He was diving in a SE direction. I saw two Hurricanes which were fighting with five Me 109s. I attacked one which was near from back of Hurricanes. He saw me because I attacked three-quarters from above. At once he turned in my direction and began to dive. I gave first burst from 300 yards [one to two seconds]. After next several bursts he was burning. I left him on the 7,000ft height.'
> (signed) P/O Pniak.

'B' Flight's Flight Lieutenant Brothers (flying N2921) claimed one Bf 109 destroyed near Canterbury, firing 640 rounds in two bursts of two seconds at 100 yards:

> 'At 1745 hours on 18 August 1940, I was leading Blue Section when I observed about 100 enemy a/c about five miles north of Herne Bay flying west. They were stepped up with fighters behind and were too far away to distinguish their type. The fighters, about twenty Me 109s, broke away and attacked us.
>
> 'I saw one behind me and on my right, so I turned sharply onto his tail and put two short bursts into him. He caught fire and dived steeply, so I followed him down and he crashed in a field near Chatham. I circled round low down and observed another a/c about half a mile east of the 109 wreck, also burning on the ground. This a/c I took to be a Hurricane.
>
> 'As I was circling, P/O Wlasnowalski appeared and joined me in formation. I looked around for more enemy a/c, but was recalled by wireless ten minutes later.'
> (signed) Peter M. Brothers F/Lt.

Brothers' victim was Leutnant Gerhard Muller-Duhe, whose aircraft was also claimed by Pilot Officer Boleslaw Wlasnowolski. The 22-year-old was killed as a result of the engagement.

Flight Lieutenant Brothers later recalled: 'We broke formation as they came in and opened fire, and I turned sharply right, onto the tail of an Me 109 as he overtook me, I gave a quick glance behind to ensure that there was not another on my tail, laid my sight on him and fired a short burst. I hit him with another short burst and he caught fire, and his dive steepened. I followed him down, he went into a field at a steep angle and a cloud of flame and black smoke erupted, and I flew over it, thinking, "Jolly good, that's one. Now, where are the rest?"'

Alongside the entry are the words 'the 109 shot down at 1745 hours near Chatham was that of Leutnant Gerhard Muller-Duhe of 7 *Staffel* of JG 26. His score was five. Curiously, he was my fifth,' Pete adding, 'he should have known better!'

Brothers also recorded that he took off and landed between craters, the sortie being one hour and thirty minutes duration.

'B' Flight's Pilot Officer Wlasnowolski (flying P3205) claimed one Bf 109 destroyed at 8,000ft, firing 600 rounds in three or four, two second bursts at 300-200 yards:

> 'I was flying next to Flight Lieutenant Brothers when I saw an Me 109 behind and at the same height. I turned and attacked him, he turned away diving towards the ground and went up in flames. I circled round and saw two aircraft on fire on the ground, the ME 109 had yellow wingtips. The place was near Chatham.'
> P/O Wlasnowolski.

Landing back at Biggin Hill, Pilot Officer Wlasnowolski taxied into a bomb crater.

During the attack No. 501 Squadron lost Flight Lieutenant George Stoney, killed in combat with Hauptmann Josef Fözo of II./JG 51, while leading his squadron towards the bombers. It had been a particularly bad day for the squadron, having lost four Hurricanes a little after noon. However, No. 501 Squadron quickly counter-attacked, destroying two Bf 109s. One of them was flown by Horst Tietzen, an ace with twenty victories, making him at that time the Luftwaffe's fourth highest claimant. The other fatality was Hans-Otto Lessing. The fighter's real targets, the Dorniers, escaped unscathed.

Some of the broken formation did hit Kenley, also bombing the nearby railway to the north and the east of the airfield, others hit Croydon, three miles to the north-east of their initial dropping point.

RAF fighter pilots claimed 126 enemy aircraft shot down during the day, although the actual figure was closer to seventy-one. The Germans countered these figures with their own, with 147 RAF fighters claimed destroyed for the actual loss of only thirty-six. The actual RAF losses were between twenty-seven and thirty-four fighters destroyed, with a further thirty-nine damaged. Ten pilots were killed and a further nineteen wounded, eight only lightly so.

Between 17 and 22 August, No. 266 Squadron operated out of Biggin Hill. On 18 August, Pilot Officer R.J.B. Roach shared in the destruction of an He 115 off Dunkirk. Pilot Officer Roach would add to his total in the following weeks, shooting down a Do 17 on 7 September, but was shot down by defensive fire from an He 111 four days later, bailing out from his Spitfire (P7313) at 1620 hours over Billericay unhurt.

Chapter 9

No. 32 Squadron Keeping the Upper Hand

Brothers was rested on 20 August. On what otherwise proved to be a quiet day for the squadron, the pilots were scrambled at 1515 hours and intercepted an enemy raid over the Thames estuary. Pilot Officer Smythe (flying V6567) damaged a Do 215, firing several bursts.

Although the news had already reached the squadron from No. 11 Group, regarding Acting Squadron Leader Michael Crossley being made a Companion of the Distinguished Service Order, the award was officially promulgated in that day's *London Gazette*. The same issue also announced the awards of the DFC to Flying Officers John Humpherson, Rupert Frederick Smythe and to Pilot Officer Peter Melville Gardner:

'Appointed a Companion of the Distinguished Service Order
'Acting Squadron Leader Michael Nicholson CROSSLEY, DFC (37554).

'This officer has led his section, flight and squadron, with skill and courage and has flown almost continuously since the commencement of hostilities. Since May, he has participated in engagements against the enemy over Holland, Belgium and France, including patrols over Dunkirk and St. Valery during the evacuation operation. In August he destroyed two Junkers 88s over Portsmouth and assisted in the destruction of another over Croydon. During the latter engagement he encountered another Junkers 88 and, having expended all his ammunition, acted as above guard until two of his section finally destroyed it. Squadron Leader Crossley has now destroyed a total of eighteen enemy aircraft and possibly five others. He has displayed rare qualities as a leader; his example of courage and tenacity of purpose have proved an inspiration to other members of his squadron.'

'Awarded the Distinguished Flying Cross
'Flying Officer John Bernard William HUMPHERSON (39317).

'This officer has led his section, and on occasions his flight, with great skill. During operations in France he destroyed two enemy aircraft and probably another three. Since returning to England he has destroyed a further four enemy aircraft. He has displayed courage and initiative and has proved an excellent leader.'

'Flying Officer Rupert Frederick SMYTHE (40436).

'In July 1940, this officer, whilst leading his section, broke up a formation of six Messerschmitt 109s near Folkestone, and succeeded in destroying one. Flying Officer Smythe has destroyed six enemy aircraft. He has displayed courage and set an excellent example to all.'

'Pilot Officer Peter Melville GARDNER (40527).

'During a short time in France this officer succeeded in destroying four enemy aircraft. Since returning to this country he has destroyed a further five enemy aircraft and possibly several others. He has displayed great keenness and courage.'

Meanwhile, Winston Churchill spoke in the House of Commons, extracts from the speech appearing in the following day's press:

'The great air battle which has been in progress over this Island for the last few weeks has recently attained a high intensity.
    'It must also be remembered that all the enemy machines and pilots which are shot down over our Island, or over the seas which surround it, are either destroyed or captured; whereas a considerable proportion of our machines, and also of our pilots, are saved, and soon again in many cases come into action.'

Concerning his earlier prediction that over British soil, Fighter Command would improve their 'kill' ratio to greater than 4:1, Churchill was able to report that: 'this has certainly come true'. Despite their successes the RAF would, if the rate of attrition continued to increase, soon run out of trained fighter pilots. Meanwhile, the stepping up of production meant that Fighter Command's aircraft pool had never been stronger.
    Churchill continued, coining the phrase which was to become synonymous with the Battle of Britain:

'The gratitude of every home in our Island, in our Empire, and indeed throughout the world, except in the abodes of the guilty, goes out to the British airmen who, undaunted by odds, unwearied in their constant challenge and mortal danger, are turning the tide of the World War by their prowess and by their devotion. Never in the field of human conflict was so much owed by so many to so few.'

Following an uneventful Dover patrol on 21 August, Brothers and the squadron had better luck the following day, one on which Pete made four operational sorties.
    During a patrol of the Dover area, Brothers and Wlasnowolski latched onto a Bf 109 which they destroyed over Folkestone. Both combat reports are missing, while Brothers' logbook entries throughout the battle are brief, with only occasional

additional detail, most of which was penned in the post-war era. As Brothers said, 'You didn't have time to sit down and write out what was happening.'

Landing to rearm and refuel, Brothers was back in the air when the squadron was scrambled to defend a convoy under attack from bombers. Nothing was seen, however, as the vessels were actually being shelled by German shore batteries.

At 1755 hours, in a reciprocal action, the squadron flew a mid-Channel patrol escorting an Anson on spotting duties for an artillery bombardment of German positions. Over thirty minutes into the patrol, the Hurricanes were vectored onto twenty bombers escorted by Bf 110s and 109s. Making their interception at 3,000ft between Manston and Deal, Flight Lieutenant Brothers (flying N2921), along with Sergeant Aslin (flying V6572) and Pilot Officer Pniak (flying P6546), damaged a Do 215, which was last seen diving away into cloud with smoke trailing from both engines.

Meanwhile, Sergeant Henson was admitted to the Royal Herbert Hospital, Woolwich, suffering from wounds received in combat.

During the afternoon No. 610 Squadron had flown on a patrol of Folkestone at 15,000ft, when they were attacked from out of the sun by twenty-plus Bf 109s. Four Spitfires were rendered unserviceable, including that of Sergeant D.F. Corfe (R6695 'O'), which was lost when he was shot down by cannon fire and crashed near Hawkinge. Corfe bailed out safely.

Brothers flew on a thirty minute scramble from Hawkinge on 23 August. Meanwhile, Pilot Officer Pfeiffer engaged the enemy but was unable to make a claim. His own Hurricane (P2795) was shot up and he was forced to make a crash-landing back at Hawkinge. Pfeiffer was admitted to Kent and Canterbury Hospital slightly injured.

Brothers made four operational sorties on 24 August totalling four hours flying time. During the day news of Brothers' Distinguished Flying Cross reached the squadron, the letters DFC being added after his name in all subsequent ORB entries. The Luftwaffe mounted a series of heavy attacks on Fighter Command's airfields, concentrating on No. 11 Group's seven Sector Stations at Tangmere, Debden, Kenley, Biggin Hill, Hornchurch, North Weald and Northolt – it was on these bases that the defence of the whole of the south-east and London depended. Meanwhile, He 111s targeted Hornchurch, No. 32 Squadron scrambling to break up the attacks.

Brothers made a squadron scramble at 1430 hours. Once in the air the pilots pushed their aircraft into a battle climb to put themselves in a better position to attack a raid approaching Dover. Here they were jumped by a *staffel* of Bf 109s. The action proved indecisive and no claims were made by either side, the Hurricanes landing after ninety minutes in the air.

Brothers flew on one of two section patrols made between 1545 and 1645 hours, with orders to patrol Hawkinge, engaging fifteen Bf 109s over Folkestone. Pilot Officer Gillman (flying V6565) and Sergeant Higgins (flying P3879) destroyed a Bf 109 which crashed into the sea. Pilot Officer Barton (flying V6565) damaged another fighter. Sergeant Aslin (flying N2524) attacked a Bf 109 which made off with smoke pouring from it. During the same dogfight Flying Officer Smythe (flying V6568) was shot down and crashed, being taken to the Royal Masonic Hospital, Hammersmith, wounded. Pilot Officer Pniak claimed one Bf 109 probably destroyed, but had to bail out over Folkestone and was admitted into hospital with slight knee and ankle injuries from a heavy landing. Pniak's Hurricane (V6572) crashed at Rhodes Minnis, near Lyminge.

Another casualty was Pilot Officer E.G.A. Seghers (flying V6567), who was shot down by a Bf 109 and bailed out, landing in the sea uninjured, his Hurricane crashing in flames on Elham and Lyminge road. Seghers was quickly picked up and was back in the air the following day. Meanwhile, Squadron Leader Crossley (flying P3481) was shot down in combat over Folkestone, making a wheels-up landing, skidding across a field on Valley Farm at 1630 hours.

'A' Flight's Sergeant Higgins (flying P3879) claimed one Bf 109 destroyed, firing 2,400 rounds in twelve short bursts closing to 100 yards:

'The squadron intercepted from twelve to twenty Me 109s [at 10,000ft] off Folkestone. Each pilot took on one of the enemy, a dogfight ensuing. I attacked an Me 109 at about 300 yards, remaining on his tail for several minutes. Continually the rounds struck the E/A. then finally a gentle dive resulted, the Me 109 hitting the water about ten miles out to sea off Folkestone.'
(signed) W.B. Higgins, Sgt.

Yellow Section's Pilot Officer Barton (flying V6565) claimed one Bf 109 damaged:

'After engaging [fifteen] Me 109s over Folkestone at 15,000ft for some five minutes, I chased one of them across the Channel. He was taking fairly skillful avoiding action, but I managed to give him four bursts of approximately two seconds each at 300 to 200 yds range during the fight.'
(Signed) Barton.

Flight Lieutenant P.M. Brothers (flying N2921), destroyed a Bf 109, firing 1,500 rounds in three second bursts at 150 yards. The engagement began four miles north-west of Dover:

'I was leading Blue Section at 1600 hrs on 24 August 1940, when we were attacked by twelve Me 109s which had been circling above us for some time. As we climbed up to them they climbed away and kept their distance until an opportune moment, when they dived on us. I fired short bursts at two or three and then lost them owing to 'blacking out'. I climbed up 20,000ft and engaged them again, and managing to get on the tail of one. I gave him two, three second bursts. Part of his starboard wing came away and he dived into the sea about ten miles SE of Dover. I followed him down, then returned to base.'
(signed) Brothers.

Brothers later added in pencil 'Lt. Achleitner of 111./JG 3. Bailed out. PoW.' against the original entry, which was for a 'Dover Patrol' of one hour and fifteen minutes duration. Pilot Officer Pniak (flying V6572), claimed one Bf 109 probably destroyed with four, two second bursts at 150 yards:

'I was flying No. 3 of Blue Section when we met twelve Me 109s at about 20,000ft [near Dover]. They were above us and attacked us. I was attacked by an Me 109 from head-on and above. I circled round on his tail and closing to 150 yards gave him two, two second bursts, he started to smoke from the engine, I followed him and gave him two more bursts, much black smoke came from the aircraft and he was diving.'

Moments later Pniak's Hurricane burst into flames:

'The flames were so big, that I turned my plane on one side and jumped [over Folkestone]. I landed very fast because my parachute was not open and full of big holes. I landed three miles NW of Hawkinge, my ankle and knee were injured and I was taken to hospital.'
Plt Off Pniak.

Brothers made two more sorties, landing back at Biggin Hill at 1730 hours. Meanwhile, enemy shore-based guns had shelled Hawkinge.

Scrambled to Ramsgate, No. 610 Squadron engaged the enemy. Sergeant Hamlyn claimed one Ju 88 and a Bf 109 as destroyed. Meanwhile, Sergeant N.S.J. Arnfield (flying R6686) bailed out following combat with JG 51 off Ramsgate at 0850 hours.

The squadron patrolled at 1035 hours and engaged six Bf 109s, destroying three, Hamlyn claiming one along with a Ju 88. He fired two bursts at 250 yards, 'Ju 88 astern and above attack aiming at port engine' and, 'Me 109 astern aiming at centre of fuselage'. Pilot Officer D.M. Gray was wounded (flying X4102 'K') and shot down by a Bf 109 over Dover.

A further interception was made between 1545 and 1645 hours, when the squadron sighted twenty Ju 88s in tight formation, with twenty Bf 109s providing an escort, 15–20 miles north of the Isle of Sheppey. The squadron claiming four Bf 109s destroyed, two by Sergeant Hamlyn, one each by Flight Lieutenant Norris and Sergeant Baker, while one Bf 109 was probably destroyed by Pilot Officer Pegge. Pilot Officer C. Merrick (flying L1037 'D') was shot down, slightly wounded, following combat with a Bf 109, crash-landing at Fyfield. Meanwhile, Pilot Officer D.H. Hone (flying V 7318) was hit in the glycol tank by return fire from a Do 17, making a forced-landing near Meopham.

During the day, Sergeant Ronald Fairfax 'Ronnie' Hamlyn had three times waited outside Station Commander Grice's office, getting as far as standing before the Group Captain awaiting his pronouncement on an earlier landing incident. The young sergeant returned from his third and final scramble only to be told that instead

A very young Pete Brothers with his mother, Maud, at the family home. (*Pete Brothers Collection via the family*)

Pete sitting in the driving seat of the family's Coventry-built Crouch car, pictured outside the family home. (*Pete Brothers Collection via the family*)

Pete's father, Jack Brothers. (*Pete Brothers Collection via the family*)

Studio photograph of Pete Brothers, then aged seventeen. Note the lapel badge with its winged motif, possibly an early Lancashire Aero Club badge. (*Pete Brothers Collection via the family*)

Brothers as a civilian pilot (1935). (*Pete Brothers Collection via the family*)

Pre-war training with No. 32 Squadron, 17 May 1937. (*Pete Brothers Collection via the family*)

Pete Brothers on a mock-scramble, 17 May 1937. (*Pete Brothers Collection via the family*)

Brothers pictured in full ceremonial dress, 1939. (*Pete Brothers Collection via the family*)

Pete and Annette's wedding day photo taken on 22 March 1939. (*Pete Brothers Collection via the family*)

No. 32 Squadron's 'A' Flight's Gloster Gauntlets in squadron formation. (*Pete Brothers Collection via the family*)

Pete's 'B' Flight, No. 32 Squadron, May 1939. (*Pete Brothers Collection via the family*)

Line-up of Officers, Biggin Hill Staff, 1940. Centre front row, Group Captain Grice with 'Humph' Russell to the right. (*NJT Collection via PMB*)

No. 32 Squadron's 'B' Flight, early 1940. (*Pete Brothers Collection via the family*)

No. 32 Squadron Hawker Hurricane, Biggin Hill, 1940. (*NJT Collection via PMB*)

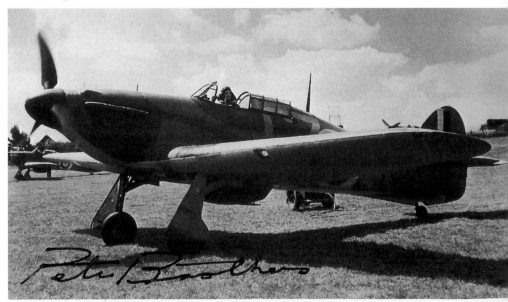

Flight Lieutenant Michael Crossley receiving the DFC from the hand of His Majesty King George VI. (*NJT Collection via PMB*)

Flight Lieutenant P.M. Brothers pictured between scrambles, 1940. (*NJT Collection via PMB*)

No. 32 Squadron at their advanced landing ground at Hawkinge, August 1940. (*Pete Brothers Collection via the family*)

No. 32 Squadron, August 1940. Standing:
(l–r) Pfeiffer, Humpherson, Gardner, Crossley,
Grice, Pain. Seated: (l–r) Eckford, Pniak and
Wlasnowalski. (*Pete Brothers Collection via the
family*)

Pete Brothers during the Battle of
Britain, August 1940. (*NJT collection
via PMB*)

Brothers flying a Spitfire Mark Vb with No. 457 Squadron. (*Pete Brothers Collection via
the family*)

Pilot line-up of No. 457 Squadron, March–
April 1941: (l-r) F/Lt North, Sgt Clark,
Sgt Burgess, P/O MacLean, Sgt Munro,
P/O Newton, Sgt Blake, Sqdn/Ldr
Brothers (CO), P/O Edwards, F/Lt Sly,
Sgt Parbery, P/O Russell, P/O James. (*Pete
Brothers Collection via the family*)

No. 457 Squadron in loose formation over
RAF Redhill, spring 1941. (*NJT Collection*)

No. 602 Squadron's pilots, many of whom served under Brothers. (Top) Sgt Gourlay,
Sgt Atkins, Sgt Sorge, Sgt Spence, Sgt Turner. (Middle) F/O Hargreaves, P/O
J. Yates, Sgt W.W.J. Loud, Sgt Jones, Sgt Codon, Sgt Hanscon. (Bottom) F/O Sampson,
F/L Bocock, S/L M.L. ff. Beytagh, F/L Niven, F/O J. Topham (*Pete Brothers
Collection via the family*)

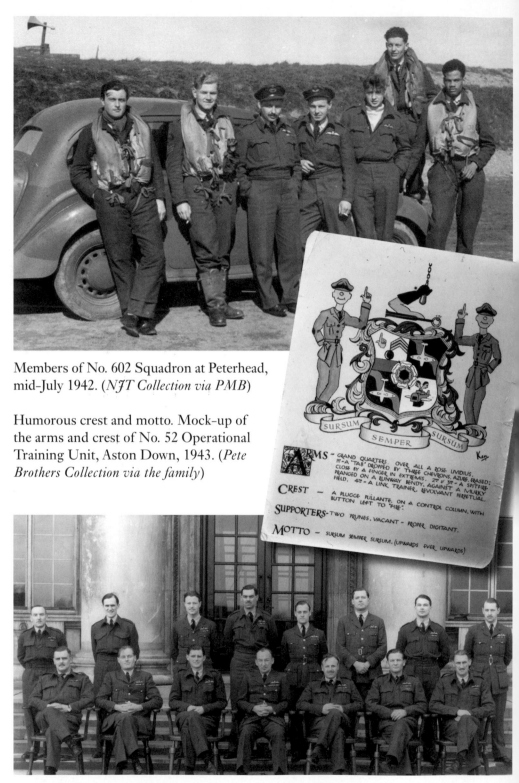

Members of No. 602 Squadron at Peterhead, mid-July 1942. (*NJT Collection via PMB*)

Humorous crest and motto. Mock-up of the arms and crest of No. 52 Operational Training Unit, Aston Down, 1943. (*Pete Brothers Collection via the family*)

Brothers (back row, fifth from left) attending No. 10 Senior Officer's Course at RAF Cranwell, February 1945. (*Pete Brothers Collection via the family*)

A post–war studio photograph of Brothers. (*Pete Brothers Collection via the family*)

Pete's Auster in Kenya, 1947. (*Pete Brothers Collection via the family*).

No. 57 Squadron line-up at RAF Waddington in preparation for their service in Malaya. (*Pete Brothers Collection via the family*)

No. 57 Squadron's Lincolns in formation. (*Pete Brothers Collection via the family*)

Pete Brothers pictured en-route to Singapore in one of No. 57 Squadron's Lincoln bombers. (*Pete Brothers Collection via the family*)

No. 57 Squadron's Lincolns in Singapore during the Malaya Emergency. (*Pete Brothers Collection via the family*)

Wing Commander Brothers and his crew alongside his Valiant bomber, RAF Marham, 1958. (*Pete Brothers Collection via the family*)

Pete's Valiant bomber, RAF Marham. (*Pete Brothers Collection via the family*)

Military Air Traffic Operations (MATO), RAF Uxbridge posting 1966. Pete pictured centre. (*Pete Brothers Collection via the family*)

A-O-C Conference 1968 (PMB not in photograph). (*Pete Brothers Collection via the family*)

Pete Brothers in his last appointment, as Head of the RAF's Public Relations. (*Pete Brothers Collection via the family*)

Pete with Carolyne Grace's privately owned Spitfire ML407. (*Pete Brothers Collection via the family*)

Air Commodore Pete Brothers on his appointment as Master of the Guild of Air Pilots and Navigators, 1973. (*Pete Brothers Collection via the family*)

Pete celebrating his 80th birthday with some special friends, (l-r) Christopher Foxley-Norris, Dim Strong, Peter Reynolds (son-in-law of Dick Abrahams), Mark Wallington (PMB's son-in-law), Dusty Miller, Pete Brothers, Ken Rees, a Great Escaper and married to Annette Brothers' cousin, Mary. (*Pete Brothers Collection via the family*)

Spectating at the Bentley Priory fly-past, H.R.H. Prince Charles and Pete Brothers. (*Pete Brothers Collection via the family*)

of a fine he was being recommended for the DFM. The award was announced in the *London Gazette*, 13 September 1940:

(580244) Sergeant Ronald Fairfax HAMLYN.

'In August 1940, whilst on an offensive patrol, Sergeant Hamlyn attacked and destroyed one Junkers 88, and one Messerschmitt 109. A few hours later he engaged a Messerschmitt 109, chased it across the English Channel and finally shot it down over Calais, where it crashed in flames. Shortly afterwards he attacked and destroyed two further enemy aircraft, thus making a total of five in one day. Altogether this airman pilot has personally destroyed at least seven enemy aircraft. He has displayed great courage and good marksmanship.'

Group Captain Grice flew over in the station's Magister to assess the situation, but on his return was pursued by two Bf 109s. Diving down to treetop level, Grice twisted and turned, clipping greenery with his tailwheel, before the Messerschmitts finally gave up the chase.

That night, raids were made against the capital, when bombs accidentally fell on a residential area. This was to prove a turning point in the Battle of Britain, with Winston Churchill ordering retaliatory raids on Berlin. Earlier the German Dictator had publicly vowed: 'If they attack out cities, we will rub out their cities from the map.' Hitler's response to the Berlin raids would change the course of the battle and the war.

But for the moment, at least, the pattern of raids continued. On 25 August, Brothers led 'B' Flight off from Hawkinge and was vectored to the Dover area, but the radar plot turned back. With the danger averted Brothers was ordered to pancake.

Brothers didn't fly on the flight strength scramble made at 1900 hours. The squadron's Hurricanes intercepted twelve Do 215s before being engaged by their escort of thirty-six Bf 109s south of Dover and heading for home. Squadron Leader Crossley (flying N2755) shot down a Do 215 in flames and sent a Bf 109 spinning into the sea. Meanwhile Pilot Officers J. Rose (flying V6547) and K.R. Gillam (N2433) were both shot down over the Channel off Dover. Pilot Officer (42053) Keith Reginald Gillman, RAF, was killed-in-action. He was the son of Richard Gordon and Gladys Annie Gillman, of River, Kent. Gillman, who was 19-years-old, is remembered on the Runnymede Memorial, Panel 8.

Gillman had served with the squadron since the beginning of May. His photograph, looking skywards wearing a 'B'-Type flying helmet and goggles was used on RAF recruitment posters, becoming one of the iconic images of the Battle.

The Hurricanes were still climbing when they engaged the enemy as Pilot Officer Rose later recalled: 'Earlier we had seen [Bf] 109s, but they were way up and away, we just thought they looked like gnats. The trouble was, we didn't have quite enough height to attack something while we were still climbing, obviously not the best way to do it. I suppose it allowed enough time for this chap to come and knock me down.'

The Hurricane's pursuit of the bombers had taken them out over the Channel and when Rose emerged from the cloud base on his parachute, he was surprised to find he was over water, 'I came down in the Channel; they'd come around that morning while we were waiting at Readiness, with little packs of flourescin.'

While some of the other pilots (presumably including Gillman) chose to wait to have the packs sewn onto their Mae Wests, Rose decided to do his there and then, while he awaited the next scramble, 'So there was this long trail of flourescin in the water. Fortunately, one of our chaps spotted this slick in the late afternoon and got a boat out from Dover.'

Before being shot down, Pilot Officer J. Rose had attacked a Do 215 at 14,000ft south-east of Dover, firing a three to six second burst at 300-200 yards. His combat report read:

'No. 2 of Red Section attacked Do 215 at same time as Red 1 attacked another. First burst down fuselage from astern and second burst at port engine. Engine had begun smoking when self attacked by Me 109. Rudder control shot away, escaped by parachute and picked up by speed boat.

'Dornier attacked by Red 1, also seen to be smoking badly before I broke away.' (signed) PO J. Rose.

'B' Flight's Pilot Officer Barton (flying V6546) claimed one He 126 destroyed mid-Channel:

'We sighted the He 126 near Dungeness. He sighted us at about the same time and went down on the water and made for France. Green 1 went in while I watched for the reported escort of 109s.

'Green 1 broke away – I went in and gave a three second burst [at] between 300 and 200 yards, during which I saw tracers going into the He 126. There was no answering fire. I broke away quickly, as I thought that Green 1 had broken away because he had sighted the escort.' (signed) Barton.

Flying as Yellow 1, Pilot Officer Proctor (flying N2921), claimed one Bf 109 destroyed, five miles south of Dover, firing 2,400 rounds:

'I attacked the escort fighters with the rest of the section and the formation split up into several dogfights. One Me 109 settled on the tail of one of our a/c so I gave my first burst [four seconds at 250 yards closing to 50 yards, expending the rest of his ammunition at 150 yards] at fifteen degrees deflection from astern. The E/A dived and climbed up to a stall turn, but I followed all the while except when recovering from a spin. After my first burst the E/A dived straight down towards the French Coast and crashed in flames four miles south-east of Cap Griz Nez.' (signed) PO Proctor.

This brought Proctor's total to seven destroyed and one shared destroyed, having claimed five enemy aircraft while flying in France with No. 501 Squadron. Proctor was awarded the DFC, *London Gazette*, 18 March 1941, when he was credited with eleven 'kills'.

Also scrambled were the Spitfires of No. 610 Squadron, which intercepted between six and a dozen Bf 109s of Major Adolf Galland's JG 26 near Dover. The Spitfires climbed into the attack, claiming one Bf 109 destroyed, the pilot being picked up out of the Channel. Flying Officer F. T. Gardiner was slightly wounded and forced to bail out of K9931 'P'.

No. 616 Squadron lost Sergeant Westmorland – killed. While Sergeant Wareing was taken as a PoW when he was shot down near Calais by Oberleutnant Kurt Ruppert, Kapitan of III./JG 26. Sergeant (741143) Thomas Emrys Westmorland, RAFVR, is remembered on the Runnymede Memorial, Panel 200.

Meanwhile, No. 79 Squadron returned for a further brief posting to Biggin Hill between 25 August and 8 September. Flight Lieutenant Haysom was awarded the DFC for his role during his stint flying out of Biggin Hill, *London Gazette*, 29 April 1941:

'Flight Lieutenant Geoffrey David Leybourne HAYSOM (39736), No. 79 Squadron.

'This officer has been engaged on operational flying since the war began. He has displayed great keenness in his efforts to seek and engage the enemy, and has destroyed at least five of their aircraft.'

Haysom was later awarded the DSO (*London Gazette*, 16 February 1943).

No. 610 Squadron was scrambled on 26 August; intercepting eight bomb-carrying Bf 109s over Dover. They shot down one and claimed another probably destroyed, later attacking a formation of Do 215s and 'bagging' one. However, Flying Officer F.K. Webster (flying R6595 'O') was killed while attempting a landing at Hawkinge following combat with Bf 109s over Folkestone. Flying Officer (82682) Frank Kinnersley Webster, RAFVR, was buried at Sandown – Shanklin (Sandown) Cemetery, Section E, Grave 40. Meanwhile, Sergeant P. Else (flying P9496 'L') was forced to bail out seriously wounded following combat over Dover.

With the pilots of No. 32 Squadron much in need of a rest they were temporarily moved to Acklington. The ORB records their secondment to No. 79 Squadron, thus allowing the majority of the ground staff and infrastructure to remain at their current location:

'The under-mentioned officers and airmen attached to No. 79 Squadron, Acklington for flying duties:

Squadron Leader Crossley *	Pilot Officer Seghers *
Flight Lieutenant Brothers	Flying Officer Gardner *
Flight Lieutenant Proctor *	Sergeant Pilot Aslin

Pilot Officer Crossman *   Sergeant Pilot Bayley
Pilot Officer Eckford   Sergeant Pilot Henson
Pilot Officer Flinders   Sergeant Pilot Higgins
Pilot Officer Rose *   [Sergeant Pearce]

'Flying Officer Sir R. Leighton, the Squadron Intelligence Officer, proceeded on attachment to No. 79 Squadron, Acklington.' *

(Those marked * ceased to be attached to No. 79 Squadron on 11 September 1940.)

Meanwhile, No. 79 Squadron's pilots were seconded the other way:

'The undermentioned officers and airmen pilots of No. 79 Squadron attached to No. 32 Squadron at Biggin Hill:

Squadron Leader Heyworth *   Pilot Officer Noble
Flight Lieutenant Clerke *   Pilot Officer Parker
Flight Lieutenant Haysom *   Pilot Officer Peters *
Pilot Officer Bryant-Fenn   Pilot Officer Stones
Pilot Officer Chapple *   Pilot Officer Tracey *
Pilot Officer Laycock *   Pilot Officer Zatonski *
Pilot Officer Mayhew *   Flight Sergeant Pilot Brown
Pilot Officer Millington   Sergeant Pilot Bolton
Pilot Officer Morris   Sergeant Pilot Whitby *
Pilot Officer Nelson-Edwards *

Also posted but not included in the above list were:

Flying Officer Clift *
Flying Officer Parker *
Sergeant Parr *

(Those marked * ceased to be attached to No. 32 Squadron at Biggin Hill and returned to No. 79 Squadron at Acklington on 8 September 1940.)

No. 79 Squadron was to operate out of Biggin Hill until 7 September.

Brothers wrote in his logbook against the one hour fifty minute flight entry from Biggin Hill to Acklington, 'Bye, Bye Biggin after four years.'

Brothers recalled, 'On 28 August we were pulled out of the line for a rest and to replace our losses and train them up. Our new base was in Northumberland.'

Meanwhile, Brothers was granted seven day's leave during which he headed north to be with Annette. No doubt during this quiet time he reflected on the squadron's losses; 'Of our pre-war pilots, some had been shot down and bailed out unhurt, or burnt, or wounded, or both, but none were killed.'

As these men had fallen by the wayside, been posted to bolster other units, or completed their combat tours, new pilots had filtered through. Most had come straight from OTUs, some, like Gent, Pickering and Whitehouse, straight from No. 5 FTS, and had had to be turned away. The inexperience of these pilots trained under wartime conditions made them more vulnerable, as Brothers observed; 'Our losses were the new boys who never had the time or opportunity, not only to learn or be taught the tricks of the trade, but also to know the performance advantages and limits of their aircraft and how to exploit them. Tragically, they paid the ultimate penalty for their inexperience.'

Meanwhile, still operating out of Biggin Hill, No. 610 Squadron intercepted about twenty Bf 109s approaching the coast between Dover – Deal. They claimed two Bf 109s destroyed, with one Bf 109 probably destroyed. Pilot Officer (81367) Kenneth Henry Cox, RAFVR, was killed as a result of a flying accident due to enemy action. Cox was the son of Henry and Beatrice Mary Cox, of King's Heath, Birmingham. He is remembered at the Birmingham Municipal Crematorium, Panel 1. Cox was 24-years-old.

On the following day No. 610 Squadron was scrambled at 1530 hours and engaged a formation of sixty Do 215s, Bf 110s and Bf 109s. With good positioning and well-timed passes they claimed a mixed 'bag' of one Bf 110 destroyed, two Bf 110s and two Do 215s 'probably' destroyed, with three Do 215s damaged. Sergeant (810081) Edward Manton, AAF, was lost. He was the son of Edward Frederick and Sarah Manton, of Bebington, Cheshire. Manton, who was 25-years-old, was buried at Hawkhurst Cemetery, Plot A, Row J, Grave 62.

During a further patrol over Hawkinge they claimed one Bf 109 destroyed and a second damaged.

On 31 August, No. 610 Squadron transferred from Biggin Hill and flew north to Acklington, their place being temporarily taken by No. 72 Squadron, who themselves transferred away on 1 September.

Back with his squadron, Brothers flew two patrols on 3 September, the second an unsuccessful interception of a Do 17. This was followed by a brief rest from operations.

On the following day Adolf Hitler made a speech at the *Sportsplast* signalling the beginning of the night bombing offensive against London and other principal cities. This terror campaign, waged against the ordinary citizens of Great Britain, would prove to be the Reich-Führer's undoing:

'If the British Air Force drops two, three or four thousand kilos of bombs, then we will now drop 150,000, 180,000, 230,000, 300,000 or 400,000 kilos, or more, in one night. If they declare that they will attack our cities on a large scale, we will erase theirs!

'The English are wondering when the attack is going to begin. The English ask "Why doesn't he come?" Be calm. Be calm. He's coming. He's coming.'

Saturday, 7 September 1940, saw the beginning of a new phase of the Battle of Britain with the Luftwaffe's daylight raids transferring their focus to London, while the bombers returned by night to attack the East End and the Docks, the all-clear not sounding until 0530 hours on 8 September, by which time some 300 tons of bombs had been dropped on the capital, resulting in around 2,000 deaths or serious injuries – this was the beginning of the London Blitz.

Goering announced, on air, that he had personally taken charge of the aerial campaign, turning the Luftwaffe's attention on the city.

During the following morning, Winston Churchill visited the East End of London to see for himself the damage caused by the first night of the Blitz. The raids would not end until 10 May 1941, with only a single night without air attacks. In all, 50,000 civilians were killed and many more injured. Reporting the heavy bombing of London during the night of the 7/8 September, the German radio announced: 'For weeks the British people have been deluded into believing that the German raids on London had been repulsed. In reality no such raids took place. They did not begin until yesterday.'

Meanwhile, on 9 September, Brothers made his last flight with No. 32 Squadron, writing the following note in his logbook: 'Last flight in the Fighting 32nd Squadron: break up starts today. Aerobatics. Goodbye chaps after 4 years. Bye P2921, old faithful.'

Pete Brothers added an extract from the Squadron's Diary into his logbook:

'It seems incredible to me
To say goodbye to Peter B.
He's been with us for years and years
He's shared our laughs and shared our tears
And now he's gone – New friends to meet
So long, old pal, we'll miss you, Pete'

A provisional list of No. 32 Squadron pilots who flew during the Battle of France and Battle of Britain, 1940 (prior to 9 September 1940):

Squadron Leader Robert Alexander Chignell	Squadron CO, April 1940
Squadron Leader Michael Nicholson Crossley, DSO, DFC	Squadron CO, OBE 1.1.46
Squadron Leader John Worrall, DFC	Squadron CO, CB 1.1.63, MiD 8.6.44
Flight Lieutenant Peter Malam Brothers, DFC	DSO 3.11.44, Bar DFC 15.6.43, CBE, 1964
Flight Lieutenant Rupert Francis Henry Clerke	DFC 23.7.43
Acting Flight Lieutenant Peter Melvill Gardner, DFC	PoW 11.7.41

Flight Lieutenant John Bernard William Humpherson	DFC 30.8.40, KIA 22.7.41
Flight Lieutenant Humphrey à Beckett Russell	MiD 2.6.43 and 14.1.44, PoW May 1944, DFC 15.5.44
Acting Flight Lieutenant John Ernest Proctor	DFC 18.3.41, DFC Bar
Flying Officer Ladislav Corny Cesek (Czechoslovakia)	
Flying Officer Victor George Daw, DFC	AFC 1.1.45
Flying Officer Douglas Hamilton 'Grubby' Grice, DFC	MBE 1.1.46
Flying Officer A.J. Haskell	
Flying Officer G. Henderson	
Flying Officer J.C. Hunter	
Flying Officer R.V. Jeff	
Flying Officer D.A.E. Jones	
Flying Officer J.C. Milner	PoW, 19.5.40
Flying Officer R. Wilberforce	
Pilot Officer Sydney Ernest Andrews	killed in flying accident 9.8.42
Pilot Officer Anthony Richard Henry Barton, DFC	Bar DFC 7.7.42, killed in flying accident 3.4.43
Pilot Officer P.F. Blackford	
Pilot Officer G.L. Cherrington	killed-in-action, 8.6.40
Pilot Officer B.L. Duckenfield	
Pilot Officer A.F. Eckford	DFC 24.8.40
Pilot Officer John Flinders	
Pilot Officer Keith Reginald Gillman	killed-in-action, 25.8.40
Pilot Officer Comte Rudolphe Ghislain Charles de Hemricourt de Grunne (Belgium)	killed-in-action, 25.5.41
Pilot Officer Bernard Henson	killed-in-action, 17.11.40
Pilot Officer Norman Bagshaw Heywood	killed-in-action, 22.11.40
Pilot Officer Horner	
Pilot Officer R.R. Hutley	
Pilot Officer K. Kirkcaldie	killed-in-action, 8.6.40
Pilot Officer Lang	
Pilot Officer John Francis Pain	
Pilot Officer Jan Piotr Pfeiffer (Polish)	killed-in-action, 20.12.43

Pilot Officer Karol Pniak (Polish)   VM 5th Class 1.2.41, KW 1.4.41, Two Bars KW 20.12.43, Third Bar KW 8.3.46, DFC 1.6.42

Pilot Officer John Hedley Rothwell

Pilot Officer Jack Rose   DFC 9.10.42, MBE, CMG

Pilot Officer Rupert Frederick Smythe

Pilot Officer Peter Douglas Thompson   DFC 30.1.42

Pilot Officer John Lewis Ward   killed-in-action, 20.3.42, No. 127 Squadron

Pilot Officer Sydney Anthony Hollingsworth Whitehouse

Pilot Officer Boleslaw Andrzej Wlasnowolski (Poland)   VM 5th Class 1.2.41

Sub-Lieutenant Geoffrey Gordon Robson Bulmer, FAA   killed-in-action, 20.7.40

Flight Sergeant Guy Turner

Flight Sergeant John Sidney White

Sergeant Dennis Kenneth Ashton   killed-in-action, 26.11.40

Sergeant Donald James Aslin

Sergeant Edward Alan Bayley   killed, 10.10.40

Sergeant Herbert Ernest Black

Sergeant D. Flynn

Sergeant Raymond John Mitchell Gent

Sergeant William Burley Higgins   killed-in-action, 14.9.40 with No. 253 Squadron

Sergeant Oliver Vincent Houghton   killed-in-action, 27.8.40

Sergeant Henry Nuttall Hoyle

Sergeant Jones

Sergeant G.L. Nowell

Sergeant G. North

Sergeant Leonard Hilary Borlase Pearce   killed-in-action, 9.4.41 with No. 46 Squadron

Sergeant Tony Garforth Pickering

Sergeant J. Proctor

Sergeant Guy Turner

Sergeant R. Ware

Sergeant John Sidney White

Nos. 79 and 610 Squadrons operated out of Biggin Hill alongside Pete's No. 32 Squadron. While some of their sorties are referred to in the main body of the text, their contribution to the battle is expanded upon here:

No. 79 Squadron – Biggin Hill – 25 August 1940 to 8 September 1940:

28 August	Flying Officer P.F. Mayhew – He 59 (shared)
	Pilot Officer T.C. Parker – He 59 (shared)
30 August	Flight Lieutenant G.D.L. Haysom – Bf 109 probable
	Flying Officer P.F. Mayhew – He 111
	Pilot Officer G.C.B. Peters – He 111
31 August	Flight Lieutenant G.D.L. Haysom – Bf 109
1 September	Flight Lieutenant G.D.L. Haysom – Do 17 damaged
	Pilot Officer P.F. Mayhew – Do 17
4 September	Pilot Officer T.C. Parker – two Bf 110s damaged
	Pilot Officer G.C.B. Peters – Bf 110
6 September	Squadron Leader J.H. Heyworth – Ju 88 damaged
	Pilot Officer H.K. Laycock – Bf 109 damaged
7 September	Pilot Officer J.H. Heyworth – Ju 88 probable (shared)
	Pilot Officer G.C.B. Peters – Do 17 probable

30 August	Pilot Officer J.E. Marshal (flying V6624) shot down while attacking an He 111.
31 August	Pilot Officer G.H. Nelson-Edwards (flying N2345) crashed following combat with a Bf 109.
	Pilot Officer W.H. Millington (flying P3050) was wounded, crash-landing on fire following combat with a Bf 109.
	Pilot Officer E.J. Morris (flying P3877) was wounded in combat with a Do 17.
	Sergeant H.A. Bolton (flying V7200) crashed with battle damage. Sergeant (754530) Henry Albert Bolton, RAFVR, son of Herbert Sainty Bolton and Margaret Bolton, of West Hartlepool. He was 21-years-old and was buried in Hartlepool (Stranton) Cemetery, Plot 10 Division A, C. of E. Grave 258.
4 September	Sergeant J. Wright (flying P3676) shot down during combat with a Bf 110 and died of wounds the following day. Sergeant (522272) John Wright, RAF, was the son of Robert Wright and Agnes Wright, of Kessington, Bearsden. He was 24-years-old and was buried in New Kilpatrick (Hillfoot) Cemetery, Section D, Grave 741.

No. 610 Squadron's combat victories, casualties and awards for August/September may be summarized:

11 August	Squadron Leader E.B.B. Smith – He 59
12 August	Flight Lieutenant J. Ellis – Bf 109, Bf 109 probable
	Pilot Officer K.H. Cox – Bf 109
	Pilot Officer C.O.J. Pegge – two Bf 109s
	Pilot Officer B.V Rees – Bf 109
	Sergeant H.H. Chandler – Bf 109 damaged
	Sergeant B.G.D Gardner – three Bf 109s
14 August	Pilot Officer S.C. Norris – two Ju 87s, Ju 87 damaged
	Pilot Officer B.V Rees – Ju 87 probable
	Sergeant H.H. Chandler – Bf 109
	Sergeant D.F. Corfe – Bf 109
	Sergeant P. Else – Bf 109 damaged
	Sergeant B.G.D. Gardner – Bf 109
	Sergeant R.F. Hamlyn – Bf 109 damaged
	Sergeant C.A. Parsons – Ju 87
	Sergeant N.H.D. Ramsay – Bf 110
15 August	Flying Officer W.H.C. Warner – Bf 109 probable
	Pilot Officer K.H. Cox – Bf 109
	Sergeant S.J. Arnfield – Bf 109 damaged
	Sergeant D.F. Corfe – Bf 109 damaged
16 August	Flight Lieutenant J. Ellis – Ju 88 damaged
	Pilot Officer D.M. Gray – Bf 109 damaged
	Sergeant S.J. Arnfield – Bf 109 probable
18 August	Flight Lieutenant J. Ellis – Bf 109, He 111
	Flying Officer F.T. Gardiner – Bf 110
	Pilot Officer K.H. Cox – Bf 109
	Pilot Officer C.O.J. Pegge – Bf 109, He 111, (R6694, damaged by return fire)
	Pilot Officer B.V Rees – Bf 109, Do 215
	Sergeant S.J. Arnfield – two Bf 109s
	Sergeant H.H. Chandler – Do 17, Do 17 damaged
	Sergeant P. Else – two Do 215s damaged
	Sergeant C.A. Parsons – Do 17
24 August	Flying Officer P.G. Lamb – Bf 109
	Pilot Officer J. Aldous – Bf 109 probable
	Pilot Officer A.C. Baker – two Bf 109s
	Pilot Officer S.C. Norris – Bf 109
	Pilot Officer C.O.J. Pegge – Bf 109 probable
	Sergeant R.F. Hamlyn – four Bf 109s, Ju 88
25 August	Sergeant R.A. Beardsley – Bf 109
26 August	Flight Lieutenant J. Ellis – Bf 109
	Flight Lieutenant D.S. Wilson – Bf 109

	Flying Officer P.G. Lamb – Do 215
	Sergeant R.F. Hamlyn – Bf 109, Bf 109 probable
	Sergeant N.H.D. Ramsay – Bf 109
27 August	Flight Lieutenant J. Ellis – He 111
28 August	Pilot Officer C.O.J. Pegge – Bf 109
	Sergeant C.S. Bamberger – Bf 109 probable
	Sergeant R.F. Hamlyn – Bf 109
29 August	Flying Officer P.G. Lamb – Bf 110
	Pilot Officer J. Aldous – Do 215 damaged
	Pilot Officer A.C. Baker – Bf 109, two Do 215s damaged
	Pilot Officer S.C. Norris – Bf 110 probable
	Pilot Officer C.O.J. Pegge – Do 17 damaged
	Sergeant R.A. Beardsley – Bf 109 damaged, Do 215
	Sergeant H.H. Chandler – Do 17 damaged
30 August	Flying Officer P.G. Lamb – He 111
	Pilot Officer J. Aldous – He 111 damaged
	Pilot Officer A.C. Baker – Do 215 damaged
	Pilot Officer C.O.J. Pegge – He 111
	Sergeant R.A. Beardsley – He 111
	Sergeant H.H. Chandler – Bf 109, Bf 109 probable
	Sergeant R.F. Hamlyn – Bf 109
24 September	Sergeant R.F. Hamlyn – Two Bf 109s
	Pilot Officer S.C. Norris – Bf 109 probable

11 August	Flight Sergeant J.H. Tanner (flying R6918 'D') killed-in-action. Flight Sergeant (565125) John Henry Tanner, RAF, son of John William and Eva Tanner, of Enfield, Middlesex, husband of Helen Maria Tanner. He was 25-years-old and was buried in Calais Southern Cemetery, Plot P, Grave 17.
	Sergeant W.J. Neville (flying R6630) killed-in-action. Sergeant (74183) William John Neville, RAFVR, was the son of William James Neville and Julia Kathleen Neville, of Shepperton, Middlesex. Neville was 26-years-old and is remembered on the Runnymede Memorial, Panel 17
12 August	Flight Lieutenant E.E.B. Smith (flying K9818 'H') bailed out burnt. Flying Officer F.T. Gardiner (flying P9495 'K') slightly wounded left leg.
16 August	Flying Officer W.H.C. Warner (flying R6802 'Z') killed-in-action. Flying Officer (90344) William Henry Cromwell Warner, AAF, is remembered on the Runnymede Memorial, Panel 5.
	Pilot Officer P.H. Hugo (flying P2963) forced-landed.
22 August	Sergeant D.F. Corfe (flying R6696 'P') shot down by a Bf 109.
24 August	Pilot Officer D.M. Gray (flying X4102 'K') shot down wounded.
	Pilot Officer C. Merrick (flying L1037 'D') crashed injured

	Sergeant S.J. Arnfield (flying K9975 'S') bailed out safe (shot down by a Bf 109).
25 August	Flying Officer F.T. Gardiner (flying K9931 'P') shot down.
26 August	Pilot Officer H.K. Webster (flying R6965 'O') killed on crash-landing. Pilot Officer (82682) Frank Kinnesley Webster, RAFVR, was buried at Sundown Cemetery, Section E, Grave 40.
	Sergeant P. Else (flying P9496 'L') bailed out seriously wounded. Sergeant (1073652) John Graham Leech, RAFVR, was the son of Nelson and Gertrude E. Leech, of Belfast. Leech is remembered on the Runnymede Memorial, Panel 88.
28 August	Pilot Officer K.H. Cox (flying P9511) killed-in-action. Pilot Officer (81367) Kenneth Henry Cox, RAFVR, was the son of Henry and Beatrice Mary Cox, of King's Heath, Birmingham. Cox was 24-years-old and is remembered on the Birmingham Municipal Crematorium, Column 1.
29 August	Sergeant C. Baker (flying X4011 'O') crashed at Gatwick.
	Sergeant E. Manton (flying P9433 'E') killed-in-action. Sergeant (810081) Edward Manton, AAF, was the son of Edward Frederick and Sarah Manton, of Bebington, Cheshire. Manton was 25-years-old and was buried at Hawkhurst Cemetery, Plot A, Grave J.62.

Flight Lieutenant Ellis was awarded the DFC, *London Gazette*, 13 August 1940:

'This officer was employed on offensive patrols over Dunkirk during the evacuation of the British Expeditionary Force and led his flight with great courage. On two occasions, whilst deputizing for his Commanding Officer, he led a patrol of four squadrons, displaying great initiative and leadership. During these patrols Flight Lieutenant Ellis destroyed two enemy aircraft. Later, whilst engaged on home defence, he shot down one enemy bomber. In July 1940, whilst leading the squadron, he destroyed two enemy aircraft and on the following day he shot down a further three of eight enemy aircraft destroyed by his squadron. Flight Lieutenant Ellis has displayed courage and leadership of a high order.'

Flight Lieutenant E.B.B. Smith, was awarded the DFC, *London Gazette*, 30 August 1940:
'Acting Flight Lieutenant Edward Brian Bretherton SMITH (90340), Auxiliary Air Force.

'This officer has led his flight with great success; twenty-five enemy aircraft have been destroyed since June 1940. One day in August he led the flight almost to the French coast to attack two enemy aircraft flying over the Channel. Despite strong opposition an enemy seaplane was damaged and, whilst on the return journey, another aircraft was attacked and damaged. Flight Lieutenant Smith was the only member of his section to return from these engagements. The next day, he was involved in an attack by twelve or more Messerschmitt 109s. His aircraft was hit by two shells, damage being inflicted near the cockpit, and petrol tanks. His aircraft eventually caught fire and, although he himself was enveloped in flames, he successfully abandoned his aircraft and was rescued about eight miles out to sea. Flight Lieutenant Smith has now destroyed six enemy aircraft. He has displayed great courage and leadership.'

Acting Flight Lieutenant S.C. Norris, was awarded the DFC, *London Gazette*, 24 September 1940:
'Acting Flight Lieutenant Stanley Charles NORRIS (40561).

'In August 1940, this officer was leading his flight on an offensive patrol when twenty Junkers 88s were sighted. Flight Lieutenant Norris ordered his flight to attack them but were themselves attacked in turn by twenty Messerschmitt 109s. It became necessary to abandon the attack on the enemy bombers, and to engage the enemy fighters. During the combat Flight Lieutenant Norris destroyed one Messerschmitt 109. This officer has personally destroyed six enemy aircraft and damaged a further two. He has displayed outstanding determination and skill as a leader.'

Sergeant H.H. Chandler, was awarded the DFM, *London Gazette*, 22 October 1940:
'Sergeant Horatio Herbert Chandler (810021), AAF.

'This airman has been continuously engaged in operations against the enemy since April 1940, and has destroyed six of their aircraft. He has displayed courage, skill and determination.'

Pilot Officer C.O.J. Pegge, was awarded the DFC, *London Gazette*, 22 October 1940:
'Pilot Officer Constantine Oliver Joseph PEGGE (41317).

'Since July 1940, this officer has destroyed seven enemy aircraft. His great skill and initiative in air combat were particularly shown on one occasion when, although wounded in the eye, his aircraft damaged and the windscreen rendered opaque by bullets, he brought his aircraft back to base and made a successful landing. He has proved a fearless fighter when attacking superior numbers of enemy aircraft.'

During the period from the end of the so-called Phoney War to the end of August 1940 a number of squadrons operated out of Biggin Hill, sharing the famous Fighter Command station with Pete's No. 32 Squadron. The following table provides a summary.

Fighter squadrons serving at Biggin Hill 10 May 1940–28 August 1940

No. 213 Squadron ('A' Flight)	18.5.40	23.5.40
No. 242 Squadron	25.5.40	8.6.40
No. 229 Squadron	27.5.40	5.6.40
No. 213 Squadron	9.6.40	18.6.40
No. 141 Squadron HQ	10.7.40	21.7.40
No. 266 Squadron	17.8.40	22.8.40
No. 79 Squadron	25.8.40	8.9.40

(NB: Dates vary according to different sources and the best approximations have been adopted.)

Chapter 10

No. 257 Squadron

Formed under Squadron Leader D.W. Bayne on 17 May 1940, No. 257 (Burma) Squadron became operational on 4 July, Squadron Leader Hill Harkness assuming command eighteen days later. Many COs limited their own operational flying, relying heavily on their flight commanders and other seasoned pilots of all ranks. Despite his senior years for a fighter pilot, Harkness elected to fly operationally whenever he could.

Through necessity, No. 257 Squadron had been thrown into the battle before they were ready. Heavily engaged, and with few pre-war pilots amongst their ranks, they inevitably lost a number of men killed, wounded or badly burnt. Squadron Leader Harkness frequently led his men in Park's preferred method of attack; head-on and at closing speeds of over 500 mph. This took supreme courage, as a moment's hesitation could spell disaster, but led to the desired break-up of the bomber formations. In late August Harkness narrowly survived a direct hit on the slit trench in which he was sheltering. Despite being shaken by these events, he was quickly back in the air leading his pilots into action.

For all of his courage, Harkness appeared to have lacked flexibility in combat and was perhaps slow to reject the RAF's pre-war No. 1–6 attacks. He had flown during a period of intense operations and was now tour expired and in need of a rest.

Operating out of Martlesham Heath on 7 September, Squadron Leader Harkness (Yellow 1) led the squadron against an enemy formation of fifty-plus enemy aircraft heading up the Thames estuary. Scrambled late, there was no possibility of getting up-sun. Squadron Leader Harkness led a head-on attack against the bombers, as a consequence the squadron was bounced by their escorting Bf 109s. Flight Lieutenant Beresford (Red 1) may have been shot down at this time as it is thought that Flight Lieutenant (37150) Hugh Richard Aden Beresford, RAF, was bounced and shot down over the Thames estuary. He crashed at Elmley, Spitend Point, Sheppey. His Hurricane was not recovered until 1979, when Beresford's body was exhumed and on 16 November 1979 was buried with full military honours at Brookwood Military Cemetery, Section C24, Row D, Grave 14.

As the combat developed, Sergeant Fraser (Red 2) attacked a formation of about thirty enemy bombers, escorted by many fighters, making quarter deflection attacks from above on two Do 215s on the left of the formation. He gave two bursts of about four seconds from 250 yards, emptying all his ammunition without registering any results.

Meanwhile, Flying Officer (70469) Lancelot Robert George Mitchell, RAF, (Green 1), 'B' Flight Commander (flying V7254), was lost in combat over the Thames estuary. He was the son of Robert George and Elizabeth Sinclair Mitchell, of Keith, Banffshire. He is remembered on the Runnymede Memorial, Panel 6. Mitchell was 24-years-old.

An explosive cannon shell hit Sergeant Hulbert's wing, damaging the mainplane and puncturing his petrol tank. Hulbert (Green 3) dive-turned and made a successful landing in an obstructed stubble field at Bashford Barn Lane, Breddown, near Sittingbourne.

During the same attack Pilot Officer Cochrane (Blue 1) claimed a Do 215 or 17:

'I climbed up into sun and delivered a diving 'very steep' attack – opened fire at about 400 yards, brushing close at about 50 yards. I broke off the attack and climbed up again ready for another. Just when I was about to open fire, white smoke appeared from the Do's fuselage and almost immediately three parachutes opened. The plane did a half circle and dived into the sea. The crew landed about two or three miles away. A boat picked them up after an hour, during which time I had circled around them and directed it to them.'

On the following day, 8 September, the squadron flew two patrols. The second of these was led by Squadron Leader Harkness, who also commanded two uneventful interception patrols made on 9 September, the same day that Brothers reported for duty. Brothers was posted to replace Beresford as 'A' Flight's new commander. By then the squadron had already lost a number of seasoned pilots killed or wounded and, of the remainder, only two were pre-war airmen, the others had little air experience and were fresh from OTUs. Compared to the morale at his old squadron, 257 must have seemed at a low ebb: 'I got a lift in a Blenheim down to Martlesham Heath, walked in, to see all these glum looking chaps; having lost both flight commanders on the same day obviously the young chaps thought, "well, if the flight commanders can get shot down, what chance have we got?"'

According to the Squadron ORB and the logbooks of both Tuck and Brothers, neither man flew with Squadron Leader Hill Harkness, who Brothers felt was: '[Too] old for the game. He was probably thirty or thirty-five and he was past it from our point of view – too cautious after the heavy losses – possibly had relied on the tactical abilities of his two flight commanders.'

This opinion was confirmed by Sergeant Tucker who later said that his former CO: 'Would merely follow all instructions without question.'

In fairness to Harkness, the ORB noted that a signal had been received from No. 11 Group informing his predecessor, Squadron Leader Bayne, that No. 257 Squadron was to be ready for operations on 1 July. The entry continued: 'We were also asked by signal to estimate a date we will have twelve pilots operationally fit; to which we replied on 15 August.' Therefore at Group level it was known that the squadron had been thrown into the battle too early. Under the circumstances, Harkness, his flight commanders and pilots, had fought well and hard, and were more than worthy recipients of the Battle of Britain Clasp.

In Tuck's biography *Fly for Your Life* by Larry Forrester, published after Harkness'death, it was inferred that Harkness avoided combat, sticking instead to a vector rather than asking the controller for permission to divert onto another raid. This was supposed to have occurred on several occasions while Tuck was acting as flight commander and he is said to have requested permission to deflect from the squadron's original vector. There is no corroborating evidence of this. The squadron ORB and Tuck's logbook confirm that they never flew together. While Harkness was no longer best suited to the role he was in, it was perhaps because fighter tactics had been revolutionized and he was too slow to discard the RAF's own manuals. To Harkness the controller's orders were sacrosanct and not open to interpretation. Tuck's reported opinion of him seems unsympathetic and ignores his earlier record. Harkness had repeatedly flown operationally knowing that his own flying reactions were slower than his potential assailants and therefore that he was more likely to be shot down – Tuck flew knowing that with more hours than most on modern fighters, and with youth on his side, he was the match of any adversary.

While Squadron Leader Harkness' abilities as a tactician and marksman might have been in doubt, his courage should not be questioned. He led from the front and despite only having a half kill to his credit, had continued to fly combat operations whenever possible. Even a cursory glance at the ORBs of other squadrons at this time reveals that many COs let their flight commanders bear the greater burden in the air and were content to fly only occasional sorties.

As if a reminder was needed of the fight that the squadron had already been through, on 10 September 1940, the squadron received a visit from Pilot Officer Henderson who had just been discharged from Brightlingsea Naval Hospital. Henderson had suffered from burns and minor wounds received in combat on 31 August.

Two operational patrols were flown on the following day, the second, made between 1545 and 1710 hours, was Harkness' last sortie with the squadron before taking up a posting to Boscombe Down on 13 September, Tuck having arrived earlier that day to assume command. Nos. 249 and 257 Squadrons were scrambled with orders to intercept a force of He 111s of KG 1 and II./KG 26, with their Bf 110 and Bf 109 escorts, which by then was heading up the Thames estuary. Fifteen minutes into the patrol the Hurricanes intercepted thirty He 111s of KG 1, flying in the London Docks area, most of their fighter escort having already been drawn into combat.

During the general air battle, Victor Beamish claimed an He 111 probably destroyed south-east of London, while Sergeant W.L. Davis of No. 249 Squadron (flying V 6682) bailed out over Benenden, Kent, wounded, his Hurricane hit by return fire from an He 111.

Meanwhile, No. 257 Squadron's Sergeant Fraser crash-landed back at base, probably as a result of combat damage.

It had been a costly raid in terms of casualties on the ground. One bomb fell on a public shelter in Lewisham High Street causing 100 casualties, while another hit Deptford Central Hall, burying fifty-plus in the rubble.

Of these raids on the capital, Churchill wrote:

'These cruel, wanton, indiscriminate bombings of London are, of course, a part of Hitler's invasion plan. He hopes, by killing large number of civilians, women and children, that he will terrorize and cow the people of this mighty Imperial city and make them a burden and anxiety for the government; little does he know the spirit of the British nation.'

Tuck's recollection of his first few days as CO are at odds with the ORB. He claimed that he put the whole squadron through an intense three-day programme of battle climbs and mock combats, flying from dawn to dusk. With no time to rest, it was said that the pilots had to grab their meals at dispersals out of 'hot boxes', their only breathers coming between flights, while the 'erks' were busy refuelling the Hurricanes and checking them over. The ORB makes no mention of the programme, while the squadron continued to be operational throughout the period in question.

In his biography of Tuck, Larry Forrester explained how in order to help some of the less experienced pilots Tuck would send them up in pairs with instructions to patrol. He'd take off a little after them, flying on a shadowing flight path before bouncing them, diving down out of the sun.

One of the ways in which the squadron's pilots showed their general inexperience in combat was noted by Tuck: 'I found that as soon as they got excited they would overuse the r/t and forget all the set procedures – just as 92 had done back in the first May battles. The other great mistake was that they opened up miles out of range'.

Tuck and Brothers got on well from the very beginning, both respecting each other's flying abilities and exceptional record as tacticians. Tuck was quoted in his biography as saying, 'Pete Brothers turned out a corker. He was highly intelligent and devoted to his job – an excellent flight commander.'

Referring back to the training up of the squadron, Tuck added, 'He picked up everything first time and helped me get it across to the others. Every now and again we'd take half the squadron apiece and have a ding-dong battle'.

Robert Roland Stanford Tuck was an extrovert. Tall and slim, he had jet-black hair, which he kept Brylcreemed back. Contrary to 'King's Regulations', Tuck wore a thin moustache, which complemented a 'dueling' type scar, the result of striking a flying wire while in the process of bailing out of a Gloster Gladiator following a mid-air collision during formation acrobatics with No. 65 Squadron. It was while still with No. 65 Squadron that he converted to Spitfires in late 1938. On 1 May 1940, he was transferred to No. 92 Squadron based at Croydon. As a flight commander he played a prominent role in the Dunkirk air operations and was made CO following the loss of Roger Bushell. Tuck received the DFC (*London Gazette*, 11 June 1940) by the hands of the King at a special ceremony held at Hornchurch on 28 June 1940. The citation read:

'During May 1940, this officer led his flight, in company with his squadron, on two offensive patrols over Northern France. As a result of one of these patrols in which the squadron engaged a formation of some sixty enemy aircraft, the Squadron Commander was later reported missing, and the flight commander wounded and in hospital. Flight Lieutenant Tuck assumed command, and on the following day led the squadron, consisting of only eight aircraft, on a further patrol engaging an enemy formation of fifty aircraft. During these engagements the squadron has shot down ten enemy aircraft and possibly another twenty-four. Throughout the combats this officer has displayed great dash and gallantry.'

In June 1940, Tuck flew a captured Bf 109 against a Spitfire Mk II at Farnborough. One of the most experienced pilots on the new monoplanes, Tuck had 1,000 hours on Spitfires by the time he was posted away from No. 92 Squadron.

Many years later Brothers wrote of his posting: 'Thus began my long friendship with him [Tuck] and Douglas Bader, with whom I briefly shared a mess bedroom'.

While not flying Brothers and Tuck passed on their combat experience, giving lectures on the different speeds, engine revs and throttle settings for each type of attack. Good marksmanship was another key to survival and they passed on tips on deflection gunnery. They used models of German aircraft to help demonstrate their blind spots and to discuss tactics.

Brothers remembered giving lectures to the pilots in his flight:

'Better to attack a lone fighter from ninety-five degrees starboard and not from directly from astern as most pilots look to port. Most enemy fly in pairs or pairs of pairs, you must always look for the wingman; always fly with a bit of rudder trim on so that the aircraft was crabbing slightly. If you were jumped and you saw tracer rounds flying past you, always turn into them rather than away.'

Tuck made his first operational sorties with No. 257 Squadron on 12 September, the squadron flying several patrols. During one of these, Pilot Officer Hon. D. Coke's Hurricane (3776 'P') was badly damaged in combat over Portsmouth. Coke crash-landed slightly wounded and was admitted to the Royal Naval Hospital, Haslar, returning to the squadron on 27 September.

During the next day the Luftwaffe launched a number of smaller raids. During one, a lone bomber targeted Buckingham Palace, which received a direct hit. There had been no time for The Royal Family to take to the shelters and one bomb detonated eighty yards from the King and Queen. Miraculously they were unhurt.

Although Brothers had known about the award for over a fortnight, his Distinguished Flying Cross was promulgated in the *London Gazette* of 13 September:

'During an offensive patrol in August 1940, this officer's flight encountered about one hundred enemy aircraft. He led the flight in attack against them, but before this could be pressed home, he was himself attacked by a number of Messerschmitt 110s. Turning to meet them, he found himself in a stalled position; he spun out of it and immediately sighted and engaged a Dornier 215 which he shot down. Later in the day he destroyed a Messerschmitt 109.

Altogether Flight Lieutenant Brothers has destroyed seven enemy aircraft. He has at all times displayed great courage and initiative.'

The squadron was at Readiness from before dawn on 14 September; Brothers made two uneventful patrols (flying V7254 and L1706).

Meanwhile, in Berlin, Adolf Hitler met with his High Command, further postponing the invasion. Goering had insisted that all he needed to destroy Fighter Command was five consecutive days of bombing. He had grossly underestimated the British resolve and that of Dowding's 'Fighter Boys'.

Brothers led Blue and Yellow Sections on a scramble at 1126 hours on 15 September. Once airborne the fighters rendezvoused with No. 504 Squadron over North Weald. A little before noon, while flying in the direction of the capital, Flight Lieutenant Brothers (Blue 1) spotted a formation of twenty-five Do 215s and Do 17s, escorted by Bf 109s and Bf 110s. Calling the controller for permission to attack, Brothers gave the 'Tally-Ho!' Pilot Officers Hedges and Sergeant Robinson followed Brothers in a quarter-attack from the starboard developing into astern. They concentrated their fire on the middle back line Do 17. The Dornier's port engine and the rear of the fuselage caught fire, forcing the crew to bail out. Crossfire from all of the rear-gunners, meanwhile, was focused on Brothers' Hurricane (V7254 'L') which suffered slight damage.

Brothers had singled out a Do 17 which he shared with Pilot Officer Hedges and Sergeant Robinson:

'The only way one could whip this squadron into shape was the sort of thing I would do when we got mixed up with some German bombers and I set the chaps port engine on fire, and he followed me in and finished it off.

'What did it matter, I mean you gave away bits of your own score, but it built up the morale of the chaps you were leading.'

Brothers then made a second attack, claiming a Do 215 (Ju 88) destroyed, firing all but forty rounds in several four second bursts. His combat report expands on both combats:

'At 1200 hours I was leading Blue Section 257 Squadron in line astern with 504 Squadron when I sighted a square formation (approximately five lines of five aircraft) of Do 17s and 215s. The rest of 257 Squadron were in line astern of my section. I attacked the enemy formation from the starboard side doing a quarter attack, developing into astern. I ordered my section to concentrate their fire on one Do 17. We succeeded in setting the rear of the fuselage and port engine on fire. During the attack the enemy concentrated their fire on me. Their fire was heavy but unsuccessful as only one bullet hit the aircraft, passing through the port ammunition tank and nearly severing the port aileron control cable. I broke away downwards and attacked a lone Do 215 [Ju 88]. Crew bailed out, and it crashed about two miles south of Sevenoaks. During the attack the strain proved too much for the weakened aileron cable, which snapped. As the aircraft

was just manageable on the starboard aileron I managed to reach Biggin Hill and landed, and have it repaired.'
(signed) P.M. Brothers F/Lt Blue Section.

Brothers recalled these types of attacks and this incident in particular:

'One thing I remember was the density of the rear-gunners' fire. They'd put up a sort of a barrage that you had to go through if you wanted to get in close – to about fifty or a hundred yards, which was vital. The aim was to get that rear-gunner out of the way. There was nothing you could do to avoid it – you'd collect a few holes and just hope for the best – I was hit once in those early operations. I got shot up and the controls were broke, shot away. I was halfway out of the cockpit before I realized the aircraft was still controllable, and climbed in again.'

The Do 17 (No. 3322) that Brothers shot down was piloted by Wilhelm Raab of 9./KG 76. The former enemies met on 31 July 1981, Brothers noting the meeting in his logbook against the original combat, later commenting:

'His unit lost most of its aircraft on that low-level raid. The Germans threw everything they had at us. We did three sorties that day, all around midday, one of them was fifty minutes long, one was an hour, and the other was an hour and a bit. I got a 109 and a Do 17 at high-level. The Germans lost seventy-five aircraft that day; they never came again in such numbers.'

It later transpired that Raab's aircraft had initially been attacked by Sergeant Tyler of No. 46 Squadron, then by No. 229 Squadron's Flight Lieutenant Rimmer: 'I led Blue Section in a head-on attack. Picking out a straggler I gave a three second burst at 200 to 100 yds, followed by two quarter attacks of three seconds at 200 yds closing to 50 yds. E/A went into cloud and I followed him down, and saw him engaged by four Spitfires and three Hurricanes before he crashed on West Malling Aerodrome.' Two of the Hurricanes were those flown by Flight Lieutenant Brothers and Meanwhile, Meanwhile, Pilot Officer Mortimer of No. 257 Squadron.

Having dived for cloud, the limping bomber was then hit by Flight Lieutenant Powell-Sheddon and Pilot Officer Tamblyn of No. 242 Squadron. Meanwhile, Squadron Leader Lane, of No. 19 Squadron, also got a burst in at close range. As he pulled away the crippled bomber was attacked by further fighters, including Flight Lieutenant Villa of No. 72 Squadron, Pilot Officer Turner of No. 242 Squadron and Sergeant Wright of No. 605 Squadron. Finally the crew bailed out before their stricken Dornier crashed near houses at Underriver, south of Sevenoaks, Kent, at about 1220 hours. Of the crew, remarkably only one was killed, while three, including Feldwebel Raab, were captured.

Pilot Officer Hedges (Blue 2) and Sergeant Robinson (Blue 3) of course also claimed the Do 17 as probably destroyed (shared):

'Flying as Blue 3 with Flight Lieutenant Brothers as leader, we attacked twenty to twenty-five bombers from beam, and got a four second burst in at 250 yards range. There was considerable return crossfire from the bombers and the one at which I fired caught fire at the rear.'
(signed) P.T. Robinson.

Meanwhile, Pilot Officer Mortimer (Yellow 1) claimed a Do 215 destroyed (shared with a 'friendly fighter'):

'At 1205 hours, 18,000ft, I found myself detached from my comrades and spotted [a lone] E/A heading south. I made an attack from behind and slightly above – three second burst – with no apparent effect. I was then joined by two Hurricanes and one Spitfire and we all made varied attacks on the enemy aircraft, which seemed to be losing height. At about 4,000ft two of the E/A's crew bailed out. Eventually the enemy aircraft crashed and burst into flames. Exact position not known – possibly near Swaley.'
(signed) Plt Off P.A. Mortimer.

Yellow Section's Pilot Officer North claimed one Do 215 damaged (shared with three Spitfires):

'I was left slightly behind in the initial attack; I saw a straggling Do 215 being engaged by Spitfires, and after they had broken away, I attacked from the rear, opening fire at 350 yards, closing in to 200 yards giving five second bursts. Pieces fell from the E/A.'
(signed) Plt Off Gerald North.

Blue Section also had one success, when Pilot Officer A.C. Cochrane (Blue 1) shared in the destruction of a Do 17, firing a ten second burst at 250 yards:

'I sighted a lone Do 17, 4,000ft below. I at once swooped down on it from its starboard beam. After six or seven bursts the E/A turned over and went down in a spin, one parachutist leaving the smoking Do 17. Just above the clouds the machine blew into bits.'
(signed) Plt Off A.C. Cochrane.

Pilot Officer Mortimer (Blue 2) claimed one He 111 destroyed, shared with Pilot Officer Cochrane:

'I spotted an enemy aircraft [He 111] heading SE and losing height. I made a number of attacks and was joined eventually by P/O Cochrane (257 Sqdn) and a Spitfire. The enemy aircraft eventually landed [wheels down] on a mud bank on the east coast of Foulness Island, and four of the crew got out and were taken prisoner by Army personnel.'
(signed) Plt Off P.A. Mortimer.

These claims must be for different aircraft as PO Cochrane's shared Do 17 blew up in mid-air, while PO Mortimer's He 111 crash-landed.

Meanwhile, Pilot Officer Capon's Hurricane (Yellow 2) was damaged and he made a forced-landing at Croydon.

Brothers had been forced to land at Biggin Hill to have his Hurricane repaired and was unable to fly on the squadron scramble which was made at about 1400 hours. Ordered to patrol between Hornchurch and Biggin Hill, thirty minutes into the patrol Nos. 257 and 249 Squadrons intercepted a formation of forty Do 17s, Do 217s and He 111s approaching the Biggin Hill area from the east. The enemy formation was slightly stepped up from 18,000ft, with escorting Bf 110s some 2,000ft above, circling the bomber formation, with several pairs of Bf 109s at various heights up to 30,000ft.

As the Hurricanes approached the bombers from below, Tuck called out to his pilots, 'Into line-abreast'.

The Bf 109 escort had already seen their approach and screamed down through a narrow gap in the bomber's formation, head-on into the Hurricanes, which maintained their course and headed for the bombers.

Tuck was lining up a Ju 88 when an unseen Bf 109 shot at him. Reacting instantly, he pulled away in a tight climb, closely followed by his No. 2, Capon. Straight in front of them was a formation of Bf 110 fighter-bombers, which were making a slow wide turn. Tuck fired at one, which shuddered, falling away in flames. During the melee one of the Bf 110s put a bullet into his windscreen.

The squadron's initial attack broke up the bomber formation. Pulling away, Tuck then made a half roll onto an He 111, when a Bf 109 flew through his gunsight long enough for him to get off a good burst as it turned and banked in front of him. The Bf 109 was badly hit and rolled away, going down trailing smoke.

Meanwhile, Sergeant Robinson (Red 2) was attacked by two Bf 109s in line. Tuck peeled away to assist, forcing the enemy out of the attack after his first burst. Tuck now engaged a Bf 110 with a four second burst from above and on the starboard quarter; the enemy aircraft spiraled down in flames. Tuck was then attacked by two Bf 109s, getting a four second burst at each. One went into a steep spiral dive with pieces coming from it, Tuck claiming this as probably destroyed.

After following Red Section into the main formation of bombers, Yellow Section made individual attacks.

Pilot Officer Hedges (Yellow 2) damaged an He 111:

'I attacked an He 111 on the starboard quarter and maintained attack until astern and fired on by two Me 109s. Length of burst six seconds. White smoke appeared from the He's port engine. No return fire. Enemy aircraft falling behind main formation.'
(signed) Plt Off A.L Hedges.

Also flying out of Martlesham Heath, No. 249 Squadron's Pilot Officer K.T. Lofts' Hurricane (V6566) was damaged in combat with He 111s at 1435 hours, crash-landing at West Malling.

The day's combats had been a resounding success and No. 257 Squadron had regained some of its fighting cohesion. That night there was a party, but the moral-boosting celebrations ended in mayhem when Tuck drove into the back of Pilot Officer Frizell's car, seriously injuring both 'Cocky' Cochrane and Frizell. At a crucial time, two fighter pilots were taken out of the battle, Frizell not returning to operational flying until March 1942. Pilot Officer Arthur Charles 'Cocky' Cochrane had claimed a Do 17 on 8 August, adding a probable Do 17 on 18 August, a Do 215 on 7 September, adding a Do 17 and a half share of an He 111 on 15 September. He had been one of the squadron's early success stories, but was now hospitalized by his own CO.

Despite this setback Brothers later commented that, '15 September was one of the most important days of my life. It was the date that 257 became a squadron, and after that they never looked back.'

The following day saw only routine defensive patrols and aborted scrambles. Meanwhile, Pilot Officers Pfeiffer and Pniak arrived on posting from No. 32 Squadron. Brothers knew both men well. 'They were supremely brave and were determined to get to grips with the enemy; they had a habit of chattering over the airwaves, which Tuck tried to curb.'

The Poles were often too keen and took what were considered unnecessary risks. 'They often disobeyed orders and went after the enemy when they tried to make for home over the North Sea. On one occasion several Poles nearly ran out of fuel and had to land at a Coastal Command advanced/emergency airstrip.'

The squadron flew to Debden on 17 September; from here Brothers (flying V6558) took off on a scramble but without making contact with the enemy. Meanwhile, a German High Command signal ordering the dispersal of the invasion fleet was intercepted – the battle had been won.

The squadron was rested on 18 September. Meanwhile, No. 46 Squadron engaged the enemy over Chatham at 1230 hours. Sergeant (754867) George William Jefferys, RAFVR, was killed (flying V7442) when his parachute failed to open. Jefferys was the son of Samuel William and Henrietta Emily Jefferys, of Winterbourne, and was buried at Winterbourne Earls (St Michael) Churchyard, north of Church. Shot down during the same engagement, Sergeant C.A. Hurry was wounded and burnt, bailing out of his Hurricane (P3816), while Pilot Officer P.W. LeFevre (flying V 6554) bailed out wounded.

Also engaged were the pilots of No. 249 Squadron, who lost Flying Officer Parnall, killed when his Hurricane (V6685) was shot down over Gravesend at 1325 hours. Denis Geach Parnell was buried at St Genesius churchyard, St Gennys, Cornwall. He was 25-years-old.

On 19 September, No. 257 Squadron made a convoy patrol at 1320 hours, during which Flight Lieutenant Brothers' Hurricane (V6558), which had only recently been delivered, suffered an engine failure: 'We were miles out to sea circling these ships at about 3,000ft and suddenly I got twitchy.' Sensing that there was something wrong, Brothers checked his controls but everything seemed to be responding; the aircraft was handling as it should have and the engine responded to extra throttle. By now he had set a heading towards the shore, 'I got a few miles off and I thought "you're just getting lily-livered Brothers"'. Turning back towards the convoy, he heard a bang: 'the propeller stopped dead and oil poured over the windscreen. "I thought, Oh Christ! Bit low to bail out, think I can make the beach."' But then Brothers remembered that the beaches would most likely be mined against possible invasion. He would have to stretch his glide to clear the beach. 'I took a deep breath and shoved the nose down and built up speed, and swept in a couple of feet over the beach and through a hedge and into a field.' Removing the cowling to see what had happened, Brothers discovered that a connecting rod was sticking out of the side of the engine. 'There must have been something that made me suspicious; the main bearing had gone and the con rod had broken. I suppose it could have been making high-pitched noises. Anyhow, *Him* above had been looking after me and I made it.'

Brothers (flying V6604 'T') made a section strength patrol over base during the following morning, later making a forty-five minute convoy patrol. Meanwhile, the squadron flew out to Debden where they remained at Readiness but were not scrambled. Spirits were high: 'The general feeling was that we'd seen them off.'

On 21 September the squadron began a period of operating out of their temporary forward base at Castle Camps. Brothers made three sorties, one of which was an interception patrol (flying V6604 'T'), chasing a Do 17 which he reported 'got away in cloud'.

At 0920 hours on 23 September, No. 257 Squadron was scrambled to join Nos. 17 and 73 Squadrons, the formation being vectored over Rochford and Gravesend. The controller ordered them to climb to 20,000ft. At that moment fifteen Bf 109s and 110s were spotted with ten He 113s (actually, Bf 109s) flying above and behind. Two Bf 109s dived past No. 257 Squadron's Hurricanes onto No. 73 Squadron, hitting them from astern and out of the sun.

Tuck gave the command to break. He engaged a Bf 109 which fled towards the coast, crashing into the Channel ten miles north of Cap Griz Nez. His own aircraft was 'slightly shot up' as a result of the combat.

Meanwhile, Sergeant Donald James Aslin's aircraft (P2960) was shot down in flames by Bf 109s while over the Thames estuary, crashing at Grove near Eastchurch. Aslin, who had only been posted from No. 32 Squadron on the previous day, suffered burns before he was able to bail out, landing at the edge of Detling aerodrome. He became one of Archie McIndoe's guinea pigs.

Between 24 and 28 September Brothers flew on a number of scrambles and patrols, No. 275 Squadron largely operating in the company of Nos. 17 and 73 Squadrons. During one of these sorties, made on 28 September, the formation was jumped by Bf 109s as Brothers (flying V6802) recalled: 'On 28 September we did two patrols – "Big Wing" with 73 and 17 Squadrons. We were flying in and out of cloud, when suddenly we were jumped by some 109s. I saw one going past, attacking 17 Squadron, who were below and in front of us, leading.' Diving through the formation, the Bf 109s shot down a Hurricane before anyone had the time to respond, 'Suddenly we realized that there were several of them about, and of course, the Wing broke and everybody got involved, but without any great success.'

On 4 October Tuck, whose promotion to squadron leader had just come through, was scrambled to intercept a lone Ju 88 heading for the airfield. Making his initial contact at 1010 hours, Tuck made five attacks with bursts of approximately three seconds fired at 250 closing to 100 yards, killing most of the crew and claimed the Ju 88 destroyed:

'I sighted one Ju 88 about 100 yards in front of me and about 200ft higher. I got in a good surprise attack from below and on the beam and, think I killed most of the crew. The enemy aircraft continued east, but in a steady dive. I expended the rest of my ammunition on it and not one shot was fired at me. I then formatted on his starboard side and could see no sign of life inside it. I broke away from him at 500ft and the enemy aircraft continued on down, hit the water and exploded.'
(signed) R.R. Stanford-Tuck.

On 8 October, No. 257 Squadron transferred to North Weald, which was commanded by Group Captain Victor Beamish, DSO. Also operating out of the station were Nos. 46 and 249 Squadrons. The latter was commanded by John Grandy, one of the instructors at No. 9 FTS in 1936. Brothers recalled that their 'local' was The Thatched House, Epping, ten minute's drive from the airfield.

Beamish still regularly flew operationally and was in the habit of flying solo above or around the formation acting as a spotter, something which could make new pilots jittery.

Group Captain Victor Beamish, had recently been awarded the DSO, *London Gazette*, 23 July 1940. His citation read:

'Wing Commander Beamish took over command of an RAF station after two squadrons there had been intensively engaged in successful fighting operations over France for thirteen days and personally led them on many patrols against the enemy. In June 1940, during an offensive mission over France, six Messerschmitt 109s were destroyed, two of them by Group Captain Beamish himself, and twelve driven off. One day recently he assisted in the destruction of a Messerschmitt 110 while leading the escort to a convoy and three days later he shot down a Dornier 17. His outstanding leadership and high courage have inspired all those under his command with great energy and dash.'

During October, Sir Hugh Dowding visited North Weald, spending time with Beamish and his senior commanders. No doubt Brothers was able to reacquaint himself with the man the command affectionately called 'Stuffy'. Dowding was not only the head of Fighter Command, but had been the driving force behind the detection and command and control systems that had played such a key part in the

Battle of Britain. He had foregone retirement to see the process through. He received scant recognition from the Air Ministry at the time and would soon be sidelined in favour of Leigh-Mallory.

Brothers (flying V6802) flew on a scramble at 1530 hours on 10 October, Nos. 257 and 249 Squadrons engaging a formation of Bf 109s of JG 2. During the combat No. 249 Squadron lost Sergeant E.A. Bayley (flying V7537), who was shot down and killed; his Hurricane crashed at Cooling, Kent. Sergeant (74100) Edward Alan Bayley, RAFVR, son of Edward George and Edith Bayley; husband of Josephine Adele Bayley, of Hailsham, Sussex, was buried at Bromley (St Luke) Cemetery, Section K, Grave 198. He was 29-years-old.

Brothers (flying V6802) led the squadron off from North Weald at 0845 hours on 12 October, with orders to patrol the Hornchurch line with No. 249 Squadron. Once airborne the formation was vectored to intercept Raid No. 31 over Deal. No. 257 Squadron's Weaver Section reported a dozen aircraft at about the same altitude but about three-quarters of a mile to the rear. Suddenly, a Bf 109 flew abreast of Brothers and attacked the rear of No. 249 Squadron.

No. 257 Squadron's Blue 2 succeeded in swooping down on the Bf 109, which he believed had brought down No. 249 Squadron's Sergeant Perrin (Red 2). Flight Lieutenant Brothers (Blue 1), while flying to attack the first Bf 109, noticed several more on 257 Squadron's tail; leaving Red 2 to attack the first Bf 109, he circled round and made an astern attack on another, which he damaged.

During debriefing it transpired that, flying into the sun, Pilot Officer Gundry (Yellow 1 in 'Weaver' Section) had mistaken the Bf 109s for the Hurricanes of No. 46 Squadron acting as rearguard. Most of No. 257 Squadron's pilots didn't see the Bf 109s until they had begun the attack and were unable to warn No. 249 Squadron via the controller.

Caught by surprise, Gundry was shot down over Deal, his Hurricane riddled with cannon and machine-gun fire. He was slightly wounded in the leg and thigh by shell splinters, but succeeded in making a forced landing at Rochester aerodrome. Meanwhile, Pilot Officer Redman (Yellow 2) was hit from behind and slightly below. He crash-landed in a field at Saffrey Farm, Owens Court, Selling, south-east of Faversham, slightly wounded.

Flying on a second patrol at 1550 hours, this time over Canterbury in the company of No. 46 Squadron, the formation was vectored onto the enemy south of London Docks. Here, fifteen to twenty bomb-carrying Bf 109s were sighted dropping their payloads. Calling out a warning, Beamish dived down, making a head-on attack on the lead Bf 109, opening fire at 300 yards. Streaming black smoke, the Bf 109 rolled over and dived away vertically.

Meanwhile, No. 257 Squadron had been vectored onto another raid and headed towards Dungeness where they engaged a formation of Bf 109s at about 1700 hours. Pilot Officer Capon (flying V7298), Tuck's regular wingman, was shot down and bailed out slightly wounded, landing near Cranbrook. His Hurricane crashed at High House Farm, Stone, east of Dartford.

Squadron Leader R.R.S. Tuck, although officially on leave, was flying with his old No. 92 Squadron friends at Biggin Hill, and at 1015 hours entered into a dogfight during which he destroyed a Bf 109 near Dover:

'Attacked leader of two Mes which were in line astern of each other. I gave five short bursts from astern, in beam and quarter attacks and he dived steeply, belching thick black smoke.'
(signed) Sqn Ldr R.R. Stanford-Tuck.

Two of No. 249 Squadron's pilots were wounded during the day. Adjutant G.C. Perrin (French) was flying V7313 on patrol over Sussex at 0950 hours when he was shot down by a Bf 109. He bailed out safely.

On 15 October Brothers (flying V6802) joined his squadron on patrol in the company of No. 249 Squadron. A formation of about fifteen Bf 109s was intercepted east of Dover at 1150 hours. Pilot Officer North (flying V7351) made a forced landing at Hawkinge, following combat over the Thames estuary, while Pilot Officer Mortimer (Green 1) claimed one Bf 109 damaged:

'I followed an Me 109 down and fired a burst which appeared to knock pieces from its tail. I was attacked almost head-on and I delayed firing because of the similarity of a 109 to a Spitfire. The Me 109 fired at me, but all shots passed over my head.'
(signed) Plt Off P.A. Mortimer.

Meanwhile, No. 46 Squadron lost two of its pilots during the early afternoon. Pilot Officer P.S. Gunning (flying N2480) was shot down and killed by a Bf 109 over the Thames estuary at 1305 hours. Pilot Officer (43474) Peter Stackhouse Gunning, RAF, was buried at North Weald Bassett (St Andrew) Churchyard, Row 2, Grave 9. He was 29-years-old.

Also while flying over the estuary, Flight Sergeant E.E. Williams was killed (flying V6550), shot down at 1430 hours by a Bf 109. Flight Sergeant (56290) Eric Edward Williams, RAF, was the son of William and Amelia Williams; husband of Joan Margaret Williams. He is remembered on the Runnymede Memorial, Panel 11. He was 28-years-old.

During the same engagement Sergeant A.T. Gooderham (flying V6789) was slightly wounded and was forced to bail out.

North Weald saw little activity on the following day, although No. 249 Squadron was engaged at 1130 hours, when Pilot Officer K.T. Lofts (flying V6878) force-landed near Tenterden, Kent, following combat with a Do 215.

On 22 October, Brothers (flying V6802) led the squadron on a scramble at 1545 hours. Joined by No. 46 Squadron, they engaged a formation of seven twin-engine enemy aircraft in the Folkestone area. Anti-aircraft bursts led the squadron towards the enemy, which headed back out to sea again. Both squadrons flew along the coast where Brothers sighted the bombers approaching land again, three miles ahead of them. Yellow 1, rearguard leader, calling out the warning, '109s above and behind', as about nine shadowing Bf 109s in line-astern closed in. Brothers ordered the squadron sharply to the left. At that moment No. 46 Squadron broke up and No. 257 Squadron was obliged to follow suit.

A dogfight ensued at about 1630 hours during which twelve Bf 109 'Yellow Noses', were seen approaching the coast from the south-east at 19,000ft, grouped in threes in very open formation, in line astern.

After the squadron was forced to break up, Brothers (Blue 1) sighted a Bf 109 above him, which he engaged and claimed probably destroyed near Dungeness:

'At 1630 hours on 22 October 1940, I was leading 257 Squadron and escorting 46 Squadron. I was informed by my rearguard a/c that 109s were behind and above. Simultaneously, 46 Squadron broke up and compelled us to do likewise as we were in the middle of what appeared to be a dogfight. I half-rolled, dived to gain speed and, as I pulled up, sighted a 109 above me. I fired a burst (approximately two secs) and as he dived I fired a longer burst and observed three or four pieces flying off his fuselage and wings. I followed him down from 19,000ft until he went into cloud at 2,000ft still diving steeply. I followed and found I was about five miles out to sea and could not see the 109 anywhere. I climbed up again but was unable to locate my squadron.'
OC B Flight P.M. Brothers F/Lt Squadron No. 257.

In his debriefing, Blue 3 reported that he had seen one Bf 109 and one Hurricane dive down, apparently out of control and another Hurricane going down with smoke pouring out.

Flying Officer Martin (Red 1) caught sight of the twelve Bf 109s coming in from the coast, which were then sweeping round into sun. Red 1 followed them and opened fire in quarter attacks from below at two sections of three enemy aircraft, which scattered and raced off out to sea. Nothing definite is known of the action of Red 2, Sergeant Fraser (flying V6851). He was killed when his aircraft crashed south of Ashford at Shadoxhurst, at 1643 hours. Sergeant (741810) Robert Henry Braund Fraser, RAFVR, was the son of Adam and Mary Frew Fraser, of Glasgow. Buried at Glasgow (Craigton) Cemetery, Section F. Grave 2213, he was 20-years-old.

Meanwhile, Pilot Officer The Hon. D. Coke (Yellow 1) claimed one Bf 109 destroyed, North of Rye:

'I saw about nine Me 109s above and behind, manoeuvering to up sun of us. I warned 257 Squadron Leader. I sighted seven Me 109s in wide vic, slightly below and flying straight towards me. I don't think they saw me. I carried out a three-quarter head-on attack on the right-hand Me of the vic; I could see my bullets hitting him from the engine right through to the tail.'
(signed) Plt Off Coke.

Pilot Officer Heywood (Yellow 3) was killed when his Hurricane (R4195) crashed south of Lydd Church, near Dungeness, at 1645 hours. It is suspected that he was shot down at low altitude by a Bofors gunner. Pilot Officer (41923) Norman Bagshaw Heywood, RAF, was buried at Stretford Cemetery, Manchester, Section N, Row L, Grave 210. He was 22-years-old.

During the engagement, No. 46 Squadron lost Sergeant (754728) Joseph Pearson Morrison, RAFVR (flying R4074), who was shot down and killed at 1650 hours while on patrol over Dungeness. Morrison was buried at Newcastle-upon-Tyne (St Andrew and Jesmond) Cemetery, Section O, Uncons., Grave 277. He was 25-years-old.

Brothers' report noted that having two aircraft of No. 46 Squadron weaving in front of the squadron had a 'disturbing effect on the leading section of 257. This weaving prevented the leading section of 257 from concentrating on searching for the enemy.' He also felt that when flying in such close formation the two squadrons should prearrange to break in opposite directions.

During the mid-afternoon of 23 October, the pilots of Nos. 257 and 46 Squadrons were patrolling near Canterbury when they were bounced by a formation of Bf 109s. The enemy quickly lost their initial advantage, but neither side was able to make a claim. Further combat came on 25 October when, a little after noon, the squadron was scrambled to patrol Northolt in the company of No. 615 Squadron. Squadron Leader Tuck sighted fifty-plus Bf 109s and ordered individual attacks. Wing Commander Beamish claimed a Bf 109 probably destroyed and another damaged, while Squadron Leader Tuck claimed one Bf 109 destroyed and two more damaged. Pilot Officer's North and Coke both claimed one Bf 109 probably destroyed.

Beamish shot at the Bf 109 in the centre of the starboard side of a wide vic, Tuck taking on the outside Bf 109. Firing from slightly above, his first burst was a deflection shot fired from the beam, the second from behind. The Bf 109 turned onto its back and went down leaving a thick trail of black smoke. Beamish fired upon a second 109 as it flew across his gunsight, getting in another burst as he chased the enemy aircraft towards the coast near Dover. Firing again, Beamish saw the Bf 109 was losing altitude fast and emitting black smoke.

Squadron Leader Tuck claimed one Bf 109 destroyed and two damaged:

'We came out of the sun and took them completely by surprise. I climbed over the top of them and got in a good burst of three seconds from the astern quarter on the extreme left-hand Me 109, closing from 200 to 50 yards. I saw my ammunition striking this E/A quite plainly. He immediately half rolled out of the formation and went straight down. I attacked another Me 109 which was turning on to a Hurricane. After one burst of three seconds at this E/A he half rolled and dived away. As he started his dive, I saw about four pieces come off various parts of his a/c, but as there were still many 109s about I did not have time to follow him. (One Me 109 damaged). I attacked another Me 109 from dead astern and he dived away leaving a thin trail of black smoke. However, I spotted an a/c [Bf 109] 3,000ft below me and dived on to it. I fired from this position and saw bits fly off him and he dived away. I then got in two good bursts from dead astern at close range and saw a large cloud of sparks suddenly burst from his starboard wing root-end, and then the whole starboard wing

came off and back and narrowly missed my a/c. The enemy aircraft went into a furious spin. The pilot did not bail out.'
(signed) Sqn Ldr R.R. Stanford-Tuck.

Pilot Officer The Hon. D. Coke (Yellow 1) claimed one Bf 109 probably destroyed:

'The squadron wheeled and dived onto them from one quarter astern. I got in a three second burst from quarter astern, closing to 50 yards, and saw petrol and glycol streaming out. I followed him down and put another two second burst into him from the opposite side. Position Tonbridge Wells – Cranbrook.'
(signed) P/O Coke.

Taking part in the same sortie, Pilot Officer G. North (Yellow 3) claimed one Bf 109 destroyed:

'I turned right and dived on the nearest E/A opening fire from quarter astern giving a burst of about two seconds at 300 yards range, closing in to 200 yards dead astern, I fired a further five second burst and saw both white and black smoke stream from the enemy aircraft and pieces came away, probably from the tailplane. The E/A then dropped one wing and dived.'
(signed) Plt Off G. North.

It had been a good day for the squadron and for Tuck in particular. Not only had he added to his tally, but the award of a Bar to his DFC was announced in the *London Gazette*:

'Since the 11 June 1940, this officer has destroyed six enemy aircraft, and probably destroyed or damaged six more. One day in August 1940, he attacked three Junkers 88s, destroyed two and damaged the third. Later in the month he intercepted two Junkers 88s at 15,000ft, and in a head-on attack destroyed one. In a similar attack on the second, a cannon shell blew away his oil and glycol tank and a piece of his propeller, but he reached the coast and landed by parachute. In September 1940, he shot down one Messerschmitt 110 and probably a Messerschmitt 109, and one week later destroyed a Messerschmitt 109 over the sea. Flight Lieutenant Tuck has displayed gallant and determined leadership.'

Brothers flew on Wing patrols on the 26 and 27 October. During the twenty-seventh No. 249 Squadron lost two pilots, the first casualty occurring at 0950 hours, when Flying Officer (74348) Percival Ross Frances Burton, RAFVR, was killed (flying V6683) as a result of ramming a Bf 110 of V./LG 1 over Hailsham, Sussex. Burton was buried at Tangmere (St Andrews) Churchyard, Plot E, Row 1, Grave 480.

The squadron's second casualty was Pilot Officer J.R.B. Meaker, DFC, (flying P3834) who was killed during a patrol at 1520 hours, when he bailed out and struck his own tailplane following an attack on a Ju 88 over Sussex. Pilot Officer (42514) James Reginald Bryan Meaker, DFC, RAF, was the son of Edgar Reginald and Lucy Adelaide Kathleen Meaker, of West Dean, and was buried at West Dean Cemetery, Grave 243, Meaker was 21-years-old. He was awarded the DFC, *London Gazette*, 8 October 1940. Meanwhile, Pilot Officer H.J.S. Beazley (flying V6559) was wounded in the foot during combat.

On 28 October, Nos. 257 and 249 Squadrons were scrambled at 0945 hours and vectored onto an enemy formation flying over Maidstone. Pilot Officer Surma (Red 2) latched onto an He 111, which he claimed as a 'probable' between Romney and Folkestone:

> 'I zoomed up and made an astern attack. When I was about 300 yards behind the E/A, an He 111, the rear gunners opened fire from below.
>
> 'When I was 150-200 yards behind the E/A's tail on the port side, I gave a three to four second burst at the cockpit. I passed over him and then fired at the starboard engine from about 80 yards.
>
> 'I followed the attack up with another burst at the starboard engine. I noticed a small explosion from the engine and saw grey smoke pouring out.'
> (signed) P/O Surma.

No. 249 Squadron's Pilot Officer A.G. Lewis was wounded and bailed out of Hurricane V6617 'R' badly burnt, while over Faversham, at 1420 hours.

Later in the day No. 257 Squadron made a second joint patrol, which was flown with No. 249 Squadron. While over the Gravesend area they sighted seventy to eighty enemy aircraft and launched an attack at about 1645-1700 hours.

Flying as Red 1, Squadron Leader Tuck claimed two Bf 109s probably destroyed over Tunbridge Wells:

> 'I dived out of the sun and attacked the rearmost a/c of the enemy formation [twenty-plus Bf 109s]. At the beginning of my four second burst from above and astern, the E/A's left wing went down and he slowly turned away from the formation. I left him doing a gentle spiral turn downwards, belching out thick black smoke.
>
> 'By now, about the last five of the enemy formation were milling around. I picked on the highest of this group of five E/A, and dived down and raked him with a three-second burst which I directed twice along the full length of his belly. I closed in to about 50 yards. I saw his tail struts break off. He pulled straight up, quite gently, then stalled and went into a gentle left-hand spin, leaving a trail of white smoke.'
> (signed) Sqn Ldr R.R. Stanford-Tuck, DFC.

Sergeant Henson (Green 1) claimed one Bf 109 damaged over Dungeness:

> 'I attacked one machine, but noticed his partner firing at me from my rear. Closing my throttle, I turned, and as he overshot me, I gave him a short burst at about 50 yards range. I saw tracer entering the fuselage.

'Green 2 (Sgt Nutter) saw glycol pouring from underneath the Me 109.

'As I was attacked by at least four more enemy aircraft, I was unable to follow the damaged machine.'

(signed) Sgt B. Henson.

At 1640 hours on 29 October, Nos. 257 and 249 Squadrons were scrambled to patrol North Weald at 15,000ft. Just as No. 257 Squadron was getting airborne, a dozen bomb-carrying Bf 109 hit and run raiders of II./LG 2 made a low-level attack. Their escort of JG 26's Bf 109s, under Major Adolph Galland, following closely behind. As Tuck lifted off at the head of Yellow Section, a bomb detonated at the end of the runway, the blast flipping Sergeant Girwood's Hurricane (V6852) over Tuck's, landing on his left-hand side, on fire and sliding along on its belly.

The scene was one that Pilot Officer Neil was never able to put out of his memory, 'A Hurricane, pointing west, sat outside our dispersal hut. On its belly and on fire.'

With the fire creeping towards the cockpit Neil could see from the squadron code that it was one of 257's, 'As the flames took hold a blackened and unrecognizable ball that was a human head sank lower and lower. Then the fuel tanks gaped with whoofs of flames, the ammunition began to explode.'

Those on the scene were powerless to help, forced back by the overwhelming heat: 'The fuselage and wings began to bend and crumble in glowing agony. Finally, there was only heat and crackling silence – and ashes.'

Meanwhile, Flight Lieutenant Blatchford (Red 1) was pursued by a Bf 109, which had just bombed the aerodrome. Then Hauptmann Gerhard Schopfel, Gruppenkommandeur of III./JG 26, met him in a head-on pass, Blatchford's Hurricane being badly shot-up, with a big hole in his fuselage, pierced oil tank and damaged tail. Sergeant Nutter (Green 4) managed to get onto Schopfel's tail and fired a burst, allowing Blatchford to escape the *coup de gras*. He made a forced-landing at North Weald.

A bomb had detonated just off to the left-hand side of Red 2, Pilot Officer Suma's Hurricane (P3893), as he was running up. Somehow he managed to take-off through the hail of shrapnel and bullets. While Nowell was still climbing, a cannon shell exploded in his cockpit, probably fired by Schopfel. With the controls 'dead' and the cockpit filling with acrid smoke, the aircraft went into a spiral dive. Surma opened the hood and bailed out at about 1,000ft.

The Squadron Intelligence Officer's report explained how the young Pole made a:

'Landing in a treetop near Matching. After convincing a Home Guard that he was a Pole and not a German (Sumar was wearing a Luftwaffe jacket, liberated from the wreckage of a German bomber while in Poland in September 1939), he was given two complimentary whiskies and driven back to the aerodrome.'

In all twenty-four bombs fell on North Weald, destroying a number of aircraft on the ground and leaving nineteen personnel dead with another forty-two wounded. Five of the casualties, including Sergeant Girwood, were from No. 257 Squadron.

Sergeant (741908) Alexander George Girwood, RAFVR, was the son of Alexander and Margaret Stevenson Girwood, of Paisley. Girwood was 20-years-old and was buried at Paisley (Hawkhead) Cemetery, Section A, Grave 2026.

Meanwhile, No. 249 Squadron had got off the ground without casualties. 'Butch' Barton got one Bf 109 and two damaged, while three 'probables' were claimed by Pilot Officer Millington (who was killed-in-action the following day) and Sergeants Maciejowsjki and Stroud.

It was later discovered that the Duxford Wing could have defended the airfields, but No. 11 Group's controller was unable to call upon them at the vital time because Bader was engaged in 'chit-chat'.

During the day, two of No. 249 Squadron's pilots were wounded. Sergeant N.B. Beard (flying P3615) bailed out at noon, following combat with a Bf 109 over Linton, Kent. Meanwhile, Sergeant H.J. Bouquillard was hit in the left arm, leg and head while flying V7409 in combat with Bf 109s. He made a forced-landing on Rochester airfield.

Also flying out of North Weald, No. 46 Squadron lost Pilot Officer W. B. Pattullo, who died of injuries received when his Hurricane (V6804) crashed onto a house in Romford while returning to base from a patrol. He died the following day aged twenty-one. Pilot Officer (43379) William Blair Pattullo, RAF, was the son of Patrick William and Jessie Hood Blair Pattullo, of Eaglescliffe, Co. Durham. Pattullo was 21-years-old and was buried at North Weald Bassett (St Andrew) Churchyard, Row 2, Grave 8.

Sergeant H.E. Black died on 9 November in Ashford Hospital as a result of burns and serious wounds received when his Hurricane (P3053) was shot down by Bf 109s, crashing at Hothfield Park, near Ashford, Kent. Sergeant (740749) Herbert Ernest Black, RAFVR, was the son of Herbert Ernest and Mary Elizabeth Black; husband of Gwendoline Annie Black, of Ibstock. Black was 26-years-old and was buried at Ibstock (St. Denys) Churchyard, Grave 1242.

During the raid on North Weald, Brothers had been unable to get to a spare Hurricane and had to endure the bombing, 'I was having tea in the officer's mess when the raiders struck. Suddenly the scramble sounded. We were raided by 109s dropping bombs. We all dived under a table when the attack came in!'

Brothers had left his car, an open 3-litre Red Label Bentley, on the airfield, right outside the mess, 'They dropped a bomb right outside. I was livid to discover that a near miss had filled it with soil, which took forever to clean out!'

No. 257 Squadron flew two uneventful missions on 30 October, patrolling the base at 1137 hours and again at 1600 hours, but nothing was seen. Brothers later commenting on the realization that, 'The winter was coming and clearly there was not going to be an invasion. The Battle of Britain had been won.'

During the day, No. 46 Squadron lost Pilot Officer (43283) John Dallas Crossman, RAF (flying V6748), who was shot down and killed while over Forest Row, Sussex, by Bf 109s during a patrol at 1330 hours. Crossman was the son of George Edward and Gladys Allyne Crossman, of New Lambton, New South

Wales, Australia. He was buried at Chalfont St Giles Churchyard, Grave 13. Crossman was 21-years-old.

Meanwhile, No. 249 Squadron lost Pilot Officer W.H. Millington (flying V7536), killed in combat with Bf 109s at 1300 hours while on patrol over the Channel. Pilot Officer (42720) William Henry Millington, DFC, RAF, was the son of William Henry and Elizabeth Hay Millington, of Edwardstown, South Africa. Millington is remembered on the Runnymede Memorial, Panel 9. He was 23-years-old.

On 1 November, No. 46 Squadron lost Sergeant Roger Emile de Cannaert d'Hamale (flying V7616), who was killed when he was shot down at 1300 hours during combat with Bf 109s, crashing at Acrise, Kent. The Belgian had arrived in England on 20 June and converted onto Hurricanes the following month. He was posted to No. 46 Squadron on 13 August. The 19-year-old had earlier been shot down and bailed out safely on 11 September. His body was repatriated following the end of the war.

Brothers (flying V6802) was at the head of a formation of eight Hurricanes in the company of No. 17 Squadron on a convoy patrol during 8 November. Scrambled too late, the Hurricanes reached the convoy only to discover two vessels already sinking. Later, Flight Lieutenant Blatchford led the squadron on patrol when they were engaged by a formation of Bf 109s. Sergeant (745566) Anthony Durrant Page, RAFVR, became separated and was killed when his Hurricane (V6870) crashed at Hythe Road, Stelling Minnis and burnt out. Page was the son of L. Graham and Gertrude Page, of Pinner, Middlesex. Page, who was 21-years-old, was buried in Hawkinge Cemetery, Plot O, Row 2, Grave 34.

The only other notable event for the station was Beamish's award of the DFC, which was announced in the *London Gazette*. His citation read:

> 'The work of this station commander has been outstanding. He has displayed exceptional keenness in his engagements against the enemy and has recently destroyed one, and possibly a further seven, enemy aircraft. His coolness and courage have proved an inspiration to all.'

Meanwhile, the previous day's convoy patrol was repeated on 9 November with Brothers (flying V6802) leading the squadron in the company of No. 17 Squadron, patrolling a southbound convoy in the mouth of the Thames. The vessels were seen safely out of the squadron's sector without inident.

Brothers had the great misfortune to be on leave on 11 November, otherwise he would undoubtedly have featured heavily in the day's air activities.

The squadron was patrolling two convoys between the Thames estuary and a point fifteen miles east of Harwich when they engaged twenty-five Ju 87s and their escort of Bf 109s at about 0945 hours.

Pilot Officer North (Red 4), joined a Spitfire in attacking four Bf 109s, claiming one Bf 109 destroyed, 'I then closed in astern and fired about four seconds at 250 yds closing to 150 yds.'

North then came under attack from astern by a Bf 109:

'I turned steeply to the left, evading the attack, and as I was turning I saw the
splash as the E/A I had been attacking hit the sea.'
(signed) P/O Gerald North.

Pilot Officer Jack Kay (Green 1) claimed one Ju 87 destroyed and another damaged,
also damaging a Bf 109 fifteen miles off North Foreland:

'Saw two formations of Ju 87s approaching just above the water. I did a head-on
attack on the formation and they broke up. I turned round and did an astern
attack on one who dived into the sea. I then did a head-on attack on another Ju
87 who pulled up vertically in front of me leaving me to fire straight into his
underside.'
(signed) Plt Off Jack Kay.

Flying as Green 2 (Weaver Section), Sergeant S.E. Lucas claimed one Bf 109
damaged:

'I climbed to 8,000ft above the 109s. I saw a 109 attack a Hurricane so I dived
on it, but he saw me and turned away. A dogfight followed and I managed to put
bullets into his fuselage from a deflection shot. He then turned over on his back
and went through the clouds.'
(signed) Sgt S.E. Lucas.

During the squadron's second contact of the day, seven of No. 257 Squadron's
Hurricanes were scrambled with orders to intercept 'bandits' which were engaged
north of the mouth of the Thames.
    At 1210 hours, Pilot Officer John Redman, 'A' Flight's Red 1, claimed one Bf 109
damaged fifteen miles north-east of the Thames estuary:

'I was diving towards him and he was climbing to meet me. I fired a burst
of about two seconds duration. Seeing several small pieces come away from
E/A.'
(signed) Plt Off John Redman.

Pilot Officer Gundry (Red 2) positioned himself for attack, breaking up a formation
of enemy aircraft, but his Hurricane was hit through the hydraulic reservoir and
diagonal strut, rendering his guns useless.
    Meanwhile, Pilot Officer North (Red 4) destroyed a Bf 109 which he shot at with
a quarter stern attack from slightly below, firing at 250 yards range with a two second
burst. Subsequent attacks were made from astern closing from 250 yards to 150
yards. The enemy aircraft was eventually seen to dive into the sea.

Pilot Officer Kay (Green 1) made a diving attack on a Bf 109 and saw a profuse glycol trail issuing from the enemy aircraft, which he claimed as damaged. He made a head-on attack on the first formation of Ju 87s which broke up completely. Making a second pass, the Ju 87 dived straight into the sea. Another Ju 87 pulled up vertically in front of him and he fired straight into his underside, claiming this enemy aircraft as damaged.

Sergeant S.E. Lucas (Green 2) sighted a Bf 109 attacking a Hurricane and dived on it, but the Bf 109 broke away. Lucas fired a deflection shot and saw bullets entering the whole length of the enemy aircraft's fuselage; it immediately turned over, apparently damaged and out of control.

During the early afternoon nine Hurricanes of No. 257 Squadron were scrambled with No. 17 Squadron and were vectored onto nine Italian Fiat BR 20 bombers with their escort of forty Fiat CR 42 fighters well behind in two formations; one above the bombers and the other formation far below.

At 1345 hours, Flight Lieutenant Blatchford (Red Leader) destroyed one Fiat BR 20, sharing another with No. 46 Squadron, and also damaging two Fiat CR 42s:

'I sighted a formation of nine bombers. I then climbed about 1,500ft and led Squadron on a beam attack.

'I selected the rear starboard bomber and opened fire with a beam attack, firing a four second burst (it was later confirmed that this enemy aircraft was destroyed by a Hurricane of 46 Squadron [shared]). I passed over to the port side and did a quarter attack on the rearmost port bomber. Owing to my speed I repeated this same attack on both occasions with a two second burst. The bomber then looped violently and went into a vertical dive towards the sea, and disintegrated before hitting the water.

'But sighted a large number of fighters (Fiat CR 42) and engaged one in a quarter attack with several short bursts, which obviously were registering. The E/A waffled extensively and lost height. I claim this E/A as damaged.

'Meanwhile, I was attacked by the fighters and engaged another one which developed into a dogfight. I found I could turn as quickly as he could and after expending all my ammunition I attempted to ram him and hit his main top wing with my propeller. He immediately lost height and I claim this E/A as damaged.

'On landing, nine inches of one of the blades of my propeller was found to be splashed with blood.

'I turned towards base and on my way back I saw a Hurricane being attacked. I made a feint attack from almost head-on, and on each occasion they turned eastwards.'

(signed) Flt Lt Blatchford.

Meanwhile, Pilot Officer North (Red 2) claimed one Fiat BR 20 shared with Blue 1 and one Fiat BR 20 shared with a Hurricane of No. 46 Squadron:

'I followed Red Leader (F/Lt Blatchford) and made a beam attack from the starboard on the right-hand aircraft, observing no result. It was afterwards ascertained that this aircraft fled away and was destroyed by a member of 46 Squadron. I then made a stern attack on the aircraft flying No. 5 and he also fell away after a three second burst at 200 yards range and dived towards the east. I followed him and finished my ammunition with two attacks from quarter astern. I saw bullets hitting the fuselage, there was no return fire from the rear gunner. The E/A then dropped four heavy bombs into the sea and lowered his undercarriage; a Hurricane of 257 Squadron [Pilot Officer Mortimer, Blue 1] came down and after two short attacks from quarter astern the enemy aircraft caught fire and dived straight into the sea. One of the crew attempted to bail out but pulled the ripcord too early and his parachute caught on the tailplane, ripped, and he fell down with his parachute torn and not properly opened.'
(signed) Plt Off Gerald North.

Pilot Officer B. Davey (Red 3) claimed one BR 20 damaged (shared with a pilot of No. 46 Squadron):

'We swung round into a quarter astern attack and I picked off a bomber on the outside right-hand plane of the Italian vic, and attacked him from dead astern, coming up underneath him.
    'I opened fire at 300 yds and closed to 100 yds using all my ammunition. I saw black smoke from both his engines and burst of flames from the fuselage.'
(signed) B. Davey.

Pilot Officer P.A. Mortimer (Blue 1) claimed two BR 20 damaged and one destroyed (shared with Red 2):

'No. 5 caught fire and dived into the sea. I saw No. 3 and No. 1 carrying on in formation so attacked No. 1, which immediately started emitting smoke. After this attack I was out of ammunition.'
(signed) Plt Off P.A. Mortimer.

Pilot Officer K. Pniak (Blue 2) claimed one BR 20 bomber destroyed and another shared:

'I attacked enemy bomber (No 7 in formation) from below and behind from the distance 200 yards. I gave him one burst four seconds long. Just after, enemy plane began to smoke and fire [from the cockpit area]. He turned over on his back and dived straight into the sea. One of the enemy crew bailed out. I attacked another enemy bomber and I gave him two, four to five second long

bursts. He began to smoke and glided to the coast. At the same time another of our fighters fired at him [Pilot Officer Kay]. We followed him until he force-landed in the [Bromwell] wood near Woodbridge.'
(signed) Plt Off K. Pniak.

Pilot Officer S.E. Andrews (Blue 3) claimed one BR 20 destroyed (shared with Green 1):

'I attacked an E/A [No. 9 in the formation] with a three to four second burst which then broke from the formation after having been previously attacked by P/O Kay. The E/A dived straight into the sea, leaving a thin trail of smoke.'
(signed) Plt Off S.E. Andrews.

Pilot Officer Jack Kay (Green 1, Weaver Section) claimed two BR 20s destroyed:

'I attacked the extreme right bomber who broke upwards smoking. This machine was given a burst by P/O Andrews at this point and dived into the sea. I attacked another then in conjunction with P/O Pniak. It broke down from the formation with us following. We continued to fire at it and eventually it came in to land by the side of a wood east of Woodbridge.'
(signed) Plt Off Jack Kay.

Sergeant S.E. Lucas (Green 2) claimed one Fiat CR 42 destroyed and a BR 20 bomber damaged:

'Gave one of the bombers [No. 3 in the formation] a three second burst [attacking from the port side head-on], setting one of the engines on fire and stopping it. I broke away downwards and saw the fighters below and behind. I gave one a four second burst head-on and saw it go down in a spin and hit the sea.'
(signed) Sgt S.E. Lucas.

Sergeant Barnes (Green 3) claimed one CR 42 destroyed:

'Attacked two BR 20s in turn firing two or three, one second bursts which struck the a/c amidships. I attacked a section of four [CR 42s] (beam to quarter) the a/c leading immediately dived straight down out of control in a dive over the vertical. The remaining three turning very quickly, got inside my turn and attacked, sending only one bullet through my wing.'
(signed) L.D. Barnes Sgt.

The squadron retrieved two 'crests' off a bomber that crashed at Woodbridge, along with a bayonet sheath and two steel helmets, all of which were displayed at dispersal as trophies.

Further combat successes came during a convoy escort on 17 November, when six Bf 109s were sighted near Harwich, above and behind which were a further twenty-five to thirty Bf 109s.

During the combat, which took place at 0920 hours, Flight Lieutenant Blatchford and Pilot Officer Kay both destroyed a Bf 109. Meanwhile, Pilot Officer Mortimer probably destroyed one Bf 109, but was wounded in the left hand by a cannon shell splinter. Sergeant Henson (flying N2342) was killed, shot down by Adolf Galland, commander of JG 26, while flying ten miles east of Harwich. Sergeant (742563) Bernard Henson, RAFVR, was buried at Mount Pleasant Cemetery, Wisbech Western Division 3, Grave 2.

Meanwhile, Flight Lieutenant Blatchford (Red 1) claimed one Bf 109 destroyed:

'I led squadron up towards the sun in an endeavour to cut off the 109s who were on my starboard side. While we were converging, the 109s realized we held an advantage and they were forced to turn left-handed towards us, forcing us to attack head-on.

'I opened fire on the leader at about 300 yards with a four second burst. Immediately, I opened fire, as he went over the top I gave a short full deflection shot and I then did a right-hand turn and saw the 109 in front of me streaming profuse black smoke. I engaged the 109 again from astern. He continued to dive and I followed behind and above; he appeared to flatten out, so I put the finishing touches on him. The E/A did a 'cartwheel' and the pilot was jettisoned into the sea.'
(signed) H.B. Blatchford F/Lt.

Pilot Officer Mortimer, Blue 1, claimed one Bf 109 probably destroyed over the sea 10 miles south east of the Harwich coast:

'I saw two Me 109s passing in front of me about 350 yards away. I fired a long burst at the second one and saw black [and] glycol smoke start streaming from E/A which immediately started to turn and lose speed. I was closing in for a final attack when I was attacked from behind [left hand wounded by bullet].'
(signed) P/O P.A. Mortimer.

Pilot Officer J. Kay (Blue 2) engaged a formation of six Bf 109s, claiming one destroyed:

'One Me 109 towards which I turned was about 1,000ft above. I pulled up my nose and fired at the underside of his machine just behind the nose. I must have hit his petrol tank, as he burst into flames underneath and dived straight down through the clouds into the sea.'
(signed) P/O J. Kay.

It had been a good day for the squadron, but not one that passed off without loss.

The routine patrols continued, while a few days later, on 24 November, the squadron's ORB noted: 'Flt Lt H.P. Blatchford awarded the DFC', the gallantry award was officially announced in the *London Gazette*, 6 December 1940:

'In November 1940, this officer was the leader of a squadron which destroyed eight and damaged a further five enemy aircraft in one day. In the course of the combat he rammed and damaged a hostile fighter when his ammunition was expended, and then made two determined head-on feint attacks on enemy fighters, which drove them off. He has shown magnificent leadership and outstanding courage.'

Tuck and Blatchford would later fly over to Bircham Newton on 26 January 1941 to attend an investiture ceremony held by His Majesty the King, Tuck receiving the DSO and a Bar to the DFC. Blatchford would later lead the squadron when Tuck was posted away to command the Duxford Wing.

Tuck's award of the DSO was announced in the *London Gazette* of 7 January 1941:

'This officer has commanded his squadron with great success, and his outstanding leadership, courage and skill have been reflected in its high morale and efficiency. Since 4 October, 1940, he has destroyed four hostile aircraft, bringing his total victories to at least eighteen.'

Tuck would be awarded a second Bar to the DFC, *London Gazette*, 7 April 1941.

Meanwhile, on 7 December, Blatchford was interviewed at the BBC's Broadcasting House, giving an account of the squadron's attack on 11 November.

Back on the squadron, Blue Section was scrambled at 1710 hours on 8 December, Flying Officer The Hon. Coke probably destroying a Do 17 which he attacked and hit right along the fuselage. The aircraft put its nose down slowly, turned on its back and dived away vertically.

Later that day, at about 1640 hours, while on a weather test over the Channel, Squadron Leader Tuck sighted a Do 17 which he destroyed ten miles north of Ostend,

'When I was flying directly astern of the aircraft, about 100 yards away, the top rear gunner opened fire at me. I immediately dived underneath him and to starboard. The front gunner then fired at me as I flashed past underneath. I opened fire with an astern attack from above from about 350 yards, closing to about 100 yards. I could see my shots going straight into the nose of the E/A. I believe I must have killed the pilot on this first attack as the E/A remained in a right-hand spiral dive the whole time [Two crewmen were seen to bail out].'

Tuck was to have one further victory while flying out of North Weald. While patrolling Rochford on 12 December, Squadron Leader Tuck sighted a strong formation of Bf 109s, one of which he shot down into the sea. His logbook noting: 'Ran into about forty Me 109s. Squirted at three then singled out one. Chased him right out to sea and shot him down in water off Clacton.'

All tolled the squadron had achieved great things over the last few months, but some of its key pilots were in need of a rest. On 16 December, orders were received for the squadron to transfer to Coltishall, Norfolk, in No. 12 Group, their role being taken over by No. 242 Squadron.

With his second consecutive tour of operations over, Brothers joined No. 55 Operational Training Unit at Aston Down on 18 December.

The idea behind the OTUs was to bridge the gap between the Flying Training Schools and fully operational squadrons. Brothers' logbook reveals that he largely flew the Miles Master and the Northern American Harvard trainer, passing on his experience to pilots converting onto Hurricanes. Brothers was anxious to give the men under his tutelage the best chance in combat. In his lectures he passed on his knowledge:

'Keep your eyes on the sun – there's probably a Hun up there; never follow the Hun who dives past you at forty-five degrees but just out of range, he's drawing you in – remember the enemy hunt in pairs. Learn when to use your radio and when to remain silent. If you come across a lone pilot and have cover, attack from ninety-five degrees starboard and not from astern, as its more natural for a pilot to turn to his left to look behind him; remember, under attack a pilot always breaks to the left; always leave an aircraft above you.'

A few months into his posting, Brothers was sent on detachment to the Central Flying School attending No. 79 Flying Instructors Course. Here he uncharacteristically held back, 'Better not to do too well, otherwise they'd make you an instructor for the duration.' On his return to the OTU, Brothers found that his flight was under the Battle of France ace, William Dennis David, DFC and Bar. (Later Group Captain W.D. David, CBE, DFC and Bar, AFC.) Brothers was now supernumerary, a situation which lasted about two months, before, on 20 June, he was sent to RAF Hawarden, for a two day conversion course on Spitfires.

Pilots who flew operationally with No. 257 Squadron during the Battle of Britain:

Group Captain Stanley Flamank Vincent, DFC, AFC	CB 5.6.45, LoM (US) 1945
Wing Comander Andrew Douglas Farquhar, DFC	Wing Commander, Martlesham Heath
Squadron Leader David Walter Bayne	Commanding Officer
Squadron Leader Hill Harkness	Commanding Officer

Squadron Leader Robert Roland Stanford Tuck, DFC and Bar	Commanding Officer, DSO 7.1.41, Second Bar to the DFC 11.4.41, DFC (US) 14.6.46, PoW July 1941, Wing Commander (Flying) Duxford
Flight Lieutenant Hugh Richard Aiden Beresford,	'A' Flight Commander, KIA 7.9.40
Flight Lieutenant Walter Stafford Bowyer	KIA 24.1.42 as Sqn Ldr
Flight Lieutenant Peter Malam Brothers, DFC	Later Air Commodore, CBE, DSO, DFC and Bar
Flying Officer Howard Peter Blatchford, DFC	Later Squadron Leader, Commanding Officer. KIA 3.5.43 as Wing Leader, Coltishall Wing
Flying Officer The Hon David Arthur Coke	KIA 9.12.41 with No. 80 Squadron, DFC 26.12.41
Flying Officer Brian William Jesse D'Arcy-Irvine	KIA 8.8.40
Flying Officer James Aan MacDonald Henderson	
Flying Officer John Claverly Martin	KIA 27.8.41 with No. 222 Squadron
Flying Officer Lancelot Robert George Mitchell	'B' Flight Commander, KIA 7.9.40
Flying Officer Lionel Harold Schwind	KIA 27.9.40 with No. 43 Squadron
Pilot Officer Sydney Ernest Andrews	Killed in flying accident 9.8.42
Pilot Officer Camille Robespierre Bonseigneur	KIA 3.9.40
Pilot Officer Cardale Frederick Alexander Capon	Died air accident 1.1.41, MiD 24.9.41
Pilot Officer John Allison George Chomley	KIA 12.8.40
Pilot Officer Arthur Charles Cochrane	DFC 30.3.43, KIA 31.3.43 with No. 87 Squadron
Pilot Officer Brian Davey	KIA 12.6.41
Pilot Officer Charles George Frizell	Order of the Cloud and Banner Mochi Medal (China) 14.6.46

Pilot Officer Kenneth Cradock Gundry   KIA 22.5.42 with No. 112 (Shark) Squadron

Pilot Officer Alan Lindsay Hedges

Pilot Officer Norman Bagshaw Heywood   KIA 22.10.40

Pilot Officer David Walter Hunt

Pilot Officer Jack Kininmonth Kay

Pilot Officer W.W. McConnell

Pilot Officer Gerald Hamilton Maffett   KIA 31.8.40

Pilot Officer Percival Alexander Mortimer   KIA 7.11.42 with No. 261 Squadron

Pilot Officer Gerald North   KIA 10.2.43 with No. 232 Squadron

Pilot Officer Jan Piotr Pfeiffer (Poland)   Died air accident 20.11.40 with No. 307 Squadron

Pilot Officer Karol Pniak (Poland)   VM 5th Class 1.2.41, KW 1.4.41, DFC 1.6.42, two Bars to the KW 20.12.43, third Bar KW 8.3.46

Pilot Officer John Redman   KIA 20 April 1943 with No. 224 Squadron

Pilot Officer Franciszek Surma (Poland)   KW and Bar 10.9.41, Second Bar 30.10.41, VM 5th Class 30.10.41, KIA 8.11.41 with No. 308 Squadron

Flight Sergeant Kenneth Mervyn Allen

Sergeant Donald James Aslin

Sergeant Leslie Denis Barnes

Sergeant Herbert Ernest Black   DoW 9.11.40

Sergeant Ronald Victor Forward

Sergeant Douglas Norman Francis

Sergeant Robert Henry Braund 'Bobby' Fraser   KIA 22.10.40

Sergeant Alexander George Girdwood   KIA 29.10.40

Sergeant Bernard Henson   KIA 17.11.40

Sergeant Henry Nuttall Hoyle

Sergeant Donald James Hulbert

Sergeant Ernest Robert Jessop	KIA 15.11.41 with No. 261 Squadron
Sergeant Sidney Edward Lucas	DFC 8.8.44 with No. 149 Squadron
Sergeant Reginald Charles Nutter	DFC 14.9.45 with No. 175 Squadron
Sergeant Anthony Durrant Page	KIA 8.11.40
Sergeant Arthur John Page	KIA 24.10.40 with No. 101 Squadron
Sergeant Peter Trevor Robinson	
Sergeant Harold Frederick William Shead	DFC 3.9.43 with No. 89 Squadron
Sergeant Kenneth Barton Smith	KIA 8.8.40

Chapter 11

Leading the Aussies of No. 457 Squadron

Raised at Baginton, near Coventry, on 16 June 1941, No. 457 Squadron, Royal Australian Air Force (RAAF) was, after No. 452 Squadron, the second RAAF fighter unit formed in England in accordance with Article XV of the Empire Air Training Scheme. Until 26 September the squadron, initially a part of No. 9 Group, was equipped with old Spitfire Mk Is.

Brothers and his senior Flight Commander, Flight Lieutenant North, were on station in advance of the first major intake of pilots which arrived on 30 July. Brothers recalled the scene that greeted him: 'There were eighteen Spitfires, scattered round the airfield, pointing in all sorts of directions, as left by the ATA or whoever. I had a flight sergeant and a couple of English airmen. Then a grey-haired chap arrived and said, "Flight Lieutenant North reporting for duty."'

North, who was prematurely grey-haired at the age of twenty-one, had served with No. 43 Squadron throughout the Battle of Britain, later transferring to No. 96 Squadron.

Meanwhile, Brothers' other flight commander, Flight Lieutenant Edy, DFC, had served with No. 603 Squadron during the Battle of Britain, having won the DFC (*London Gazette*, 5 November 1940) as a bomber pilot with No. 613 (City of Manchester) Squadron. Edy had later served as a flight commander with the newly formed No. 315 (Polish) Squadron and therefore had some experience of building a unit from scratch.

A study of the remainder of his pilots' logbooks told Brothers that he would have his work cut-out to make the squadron operational. And so began a process of intensive training in which North and Edy would play key roles. As he had done at Nos. 55 and 57 OTUs, Brothers was able to pass on his combat knowledge, giving lectures and some individual tuition where he felt it necessary.

A combination of a shortage of serviceable aircraft and the need to tailor each pilot's training meant progress was initially slow but measured. But by 18 July a dozen pilots were considered to have been trained to 'No. 11 Group Standard'.

The squadron's first patrol followed four days later, while on 5 August the squadron was declared fully operational. Meanwhile, news had arrived of their posting to RAF Jurby, Isle of Man, Ramsey Section, No. 8 Group. Here, their role was to maintain convoy escorts and fly defensive patrols. From 8 September, however, the squadron effectively became an unofficial OTU, feeding fully-trained pilots to Nos. 452 RAAF and 605 Squadrons.

It had been a long held goal that No. 457 Squadron's flying personnel should be exclusively Australian and by 1 October 1941 only Brothers and his two flight commanders remained the exceptions. Brothers must have felt that his pilots were getting a raw deal when news came through of their transfer across the island to the more exposed RAF Andreas, Andreas Sector, which formed a part of No. 9 Group. The move took place on 3 October. Progress was abruptly halted by the conditions: 'Operationally the base was far from ideal; the dispersals were not ready and there were no pens, the aircraft sank into the muddy perimeter track and had to be dugout.'

Consequently, the squadron's first patrol from their new base didn't come until 10 October, further uneventful patrols and convoy escorts coming towards the end of the month. Meanwhile, Australian ground staff arrived following a ten-week sea voyage, allowing RAF personnel to be posted away.

On 29 November came the first real 'black' day for the squadron when Sergeant (400692) Raymond Thomas Brewin, RAAF (flying P7445), failed to return from a patrol, his body later being sighted floating face down. Brewin was the son of Edith Mary Brewin and stepson of Denzil Brewin, of Kew, Victoria, Australia. Brewin, who was 26-years-old, is remembered on the Runneymede Memorial, Panel 62.

There were a number of scrambles, patrols and convoy escorts in early December. During one of these operations, flown on 5 December, the squadron lost 'B' Flight Commander, Flight Lieutenant Edy, who's Spitfire Mk IIA caught fire. He tried to control the aircraft before bailing out too low. Flight Lieutenant (41566) Allen Laird Edy, RAAF, was the son of John Curtis Harrington and Minnie Louise Edy, of St Andrews, Manitoba, Canada. Edy, who was 23-years-old, was buried at Andreas, Isle of Wight (St Andrew) Churchyard, Service Plot, Grave 1. Edy, Brothers later recalled, had survived a near-death experience when shot down in flames from 19,000ft during the Battle of Britain: 'He couldn't open the hood to get out, it was jammed.' The resourceful Canadian had slowed his aircraft's descent by a series of stalls, until it plunged nose first into a wood at the bottom of a swoop. The wings were ripped off while the engine broke away, allowing Edy to crawl out from under the instrument panel, the hood still being stuck fast.

On 17 December the squadron's defence section staged a mock attack on the base. This was the opportunity for Brothers and his senior pilots to make their first flights on the squadron's new Spitfire Mk Vbs.

With no sign of a combat posting, Brothers encouraged the men under his command to make the best of a Christmas away from their families, leading the festivities in his inimitable style. The squadron ORB summed up all of the men's feelings: 'The year 1941 closes with the squadron still not having been in action, it is to be hoped that we shall be moved to some place where 'Action' can be met.'

The weeks continued to drift by without a hint of combat. Only occasionally did an enemy aircraft venture into their airspace to justify their near constant state of Available. Routine flying continued, but still with no sign of action. Tragedy struck, however, on 8 March, when during formation practice, Sergeant R. McDonell's Spitfire (BL 491) plunged from 16,000ft into the sea off Ramsey Pier, 'I was leading the squadron in formation with one of the chaps on the right, his wings folded up suddenly and he vanished down into the sea.' Sergeant (401135) Russell McDonell, RAAF, was the son of John and Hilda McDonell of Elsterwick, Victoria, Australia.

McDonell was 21-years-old and was buried at Andreas (St Andrews) Churchyard, Service Plot, Grave 3.

On the afternoon of the incident, Brothers became acutely aware that his pilots were very edgy in case their own Spitfires disintegrated without warning. Brothers knew that his men had to have unswerving confidence in both him and their aircraft and decided to act, 'I thought they needed a demonstration of confidence, so I did an aerobatic display over the airfield.'

This worked and the pilots resumed their training programme. McDonell's Spitfire was raised and his body recovered for burial. The crash investigators quickly discovered that mild steel bolts had been used on the wing root instead of high-tensile steel. Orders were immediately issued for all aircraft to be checked, 'Aircraft so fitted with mild steel bolts were to be grounded and [the bolts] changed; all my squadron, including my aeroplane, were struck off.' Thinking back to his impromptu flying demonstration and the fact that his own Spitfire had the same faulty construction, Brothers added, 'Funny if they'd all come apart! *C'est la vie!'*

Meanwhile, the squadron's fortunes turned when Brothers received the news that everyone had been waiting for, 'We were to transfer into No. 11 Group and moved to Redhill, just south of London, to take over No. 452 Squadron's frontline duties.'

The move began on 19 March. Fighter Command had recently received authorization to launch a full-scale offensive campaign deep into enemy occupied territory and the squadron became part of this effort.

The former civilian airfield at Redhill, Surrey, had, until the outbreak of hostilities, belonged to British Air Transport Ltd. and was home to No. 15 E & RFTS and the Redhill Flying Club. From August 1940, the grassed landing strip was used by the Kenley Wing, and after the onset of the London Blitz, by the night-fighters of No. 600 (City of London) Squadron and later by No. 219 Squadron.

In 1941 the airfield was upgraded with a laid perimeter track and army mesh runways. Meanwhile, dispersal pens were constructed, along with blister hangars. A larger hangar housed civilian workers from Vickers, repairing Spitfire wings.

From early 1941 the newly renamed RAF Redhill became home to No. 1 Squadron, later Nos. 258, 41 and 485 (RNZAF) Squadrons all operated out of the airfield at one time or another; in February 1942, No. 602 Squadron was added to the list. The station also became a refuelling ground for No. 12 Group.

On 24 March, the Station Commander, Group Captain Beamish, DSO, DFC, AFC, (AFC, *London Gazette*, 1 January 1938; MiD, *London Gazette*, 20 February 1940; DSO, *London Gazette*, 23 July 1940; DFC, *London Gazette*, 8 November 1940; Bar to DSO, 2 September 1941) whom Brothers had first met while with No. 257 Squadron at North Weald, where Beamish had been Station Commander, addressed the pilots at Readiness – the missions that lay ahead of them were designed to take the fight to the enemy. Brothers summed up his own feelings, which were no doubt shared by the majority of his pilots, 'After a year of defensive fighting, wearily waiting for the frantic "scramble" at the enemy's beck and call, I found it exhilarating to take to the offensive.'

The RAF's new fighter offensive included a number of different types of air operations made over enemy occupied Europe, each with a different codename:

Circus
Bombers or fighter-bombers heavily escorted by fighters. The purpose of these sweeps being to draw the enemy fighters into combat.

Ramrod
Heavily escorted bomber formations targeting specific locations.

Rodeo
A mass fighter sweep, sometimes at squadron, Wing and even multi-Wing strength.

Sweep
An offensive flight by fighters designed to draw up and clear the enemy from the sky.

At 1535 hours on 26 March 1942, the squadron took off for its first taste of action, taking part in Circus 116A, an escort to twenty-two Douglas Boston bombers attacking vessels in Le Havre harbour. As the squadron slid into formation behind their leader, Brothers headed towards their rendezvous with Nos. 485 (New Zealand) and 602 Squadrons before flying low over the Channel to avoid radar. As they approached enemy occupied Europe they climbed to avoid the coastal flak batteries. The squadron cruised well below their normal 350 mph, allowing the lumbering bombers to keep pace. Meanwhile, their progress was being closely monitored by enemy radar. As the bombers swung in towards their target, twelve Bf 109s and Fw 190s came into sight, making individual attacks.

During the ensuing combat Brothers (flying BM143 BP – A) destroyed a Bf 109E of JG 26:

'At 1602 hours I was leading 457 Squadron in a Circus operation five miles off Le Havre when E/A were reported above and at three o'clock (Up sun). I turned right, through 360 degrees and E/A were reported at six o'clock. I turned left and as I turned saw a Spitfire (BP-R) going down smoking. Ahead, an Me 109E was diving down sun. He saw me and pulled up into a steep climb. I pulled up after him and gave him a six second burst at 200 yards from quarter astern. Pieces flew off, and then half the starboard wing broke off. The E/A turned over on its back and dived down into the sea, pieces still coming off. The pilot did not leave the a/c.'
(signed) S/Ldr P.M. Brothers.

The aircraft Brothers had seen in trouble a few miles off the French coast was AB495 flown by Pilot Officer B.J. Halse. Pilot Officer (402236) Brian Joseph Halse,

RAAF, was the son of Neville and Margaret Ann Halse, of Bondi, New South Wales, Australia. Halse, who was 29-years-old, is remembered on the Runnymede Memorial, Panel, 110. He had been one of the squadron's first sergeant pilots and received his commission in mid-November, serving as 'B' Flight's second-in-command. The Squadron ORB noted:

> 'Our Commanding Officer, Squadron Leader P.M. Brothers, bagged the squadron's first Hun (an Me 109). The elation of everyone was forestalled by the loss of Pilot Officer B.J. Halse (RAAF). Should he be safe, and in German hands – Good luck to him, and we shall all be glad to hear of his safety.'

As a further note, a message had been received from No. 11 Group: 'In the opinion of Wing Commander (Flying), Wing Commander Boyd, DFC, they [457 Squadron] acquitted themselves very well.'

Of the remainder of the Wing, No. 485 Squadron's Flight Lieutenant Crawford-Compton claimed a Bf 109E destroyed near Le Havre, Pilot Officer Mackie damaging a second, while No. 602 Squadron's CO, Squadron Leader Hodson, destroyed one Bf 109 and Pilot Officer Charlesworth (Yellow 3) damaged another. Their victories were tempered by the loss of Flight Sergeant (402194) William Max Krebs, RNZAF. He was the son of William Ernest and Ruby Krebs, of Gisborne, Auckland, New Zealand. Krebs, who was 24-years-old, is remembered on the Runnymede Memorial, Panel 117.

Brothers led an uneventful Fighter Sweep over France before lunch on 28 March, while the squadron took part in a Wing Rodeo over Le Touquet – Dieppe at 1655 hours. Shortly after making landfall south of Cap Griz Nez, between forty to fifty Fw 190s and Bf 109s were sighted flying in pairs and fours. Group Captain Beamish turned the Wing sharply to port to make the interception as the Fw 190s dived towards the outgoing Biggin Hill Wing. A 'terrific dogfight' ensued, timed at 1745 hours, during which they were engaged by Fw 190s of JG 26, claiming one 'probable' and two shared, with several more damaged. One of those who damaged an Fw 190 was Flight Lieutenant North:

> 'I saw an Fw 190 diving on a Spitfire. I turned onto the tail of the Fw 190 and he pulled up steeply, and a barrel roll. I gave the other Fw a short burst of cannon and machine-gun fire and something fell off the under side of the E/A. It turned over slowly and went into a vertical dive.'
> (signed) F/Lt North.

Yellow 2, Sergeant W. 'Bill' Wright (flying AA928), was wounded but damaged another:

> 'Saw twelve Fw 190s and was able to get on the tail of one of them, I gave a four second burst and saw thick whitish smoke come from the engine.
> 'The E/A then went down in a very steep dive with dense smoke still coming from it. I did not trouble to follow it as I was convinced my burst had destroyed the E/A.

'I became aware I was being attacked and found I had been shot through the right knee.'
(signed) Sgt Wright.

Yellow 3, Pilot Officer K.E. James (flying AA857 BP 'D'), destroyed an Fw 190 which he shared with Squadron Leader Finucane:

'I saw two Fw 190s about 2,000ft below me and slightly to starboard. I dived on the rear aircraft and fired a three second burst with machine guns at about 200 yds range. (I understand that Squadron Leader Finucane followed me in and finally destroyed this aircraft and claimed half.)'
(signed) P/O K. E. James.

Yellow 4, Pilot Officer G. Russell (flying AB994), claimed an Fw 190 probably destroyed:

'Saw an Fw 190 diving for the circle, I closed in to 400 yards, firing until within 200 yards, the E/A went slowly on his back fish-tailing and apparently out of control.'
(signed) P/O G. Russell.

Meanwhile, Blue 1, Flight Lieutenant R.H. Sly (flying AB260), posted on 24 March to command 'B' Flight, destroyed an Fw 190:

'I saw two Fw 190s passing about 500ft above me. I pulled up and followed and the first Fw 190 half rolled and dived away. The second kept climbing and I followed, firing a one second burst from below and astern without result. The E/A half rolled, I followed him down and closed in to 150 yds and gave a four second burst of cannon and machine gun, seeing De Wilde strike on the port wing and a big orange flash appeared in the cockpit, and pieces flew off. The E/A went on his side and spiraled slowly down with flames coming from the cockpit.'
(signed) A/F/Lt R.H. Sly.

Sergeant William 'Bill' Wright's Spitfire was damaged but managed to get back to base. Sergeant Reilly, however, was forced to take to his parachute eight miles south of Dungeness and was pulled out of the water by the crew of an Air Sea Rescue Launch and taken to Dover. Sadly, Sergeants Bloomfield (flying AB187) and Edwards (flying BL774) were both reported as missing. Flight Sergeant (402721) David l'Anson Bloomfield, RAAF, was the son of Archie l'Anson and Ethel Bloomfield, of Dee Way, New South Wales, Australia. Bloomfield, who was 25-years-old, is remembered on the Runnymede Memorial, Panel 111. Sergeant (403043) James George Edwards, RAAF, was the son of Dr James George and Margaret Stewart Edwards, of Sydney, New South Wales, Australia. Edwards, who was 26-years-old, is remembered on the Runnymede Memorial, Panel 112.

Sergeant Bloomfield, one of the squadron's original pilots, had been recommended for a commission by Brothers. He had only recently been appointed second-in-command of 'B' Flight, following the death of Pilot Officer Halse.

Also flying on the same Wing operation, No. 485 Squadron's Flight Lieutenants Grant and Compton, along with Pilot Officer E.D. Mackie, each claimed an Fw 190 destroyed, while Flight Sergeant Liken damaged an Fw 190, and Pilot Officer Palmer claimed an Fw 190 probably destroyed.

For No. 602 Squadron, Squadron Leader Hodson 'got a couple of Fw 190s' and Maxwell an Fw 190, while Flight Sergeants J. Garden and Catarall claimed one Fw 190 each, Catrall also claiming another damaged, while Schofield got one damaged. Warrant Officer Rudolph Ptacek (787434), RAFVR, who had previously been shot down twice, was killed-in-action. Ptacek, who was born in Czechoslovakia, is remembered on the Runnymede Memorial, Panel 73.

The Wing had suffered a further grievous loss with the death of Group Captain Victor Beamish, No. 485 Squadron's ORB taking up the narrative:

'An Fw 190 came in to attack the Group Captain. Flight Lieutenant Grant gave the Fw 190 a two second burst in the belly from about 50 yards range just as the Hun opened fire on the Group Captain. Strikes were seen in the port wing and under the fuselage of the Fw 190, and it dived away vertically, pouring greyish blue smoke from its engine and a large piece, which seemed to be the left aileron, blew off, and the cannon hole in the port wing appeared to be widening as it went down. Another Fw 190 came in to attack, but Flight Lieutenant Grant attacked it with cannon from 150 yds range from port quarter astern, and the Fw 190 shuddered, continued on its course for a brief period and suddenly blew up. The Group Captain was heard by Squadron Leader Finucane asking for a fix and someone advised him to steer 310.'

Group Captain (16089) Francis Victor Beamish, DSO and Bar, DFC, AFC, RAF, was the son of Francis George and Mary Elizabeth Beamish of Castlerock, Co. Derry. Beamish is remembered on the Runnymede Memorial, Panel 64.

Beamish was awarded a Bar to the DSO, *London Gazette*, 25 September 1941:

'Group Captain Beamish commanded an RAF Station from October [*sic*] 1940 to March 1941 and during that period carried out seventy-one operational sorties in which he destroyed an enemy fighter, probably destroyed three other hostile aircraft and damaged others. Since his appointment to Group Captain he has probably destroyed two more enemy aircraft. The courage and devotion to duty displayed by Group Captain Beamish are of the highest order and he has set a magnificent example.'

Brothers recalled, 'He was a fearless, tough and dedicated officer, a born leader, revered and respected by us all, whose loss had a serious impact on the morale of the Wing. "If he can be killed," ran the thoughts of my pilots, "what chance have I?"'

The man who assumed command of the Wing was another giant of the pre-war aviation world, Wing Commander Richard 'Batchy' Atcherley (later Air Marshal Sir Richard Atcherley, KBE, CB, AFC and Bar), an ex-member of the Schnieder Trophy Team. 'And so,' related Pete, 'started a long association with this most memorable of characters.'

Meanwhile, before breakfast on 29 March the squadron flew on an uneventful convoy patrol off the French Coast and on their return were ordered to stand down. Brothers took the opportunity to invite Wing Commander (Flying) Boyd, DSO, DFC and Bar, over to celebrate his award of the DSO. Boyd's award was promulgated in the *London Gazette* of 7 April 1942. The citation read:

'Since December 1941, this officer has led a Wing on many occasions. Much of the outstanding success which has been obtained can be attributed to the leadership, skill and fighting spirit of this officer. Since being awarded a Bar to the Distinguished Flying Cross, Wing Commander Boyd has destroyed a further twelve enemy aircraft, bringing his total to twenty-two.'

The squadron ORB for 31 March acknowledged the very mixed fortunes of the squadron's blooding:

'During our first week of action, the squadron has already three Huns to its credit and also a few 'possibles'. We have unfortunately lost one pilot by flying accident, and three are missing on active service, and one severely wounded. The squadron went straight into action on arrival, and has now found it's feet – let us hope from now on we shall give far more than we take.'

That evening Brothers and his pilots attended a Wing party held in their honour at the Tudor Rose, near Kenley. No. 602 Squadron's ORB noted: 'Squadron Leader Brothers was chaired around the lounge by his enthusiastic pilots towards the end of the evening.'

At 0945 hours on Easter Sunday, 4 April 1942, Flight Lieutenant North commanded the squadron on Kenley Wing's Circus 119, making their rendezvous with the rest of the Wing under Squadron Leader Wells, DFC and Bar. Their role was as escort to twelve Bostons and four Wellingtons raiding St Omer railway yard. After turning at Aire, the bombers were attacked by forty-plus Fw 190s. Two of the Bostons were damaged and flew back on one engine, closely escorted by the fighters.

Flight Lieutenant North (Red 1) claimed one Fw 190 damaged over St Omer:

'I saw two Fw 190s coming down to attack the bombers from four o'clock and above. I pulled up and made a head-on attack on the E/A closing to about 100ft. I saw two jets of black smoke coming from E/A as my ammunition hit it.' (signed) F/Lt North.

The overall tally was fourteen enemy aircraft claimed, for the loss of four aircraft. No. 457 Squadron's 'A' Flight lost Pilot Officer C.G. Russell (flying BP859). He had been one of the squadron's original pilots and second in command of the flight. Russell had broken formation and turned to go after an enemy aircraft. He bailed out and became a PoW. Meanwhile, Sergeant (402726) Arthur Bolwell Burgess, RAAF (flying AB994), was killed-in-action. He was the son of Arthur and Ruby Stuart Burgess, of Kelso, New South Wales, Australia. Bolwell, who was 24-years-old, is remembered on the Runnymede Memorial, Panel 112.

Meanwhile No. 485 Squadron lost Pilot Officers T.T. Fox (flying P8724) and E.F. Chandler (flying BM231), both last seen in the target area and going down in a gradual dive, trailing smoke. Pilot Officer (411392) Thomas Tristan Fox, RNZAF, was the son of Thomas and Marion Agnes Fox; husband of Doreen Fox, of Minnedosa, Mannatoba, Canada. Fox was 21-years-old and was buried at Longuenesse (St Omer) Souvenir Cemetery Special Memorial, Plot 9, Row A, Grave 1.

Pilot Officer (402543) Edward Fred Chandler, RNZAF, was the son of Edward Fred Chandler and Evelyn Marguette Chandler of Tapu Auckland, New Zealand. He was 24-years-old and is remembered on the Runnymede Memorial, Panel 115.

In retaliation, Pilot Officer Ian McNeil claimed a probable Fw 190, while Flight Lieutenant W. Crawford-Compton and Sergeant Doug Brown each damaged an Fw 190.

Between 8 and 10 April the squadron flew on an uneventful Wing patrol and a Rodeo. Another Wing patrol over France (Circus 122) was made on 12 April, when Wing Commander Boyd damaged two Fw 190s, while Pilot Officer J.B. Niven of No. 602 Squadron damaged another.

On 13 April, the squadron flew as a part of a Group operation over France, while on the following day they made up a bomber escort as a part of the Kenley Wing (485, 457, 602 Squadrons), under Squadron Leader Wells. Twelve miles east of Calais No. 602 Squadron dived to attack about fifteen enemy fighters, but sighted thirty-plus Fw 190s looking to attack them and formed a defensive circle. One by one they dived for the Channel, which they crossed at 50ft. The squadron claimed several successes. Pilot Officer Niven destroyed an Fw 190, Pilot Officer De La Poype damaged a second, and Flight Sergeant Willis another.

Back in the air at 1740 hours the squadron took off as part of the Kenley Wing, carrying out a Fighter Patrol over the French Coast. Pilot Officer D.H. McLean (flying BL636 'P') claimed an Fw 190 probably destroyed between Desvres and St Inglevert:

'I was flying as Blue 2, 457 Squadron on fighter sweep. I saw a number of Fw 190s diving from up sun towards us, and over me. We turned 180 degrees, and shortly after, one Fw 190 dived past me firing at another Spitfire.

'I fired a long burst of cannon and machine guns from quarter to astern closing in to 70 yards.

'I saw pieces fly off the aircraft but could not identify what they were. Smoke poured from the E/A, which went spinning down and obviously out of control.'
(signed) P/O MacLean.

Flying an uneventful Rodeo on 15 April, the squadron was in action again on the following day, taking off at 0635 hours on Kenley Wing's Circus 126, an escort to Hurri-bombers targeting the area between Dunkirk and Mardyck. No. 485 Squadron's Flight Lieutenant Ian Grant hit an Fw 190 which was seen to go down vertically 'belching smoke' and 'out of control', while Squadron Leader Finucane (Coiner Leader) probably got another south of Mardyke:

'We sighted four more Fw 190s and attacked. I picked on the last one and gave a two second burst from 15 degrees [at 230 – 260 yards]. Enemy aircraft started to half roll and gave a lurch. A few pieces fell off and the Fw 190 dived down. It left a trail of dirty grey smoke behind it.'
(signed) S/Ldr Finucane.

No. 457 Squadron's Red 1, Flight Lieutenant H.L North (flying BM188), claimed one Fw 190 probably destroyed while acting as high cover. Having fired a two second burst at one of four Fw 190s diving to attack No. 485 Squadron, North peeled off to strike a second enemy fighter:

'I then concentrated on the last E/A, range about 500 yds closing to 300 yds with two, two second bursts of cannon and machine gun, full ring deflection. I saw black smoke burst from E/A.'
(signed) Fl/Lt North.

The squadron's second operation of the day was an uneventful Rodeo over Le Touquet, Hardelot Guines and St Inglevert.

On 17 April, Brothers' squadron flew a Wing escort to Marquise aerodrome for eight Hurri-bombers. Later, Brothers led the squadron on Circus 130, which proved to be an uneventful bomber escort flown as a part of the Kenley Wing, the Bostons bombing the power station at Grand Quevelly. The operation was flown with only ten minutes warning, causing Brothers to 'phone Group to complain at the lack of intelligence available in advance of take-off.'

During the afternoon of 24 April the squadron flew as a part of the Kenley Wing on Circus 132, a bomber escort to Flushing Harbour. The operation was later repeated as Circus 133, an escort to a dozen Bostons. Brothers experienced radio trouble and so was forced to return early, missing out on the action.

Of the rest of the Wing, No. 457 Squadron engaged a formation of six Fw 190s flying at about 3,000ft beneath them. Pilot Officer Watson (Yellow 1) claimed one as damaged at 1745 hours:

'I saw 485 Squadron diving on six Fw 190s, I followed one of these which was doing a roll. I then pulled up my nose and squirted [cannon strikes observed on the fuselage] and when next I looked, the plane was going down in a slow spin.'
(signed) P/O P.H. Watson.

Eight of No. 485 Squadron's pilots fired their guns, with Squadron Leader Wells, Flight Lieutenant W. Crawford-Compton and Flight Lieutenant J.R.C. Kilian each claiming one as destroyed, a fourth was probably destroyed by Pilot Officer Palmer.

Circus No. 137 was flown in the afternoon of 25 April. The Wing formed up with the Biggin Hill and Hornchurch Wings, to provide an escort to thirty-six Bostons targeting Abbeville railway yards, Morliax airfield, Cherbourg, Le Havre and Dunkirk. The controller warned of large numbers of enemy aircraft approaching from the St Omer area. During the ensuing combat Squadron Leader Wells damaged an Fw 190.

The Kenley Wing swept towards Namport where three separate *staffeln* of Fw 190s were sighted. Flight Lieutenant J.H. Lacey of 602 Squadron damaged two, but Group Captain Corner, of Fighter Command HQ's Staff (Medical Officer), who was flying No. 602 Squadron's BM187, was shot down, bailing out over the Channel too low. Group Captain Hugh Wolfe Corner, AFC, MD, CHB, MRCP, RAF, was the son of William and Hedwig Dorothea Corner; husband of Emily Vera Corner, MD, FRCP, of Gerrard's Cross, Buckinghamshire. He is remembered on the Runnymede Memorial, Panel 64. Meanwhile, Sergeant (1282703) Paul Frederick Green, RAFVR (flying BM228), was seen going down in a spin near Frevert. Green is remembered on the Runnymede Memorial, Panel 151.

The squadron flew on Circus 138 during the morning of 26 April, but made no claims, although Squadron Leader Finucane and No. 602 Squadron's Flight Sergeant Thorne shared in the destruction of one Fw 190, Thorne damaging a second.

Airborne again at 1705 hours, Brothers led the squadron off on a multi-wing Rodeo to Mardyck under Wing Commander Loudon, DFC. Around fifty enemy fighters came down out of the sun and attacked No. 485 Squadron, which was acting as top cover. Unaware of the attack, Wing Commander Loudon led No. 602 and No. 457 Squadrons on towards Audricq and Ambleteuse.

Outnumbered and at a tactical disadvantage, No 485 Squadron had a tough fight. Pilot Officer Mackie probably destroyed one Fw 190, but his own aircraft was damaged by a 40mm shell from ground fire. Flight Sergeant Goodlet and Flying Officer Pattison were forced to bail out, while Flight Sergeant (404395) John Raby Liken, RNZAF, parachuted down into the Channel and died in hospital that night. He was buried at Whyteleafe (St Luke) Churchyard, Row I, Grave 29. During the same engagement Pilot Officer Ralph was set upon by four Fw 190s, received several hits and was wounded in the left foot. He feigned being out of control and made his escape.

No. 457 Squadron's Spitfires were also involved in a separate air battle. Most of the pilots fired their guns. The combats were timed at 1800 hours.

Pilot Officer MacLean (Red 3) claimed one Fw 190 damaged while flying between Calais and St Omer:

'Three Fw 190s dived down past the Squadron and the Squadron Leader ordered us to "each take one"'.

'I fired a four second burst at the second Fw 190 and saw my shells flashing on and around the aircraft [witnessed by Brothers].'
(signed) P/O MacLean.

Flight Lieutenant R.H. Sly (Blue 1) claimed one Fw 190 damaged, shared with Sergeant Blake, five miles south of Calais;

'I noticed one Fw 190 coming up behind Blue 4. I called a break and did a steep climbing turn to the right and half rolled off the top coming down vertical onto the E/A which was still flying level about 150 yards behind Blue 4. I fired a short burst from about 300 yards. E/A pulled up below him again, fired a short burst at about 200 yards. He did a very large barreled half roll and I followed, and fired two or three bursts in the dive seeing tracer striking the E/A.'
(signed) F/Lt Ray H. Sly.

Scrgeant A.H. Blake (Blue 2) wrote:

'I saw an Fw 190 position himself on Blue 4's tail. I warned Blue 4 by RT and immediately stall turned and half rolled after Blue 1 who had seen E/A almost simultaneously. Blue 1 fired short burst at range of 250 yards and I followed with two second burst of cannon and machine gun. E/A half rolled and dived being followed by both Blue 1 and myself. I was able to fire a two second burst at E/A whilst diving vertically.'
(signed) Sgt A.H. Blake.

On 27 April the squadron flew on a Rodeo over Gravelines and St Omer at 1030 hours, making a second mission, Circus 141, at 1430 hours in the company of the Northolt and Biggin Hill Wings. Their role was to act as escort for twelve Boston bombers targeting Lille. During the debriefing the pilots reported attacks by enemy fighters of JG 26 just prior to reaching the target; all of the squadron's aircraft were engaged.

One of the Bostons was damaged and Wing Commander Loudon ordered six aircraft from No. 602 Squadron and three from No. 457 Squadron to provide close escort. Pete's flight commanders both made a claim, while Pilot Officer Palmer of No. 485 Squadron was forced to bail out following combat. Flight Sergeant (402730) Marshall Edmund Parbery, RAAF (flying BM159), was last seen just before the formation reached Lille. He was the son of Charles Percival and Merle Edith Parbery, of Bega, New South Wales, Australia. Parbery, who was 23-years-old, is remembered on the Runnymede Memorial, Panel 111.

Flight Lieutenant H.L. North (Red 1) damaged an Fw 190:

'When approaching the target the bombers were attacked by about ten or twelve Fw 190s. I attacked one Fw 190, range 300 yards, which was diving on the bombers and saw what appeared to be flashes from E/A as my ammunition struck. The E/A continued to dive, with large puffs of black smoke coming from front of E/A.'
(signed) F/Lt H.L. North.

Detailed to escort the damaged Boston, Blue 1, Flight Lieutenant R.H. Sly (flying BM240 'E'), claimed an Fw 190 probably destroyed and another damaged:

'From St. Omer to the French coast we were constantly attacked by many Fw 190s. I dived on one which was firing at the bomber and fired a two second burst from 200 yds almost astern, observing cannon strikes on the tailplane and a large piece fell off. The E/A flicked over and started to spin, but I was then attacked by another Fw 190 from port stern quarter and a few bullets hit my machine. I claim this E/A as probably destroyed.

'I fired several short bursts at E/A attacking the bomber and noticed cannon strike half way out on the wing of an Fw 190 [one second burst at 150 yards]. I claim the E/A as damaged.

'The bomber by this time had white smoke pouring from the starboard engine and it turned back into France and headed south, evidently preparing to make a forced landing.'
(signed) F/Lt R.H. Sly.

The squadron was at Readiness from early in the morning of 28 April and at 0555 hours took off with the Kenley Wing providing return cover for Hurri-bombers. Airborne again at 1035 hours, the squadron accompanied No. 485 Squadron on an escort to six Bostons targeting the marshalling yards at St Omer.

On 29 April Brothers was at the head of the squadron when they flew with the Kenley Wing as Draw Wing on a diversionary raid for six Bostons targeting Dunkirk docks as part of Circus 145. The Wing made a sweep into France in the company of the Biggin Hill and Northolt Wings. A number of Fw 190s were engaged in the Cap Griz Nez area, with most of the pilots firing their guns.

Brothers (flying BM143 'A') claimed an Fw 190 probably destroyed:

'At 1550 hours I was leading 457 Squadron at 23,000ft over Griz Nez. E/A were reported astern of us and I turned round to port when I saw approximately twelve Fw 190s on my left and above, flying singly and in pairs and fours. I attacked one which immediately dived inland and after losing 4,000ft I broke off and climbed up and fired short bursts at two more E/A. Two more Fw 190s passed on my left at 24,000ft, so I turned and attacked the rear one from quarter astern. I saw strikes on the fuselage round the cockpit and the a/c turned on its back and dived. I followed him down in case he pulled out, but he went into a slow right-hand spin. At 15,000ft I saw that the other E/A was diving on me. I broke away underneath him. I had expended most of my ammunition and being alone I set course for home. Two more 190s dived on me as I crossed the French Coast, but broke away when I turned towards them.'
(signed) S/Ldr P.M. Brothers.

During the same combat Pilot Officer MacLean (Red 3) damaged an Fw 190 which was lining up to fire at Brothers' Spitfire:

'Flying behind the squadron leader, I saw him roll and attack an Fw 190 below, then saw another E/A, also an Fw 190, diving in front and above me on the squadron leader's tail. I pulled up my nose and fired a short burst of cannon at the E/A which immediately turned right and dived away. I followed, firing a further burst of three or four seconds and saw strikes on the fuselage.'
(signed) P/O MacLean.

Brothers landed at Kenley aerodrome, his pilots being driven over to join him. Brothers had the honour of presenting the squadron to His Majesty, King George VI who by then had already heard details of the raid at Operations. The King shook each man warmly by the hand, asking questions about their recent sortie and offering a few words of encouragement.

On 30 April the squadron formed a part of the Kenley Wing, under Wing Commander Loudon, joining the Biggin Hill Wing on Circus 148. Their role was to fly as Target Support to six Bostons. North-west of their target, Le Havre, a formation of Fw 190s was engaged, several being damaged. No. 602 Squadron's Squadron Leader Finucane, together with Flight Sergeants G. Willis and Thorne, each probably destroyed an Fw 190, while No. 457 Squadron's Pilot Officer E.P.W. Bocock destroyed one, and Pilot Officer J. Dennehey damaged another.

The day's second mission was as a part of the joint Wing Rodeo 7, which passed off without incident.

The Squadron ORB reviewed their first month's combat operations:

'We have suffered the loss of one officer, prisoner of war, and two sergeants missing; we have done no fewer than thirty-two sweeps, offensive patrols and offensive actions over enemy territory – this has probably been the most active month since the Battle of Britain.'

On 1 May, Flight Lieutenant North led the squadron on Circus 150 as a part of the Kenley Wing. Their role was to act as high cover to eight Hurri-bombers targeting the Marquise shell factory. Also taking part were the Tangmere and Northolt Wings. Two other bomber raids took place simultaneously, targeting St Omer and Calais.

While on the return leg, between Marquise and Griz-Nez, the formation was attacked by Fw 190s. No. 602 Squadron probably destroyed three, one each by Flight Lieutenant Bocock, Flight Sergeants Thorne and W. J. Loud, while the former damaged a second. Pilot Officer Maxwell was reported as missing. Meanwhile, No. 485 Squadron's Pilot Officer Falls was seen to bail out over Cap Griz Nez.

Six of No. 457 Squadron's pilots fired their guns between Cap Griz Nez and Calais, their combat timed at about 1925 hours.

Red 1, Pilot Officer MacLean (flying BL636 'P'), engaged and destroyed an Fw 190, his own aircraft being hit:

'Red Leader and Section dived on two enemy aircraft.

'I broke away with number two to attack about eight enemy aircraft which were diving on the section.

'I fired one long burst from 250 yds into one enemy aircraft and saw what appeared to be a large portion of hood fly off the aircraft, which immediately went into a vertical dive.'
(signed) P/O MacLean.

Meanwhile, Sergeant G. Gifford (Yellow 3) claimed one Fw 190 damaged:

'I observed two Fw 190s attacking us from the front, and pulled down onto them as they passed under me. I fired one half second burst into the last of the two enemy aircraft, but did not observe any direct hits.

'I then pulled round and brought my sights onto the other enemy aircraft which was now approximately 300 yds in front. I fired two, three second bursts and my tracer bullets showed a path directly into the enemy aircraft. I also saw one or two cannon strikes.

'At the end of my second burst the enemy aircraft gave a couple of shudders, slowly turned onto its back and dived down.'
(signed) Sgt G. Gifford.

Sergeant Little's aircraft was hit in the port wing by a cannon shell, while an armour piercing machine-gun bullet pierced the cockpit hood.

Flight Lieutenant North (flying BM188) and his No. 2, Sergeant A. Peacock (flying BM251), both failed to return. Pilot Officer McLean reported seeing them diving after a German fighter with a pack of ten or more Fw 190s following them down. North had been Brothers' right-hand man since the death of Flight Lieutenant Edy. Flight Lieutenant (41608) Harold Leslie North, RAF, son of William Charles Dingey and Ruby Rogers North, of Dunelin, Otago, New Zealand. North, who was 22-years-old, is remembered on the Runnymede Memorial, Panel 66. Sergeant (403371) Andrew Francis Peacock, RAAF, son of Harold and Charlotte Agnes Pearl Peacock, of Canberra, Australia. Peacock, who was 21-years-old, is remembered on the Runnymede Memorial, Panel 113.

The squadron made two uneventful sweeps on 3 May as a part of the Kenley Wing. Following the morning's Rodeo, on 4 May, as a part of the Kenley Wing, Brothers led the squadron on Rodeo 18, taking off at 1900 hours before making a Wing rendezvous over Kenley, meeting the Hornchurch and North Weald Wings coming out.

The Wing flew inland and, while over the Forest of Boulogne, engaged twenty Fw 190s, with No. 485 Squadron flying bottom cover claiming one Fw 190 destroyed. Flying Officer M.M. Shand and Flight Sergeant A.R. Robson claimed another probable, while Flight Sergeant D.M. Russell was shot down and killed. Flight Sergeant (403553) David Malyon Russell, RNZAF, was the son of John and Beatrice Hawes Russell, of Pukekohe, Auckland, New Zealand; husband of Violet Ada Russell, of Manurewa, Auckland. He was 25-years-old and was buried in Whyteleafe (St. Luke) Churchyard, Row I. Grave 30.

More than half of the No. 457 Squadron fired their guns, although the only claim was by Sergeant Gifford who damaged an Fw 190:

'I saw four Fw 190s about 500ft above and in front, two of the enemy aircraft broke away to the right, the remaining two continuing on towards my section. I pulled up towards these enemy aircraft and fired a three second burst into the nearest one [200 and 250 yards], and I observed cannon strikes in his fuselage. This enemy aircraft rolled and began diving, and I gave another three second burst, the only visible result of this burst was a trail of white smoke streaming out behind.'
(signed) Sgt G. Gifford.

The squadron flew on two uneventful Rodeos on 5 May as part of the Kenley Wing. During the second of these, Rodeo 20, the Northolt and Tangmere Wings followed on at five minute intervals. In between missions Brothers arranged for the pilots to view Sergeant Gifford's combat film from the previous day's engagement. The accuracy of his aim drew cheers and warm applause, with the fighter being clearly seen to go down spiraling out of control and emitting white smoke. The Fw 190 was subsequently upgraded to a 'kill'.

At 1120 hours on 6 May the squadron flew with the Kenley Wing, under Wing Commander Wells, joining the Debden Wing in escorting six Bostons targeting Caen on Circus 159.

Brothers commanded the squadron on Circus 160, the squadron's second operation of the day, taking off at 1735 hours. The Wing flew as escort for six Bostons targeting the Calais parachute factory and the Boulogne Docks, with six more bombers escorted by the Biggin Hill and two other Wings. Brothers experienced radio trouble. Unable to lead the squadron or be warned of enemy attacks, he was forced to turn back early.

The squadron flew on Circus 164, flying as escort for six Bostons bombing the Ostend Docks, and Circus 166, an escort to a formation of eight Bostons attacking the port and railway yards at Dieppe during the 7 and 8 May.

At Readiness from dawn on 9 May, the squadron had a full day of operations, flying four scrambles and patrols before breakfast.

At 1230 hours Flight Lieutenant Watson headed the squadron as a part of the Kenley Wing, flying as high and top cover on Circus 170, a mission to escort Bostons raiding marshalling yards at Hazebrouck. Reaching the target they turned towards Ostend, but were jumped by twenty-plus Fw 190s of JG 26 flying in sections of four. During the ensuing melee a Spitfire was seen being hit by severe cannon fire from an enemy aircraft flying only 50 yards behind. Pilot Officer Newton went after them, but could only fire at the enemy aircraft when the Spitfire had dived away. He got in two bursts at very short range, but made no claim. Meanwhile, Sergeant Gifford (Yellow 1) attacked two enemy aircraft, damaging one:

> 'I noticed two Fw 190s diving on my section from behind and above. I turned into the attacking aircraft and gave the nearest enemy aircraft a two second burst, which immediately dived. The second enemy aircraft had started a climbing turn to starboard, and I allowed deflection cannon strikes on his mainplanes, and he rolled onto his back with white smoke streaming out behind. I then noticed this enemy aircraft go into a steep dive.'
> (signed) Sgt G. Gifford.

The squadron was continually attacked on their return leg, during which they lost Sergeant Smith (flying BM180), who Brothers had recommended for a commission. He was last seen by his No. 2 in a dogfight over the Channel, midway between Mardyck and Dover, at about 20,000ft. Another casualty was Sergeant Halliday (flying AA851), who was on his third operation. His Spitfire had been hit and caught fire and he bailed out near Deal – too low. Sergeant (400942) William James Smith, RAAF, son of Samuel William and Freda Constance Adelaide Smith, of Whittlesea, Victoria, Australia. Smith, who was 24-years-old, is remembered on the Runnymede Memorial, Panel 113. The wreckage of Smith's Spitfire was discovered by a team led by Andy Saunders, on farmland near Cassel in November 2011 (while investigating what was thought to be another crash site). William James Smith was finally interned at the Commonwealth War Graves Commission section of Cassel Cemetery the following April. Sergeant (407426) Richard Arthur Halliday, RAAF, son of Richard Blair and Maggie Muriel Halliday, husband of Una Joyce Halliday, of Springton, South Australia. Halliday, who was 27-years-old, was buried in Aylesham Cemetery, Block O, Row, Grave 2.

At 1415 hours the squadron took off to act as a Diversionary Wing for Circus 171, a bombing raid on an oil depot at Bruges.

On 12 May, Brothers played host to AOC Air Vice-Marshal T.L. Leigh-Mallory. Following their meeting, Leigh-Mallory gave the pilots a talk on tactics before the pair travelled to Kenley to attend a party at the officer's mess.

Two days later, Kenley Wing's No. 602 Squadron, commanded by Squadron Leader 'Paddy' Finucane, DSO, DFC and Bar, was posted back to Redhill.

On 15 May, Brothers and Flight Lieutenant Watson travelled to No. 11 Group HQ where they were informed of the prospect of the squadron receiving an overseas posting. The Japanese were overrunning Burma and the Philippines, threatening Australia and New Zealand. Following talks between the Australian Parliamentary Minister, Dr H.V. Evatt, and Winston Churchill, it was agreed to deploy the Australian Nos. 452 and 457 Squadrons, along with No. 54 Squadron, to defend northern Australia.

Meanwhile, No. 457 Squadron flew three convoy escorts during the morning of 17 May, while Brothers led an air-sea rescue patrol, in the wake of the Kenley Wing's

Ramrod 33, which had included the Spitfires of Nos. 485, 402 (RCAF) and 602 Squadrons.

No. 602 Squadron's ORB reveals that Flight Lieutenant Major was shot down and bailed out off Cap Griz Nez. Pilot Officer Dennehey dropped his dingy but Major was unable to reach it. Brothers explained, 'We saw the high-speed launches picking up Major but he was already dead.'

Flight Lieutenant (33352) Peter Anthony Major, RAF, was the adopted son of John Lewis Major and Constance Theodora Major, of Eynsford, Kent. He was buried in Brookwood Military Cemetery, Block 21, Row B, Grave 15. He was 24-years-old.

On 18 May the squadron took off at 1055 hours as a part of a Kenley Wing Rodeo, led by Wing Commander Wells. Meanwhile, there was welcome news for the Wing; No. 485 Squadron's Pilot Officer L.P. Griffiths was awarded the DFC, while Flight Sergeant Robson (NZ 403990) was awarded the DFM.

On the following day, Nos. 457 and 602 Squadrons flew on a Kenley Wing Rodeo, which passed off without incident.

Meanwhile, a signal was received announcing the award of the DFC, on Brothers' recommendations, to Flight Lieutenant H.L. North and Acting Flight Lieutenant P.H. Watson. The news coincided with a visit from Mr W.J. Barr of the Australian Newspaper Service who interviewed Watson and some of the pilots and ground staff.

Both awards were officially announced in the *London Gazette* of 5 June 1942. Flight Lieutenant H.L. North's citation read:

'This officer has commanded a flight since the squadron was formed. He has performed much valuable work both during the training of the squadron and on its operational activities. Displaying great courage and initiative, Flight Lieutenant North, who previously served with another unit and fought in the Battle of Britain, has destroyed at least five enemy aircraft.'

Pilot Officer P.H.W. Watson's award announcement read:

'This officer is a most capable leader who displays great coolness and courage in action. He has participated in over forty sorties and his inspiring example has proved a great source of encouragement to other members of his flight.'

The 21 May was another red-letter day, as Air Vice-Marshal McNamara, DFC, MC, accompanied by Dr H.V. Evatt, visited Redhill. Brothers recalled that: 'Doctor Evatt came to visit my Aussie squadron at Kenley and he kicked me out of the briefing room because I wasn't Australian, and told the chaps they were going home and they said they weren't going home without their "Squaddie".'

While Brothers appreciated their loyalty, he wasn't keen on the simultaneous posting: 'I thought Christ, I don't want to go there. I'll be stuck there for the rest of the war – there's no future in it promotion-wise or anything else. I'd have been forgotten totally by the RAF. I've got to get out of this.'

'I went to see the Air Vice-Marshal Hugh "Dingbat" Saunders, the SASO of No. 11 Group, who said there was nothing he could do. He said, "Dr Evatt has just seen Winston Churchill and your name cropped up, and Churchill said he could think of no better person than an experienced Battle of Britain Ace to lead the battle for Australia."'

Brothers knew that he couldn't hope to gain an interview with Churchill, but perhaps he could persuade Dr Evatt that he should remain in England. Their meeting in his Hyde Park hotel didn't go to plan and Brothers left feeling he had got nowhere, 'I said, "I gather you are expecting me to go to Australia and I am not going."'

'He said, "Rest assured dear boy, you will be awarded every possible decoration in Australia."'

'I said, "My Aussie chaps can handle it on their own. They don't need me." It was like water off a duck's back and I didn't think I'd got anywhere.'

With their posting pending the squadron continued on ops. On 24 May the squadron flew with the Kenley Wing on Rodeo 48. The formation joined forces with the Biggin Hill and Tangmere Wings before heading for France. Wing Commander Wells damaged a Bf 109 off Griz Nez, (Wells would be awarded the DSO, *London Gazette*, 28 July 1942, for his work as Wing Leader) while No. 485 Squadron's Flight Lieutenants Crawford-Compton and J.R.C. Kilain, both claimed an Fw 190 and Pilot Officer J.J. Palmer probably destroyed another.

During the following day Brothers was summoned to RAAF Overseas Headquarters where he learnt details of the coming move, briefing his men on 26 May.

Brothers pal, Group Captain Atcherley (flying BM235) was shot down during the day and was picked up out of the Channel, 'Wishing to hear his story first hand, I rushed to the hospital.'

Brothers found his friend wandering around the wards, his arm in a sling, chatting. The Group Commander explained, 'Well, Pete, knowing that a Spitfire was more than a match for a 109 I decided to patrol St Omer [one of the Luftwaffe's fighter bases in France] at 20,000ft and knock them down as they came up.'

Unfortunately, the enemy seemed to take no notice of him. Atcherley continued, 'Getting short of fuel, I set off home. Halfway across the Channel I suddenly saw some 109s behind me. There was a loud bang, the throttle lever, and a finger, left my hand, the cockpit filled with smoke and the aircraft went out of control.'

Having successfully bailed out, Group Captain Atcherley struggled to get into his dinghy, 'Getting rid of my parachute, I tried to inflate my dinghy. The trouble with being a station commander is that you make everyone else do dinghy drill, but don't do it yourself. Eventually I opened it and dragged myself in.'

Meanwhile, the squadron flew two uneventful Rodeos on 29 May, their last sorties in the European Theatre. Having been withdrawn from operations, Brothers recalled that on 30 May: 'We packed up the aircraft, crated them, and I sent the chaps on leave, except for the ground crew, and I was sorting out admin. Forty-eight hours before the boat was due to sail from Liverpool I went home. All my kit had gone on the boat and I was due to report on the Monday morning.'

The Squadron ORB noted on 31 May: 'The squadron, from being one of the best fighting units in No. 11 Group, has been immobilized by a stroke of the pen and ordered overseas for other duties.'

By this time its pilots had been credited with five confirmed kills and another four 'probables', with seven more damaged.

Transferring to Kirton-in-Lindsey on 1 June, the squadron remained there for less than a month, surrendering their aircraft at Church Fenton on 16 June, two days before sailing for Australia on the Motor Vessel *Stirling Castle*. Also on-board were No. 452 Squadron RAAF and No. 54 Squadron, together they would form No. 1 Fighter Wing, or Churchill Wing.

But despite his fears, Brothers did not sail with them: 'On the Sunday evening the phone rang. It was a chap from 11 Group saying Dr Evatt had just flown off to see Roosevelt; and as he's out of the country I was to report to the HQ of 11 Group on the Monday. I did that and they told me I was taking over 602 Squadron.'

And so, in the south-west Pacific theatre of operations, No. 457 Squadron was to be led by Squadron Leader Ken E. James.

Quite how Pete avoided the move is not totally clear. There may be a hint in Brothers' service record which shows that he was officially transferred away from the squadron on 4 June, receiving a posting to No. 11 Group, Uxbridge, before a week-long stint in the role of Acting Wing Commander (Flying) RAF Hornchurch, which began on 13 June. Wing Commander R.P.R. Powell, DFC, had been wounded in the neck and head by shell splinters on 2 June while leading the Wing on Circus 182. The Hornchurch Wing then consisted of No. 64 Squadron (Squadron Leader Wilfred G.G. Duncan-Smith, DFC and Bar), No. 81 Squadron (Squadron Leader Ronald 'Rass' Berry, DFC), No. 122 Squadron (Squadron Leader Leon Prevot) and No. 154 Squadron (Squadron Leader Donald C. Carlson). The Wing flew a number of operations, including Circus 192, under what would have been Brothers' period in post.

In his autobiography, however, Group Captain Duncan-Smith, DFC, noted, 'For the next three weeks I led the Wing until Paddy Finucane was posted from Biggin Hill to take over as Wing Leader.'

It makes more sense for Duncan-Smith to have been 'made-up' into the role of Acting Wing Commander (Flying), while the time span mentioned in his biography is correct, against Brothers' posting which sat uncomfortably in the middle of the period between Wing Commander Powell's injury and 'Paddy' Finucane's appointment. Posting errors, even at such a high level, however, were not unheard of. One such example was the simultaneous posting of both Wing Commanders, E.H. Thomas, DFC, and R.H. Thomas, DSO, DFC, to the Hornchurch role, post-Dieppe. In Brothers' instance the 'posting' certainly would have got the Air Ministry off the hook as regards flying in the face of the agreement between Churchill and Dr Evatt as to who would command 457 Squadron in the south-west Pacific theatre.

Nominal Roll of No. 457 Squadron Pilots 16 June 1941–31 May 1942:

Squadron Leader Peter Malam Brothers, DFC, RAF	Squadron Commander
Flight Lieutenant Allan Laird 'Jake' Edy, DFC, RAAF	'B' Flight Commander, KIA 5.12.41
Flight Lieutenant John Albert Axel Gibson, DFC, RAF	'B' Flight Commander
Flight Lieutenant Kenneth E. 'Skeeter' James	'B' Flight Commander
Flight Lieutenant Harold Leslie 'Knockers' North, DFC, RAF	'A' Flight Commander KIA 1.5.42
Flight Lieutenant Raymond Harold Charles Sly	'B' Flight Commander DoW Malta USS *Wasp* 9.5.42
Flying Officer Francis Bruce Beale, RAAF	KIA 28.5.43 Darwin area
Pilot Officer F.B. Beak, RAAF	
Pilot Officer Douglas R. 'Doug' Edwards, RAAF	
Pilot Officer John G. Gould, RAAF	
Pilot Officer Brian Joseph Halse, RAAF	KIA 26.3.42
Pilot Officer F.D. Hamilton, RAAF	
Pilot Officer Ian S. Mackenzie, RAAF	
Pilot Officer Donald H. MacLean, RAAF	
Pilot Officer H. Meadows	
Pilot Officer John S. 'Snapper' Newton, RAAF	
Pilot Officer A.P. Peacock, RAAF	
Pilot Officer George G. Russell, RAAF	PoW 4.4.42
Pilot Officer Hartley V. Shearn	Temp 'B' Flight Commander, DFC 6.10.53 for Korea with No. 77 Sqn
Pilot Officer Warwick James Turner, RAAF,	D. flying accident 1.4.45 with No. 2 (F) OTU Australia
Pilot Officer Philip H. Watson, DFC, RAAF	

Sergeant Robert E. Anderson, RAAF	Wd with No. 41 Sqn 18.12.44
Sergeant Dormer G. Andrews, RAAF	PoW with No. 127 Sqn 3.11.42
Sergeant Edwin R. Bassett, RAAF	D. flying accident
Sergeant Ronald H. Bevan, RAAF	
Sergeant Allen Martin Blackburn, RAAF	D. flying accident 29.9.42
Sergeant Alfred Henry 'Harry' Blake, RAAF	KIA 28.5.43
Sergeant David l'Anson. Bloomfield, RAAF	KIA 28.3.42
Sergeant Robert K. Boyd, RAAF	Volunteered for service in the Far East
Sergeant Raymond Thomas Brewin, RAAF	KIA 29.11.41
Sergeant Arthur Bolwell Burgess, RAAF	KIA 4 4 42
Sergeant Thomas F. 'Tommy' Clark, RAAF	Wd. 28.6.43
Sergeant Creeswell, RAAF	
Sergeant C. Cumaley, RAAF	
Sergeant James George Edwards, RAAF	KIA 28.3.42
Sergeant Robert C. Ford, RAAF	
Sergeant Bernard Macolm Geissmann, RAAF	KIA with No. 452 Sqn 6.11.41
Sergeant Gordon Lindsay Charles 'Joe' Gifford, RAAF	KIA 2.5.43
Sergeant Clifford Gumblcy, RAAF	
Sergeant Richard Arthur George Halliday, RAAF	KIA 9.5.42
Sergeant William S. Hardwick, RAAF	
Sergeant Leslie J. Hart, RAAF	
Sergeant Norman V. Hobbs, RAAF	PoW with No. 266 Wing, Java, March 1942
Sergeant John R. Jenkins, RAAF	
Sergeant Robert J. Kenyon, RAAF	
Sergeant Bruce Little, RAAF	
Sergeant Russell McDonell, RAAF	KIA 8.3.42

Sergeant Frederick R. J. 'Darky' McDowell, RAAF

Sergeant Alexander C. McPherson, RAAF

Sergeant Ian S. Morse, RAAF

Sergeant Ormrod

Sergeant Marshall Edmund Parbery, RAAF   KIA 27.4.42

Sergeant Andrew Francis Peacock, RAAF   KIA 1.5.42

Sergeant Alexander J. Platen, RAAF

Sergeant Stuart W. Reilly, RAAF

Sergeant Norman Frederick Robinson,   KIA 6.7.43
RAAF

Sergeant William J. Smith, RAAF   KIA 9.5.42

Sergeant Reginald Stevens, RAAF   DFC 17.7.43, Bar 12.9.43, CO of
No. 3 Sqn RAAF

Sergeant (400740) Niel O. Thomas, RAAF   PoW as Plt Off with No. 127 Sqn
20.5.44

Sergeant Guy W. 'Glop' Underwood, RAF   PoW with No. 135 Sqn 26.2.42

Sergeant Rex W. Watson, RAAF

Sergeant Kevin J. Wyllie   PoW with No. 266 Wing Java,
March 1942

Nominal Roll of pilots passing through No. 457 Squadron for pre-operational training:

Pilot Officer William Friend, RAAF

Pilot Officer Alfred Glendinning, RAAF   later Flt Lt, DFC 23 April 1943

Pilot Officer Kirkman

Pilot Officer William McG 'Bill' Lockwood,   PoW with No. 242 Sqn March 1942
RCAF

Pilot Officer Peter William Lowe, RAF   KIA with No. 605 Sqn 15.2.42

Pilot Officer James I. McKay, RCAF

Pilot Officer Lockwood G. Munro, RAAF   later 'B' Flight Commander (1945)

Pilot Officer K.A. Murdock

Pilot Officer Mark Ernest Sheldon, RAAF	KIA with No. 75 Sqn 11.8.42
Pilot Officer Richard W. Winn, RAAF	PoW with No. 450 Sqn 14.1.43
Sergeant John Philip 'Phil' Adams, RAAF	KIA with No. 452 Sqn 26.9.43
Sergeant John G.S. 'Joe' Beckett, RAAF	
Sergeant Arthur Brown, RAF	KIA as Plt Off with No. 258 Sqn
Sergeant Arthur H. Clinch, RAAF	PoW with No. 33 Sqn 29.5.44
Sergeant Raife J. Cowan, RAAF	
Sergeant Alexander N. Cresswell, RAAF	
Sergeant John M. Emery, RAAF	
Sergeant Ronald Irvine Ferguson, RAAF	KIA with No. 11 Sqn 7.9.43
Sergeant Colin Vernon Finlay, RAAF	KIA with No. 185 Sqn 14.5.42
Sergeant John William Spencer Fletcher, RCAF	KIA with No. 185 Sqn 28.4.42
Sergeant Graham, RAF	
Sergeant M.B. Green	
Sergeant Paul Frederick Green, RAFVR	KIA 25.4.42
Sergeant John J. Harrison, RAAF	
Sergeant David J. Howe, RCAF	
Sergeant Hughes	
Sergeant Edgar Purton Jackson, RAAF	KIA with No. 452 Sqn 13.10.41
Sergeant Howard C. Lester, RAAF	Wd. with No. 185 Sqn 10.3.42
Sergeant Huon Tasman Nation, RAAF	D. flying accident No. 1 METS 23.10.42
Sergeant Oliver Ogle Ormrod, RAF, DFC	KIA as Plt Off with No. 185 Sqn 22.4.42
Sergeant John Robertson Ross, RAAF	KIA as Plt Off with No. 452 Sqn 20.10.42
Sergeant William J. Wilkinson, RAAF	No. 5 Sqdn, KIA with No. 452 Sqdn 7.9.41
Sergeant Williams, RAAF	
Sergeant William H. Wright, RAAF	

Chapter 12

A New Command: No. 602 Squadron

Brothers was posted to 602 (City of Glasgow) Squadron, arriving back at Redhill on 20 June 1942, in time for 'Paddy' Finucane to formally hand over the reins, 'That evening we all drove to the White Hart near Reigate where we gave Paddy, who had just been promoted as Wing Commander (Flying) Hornchurch Wing, a proper send-off.'

While leading No. 457 Squadron, Brothers had often been frustrated by his new squadron's apparent lack of discipline in the air and issues with aircraft recognition. Brothers cited two instances during Circus operations: 'On the way back, halfway across the Channel, there was no sign of Paddy and his chaps above us. All hell broke out on the radio – "look out Paddy, there's one behind you, blah, blah."' With the bombers nearly home, Brothers pulled away and radioed Finucane who gave his position as 'twenty miles in from Calais.' Brothers took his fighters in for the attack, 'we swept round up sun, saw a great melee of wings flashing; dived into this, and they were all bloody Spitfires'.

His actions in turning to give No. 602 Squadron assistance that they didn't need, cost Brothers a 'bollocking from the wing leader.'

On another occasion the Wing got split up on their return flight, 'We saw aircraft overhauling us, and someone said, "Aircraft following behind." I said, "Okay, keep an eye on them." Streaming home, they suddenly attacked us.'

During the melee Brothers identified a Spitfire diving down to attack him, 'We tangled around, and they were all Spits; they were 602'.

Not unnaturally, Brothers registered his annoyance in no uncertain terms. Now in charge of No. 602 Squadron, Brothers considered they needed tightening up, 'I rang Group, and said, "Would you make 602 Squadron non-operational whilst I teach them aircraft recognition and tactics?" I pulled them out of the line. They were all horrified, however, it taught them a bit of a lesson.'

Back on ops, Brothers' squadron flew with No. 402 Squadron on Rodeo 76, a sweep made with the Northolt Wing on 22 June. Two uneventful convoy patrols followed during the morning of 26 June. Meanwhile, at 1645 hours Brothers led them on a mission providing top cover to Circus 194, a raid on Le Havre made by a dozen Bostons. Thirty miles short of Etretat, the squadron was attacked by about twelve Fw 190s. Further attacks took place with combats down to sea level.

During the initial engagement Brothers damaged two Fw 190s west of Etretat, his combat report read:

'At 1720 hours on 26/6/42 I was Red 1 leading 602 Squadron as close escort for twelve Bostons, which were bombing Le Havre.

'About ten miles north of Etretat on the way home, the squadron was jumped from behind by about twelve Fw 190s. I turned to port and fired a full deflection shot at two Fw 190s flying in line astern, also turning, thus giving me a shot at their 'bellies'. Both cannon and machine guns were used. I observed strikes on both these a/c but no results were seen, so they are claimed as damaged.

'Having broken off combat and followed the main formation, I heard Yellow 1 call for assistance at about 1740 hours. I turned round and immediately saw several Fw 190s at sea level chasing Yellow 1.

'Before I got a shot in, Red 2, opened up and I saw one Fw 190 crash into the sea after he broke away.

'I fired a short burst at long range at two separate E/A, but they were too fast and got away. No results were observed. I used my cine camera gun.'
Officer Commanding 602 Squadron, Redhill
P.M. Brothers S/Ldr.

Sergeant A. Strudwick (Red 2) was one of those who turned back to Yellow 1's aid. He destroyed an Fw 190 about thirty miles north of Cap D'Antifer:

'We sighted three Fw 190s chasing one Spitfire, on our port side at almost sea level. The chase lasted for two to three minutes, then two of the E/A turned sharply to port. I selected the third E/A and followed it round in the turn. Opening fire with both cannon and machine gun at 250 yards.

'I observed cannon strikes on E/A's port mainplane and side of fuselage. It immediately flicked onto starboard wing and was skidding badly.'
(signed) A. Strudwick, Sgt.

'Shortly after Sergeant Strudwick broke away I saw the E/A, an Fw 190, crash into the sea.'
(signed) P.M. Brothers S/Ldr.

Sergeant Schaefer (Red 3) also joined in the attack, damaging an Fw 190 twenty to thirty miles north of Cap D'Antifer:

'As I drew near I saw two Fw 190s coming towards me, they turned left, apparently not seeing me. I was able to come in and do a quarter attack on the rear E/A at a distance of 400 yards. I gave a three second burst, then tightening my turn I was able to give him another three or four seconds burst (one cannon jammed). He went down low on the water, apparently well under control, but with black smoke issuing from around the cowling.'
(signed) Sgt Schaefer.

Flight Lieutenant Fifield (Yellow 3) claimed one Fw 190 damaged:

'On leaving the target after bombing, myself and Yellow 4 (P/O Rippon) were attacked by three Fw 190s. I broke to starboard into them as they were just about

300 yards astern. They in turn broke to port, presenting a slight deflection shot. I then gave the last one a three second burst with cannon and machine gun. Sgt Buley, who was Yellow 2 in the same squadron, observed an Fw 190 diving vertically down with a trail of brownish smoke coming from the underside and whitish grey smoke coming from the top engine cowling.'
(signed) F/Lt J. Fifield.

Flight Lieutenant Bocock, DFC, (*London Gazette*, 7 April 1942) destroyed an Fw 190 thirty miles north of Cap Griz Nez:

'I saw one Spitfire chased by three 190s with more behind down below to port, so turned to attack, calling up Red leader [Brothers] to cover my tail, but could not get closer than 800 yards or so of the three 190s which were about 300 yards behind Yellow 1, and slightly to the starboard of him.

'I fired a short burst of about one second at the right-hand E/A to make them break. I saw Red 1 on my right do the same, at the same time Yellow 1 turned hard port, followed by one E/A. I turned to port, climbed and then made a steep diving turn to cut off the single E/A and fired a short burst at him with the cannons and machine guns from the port quarter at about 250-300 yds before breaking onto one of the two other E/A; used all the rest of my ammunition (including two seconds of cannon) in one burst. I saw two H.E. cannon strikes on the fuselage just behind the cockpit and de Wilde strikes on the port wing and root. At the end of my attack, the E/A seemed to have slowed down considerably and was flying erratically.'
(signed) F/Lt Bocock.

Sergeant Morrell was posted as missing following the operation. Sergeant (1380942) Francis William Morrell, RAFVR, was the son of Henry John and Eleanor Mary Morrell, of Bushey Heath, Hertfordshire. He is remembered on the Runnymede Memorial, Panel 90. Morrell was 20-years-old.

On 28 June the squadron's first Spitfire IX arrived and was test flown by Brothers and a number of his more senior pilots. The squadron's ORB noting: 'Results were favourable and the pilots expected it to "beat-up" the Fw 190.'

During the following day the squadron flew on Kenley Wing's Circus 195, acting as target support for twelve Bostons bombing the Hazebrouck marshalling yards. No enemy air activity was encountered.

On 30 June Brothers led the squadron to Kenley, from where they operated until 8 July, flying uneventful scrambles, escorts and fighter patrols. It was at about this time that Brothers and his old friend Richard Atcherley, marked their reacquaintance; 'He and I celebrated in London, after which he insisted on lying flat on his back, in the "blackout?" in the middle of the road near Hyde Park Corner'.

He was approached by a 'bobby', who shone his torch on the Group Captain, lying prostrate with his 'scrambled-egg' cap on his chest, requesting, 'Do you mind just getting up and going home, Sir?'

To which Atcherley replied, 'Can't you see I am King George the Fifth lying in State?'

The pair made their way to their hotel in the small hours without attracting the further attention of the officers of the law, reporting for duty the following morning bright and breezy.

Back operating out of Redhill, the squadron flew as a part of the Kenley Wing on Circus 199 during the afternoon of 13 July. Together with the Biggin Hill Wing they acted as a diversion for twelve Bostons targeting marshalling yards at Boulogne.

Flying Officer Innes-Jones (flying BM182) was shot down by JG26, whose pilots claimed four Spitfires in the same action, two of them, Flight Lieutenant J.R.C. Tyre (flying BM650) and Flight Sergeant F.A. Duff (flying BL782) belonging to No. 401 Squadron. Of the casualties, Flying Officer (40769) Edgar Mostyn Innes-Jones, RNZAF, was 30-years-old. He has no known grave and is remembered on the Runnymede Memorial, Panel 114. Flight Lieutenant (C/1370) James Russell Courtney Tyre, RCAF, was the son of Cecil Watson Claire Tyre and Gertrude Ellen Tyre; husband of Frances M. Tyre, of Saanichton, Vancouver Island, British Columbia, Canada. He was 25-years-old and was buried in Abbeville Communal Cemetery Extension, Plot 7, Row A, Grave 5. Flight Sergeant (R/78406) Frank Alexander Duff, RCAF, was the son of Peter A. Duff and Esther J. Duff, of South River, Ontario, Canada. He was 23-years-old and was buried in Villeneuve St Georges Old Communal Cemetery, Grave 113B.

Meanwhile, the squadron was rested as orders were received to transfer to No. 14 Group's RAF Peterhead, Aberdeenshire, 'B' Flight initially operating out of Coastal Command's airfield at Dyce. Their new base had no running water, while sanitation was chemical and washing was communal.

The squadron flew to Martlesham on 16 July, surrendering their Spitfires to No. 416 Squadron, commanded by Squadron Leader Paul Webb, DFC. Meanwhile, they flew by Harrow to Peterhead where No. 416 Squadron's Spitfire Vb's awaited their arrival. The squadron's primary role was to fly defensive shipping patrols, while a number of scrambles were also made over the following weeks, but without sighting the enemy.

Grave news reached the squadron during the transfer. Wing Commander Finucane, DSO, DFC and two Bars, had been reported as missing-in-action while commanding the Hornchurch Wing. Hit by ground fire, Finucane ditched in the Channel and drowned: 'That Wednesday evening he should have attended a farewell party at Redhill where he would have been presented with a silver cigarette box. Instead it was forwarded to his father.'

It was devastating news but Brothers had to pick his men up and carry on as best he could.

The monotony of routine patrols was broken on 16 August, when eighteen of the squadron's Spitfires flew down to Biggin Hill, then also home to the USAAF No. 307 Pursuit Squadron. They made familiarization flights the following morning, before enduring the less than tactfully titled film 'Next of Kin'.

Brothers had already been briefed: '602 was to play a part in a major offensive', but as yet knew few of the exact details. Meanwhile, the squadron flew on a feint Rodeo to the French coast at 1520 hours, the real target being Rouen, which was bombed by a dozen Flying Fortresses.

As a further build-up to the main operation which was to take place on the following day, Brothers got permission to lead the Wing on a Rodeo over Dunkirk/ Cap Griz Nez on 18 August, Nos. 133 and 222 Squadrons providing top cover. Taking off at 1300 hours, the Wing crossed the French coast ten miles east of Dunkirk and flew west along the coastline at 21,000ft. The formation turned inland towards the Luftwaffe's fighter base at St Omer to, as Brothers put it, 'stir them up!'

The controller informed Brothers of two enemy formations taking off to answer their attack. Johnny Niven reported six Fw 190s of JG 26 approaching from below and the starboard quarter. In response Brothers ordered Yellow Section to peel off to make the attack. Flight Sergeant Gledhill, acting as No. 4, was caught slightly napping and his Spitfire (BL 937) was shot down, and he became a PoW.

Meanwhile, a formation of ten-plus Fw 190s came in to attack No. 222 Squadron. Both Brothers and a pilot from 222 Squadron fired at one enemy fighter which placed itself between the two squadrons.

Brothers claimed the Fw 190 as destroyed while flying over Griz Nez at 21,000ft. He fired a three second burst at 200 yards, expending eighty cannon shells and 320 machine-gun rounds:

'At 1400 hours on 18/8/42, I was leading 602 Squadron, with 222 Squadron to port above and 133 Squadron above them. When approaching, twelve to fifteen Fw 190s dived out of the sun on us from the port side. I turned into this attack, but could not get a shot at them. About thirty seconds later four Fw 190s flew in front of me in line astern. I fired a burst at No. 3 at 200 yards, seeing strikes, and he suddenly flicked onto his back and spiraled down. None of the four could see me as they were turning away and offering a belly shot.

'Shortly afterwards I saw a splash in the sea just off the coast between St. Inglevert and Cap Griz Nez, but I had lost sight of the Fw 190 because I was engaging the three who were left. They climbed away from me, and as we turned for home we were jumped by another four Fw 190s, but without result on either side. Camera exposed.'

(signed) P.M. Brothers S/Ldr, OC 602 Sqdn.

The New Zealander, Pilot Officer Davey, saw the Fw 190 strike the water and it disappeared without trace. Davey's Spitfire (AB370) was hit and spun down several thousand feet before he was able to gain control. He managed to make a forced-landing near Lympne.

Bounced by ten Fw 190s which came down from 4,000ft above their own formation, No. 222 Squadron had to concentrate on defending itself, which it did, but without being able to make a claim.

Meanwhile, Flight Lieutenant Blakeslee, DFC, (*London Gazette*, 14 September 1942) of No. 133 Squadron claimed an Fw 190 destroyed:

'I saw six Fw 190s, with four more some way behind them, approaching us from the south at about 18,000ft. I broke to the left with my section and making an orbit, came in behind these E/A. I fired at one of these from 300 yds range from dead astern and slightly above, giving a good three second burst with cannon and machine gun. I saw an explosion in the cockpit of the E/A, caused by cannon shells. The E/A went into a spin emitting smoke. A few seconds later Red 2 (F/O Sperry) saw the pilot bail out and the aircraft, which was still spinning, crash into the sea just off Sangatte.'
(signed) F/Lt Blakesee (USA).

Brothers was still going over the day's events when he was informed that the base had gone into shutdown. Summoned to the Intelligence Office, he joined the tight group of COs and senior flight commanders to receive their briefing. At 2100 hours a wider briefing was held, addressed by the Station Commander, Group Captain J.R. Hallings-Pott, DSO, AFC; they were to take part in a Combined Operations mission the following day. Codenamed Operation Jubilee, the raid was on the French port of Dieppe. The plan was to land 4,000 Canadian troops to secure the harbour and put its installations and the neighbouring airfield out of action.

The squadron was then briefed by Wing Commander E.H. 'Tommy' Thomas, DFC, while Intelligence Officer, Squadron Leader B.E. le Torre, outlined the station's role. Thomas would lead the Wing, which included Nos. 165, 222 and 602 Squadrons.

Air cover would be maintained throughout the raid. Pilots running short of fuel were directed to land at either Friston or Beachy Head. A small landing strip would be available behind Dieppe for those who needed to make a forced-landing: 'We were informed that there would be a vehicle waiting for us and that they would take us back to the port from where the navy would get us out.'

On 19 August the squadron was awoken at 0315 hours, over an hour before the pilots took breakfast. Gathering his pilots at dispersal, Brothers gave them a further update. They were to fly to the north of the main assault vessels and the harbour: 'Once over the target, split into your sections and fly in wide circles, keeping an eye out for any enemy activity,' adding, 'this will most likely come from the north.'

Waiting at dispersal, Brothers' pilots grabbed a bite to eat before getting ready for take off: 'Our first patrol was scheduled for 0530 hours. We were to land, refuel, and if necessary, rearm, and then be back in the air for a second 'show' at 0900 hours. A third op was scheduled for 1130 hours, and the last mission was to be in the air at 1630 hours.'

Airborne at 0550 hours they were followed minutes later by No. 222 Squadron and 307th Pursuit Squadron, USAAF. Heading south, the Biggin Hill squadrons picked up Nos. 133 and 401 Squadrons over Lympne. Brothers led the Spitfires towards the coast at Beachy Head seeing the sun rise over France. The first phase of the raid was already in progress. Below were the support ships and a long line of troop barges, which stretched across the open waters, pointing towards their destination. As the formation drew to within twenty miles from Dieppe, they could see the telltale flashes of explosions and gun muzzles, the enemy turning their guns on the landing craft.

The Biggin Hill squadrons were soon in action. No. 401 Squadron's combat claims for the Dieppe Raid, 19 August included:

Squadron Leader L.B. Hodson	Do 217
Flight Lieutenant James Whitham	Fw 190
Pilot Officer Stanley Cyril Cosburn	Two Do 217s damaged (awarded the DFC, *London Gazette*, 15.1.43)
Pilot Officer Harold Andrew Westhaver	Fw 190
Pilot Officer G.B. 'Scotty' Murray	Fw 190
Flight Sergeant Robert Mehew 'Zip' Zobell	Do 17 (wounded)
Sergeant Donald Robert 'Don' Morrison, DFM	Fw 190

During the day's operations No. 401 Squadron lost three Spitfires: Pilot Officer Donald Robert 'Don' Morrison, DFM (*London Gazette*, 30 June 1942), destroyed an Fw 190, but bailed out of Spitfire BS119 following combat (rescued) and was later awarded the DFC; Sergeant L.J. Armstrong (flying BS107) was shot down by an Fw 190 and made a PoW; Flight Sergeant M.H. Buckley (flying BS157) was killed-in-action, shot down by an Fw 190. Flight Sergeant (R/66343) Morton Haist Buckley, RCAF, was the son of Morton Major Buckley and Gladys Haist Buckley, of Fonthill, Ontario, Canada. He was 22-years-old and is remembered on the Runnymede Memorial, Panel 103. Another of the squadron's casualties was Sergeant (613110) Henry Morton, RAF, who died of wounds on 14 October. Morton was buried in Cirencester Cemetery, Plot 10 Church of England, Row O, Grave 5.

Meanwhile, Flight Sergeant Robert M. 'Zip' Zobell, RCAF, was wounded in combat, but claimed a Do 17 into which he fired all of his ammunition.

No. 133 (Eagle) Squadron was one of three American squadrons to take part in Operation Jubilee. Acting Squadron Leader D.J.M. 'Don' Blakeslee, DFC (USA) led the squadron on their first offensive at 0720 hours, during which they made the following claims:

Acting Squadron Leader D.J.M. 'Don' Blakeslee, DFC	Fw 190
Pilot Officer W.H. Baker	Fw 190
Flight Sergeant Dixie Alexander	Fw 190 probably destroyed

The raid quickly fell into confusion with the land forces taking terrible casualties. The air offensive fared little better.

No. 222 Squadron had been detailed to fly its first operation of the day in support of No. 602 Squadron, but in the event their missions soon moved out of synchronization. Reading through the pages of No. 222 Squadron's ORB indicates that they were over Dieppe between 0620 and 0700 hours, while their second patrol was to provide cover for the embarkation of troops at 1015 hours. Their third operation was made between 1300 and 1430 hours to cover the withdrawal. Finally, between 1700 and 1820 hours they provided cover as the last vessels made their way back, closing on Beachy Head. They patrolled but made no combat claims, although during this latter patrol Sergeant Evans' aircraft was damaged in combat.

Meanwhile, patrolling from south to north, No. 602 Squadron operated with one section at 10,000ft, the remaining two stepped down to 8,000ft. Two Fw 190s were sighted at 8,000ft over Dieppe by Flight Lieutenant Niven, who led his wingman, Pilot Officer Sampson, in going for the one on the right, Niven the other. As the enemy pulled away from their strafing, they flew straight through the Spitfire's gun sights.

Pilot Officer R.W.F. Sampson (Yellow 2), who had seen the enemy first and called out the warning, claimed one Fw 190 damaged at 0635 hours, firing ninety-six cannon and 120 machine-gun rounds at 400 yards:

'I followed Yellow 1, turning with E/A starboard. I saw Yellow 1 pick out the port aircraft so I took the starboard aircraft and delivered a short burst of one second each of cannon and machine gun. The E/A went into a spiral to starboard, diving down towards Dieppe emitting very thick white smoke.'
(signed) R.W.F. Sampson PO.

Meanwhile, Brothers destroyed an Fw 190. Thankfully, No. 602 Squadron escaped casualties during this first operation.

As the Spitfires of No. 602 Squadron ground to a halt at around 0730 hours, the pilots undid their harness straps and climbed down off the wings, while the riggers, fitters and armourers quickly got to work. Following the usual routine, the aircraft were checked over, refuelled and rearmed, ready for the next operation.

The pilots were buoyant at debriefing, the squadron's ORB recording the mission as 'a walk over'.

Brothers gave the next briefing while his pilots grabbed a cuppa and bite to eat out of hot-boxes provided at dispersals. The squadron was to be in the air again at 0830 hours, flying at 4–5,000ft to the south of the armada, which was by then stretched out some six miles off the French coast. Their role was to hunt for the expected bomber attacks.

For operational reasons, however, their take-off was delayed by over one and a half hours before they finally got the order to patrol in the company of No. 133 Squadron.

Before taking off on their second operation, Brothers gave a final briefing, adding: 'And remember, the Navy will fire at anything flying under 8,000ft, so be particularly careful when approaching convoys!'

During their second patrolling sweep, Pilot Officer Sampson reported sighting three Do 217s from KG 2 which appeared to be heading towards the harbour. Brothers gave the 'Tally-ho!' One was attacked by Bocock, Niven took on another and Sampson the furthest.

Flight Lieutenant E.P.W. Bocock (Blue 1) claimed one of two Fw 190s that had got onto his tail as damaged, having out-turned it and put a burst into its tail, Marryshow damaging the other. During a subsequent attack he claimed a Do 217E destroyed just inland of Dieppe at 1,500ft, firing 310 cannon and 1,240 machine-gun rounds:

> 'I managed to keep my sight on target, and hit the Fw 190 low on port side of fuselage with a cannon shell, seeing a puff of brown smoke and resultant blackish-brown trail; the E/A dived away inland jinking violently.
>
> 'Later, I saw several Do 217Es attempting to dive bomb shipping. I headed one off and opened fire with cannons and machine guns from about 30 degrees port quarter at 400 yards, closing to line astern at 250-200 yds. I hit E/A in port engine and fuselage with cannon shells, and dorsal gun turret and pilot's cockpit with de Wilde machine gun ammunition [short bursts of up to twelve seconds]. A stream of oil came from the port engine; the pilot feathered that airscrew as he flew. The engine was giving off a thick smoke trail, and the E/A lost speed very quickly, eventually crash-landing fifteen miles S.E. of Dieppe.' (signed) F/Lt E.P.W. Bocock.

Sergeant P. Hauser (Blue 2) claimed one Do 217E destroyed five miles inland from Dieppe at 4,000ft, expending 160 cannon, 640 machine-gun rounds:

> 'I then saw a Do 217E ahead of me and slightly below. I got dead astern of the E/A and fired three bursts totaling about eight seconds with cannon and machine gun, the range being between 300-400 yds. The E/A crashed into a small wooded area.' (signed) Sgt P. Hauser.

Flying Officer Rippon (Blue 3) claimed a Do 217 and a Ju 88 damaged, firing 280 cannon and 1,120 machine-gun rounds:

> 'Sighted Do 217E [at 2,000ft] flying south-east, west of Dieppe. I reported to Blue 1, F/Lt Bocock, who turned to attack. E/A turned to port and dived below cloud, Blue Section following. Below cloud I saw further Do 217E to port of first, so I left latter to Blue 1 and 2 and attacked the second one from astern as he dived away, opening fire [eight second burst] at 400 yds. Saw strikes on port mainplane from which a large piece flew off. Was then attacked by two Fw 190s and had to break off engagement.'

Flight Lieutenant John B. Niven (Yellow 1) damaged a Do 217, firing a six second burst (120 cannon, 600 machine-gun) at 400 yards:

> 'I attacked from quarter astern, using cannon and machine gun, and broke away when my cannon had finished. All return fire from the Dornier ceased after about three seconds; it was in a gentle dive with brown smoke pouring from its port engine. This is confirmed by P/O Sampson, Yellow 2.' (signed) John B. Niven F/Lt.

Sampson (Yellow 2) was able to claim two Do 217s damaged, having fired 120 cannon and 1,320 machine-gun rounds at 200 yards closing to 50 yards:

'Yellow 1 reported two Do 217s flying in a SW direction about 2,000ft above. The section climbed to attack as they turned to port and I picked out the rear E/A, giving him two long bursts of cannon and machine gun. I observed strikes on the port wing near the port engine and saw petrol flowing out.'

Sampson had been distracted by return fire and had opened fire too early. Johnny Niven called out a warning that two Fw 190s were on his tail and Sampson broke off the engagement.

Fifteen minute later, at 1115 hours, Sampson engaged a second Do 217:

'Yellow 1 made an attack from starboard, breaking to port and I went in after him, firing three second burst at 300 yards and then a further four second burst of cannon and machine-gun [with] strikes on the main fuselage and port wing root.'
(signed) P/O R.W.F. Sampson.

Sergeant W. Lethbridge damaged one Do 217, firing a five second burst of 105 cannon, 400 machine-gun rounds at 100 yards. [1120 hours]:

'When first seen, Do 217 was 500ft below and flying in the opposite direction to me. I turned and flew into line astern with him. I held my fire until close; I saw bullets strike tail assembly.'
(signed) Sgt W. Lethbridge.

Attacking behind Blue Section, Sergeant C.A. Booty (Yellow 2) came in for the attack, probably destroying a Bf 109 off Nieuport at 6,000ft:

'When I saw Me 109E below and turning to port, I half rolled into attack firing cannon and machine gun [two to three second bursts at 200 to 100 yards]. I saw pieces fly off from the wing root: he hung on his turn, slowly turning on to his back. F/Lt Williams, DFC, circled behind this E/A and had his windscreen covered with glycol.'
[Not signed by Booty]

Sergeant W.J. Loud (Yellow 3) claimed one Do 217 destroyed (shared with his No. 2, Sergeant Caldecott) and one Do 217 damaged. Total rounds fired 120 cannon and 600 machine-gun rounds [at 1100 hours and two miles north of Dieppe]:

'I climbed to 9,000ft, then turned onto the tail of one of them, opening fire [five second burst] at about 500 yds with cannon. I fired all my cannon shells into it and saw the port side of the tail break off, and the port engine catch fire. I was then about 100 yds from it, so I continued firing with machine gun. The Do 217 then went into a spiral dive towards the sea. My No. 2 then fired a burst at it, and it crashed into the sea. As I broke away one of the crew bailed out [Bocock reporting seeing the aircraft catch fire before rolling onto its back, three crew members bailing out as it dived vertically into the sea].

'A little later I attacked another Do 217 from twenty degrees above and directly behind. I opened fire [eight second burst] at 350 yds with machine gun, gradually closing in. I observed strikes on the fuselage and upper wing root.'
(signed) W.J. Loud (Sgt).

Sergeant W.E. Caldecott, flying as Yellow 4, [1100 hours, half a mile off Dieppe at 7,000ft] claimed one Do 217E destroyed (shared with Sgt Loud), firing 140 cannon and 560 machine-gun rounds:

'Yellow 3 (Sgt Loud) made a climbing turn to port to attack the nearest Do 217 and I followed climbing a little higher and dived down on top of my leader, opening fire with cannon at about 500yds with a two second burst. The E/A went into a gentle dive, which I followed and opened fire with cannon and machine gun at about 400yds for three to four seconds. The port engine burst into flames and one of the crew bailed out. F/Lt Bocock observed the plane crash into the sea.'
(signed) W.E. Caldecott, Sgt.

Meanwhile, Sergeant Julian Marryshow (Red 4) had shouted out a warning to Bocock (Blue 1), allowing him to avoid the fire of one Fw 190 and momentarily get onto the tail of his second would-be assailant. Marryshow claimed the first Fw 190 as damaged, firing forty cannon and 160 machine-gun rounds in a two second burst at 250-300 yards [1100 hours, five miles N.E. of Dieppe at 8,000ft.]:

'Red 3 and myself broke to attack two Fw 190s. I managed to get in a short deflection shot at one. Bits came off his plane and he peeled away; there were about three more Fw 190s coming down on my tail.'
(signed) Julian Marryshow.

As Brothers formed the squadron up, a formation of Fw 190s were seen. The Spitfires turned to engage but the enemy declined battle.

The patrol had lasted for two hours, and due to the additional fuel expended during combat, the Spitfires were forced to land at Friston. Pilot Officer Goodchap (flying BL932) crash-landed in France and became a PoW. The ORB's overall take on the mission was recorded thus: 'Very good show this, for they milled around right in the thick of it.'

During an engagement timed at 1100 hours, No. 165 Squadron, flying with the Wing recorded the following 'kills':

Squadron Leader Hallowes	Do 217, Do 217 damaged
Acting Squadron Leader J.L. Herbert	Do 217
Flight Lieutenant Ernest W. Campbell-Colquhoun	Do 217 (shared)
Pilot Officer L.R. Disney	Ju 88 damaged (shared)
Pilot Officer Headley C. Richardson	Ju 88 damaged (shared)
Pilot Officer Penderson B. Warren	Do 217 (shared)
Pilot Officer D. Warren	Do 217 (shared)

Meanwhile the pilots of No. 133 Squadron had also engaged the enemy at around 1100 hours, making the following claims:

Squadron Leader Blakeslee, DFC – damaged two Fw 190s and a Do 217
Flight Lieutenant E.G. Brettell – destroyed an Fw 190
Pilot Officer R.N. Beaty – Do 217 and Fw 190 damaged
Pilot Officer Eric Doorly – Do 217 damaged
Pilot Officer Don S. Gentile   Ju 88 and Fw 190
Pilot Officer Richard G. Gudmundsen – Do 217
Pilot Officer George B. Sperry – Fw 190 destroyed
Pilot Officer G.G. Wright – Fw 190 damaged.

No. 133 Squadron's third operation began at 1225 hours, when they made the following claims:

Acting Squadron Leader Blakeslee, DFC – Fw 190 probably destroyed
Flight Sergeant Dixie Alexander – Do 217
Flying Officer James C. Nelson – Do 217 probable

During their fourth operation No. 133 Squadron made only the one claim:

Flight Sergeant Alexander – Fw 190 probably destroyed

The squadron's pilots distinguished themselves throughout the whole day's operations, resulting in a number of gallantry awards.

Acting Flight Lieutenant Brettell was awarded the DFC, *London Gazette*, 29 September 1942:

> 'Acting Flight Lieutenant Edward Gordon BRETTELL (61053), Royal Air Force Volunteer Reserve, No. 133 (Eagle) Squadron.

> 'This officer has participated in 111 sorties over enemy occupied territory. He has always displayed the greatest keenness to engage the enemy. On one occasion he was wounded in combat and, on recovery, he resumed operational flying with renewed zest. He is an excellent flight commander.'

Brettell was later shot down and taken as a PoW, only to be murdered on 29 May 1944 by the Gestapo following The Great Escape.

Another of those to earn a gallantry award was Pilot Officer Baker who was awarded the DFC, *London Gazette*, 2 October 1942:

'Pilot Officer William Henry BAKER (108626), Royal Air Force Volunteer Reserve, No. 133 (Eagle) Squadron.

'Pilot Officer Baker has been engaged in numerous operational sorties over enemy territory. Throughout he has displayed the greatest keenness and enthusiasm for operational work and his courage and determination have been an example of a high order. Pilot Officer Baker has destroyed two and probably destroyed two other enemy aircraft.'

Meanwhile, No. 602 Squadron's third operation of the day began at 1300 hours, the ORB noting: 'Squadron went off again almost on empty stomach. Gave them sandwiches and lemonade. Wonder what they'd do on beer and oysters!'

The squadron's mission was to cover the evacuation against heavy raids mounted by Bf 110s and bomb carrying Fw 190s. At his briefing Brothers reiterated his earlier cautionary note: 'Keep clear of the ships because they have been bombed by enemy single-seater aircraft and will fire at anything approaching them, regardless of your altitude.'

As the Spitfires approached the Royal Navy vessels, it was clear that they were under attack, the ack-ack gunners putting up a fierce fire in what the Squadron's ORB recorded as a 'shaky do'.

While patrolling five miles off Dieppe, Johnny Niven, Yellow 1, spotted two Fw 190s only 100 yards ahead and climbing away from their bombing run. Niven and his No. 2, Pilot Officer Sampson, attacked the fighters which crossed their flight path, both setting their targets on fire.

Flight Lieutenant John B. Niven (flying BM451) claimed one Fw 190 damaged (at 1350 hours) firing twenty cannon rounds:

'After about fifteen minutes patrol I observed a number of Fw 190s (six plus) to the south. I attacked a pair of them which were slightly separated from the rest. I selected the port a/c and approached from the port beam, eventually closing to dead astern. I held my fire till the last minute and then opened up from 100 yds [five second cannon burst], throttling back to save colliding with him. I hit him all over the wings and cockpit region with cannon shells, and he turned onto his left side and fell away slowly, with bits coming off. My own aircraft was then shot to bits [fuel tank ruptured by ack-ack from one of the RN vessels] and I flew over the ships and bailed out.'
(signed) John B. Niven F/Lt.

Brothers orbited the dingy until Niven was picked up by the RN's motor-launch ML193, before being transferred to Landing Craft F6. Once ashore he was taken to

Brighton Municipal Hospital with an ankle injury. Niven returned to the squadron three days later. Pilot Officer J.B. Niven, RAFVR, had earlier been awarded the DFC (*London Gazette*, 15 May 1942):

> 'This officer has taken part in seventy operational sorties and he has destroyed two and probably destroyed a further two hostile aircraft. He has displayed ability and courage, setting a fine example to his fellow pilots.'

Niven continued to fly on combat sorties and was awarded a Bar to the DFC, announced in the *London Gazette*, 1 December 1944.

Sampson (Yellow 2) claimed one Fw 190 destroyed, expending 100 cannon and 300 machine-gun rounds:

> 'I was on the left of Yellow 1 and observed strikes on one Fw 190 from, I imagine, Yellow 1. I opened up at the other aircraft with a three second burst of cannon and machine gun, and closed to about 150 yards and fired from about thirty degrees for two seconds with cannon and machine gun. I observed cannon strikes on the engine and cockpit and the machine went into the sea near the ships, shedding pieces as it went down and apparently on fire.'
> (signed) R.W.F. Sampson.

Two Spitfires were lost, with Pilot Officer Goodchap taken as a PoW.

No. 602 Squadron's ORB noted: 'Cold luncheon revived the boys and they are ready for more fun – such as it is. Score to date for Squadron – four destroyed, and ten damaged for the loss of two pilots and two planes.'

No. 602 Squadron's fourth patrol, a sweep out over the Channel, began at 1700 hours, lasting an hour, on return from which they were stood down. That evening Brothers took the pilots to London's West End to wind down at the Chez Nina, Denman Street. They had plenty to celebrate.

The Press coverage of the air operations boasted: 'More than 600 sorties flown.' 'Tremendous Air Battle – Many German Aircraft Destroyed.'

The headlines steered away from the terrible losses sustained by the land forces, mainly Canadians.

A summary of the other squadrons flying with Brothers' No. 602 Squadron is included to help give the wider picture as they would have seen it.

No. 222 Squadron made no combat claims during the day's operations, although their CO, Squadron Leader Oxspring, (on secondment from No. 72 Squadron) was awarded a Bar to his DFC.

Acting Squadron Leader Robert Wardlow Oxspring's award was announced in the *London Gazette*, 15 September 1942:

> 'Acting Squadron Leader Robert Wardlow OXSPRING, DFC (40743), No. 72 Squadron – temporarily seconded to command No. 222 Squadron.

'This squadron commander has rendered much valuable service. His skill, whether in attacks on the enemy's ground targets and shipping or in air combat, has been of a high order. He has destroyed at least seven enemy aircraft.'

Meanwhile awards were also made to No. 401 Squadron pilots:

Acting Flight Lieutenant Whitham, DFC, *London Gazette*, 15 September 1942.

'Acting Flight Lieutenant James WHITHAM (Can./J.15281), Royal Canadian Air Force, No. 401 (RCAF) Squadron.

'This officer has completed a large number of sorties over enemy occupied territory. He is an excellent flight commander whose fine fighting qualities have been well illustrated when leading his section in attacks on the enemy's targets. Besides his good work in the air, Flight Lieutenant Whitham is a tireless worker on the ground and has proved a source of inspiration to all.'

Pilot Officer Murray, DFC, *London Gazette*, 25 September 1942.
'Pilot Officer George Bremner MURRAY (Can/J.15476), Royal Canadian Air Force, No. 401 (RCAF) Squadron.

'Pilot Officer Murray has carried out numerous sorties. He is an excellent leader whose resource and skill in action have proved inspiring. He has set a praiseworthy example to others.'

Squadron Leader Hodson, DFC, *London Gazette*, 29 September 1942.
'Squadron Leader Keith Louis Bate HODSON (Can/C.807), Royal Canadian Air Force, No. 401 (RCAF) Squadron.

'This officer has participated in a large number of sorties. He is a skilful pilot, whose personal example has inspired the squadron he commands. Much of the success it has achieved can be attributed to Squadron Leader Hodson's excellent leadership.'

No 307 Pursuit Squadron lost Lieutenant Wright killed-in-action, while Lieutenant Torvea was shot down and taken as a PoW. However, the squadron was able to make its first claims against the enemy, with Captain Robertson and Lieutenant John White being credited with an Fw 190 destroyed and an Fw 190 probably destroyed, while Lieutenant Whisonant damaged another.

Meanwhile, back with No. 602 Squadron's deployment, Brothers got permission to make a fighter sweep inland of Dieppe on 20 August before the squadron transferred back north, but the Luftwaffe, stretched by the previous day's combats could not be persuaded to take off, 'Below we could see debris, while smoke rose over the harbour.' Later that day the squadron flew north back to Peterhead.

A party was held in the officer's mess where the previous day's successes were celebrated. Pilot Officer Goodchap's fate, however, remained unknown and this must have put a damper on events.

The following weeks saw a return to the previous routine with occasional convoy escort and patrols, while the base was visited by a number of senior officers including the AOC No. 14 Group, Air Vice-Marshal R. Collishaw, CB, DSO, OBE, DSO, DFC, and AOC-in-C, Air Chief Marshal Sir Sholto Douglas, KCB, MC, DFC, accompanied by AOC, Air Vice-Marshal R. Collishaw. The most likely reason for these top-level visits, other than to discuss with Brothers his squadron's part in the Dieppe Raid.

While the squadron's role in providing air cover for the raid had proved successful, Brothers was able to voice his opinion on the air operation's shortcomings. Little did he then know, but his tactical savvy had already been noted and that he was destined for a very important role within Fighter Command.

Over the following few weeks there would be little activity beyond the regular aerial reconnaissance missions flown by the enemy, but which had to be countered by the Spitfire VIs.

On 10 September, No. 164 Squadron's Spitfires arrived to take over duties at Peterhead. They surrendered their Spitfire VIs to No. 602 Squadron which was posted to Skeabrae and Sumburgh, with a section from 'B' Flight being detached to Skatsa. Their new role was to protect Scapa Flow.

Here, their first taste of action came on 16 September, Flight Sergeant J.F. Kistruck and Sergeant G.F. Emes were scrambled and vectored onto an He 111, which had bombed the Fair Isle. In a pursuit which took them about 100 miles out to sea, both pilots expended all of their ammunition.

Flight Sergeant Kistruck (Blue 1) claimed one He 111 damaged (shared):

'Delivered quarter attack from starboard 150 yds closing to 50 yds. E/A was at 50ft. Blue 2 observed hits on rear gun position and fuselage. Believed rear gunners put out of action; rear gun stationary and red patch beside gun position. Oil running from starboard engine to trailing edge.'
(signed) F/Sgt J.F. Kistruck.

Sergeant Emes, (Blue 2) made four passes, firing at 175 – 20 yards, 'observing strikes along the fuselage and starboard engine, on pilot's cockpit and port mainplane', and claiming the He 111 as damaged at 50ft down to sea level (shared). This was the last of the squadron's combat victories under Brothers' command, as on 2 October he was posted away as Wing Commander (Flying), RAF Tangmere, to coordinate the wing's offensive role.

Flight Lieutenant E.P.W. Bocock, DFC, assumed command, pending the arrival of former Battle of Britain pilot, Squadron Leader Michael F. Beytagh, on 5 October.

While Pete's time with the squadron had been fairly brief, he had once again displayed his supreme abilities as a commander and tactician.

A Provisional List of Pilots who flew with No. 602 Squadron, 20 June – 2 October 1942:

Squadron Leader Peter Malam Brothers, DFC	Commander. Later Air Commodore, CBE, DSO, Bar to the DFC
Squadron Leader A.C. Stewart	Supernumary Squadron Leader
Flight Lieutenant E.P.W. Bocock, DFC	
Flight Lieutenant J.S. Fifield	
Flight Lieutenant J.B. Niven, DFC	Later Squadron Leader, Bar to the DFC 1.12.44 (CO of 602)
Flight Lieutenant Williams, DFC	
Flying Officer E.M. Innes-Jones	
Flying Officer E.D.M. Rippon	
Pilot Officer P.D. Davey	
Pilot Officer R.P.R. De-la-Poype	
Pilot Officer J.R. Dennehey	
Pilot Officer M.F. Goodchap	PoW 19.8.42
Pilot Officer G. Gray	
Pilot Officer R.W.F. Sampson	
Pilot Officer C.R. Tait	
Flight Sergeant K.D. Gledhill	
Sergeant L. Adkins	
Sergeant C.A. Booty	
Sergeant D.J. Buley	
Sergeant W.E. Caldecott	
Sergeant G.F. Emes	
Sergeant P.L. Hauser	
Sergeant A. Irvine	
Sergeant Hanscom	
Sergeant W.V. Jones	
Sergeant J.F. Kistruck	
Sergeant W.U. Lethbridge	
Sergeant W.J. Loud	
Sergeant J. Marryshow	
Sergeant Francis William Morrell	KIA 26.6.42
Sergeant B.A. Schaefer	
Sergeant S.B.A. Smith	
Sergeant F.S. Sorge	
Sergeant A. Strudwick	
Sergeant A.J. Tysowski	
Sergeant D.L. Warr	
Sergeant W.T. Whitmore	

Pilots Temporarily Posted to No. 602 Squadron
Pilot Officer S.O. Kelly
Pilot Officer R.O. Mitterling
Pilot Officer O. O'Brien
Pilot Officer F.M. Strole
Sergeant E.H. Francis
Sergeant Nordstrand
Sergeant J.G. Sanderson

Chapter 13

Wing Commander (Flying) Tangmere Wing

In October 1942, Brothers, already identified as one of the RAF's outstanding fighter tacticians, was appointed Wing Commander (Flying), taking over the Tangmere Wing, formerly led by Douglas Bader. Shot down, probably by 'friendly' fire, Bader had been taken as a PoW on 9 August. Wing Commander Don Finlay, DFC, had held the post as a stopgap until 14 August, when Group Captain Clifford Anthony 'Paddy' Woodhouse, DFC, took over the helm. During 1940-41, when multiple RAF fighter squadrons flew offensive patrols over enemy occupied Europe, it was the most senior CO who assumed command, although there are many stories of the more experienced junior officers leading operations. Under the new Wing system a Wing Commander (Flying) was appointed. He had to be able to think clearly and quickly under extreme pressure, as the safety of the entire Wing depended on his judgement. Brothers considered the role at Tangmere as 'one of the best jobs in Fighter Command'.

Tangmere lies three miles to the east of Chichester, under the Goodwood Downs, which could be a hazard for those using the secondary north-south runway. The main runway, which lay east-west, lined up roughly with Chichester Cathedral's spire. At 270ft, this was both a useful landmark and a potential danger.

Under Douglas Bader, the Wing, known as the 'Green Line Bus', had composed of Nos. 616, 610 and 145 Squadrons. Since his loss the squadrons had been shuffled about, the new line-up included Nos. 485 (RNZAF) and 165 Squadrons, with No. 610 Squadron flying operations from February 1943. Commanded by Squadron Leader Hallowes, DFM and Bar, who had taken over just prior to the Dieppe Raid, No. 165 Squadron was posted to Tangmere on 1 November 1942.

No. 165 Squadron flew on a Circus operation on 8 November, providing rear cover for Flying Fortress bombers targeting Lille. Pilot Officer (118532) George Cruise Griffin, RAFVR, was killed during the operation when his Spitfire was hit by flak and plunged into the sea seven miles off South Foreland, the squadron's first casualty. Griffin was buried in Oulton Franciscan Cemetery, Solihull, Section G, Grave 462.

Meanwhile, Squadron Leader H.J. Hallowes claimed one Fw 190 as damaged, the combat being timed at 1233 hours:

'An Fw 190 sighted south of Dunkirk attacking one Fortress which was straggling. Red Section dived from 25,000ft to 13,000ft to attack. The Fw was turning in to carry out a quarter attack when I opened fire from approximately 400 yards using quarter attack. After a burst of two seconds, hits were observed in the region of the cockpit of the Fw 190 on the port side, Red Section were then attacked by two Fw 190s from above and behind'.

Hallowes attacked two of the Fw 190s that were on Red 4's tail, doing enough to put them off their aim. Meanwhile, Sergeant Keating engaged several Fw 190s, observing strikes, but was unable to make a positive claim.

On 14 and 18 November, Brothers detailed No. 165 Squadron to fly on two diversionary sweeps in the Cherbourg area.

Meanwhile, on 6 December they took part in Circus 241, acting as rear support for a raid on the Lille Fives Loco Works. Six days later the squadron made a diversionary sweep in the Cherbourg area for Circus 244, a raid by seventy-two Fortresses and eighteen Liberators, targeting the aircraft park at Romilly. On landing the Spitfires were quickly turned around to provide rear support for the formation's return.

Christmas Eve saw an open party in the sergeant's mess, the roles being reversed the following day, when an excellent meal was provided and, 'though the service was inexpert, it was enthusiastic.' Brothers arranged for an afternoon sing song in the station's theatre followed by a Variety Show and a dance in the evening.

The year ended on something of a damp squib for Brothers who, on 30 December, commanded the Wing on Circus 245. Discovering a fracture in his oxygen pipe, he was obliged to hand over to Squadron Leader Hallowes.

On 2 January 1943, No. 485 (RNZAF) Squadron began operating out of Tangmere's satellite airfield at Westhampnett, having recently transferred out of No. 12 Group, where they flew out of Kingscliffe. Rejoining frontline operations, they operated with both the Tangmere and Appledore Wings.

On the following day Wing Commander Brothers was at the head of the Wing on Circus 247 to Abbeville airfield. It seemed that he was dogged with bad luck and was forced to hand over to Flight Lieutenant E.W. Colquhoun due to oil pressure issues.

During the Wing's second operation, Brothers led Nos. 165 and 485 Squadrons on Rodeo 142, an uneventful swept in over the Somme estuary, flying out over Wimereux.

On 4 January, Brothers attended a Group conference where he learnt that No. 602 Squadron, which had missed out on the previous ops due to practice for its new role, would train as night-fighters on evenings with a full moon, while continuing to fly daylight operations for the remainder of the month. This was far from ideal and Brothers voiced his opinion, but to no avail.

During the early afternoon of 9 January, Brothers commanded the Wing as top cover on Circus 248 to Le Touquet. Six Fw 190s were seen over Abbeville, Brothers leading the chase, but it soon became obvious that they could not be overhauled and he reluctantly gave the order to break off the pursuit. This may have been the occasion mentioned by Wing Commander Duncan-Smith, DFC, who recalled in his biography tagging along as Brothers' No. 2 on a sweep while a staff officer at Fighter Command, 'I had a Spitfire V and made full use of it, I visited Peter Brothers, one of the Command's most successful pilots and Wing Leaders at Tangmere, persuading him to let me fly as his number two'.

On his return to Fighter Command, Duncan-Smith was given a proverbial 'rocket' for taking an unnecessary risk, 'It was well worth it, however, since it helped restore my enthusiasm for a return to operational flying. It is true to say, "The more you fly the more you want to fly."'

Meanwhile, Brothers had the privilege of informing Squadron Leader Hallowes, DFM and Bar, of his award of the DFC, the decoration being promulgated in the *London Gazette* of 19 January 1943.

'Distinguished Flying Cross.
'Acting Squadron Leader Herbert James Lempriere HALLOWS, DFM (45010), No. 165 Squadron.

Hallowes' DFM and Bar were both announced in the *London Gazette* of 6 September 1940 and give some indication of the calibre of Pete's squadron commanders.

'Awarded the Distinguished Flying Medal.
'563179 Sergeant Herbert James Lempriere HALLOWES.

'In June 1940, Sergeant Hallowes was attacking an enemy aircraft over Northern France when he was himself attacked. His engine being disabled, he proceeded to glide back to friendly territory but was again attacked when about to abandon his aircraft by parachute. He dropped back into his seat and as the enemy aircraft passed he delivered such an effective burst of fire as to destroy his opponent. He then made a successful parachute landing.'

'Awarded a Bar to the Distinguished Flying Medal.
'563179 Sergeant Herbert James Lempriere HALLOWES, DFM.

'Since the commencement of hostilities this airman has personally destroyed twenty-one enemy aircraft. He has set a fine example of bravery and resolute bearing on many occasions.

'Squadron Leader Hallowes is an outstanding and relentless fighter. He has destroyed nineteen and damaged many other enemy aircraft. His skill and unswerving devotion to duty have set an example in keeping with the highest traditions of the Royal Air Force.'

On 21 January, Brothers led Nos. 165 and 485 Squadrons on Circus 252, 'Our role was to bounce any enemy aircraft attempting to take off from Abbeville.'

With the Wing on its return leg, a formation of sixteen Fw 190s was seen over Berch, two miles ahead of No. 485 Squadron. Wing Commander Brothers closed to within 200 yards of a straggler and fired a short burst before it dived down and made for home. Not having seen any obvious signs of damage, Brothers didn't make a claim.

On the following afternoon, Brothers (flying BL907) led Nos. 165 and 485 Squadrons on an uneventful Circus between Herck and Le Touquet, as part of the Appledore Wing. He repeated the operation on 26 January, flying as a part of the 'Bouncing' Wing on Circus 256. While recrossing the coast at Le Touquet, ten Fw 190s were spotted. Several dogfights endued, during which Wing Commander Brothers destroyed an Fw 190, four miles west of Hardelot, the pilot being seen to bail out before the fighter hit the sea:

'At approx 1400 hours on 26.1.43 I was leading 485 (NZ) Squadron's Red Section at 500ft, flying north of the French Coast, when I met ten Fw 190s flying north at the same height. I turned port towards them, but they climbed round to port and came down out of the sun. I took one head-on, but he pulled away and I fired a short burst at him from quarter ahead and below. As he flashed past I saw smoke streaming from him and he pulled up into a steep climb, jettisoned his hood and bailed out. I then called down my top cover, 165 Squadron, as they were in a favourable position to bounce the 190s, and they came down out of the sun. In the meantime, I fired two short bursts at two other E/A at long range, as by then my port cannon had a stoppage and I wanted to stop them coming down out of the sun. As we were at the end of our sweep and were getting short of fuel, I ordered the wing to return to base, the 190s having broken off combat and headed back across their coast. The Fw 190s camouflage was grey-green with a black cross in a white circle.'
(signed) P.M. Brothers, W/Cdr.

Another Fw 190 was destroyed by No.165 Squadron, which came down to engage, while Squadron Leader Grant was chased by an Fw 190, but managed to shake it off by violent weaving.

Flying Officer Bruce Warren (Yellow 1) destroyed an Fw 190, which was seen to spin-in, performing tight turns during the combat. Meanwhile, Sergeant Donaldson (Yellow 2) returned with holes in both mainplanes and through his tail unit, following an engagement with another Fw 190.

A little before midday on 2 February, Brothers commanded the Tangmere Wing, now including Squadron Leader James Edgar 'Johnnie' Johnson's No. 610 Squadron, on No. 11 Group's Circus 257 which was flown under Appledore control. Johnnie Johnson, DFC and Bar would become the RAF's highest scoring fighter ace with thirty-eight confirmed 'kills', and the most decorated (DFC, *London Gazette*, 30 September 1940; Bar, *London Gazette*, 26 June 1942; DSO, *London Gazette*, 4 July 1943; Bar, *London Gazette*, 24 September 1943; second Bar, *London Gazette*, 7 July 1944; DFC (US), *London Gazette*, 18 January 1944; Order of Leopold (Belgian) 1947; CdG (Belgian), 1947; Air Medal (US), December 1950; Legion of Merit (US), October 1951; CBE, *London Gazette*, 1 January 1960; CB, *London Gazette*, 1 January 1965).

The Spitfires swept over Abbeville airfield where two aircraft were seen taxiing, but much to Brothers' disgust they did not take off.

Brothers' debriefing notes were typed up and extracts distributed as a part of the RAF's daily bulletin. The following day the national press quoted his remarks on landing, the *Daily Sketch* headline read:

200 RAF RAIDERS – NO NAZIS

"More than 200 RAF fighters attacked France and Belgium yesterday. They carried out offensive sweeps and also escorted bombers which attacked Abbeville and Bruges", say the Air Ministry.

'The raid on Abbeville was carried out by Ventura bombers which attacked the marshalling yards. This raid was marked by the total absence of opposition. A Spitfire Wing circled the Abbeville aerodrome, but although Fw 190s could be seen taxiing round the perimeter track, none took the air.

"'THEY WOULDN'T FIGHT." The Wing Commander said, "They obviously did not want to fight and we came home because we were so browned off. When we took a look at Boulogne Harbour, where there is usually flak, the Hun didn't put one shot at us."

Brothers led the Wing (Nos. 610 and 485 Squadrons) on a repeat raid on the following day, with similar results.

The Wing was despatched on a Rhubarb on 6 February, when No. 165 Squadron destoyed two locos and three vehicles. Rhubarbs were freelance fighter sorties. These often involved small sections of fighters, mainly operating in pairs, attacking trains, road transport, airfields and targets of opportunity.

Two of No. 485 Squadron pilots also attacked railway targets near Neville, with the loss of Pilot Officer Bruce Gordon (flying BM513), who was shot down and became PoW No. 200 in Stalag Luft III, Sagan. Meanwhile, Sergeant H.R. Parker, and Pilot Officer J.T. Skibinski, making up No. 610 Squadron's Green Section, were last seen twenty miles north of Cherbourg. Sergeant (414331) Howard Russell Parker, RNZAF, was the son of Thompson Ferguson Parker and Lucy Alice Parker; husband of Olive Thelma Parker, of Auckland, New Zealand. He was 24-years-old and is remembered on the Runnymede Memorial Panel 198.

Two days later Brothers arranged for some of the Wing's pilots to view the recent Rhubarb's gun-camera films, when the senior Intelligence Officer, 'waxed lyrical about them.'

The strafing ops continued and, on 9 February, four Spitfires of No. 165 Squadron flew in pairs on Rhubarb operations to the Valmont area, shooting up a loco and an armoured lorry.

The second pair, Flying Officer R.G. Lewis and Sergeant J.H. Curry, operating in the Yvetot area, were not heard of again. Flying Officer (67061) Richard Granville Lewis, RAFVR, was the son of the late Pilot Officer Granville Vernon Loch (died on active service 5 October 1917) and Myfanwy Jacob Lewis, of Ewell, Surrey. Lewis was buried in Grancourt War Cemetery, Grave A 8. Sergeant (1335808) John Henry

Curry, RAFVR, was the son of Mr and Mrs J.H. Curry, of Charlton, London, and is remembered on the Runnymede Memorial, Panel 136.

During the morning of 10 January 1943, the whole Wing flew on Circus 261, providing close escort to Ventura bombers targeting the marshalling yards at Caen. Brothers was forced to return early, handing over command to Squadron Leader 'Reg' Grant.

No. 610 Squadron lost three aircraft and pilots to the Fw 190s, which their CO later confessed 'outclassed' their Spitfire Vs. The casualties included Squadron Leader A.E. Robinson (flying EE767 'W'), shot down by JG 2 and Flight Sergeant Harold Richard Harris (flying EE724 'T'), shot down by Unteroffizier Walter Leber. Both pilots had peeled off to give protection to Sergeant Lisowski, whose engine had run rough but picked up and who landed safely. Squadron Leader (39472) Anthony Edward Robinson, RAF, was the son of Alfred Edward Robinson and of Florence Emily Maria Robinson (née Crowther); husband of Joan Patricia Myrtle Robinson (nee Leigh), of North Stoke, Oxfordshire. He was 28-years-old. Squadron Leader Robinson was buried at Grandcourt War Cemetery, Grave A, 5. Flight Sergeant (413066) Harold Richard Harris, RNZAF, was the son of Harold William Harris and of Mabel Harris (née Daniels), of Wellington, New Zealand; husband of Dorothy Joyce Harris, of Wellington. Harris was 26-years-old. He is remembered on the Runnymede Memorial, Panel 199.

Meanwhile, after leaving the Caen area, Flight Lieutenant W.A. Laurie, DFC, saw Flying Officer L.A. Smith, DFC (flying BL256 'R'), being attacked from astern by two Bf 190s. He bailed out just off the French coast, but was lost. Two aircraft hit the sea; one was believed to be an Fw 190 claimed by No. 165 Squadron. Flying Officer (114060) Lawrence Arthur A. Smith, DFC, RAFVR, was the son of Arthur Alfred and Edith Mary Smith; husband of Elsie Ellen Smith, of Barnehurst, Bexleyheath, Kent. Smith was 22-years-old. He was buried in Bayeux War Cemetery, Grave XXVIII, J13.

During the same engagement, Spitfire AB259, flown by Pilot Officer K.S. Wright, was attacked by two Fw 190s and damaged, before fire from Flight Lieutenant Laurie put the enemy off their aim. Wright headed for cloud and made base. Meanwhile, No. 610 Squadron destroyed one Fw 190.

When the Wing was drawn into combat near the L'Orne estuary, No. 165 Squadron, on their last operation with the Wing, was able to make a number of claims.

Flight Lieutenant E.W.C. Colquhoun, flying as Red 1, destroyed one Fw 190:

'We saw eight or nine 190s attacking two Spitfires over the French coast at the estuary of the L'Orne. I saw a 190 attacking a Spitfire at about 1,000 yards; the Spitfire caught fire, the tail unit fell off and the pilot bailed out. The Fw 190 did not become aware of me until I was about 300 yards behind him, when I fired another burst of machine gun as he was pulling away from me.

'He then did a flick half roll, and I followed him firing short mixed until he came out 250 yards in front of me, going much slower.

'I closed to less than 100 yards firing cannon and machine gun continuously; his hood came off and pieces broke off the fuselage. I was then forced to break away owing to two Fw 190s behind me.'

Flying Officer B. Warren (Yellow 1) damaged an Fw 190 off L'Orne Estuary:

'I looked behind and saw six Fw 190s about to attack. I ordered the section to break starboard and, after a complete turn, was able to fire from quarter port astern at an Fw 190 which was climbing at a range of 350 yds. I saw red flashes on his port wing. The E/A rolled on his back and dived away.'

Sergeant Osborne (Yellow 2) damaged an Fw 190:

'I continued to follow Yellow 1 and he fired at another Fw 190 ahead of him and then broke away starboard. I followed this Fw 190 and at about 800 yds range gave a five second burst of cannon and machine gun and observed strikes on Perspex and around cockpit.'

Brothers was assigned to desk duties on 13 February and so briefed Squadron Leader Grant, who deputized, leading Nos. 485 and 610 Squadrons on Rodeo 168 over Northern France. At 1215 hours the Wing was drawn down to engage sixteen Fw 190s in the Hardelot area, when they were bounced by a further twenty Fw 190s.

In the frantic dogfight that followed, Squadron Leader Grant destroyed the Fw 190 which was attacking his youngest brother, Flying Officer I.A.C. Grant, but not before the 190 had scored several hits. The Squadron Leader could only look on as his brother's Spitfire fell out of the sky, leaving behind him a trail of smoke. Flying Officer (391351) Ian Allen Charles Grant, RNZAF, was the son of William Edward and Gertrude Isabella Grant, of Mission Bay, Auckland, New Zealand. Grant, who was 27-years-old, is remembered on the Runnymede Memorial, Panel 197. Ian Grant had served with No. 151 Squadron during the Battle of Britain.

Flying Officer Hume destroyed another:

'I cut across the turn and got on the tail of one of the tail-end E/A who tried to evade me by doing a tight turn to port. I fired a long burst with the E/A under the nose, guessing his position by the position of the No. 1 E/A and varying the deflection. I pulled away slightly and saw the E/A go down gradually into a dive and eventually dive into the sea about a mile off Hardelot. It was confirmed by W/O McGregor and S/Ldr Grant.'

During the same combat Flying Officer Brown claimed an Fw 190 damaged:

'In the general melee my No. 2 was attacked and, though called on the R/T, failed to break. An Fw 190, climbing from the opposite direction to our section, was in a good position to attack and I delivered an attack of about one and a half seconds with cannon and machine guns [a deflection shot at 200-250 yards] and noticed one cannon strike (HE) between the pilot's cockpit and the tail unit on top of the fuselage.'

Meanwhile, Flying Officer A.R. Robson and Sergeant R.J. Steed were shot down in combat with Fw 190s. Flying Officer Robson (flying EP107) had been able to damage an Fw 190 before his own aircraft was hit and he was forced to crash-land at Boulogne. He was captured and sent to Stalag Luft III (PoW No. 201). Sergeant (414354) Revell Jackson Steed, RNZAF, was killed. Sergeant Steed was the son of Lynn Arthur Steed and Olive Steed (née Jackson), of Gisborne, Auckland, New Zealand. Steed, who was 23-years-old, was buried in Abbeville Communal Cemetery, Plot 6, Row L, Grave 19.

Johnnie Johnson flew No. 610 Squadron into the attack, remaining above No. 485 Squadron to give them top cover, which was needed when they took on fifteen Fw 190s. Not long after the engagement began a further formation of twenty Fw 190s bounced them. At least seven pilots fired their guns, with only Johnson making a claim, firing several short bursts at an Fw 190 which was observed diving vertically and smoking heavily, burning wreckage appearing below.

On 16 February, Flight Lieutenant E.G.A. Seghers, who had served during the Battle of France (Belgian Croix de Guerre) and later with Nos. 46 and 32 Squadrons during the Battle of Britain, was appointed Acting Squadron Leader. He took over command of No. 165 Squadron – Squadron Leader Hallowes being posted away. Later that day news came through that Seghers had been awarded the Distinguished Flying Cross.

The Windmill Show came to Tangmere on 28 February, providing a cabaret. Following the evening performance a dance was given in the officer's mess. This concluded at 0115 hours and, as one might have expected, was well attended.

Back on operations, Wing Commander Brothers led Nos. 485 and 610 Squadrons on a sweep down the Cherbourg Peninsula on 8 March, 'We provided rear cover to a formation of Fortresses bombing Rennes.'

This was Brothers' last operation at the helm, handing over to Wing Commander Rhys Henry Thomas, DSO, DFC. One of the forgotten heroes of Fighter Command, Thomas had flown as a pilot officer with No. 266 Squadron during the Battle of Britain. He was transferred to the newly formed No. 129 Squadron on the request of its CO, Squadron Leader Dennis Armitage, who wanted him as a flight commander. A supreme tactician, Thomas was awarded the DFC (*London Gazette*, 22 May 1942), the recommendation noting that in early 1942 he had led Wing strength formations while only a flying officer. He later assumed command of No. 129 Squadron and led them in their close ground support role during the Dieppe Raid, for which he was awarded the DSO (*London Gazette*, 11 September 1942). Thomas served as Wing Commander (Flying) Hornchurch and at Tangmere. As an Acting Group Captain with 2nd Tactical Air Force, he played a key role in the day-to-day planning of their air offensive; one of his Wing Commanders, 'Johnnie' Johnson, remembered him as 'very press-on.' It was only on 15 September 1995, that R.H. Thomas was officially acknowledged by the Battle of Britain Association as having earned the coveted clasp, following research presented by the author.

Meanwhile, in recognition of his gallantry and leadership during his most recent tour of operations, Pete Brothers was awarded a Bar to his DFC. The award was announced in the *London Gazette*, 15 June 1943:

> Air Ministry, 15 June, 1943.
> ROYAL AIR FORCE.
>
> 'The KING has been graciously pleased to approve the following award in recognition of gallantry displayed, in flying operations against the enemy: —
>
> 'Bar to Distinguished Flying Cross.
> 'Acting Wing Commander Peter Malam BROTHERS, DFC (37668), Reserve of Air Force Officers.
>
> 'This officer has displayed outstanding keenness and efficiency. Within recent months he has led a wing in many operations and, by his skilful work and personal example, has contributed in a large measure to the high standard of operational efficiency of the formation. He has displayed great devotion to duty.'

The following pilots flew under P.M. Brothers when he was Wing Commander (Flying) Tangmere.

Nominal Roll of Pilots who flew with No. 165 Squadron, October 1942– March 1943

Squadron Leader H.J.L. Hallowes, DFC
Squadron Leader A.C. Stewart
Flight Lieutenant E.W. Colquhoun
Flight Lieutenant K.T. Lofts

Flight Lieutenant Eugene Georges Achilles Seghers (Belgian), RAFVR	KIA No. 91 Squadron 26.7.44
Flying Officer A.J. Brooks	
Flying Officer J. Carlier	
Flying Officer Michael John Glover, RAFVR	KIA 17.1.43
Flying Officer Richard Granville Lewis, RAFVR	KIA 9.2.43
Flying Officer G.B. Sylvester	
Flying Officer B. Warren	
Flying Officer I.A. Watson	
Flying Officer A. Van Den Houte	
Pilot Officer L.R. Disney	
Pilot Officer George Cruise Griffin, RAFVR	KIA 8.11.42
Pilot Officer A. Imbert	

Pilot Officer H.C. Richardson
Pilot Officer W.E. Schrader
Pilot Officer W.F. Sooman
Pilot Officer B. Warren
Flight Sergeant John Henry Curry, RAFVR   KIA 25.7.43
Sergeant J. Coward
Sergeant G. Donaldson
Sergeant I. Forbes
Sergeant R. Keating
Sergeant A.J. Osborne   possibly KIA No. 236
                                                Squadron 5.7.44

Sergeant J. Quinn
Sergeant E.S. Shipp
Sergeant L.A. Smith
Sergeant T.D. Stewart

Nominal Roll of Pilots who flew with No. 485 Squadron, January–March 1943:

Wing Commander Peter Malam Brothers, DFC and Bar, RAF	Later Air Commodore, CBE, DSO, DFC and Bar
Squadron Leader R.W. Baker, RNZAF	
Squadron Leader Reginald Joseph Cowan Grant, DFC, RNZAF	Bar to DFC 15.6.43
Flying Officer John Albert Ainge, RNZAF	KIA 24.9.43
Flying Officer Ian Allan Charles Grant, RNZAF	KIA 13.2.43
Flying Officer M.R.D. Hume, RNZAF	
Flying Officer J.G. Pattison, RNZAF	DFC 23.7.43
Flying Officer A.R. Robson, DFC, RNZAF	PoW 13.2.43
Pilot Officer R.W. Baker, DFC, RNZAF	
Pilot Officer M.G. Barnett, RNZAF	DFC 1944
Pilot Officer John Grant Dasent, RNZAF	KIA 22.12.43
Pilot Officer P.H. Gaskin, RNAF	
Pilot Officer B.E. Gibbs, RNZAF	
Pilot Officer L.B. Gordon, RNZAF	PoW 6.2.43
Pilot Officer M.R.D. Hume, RNZAF	

Pilot Officer E.D. Mackie, RNZAF — DFC 18 May 1943, Bar 24 September 1943, DSO 4 May 1945, DFC (US) July 1945

Pilot Officer M. Metcalfe, RNZAF

Pilot Officer George John Moorhead, RNZAF — KIA 30.5.43

Sergeant D.G.E. Brown, RNZAF

Sergeant S.F. Brown, RNZAF — DFC 14.9.45

Sergeant G.M. Buchanan, RNZAF

Sergeant Fraser Dudley Clark, RNZAF — KIA 22.8.43

Sergeant Thomas William Jackson Denholm, RNZAF — KIA 13.4.43

Sergeant A.V. Frewer, RNZAF

Sergeant J.A. Houlton, DFC, RNZAF

Sergeant R.J. Steed, RNZAF

Sergeant I.P.J. Maskill, DFC, RNZAF

Sergeant Donald Stuart McGregor, RNZAF — KIA No. 598 Squadron 9.5.44

Sergeant I.J. McNeil, RNZAF

Sergeant G.H. Meagher, RNZAF

Sergeant Herbert John Oxley, RNZAF — KIA 4.4.43

Sergeant K.H. Salt, RNZAF

Sergeant C.J. Sheddan, RNZAF — DFC 12.6.45

Sergeant K.N.R. Sissonn, RNZAF

Sergeant R.J. Steed, RNZAF

Sergeant W.T.H. Strahan, RNZAF

Sergeant F. Transom, RNZAF

Sergeant H.S. Tucker, RNZAF

Sergeant G.R. Wilson, RNZAF

Nominal Roll of Pilots who flew with No. 610 Squadron circa 2–13 February 1943:

Squadron Leader James Edgar Johnson, DFC and Bar (DSO 4.6.43, Bar 24.9.43, second Bar 7.7.44, DFC (US) 18.1.44, Order of Leopold (Belgian) 1947, CdG (Belgian) 1947, Air Medal (US) Dec 1950, Legion of Merit (US) October 1951, CBE 1.1.60, CB 1.1.65)

Squadron Leader A.E. Robinson (Australian)	KIA 10.2.43
Flight Lieutenant D.C. Collinge	
Flight Lieutenant W.A. Laurie	
Flight Lieutenant G. Volkersz	
Flying Officer A.S. Barrie	
Flying Officer C.G. Hodgkinson	PoW
Flying Officer George Samuel Malton (Canada)	KIA 28.3.43
Flying Officer L.A. Smith, DFC	KIA 10.2.43
Lieutenant Arnt Hvinden (Norway)	
Lieutenant 'Gerry' Volkersz (Netherlands)	
Pilot Officer S.C. Creagh	
Pilot Officer A.H. Davidson	
Pilot Officer J.T. Skibinski, MBE	Missing 13.2.43
Pilot Officer J.G.A. Small	
Pilot Officer K.S. Wright	
Flight Sergeant G.W. Worley	
Sergeant H. Fallon	
Sergeant Harold Richard Harris (New Zealand)	KIA 10.2.43
Sergeant T. Lisowski	
Sergeant K. Michalkiewicz	
Sergeant Howard Russell Parker	KIA 6.2.43
Sergeant E.S. Roberts	
Sergeant J. Smith	
Sergeant William Alexander Wyse, RAFVR	KIA 28.3.43

Chapter 14

Wing Commander (Flying) Culmhead Wing

B rothers was given a much deserved break from combat operations and on 2 April 1943 was posted to No. 52 OTU, Aston Down, as Officer Commanding Training Wing, under the command of Group Captain Fred Rosier, DSO (later Air Chief Marshal Sir Fredende Rosier, GCB, CBE, DSO). This was a rare opportunity for Annette and Pete to live together, renting Well Hill House in Minchinhampton, with their daughter, Wendy, who had been born on the 9 March that year. Fred Rosier and his wife, Het, became lifelong friends and it was a brief, happy period during the rigours of the war years.

On 1 August Brothers was appointed as Chief Flying Instructor, No. 61 OTU Rednal, near Shawbury: 'I was sent down on rest, transferred to [a] Spitfire OTU near Shawbury where the station commander [Group Captain Don Finlay, DFC] was not exactly an old friend of mine.'

The pair had clashed when they served at RAF Tangmere, Finlay as Wing Commander (Engineer). One day matters had come to a head and Brothers told Finlay in no uncertain terms that he should lighten up: 'You know, what you need is to get a pint of Scotch inside you and make yourself into an ordinary chap.'

Now a Group Captain and Officer Commanding RAF Shawbury, Finlay was on the spot to greet Brothers when he landed in his personailized Spitfire, which he brought with him from his role as Wing Commander (Flying) Tangmere, 'Finlay looked at my aircraft and said: "We haven't got enough aircraft on this unit for every pilot to have his own machine."'

'Stupidly, I said, "I fully realise that sir, that's why I've taken the precaution of bringing my Spit." This didn't go down well with the stiff Finlay.'

Brothers began a short spell on the staff of HQ, No. 10 Group, at Rudloe Manor near Bath on 22 November, 'initially in charge of training', taking over from Group Captain Thomas Frederick Dalton 'Tom' Morgan, DSO, DFC and Bar, during his temporary absence on sick leave. As Acting Group Captain (Operations), Brothers was involved in planning air operations, under the AOC, Air Vice-Marshal Sir Charles Steele, CB, DFC (later Air Marshal Sir Charles Steele, KCB, DFC). Brothers' role included giving the Wings their tasks, timings and rendezvous points. The tactics of the mission would be worked out by the Wing Leader, 'I was acting Group Captain ops, and at midnight every night, we had a telephone conference with the other groups.'

The work was important, but while it was interesting to play a part in the strategy of the air offensive, Brothers was keen to get back into the air, and was fully aware that the RAF would need men with his knowledge and air experience if they were to guarantee the success of the liberation of continental Europe.

Brothers was sent to the Headquarters Air Defence of Great Britain on 4 April, attending No. 3 Air Support [Fighter Leaders] Course at Milfield three days later, making his last flight with them on 21 April 1944.

A return to operations came on 23 April 1944, when Brothers was appointed to No. 10 Group's Exeter Wing, as Wing Commander (Flying), 'My Wing consisted of 610 Squadron [Spitfire XIV], Squadron Leader R.A. Newbury, DFC: 616 Squadron [Spitfire VII], Squadron Leader L.W. Watts, DFC; 131 Squadron [Spitfire VII], Squadron Leader J.J. O'Meara, all based at Culmhead. At Colt Head I had 41 Squadron [Spitfire XII], Squadron Leader R.H. Chapman, and at Exeter, 126 Squadron [Spitfire IXB], Squadron Leader W.W. Swindon [after 20 June, Squadron Leader J.A. Plagis, DFC and Bar]. 263 Squadron [Typhoons], Squadron Leader Henri Gonay [Croix de Guerre (Belgian)], was at Harrowbeer.'

It was intended that in the lead-up to D-Day the Exeter Wing should fly fighter sweeps and escorts for daylight raids over North Western Europe. Following the landings they provided close ground support, flying regular ground strikes. Brothers' squadrons operated at anything from single sortie to multiple Wing strength.

Soon after assuming command, however, Brothers realized that his Wing was too widely dispersed to operate efficiently: 'This was too scattered to control, so I moved 126 to Culmhead and later persuaded Tom Morgan to rename us Culmhead Wing and to form the Harrowbeer Wing [based at Perranporth] using 126 [along with Nos. 41 and 263 Squadrons], who had less range than our Spit XIs and VIIs, and "Birdy" [Wing Commander H.A.C. Bird-Wilson, DFC and Bar – later Air Vice-Marshal Arthur Harold Cooper Bird-Wilson, CBE, DSO, DFC and Bar, AFC and Bar] came and took over.'

Brothers had a meeting with No. 10 Group Operations Officer, Group Captain 'Tom' Dalton Morgan: 'I explained my case; every time I went to visit a squadron away from Culmhead I would be recalled halfway there with orders that his office had ordered a Wing Sweep. This usually resulted in me rushing back to Culmhead in time to see the Wing departing, with me lacking sufficient fuel to join them. I therefore suggested to him that he form a second Wing at Harrowbeer with the two Spits units and the single Typhoon squadron, which he duly did.'

Brothers would be in regular contact with 'Tom' Morgan over operational matters until Morgan was posted to HQ 2nd Tactical Air Force prior to D-Day, the role for which he was later awarded the OBE (*London Gazette*, 14 June 1945).

Sitting in the Blackdown Hills five miles to the south-east of Wellington, Culmhead had opened as RAF Church Stanton on 1 August 1941, operating as a satellite to RAF Exeter. The first units to use the station were Nos. 302 (Poznaski) and 316 (Warszawski) Squadrons, flying the Hurricane IIb.

When Brothers arrived at Culmhead the base was in transition. The Royal Navy's No. 24 Fighter Wing had flown in from Ballyherbert on 20 April. Commanded by Lieutenant Commander N.G. Hallett, DSC, the Wing, which consisted of Nos. 887 and 897 Squadrons, flew convoy escorts and anti-shipping patrols in the Channel, also taking part in the occasional Rodeo. Their Mk III Seafires would make a total of 400 sorties during a three-week period before transferring to HMS *Infatigable*.

Meanwhile, on 2 May, No. 610 Squadron joined No. 10 Group's Roadstead 101, providing close escort to Typhoon fighter-bombers targeting shipping.

Brothers' first op out of Culmhead, however, came a few days later when he joined No. 887 Squadron's Seafires on Rodeo 128 to Rennes and Gael airfields, damaging gun positions and buildings. Brothers went along for the ride, making his first sortie on the Spitfire XIV, 'The Mark XIV was the real performer thanks to its Griffin engine. It was a truly impressive machine, being able to climb almost vertically.' Although he never took on an Fw 190 while flying the Mark XIV, Brothers added, 'It gave many Luftwaffe fighter pilots the shock of their lives, when, having thought that they had bounced you from a superior height, they were astonished to find the Mark XIV climbing up to tackle them head-on, throttle wide open. I would have liked to have had a whole Wing of these aircraft.'

The Griffin engine's torque made the Mark XIV a handful on take-off, even for an experienced pilot like Brothers, 'Even with full aileron, elevator and rudder, this brute of a fighter took off slightly sideways.'

On 22 May Brothers detailed the recently arrived No. 616 Squadron's 'A' Flight to fly on Rhubarb 255, in the Reimes to Laval area, attacking three trains, but losing Pilot Officer Prouting, shot down by flak from an armoured train in the Follingy Yards. Pilot Officer (175505) George Edward Prouting, RAFVR, was the son of Gilbert and May Prouting, of Cosham, Hampshire. He was 22-years-old and was buried in Equilly Churchyard, Cherbourg peninsula.

Early the following morning No. 616 Squadron flew on Rhubarb 256, strafing a radar station, two trains and a staff car. Brothers explained that, 'on these missions we hit anything that took our fancy; vehicles, trains and airfields.' The same day they also provided an escort to Mitchell bombers targeting Dinard airfield on Ramrod 131. For many like Brothers, the pattern of raids which heralded the invasion must have had echoes of the Luftwaffe's aerial campaign over Britain in advance of what Hitler had planned to be the invasion and conquest of these isles.

Meanwhile, on 24 May, No. 610 Squadron transferred away from Culmhead, becoming a part of the Harrowbeer Wing. They were replaced by Nos. 126 and 131 (County of Kent) Squadrons, both equipped with Spitfire IXs (the latter effectively swapping stations with No. 610 Squadron).

On 28 May, Nos. 131 and 616 Squadrons flew Rhubarb 258 over Western France, while No.126 Squadron made a reconnaissance to Batz and Ushant. Over the following few days Brothers' squadrons flew on a number of Rhubarbs and Rodeos, No. 131 Squadron losing Warrant Officer Atkinson to flak on 29 May. Warrant Officer (413332) William James Atkinson, RAAF, was the son of Clifford and Elsie Atkinson, of Cremorne, New South Wales, Australia. He was 21-years-old and is remembered on the Runnymede Memorial, Panel 259.

Brothers detailed No. 616 Squadron on further Rhubarb operations on 1 June, the Spitfires claiming two locos and a number of railway wagons and lorries, along with a gun position. A convoy patrol followed on the 4 June.

It was at about this time that Brothers attended a high-level Fighter Command conference in the company of Richard Atcherley, as ever a 'disruptive' influence, 'Inevitably, with such a large gathering, progress was slow and Batchy's interest flagged. Quickly drawing four lines on his conference pad he inserted a cross, pushed it to me and the game was on. Time passed, the pad grew thinner as sheets were used, and honours were about even when we heard the C-in-C [Sir Trafford Leigh-Mallory] say, "What do you think, Batchy?"

"I'm sorry Sir, I did not hear the question as I was playing noughts and crosses with Pete."' While Brothers looked embarrassed and waited for a severe put down in front of his peers, Batchy's amiable honesty defused what might have been a tricky situation, the incident bringing a little humour to an otherwise dry presentation.

Meanwhile, Culmhead went into lock down on 5 June in preparation for the D-Day landings. Overnight the aircraft were painted with black and white identification stripes on the underside of their wings and the rear of their fuselage, 'These distinctive markings were intended to allow air recognition and prevent casualties from "friendly" fire.'

On 6 June, known ever since as D-Day, Brothers (flying No 131 Squadron's Spitfire VII NX – U), led No. 131 Squadron on Rodeo 156 to Gael, Vannes, Karlin and Bastard, noting in his logbook; '131. Pranged three engines, two cars and odd lorries.'

Brothers made sure his pilots flew at over 6,000ft on these operations, to avoid the perils of light flak. It was during one of these sweeps that once again he demonstrated his tactical mastery, taking on and destroying a flak train, 'One of my pilots spotted a flak train steaming along below us.' Brothers acknowledged his call, but ordered the formation to maintain course, giving the enemy the impression that they hadn't been observed. 'After flying on for a further twenty miles, I gave the order to drop down to the deck and turn back in towards the train.' Following the progress of the smoke plume as the train vanished into thick wood, Brothers lined up ready to lead a single attacking pass. 'We timed our approach perfectly, and as the engine emerged from the wood I squared it up in my gunsight and gave it a broadside of cannon. The remainder of the Spitfires quickly followed suit, and by the time the deadly flak batteries had emerged from the wood we were on our way, having left the engine a hissing wreck.'

Meanwhile, having completed several convoy patrols over the D-Day Armada, No. 616 Squadron flew a Rodeo, destroying two goods trains, a staff car and around five military trucks. Brothers added a further commentary in the leaves of his logbook:

'D-DAY. Last night and this morning, British and Allied forces set foot on Hitler's "European Fortress". Landings all according to plan, with only slight opposition and few casualties. Out of 1,100 British and American troop carrying a/c, only twenty-three were lost. 4,000 ships taking part and 11,000 aircraft. Air opposition nil. Bridgehead firmly established and troops "pressing on", behind Caen.'

Brothers' note was optimistic. While the tanks of the Staffordshire Yeomanry did reach the outskirts of the city, they had to retire due to lack of infantry support – it would be another six weeks before the key objective of Caen was in Allied hands.

Brothers later wrote; 'With great excitement we participated in the invasion of Europe, sweeping over the beach and deep into France, top dogs now, hammering the enemy in the air and on the ground.'

On the following day, Nos. 126, 131 and 616 Squadrons were involved in successful Rhubarb and Rodeo operations. Meanwhile, in the early evening, Brothers (flying NX – X) led No. 616 Squadron on Rodeo 164 to the Brest Peninsular, strafing three locos, seven enemy vehicles and a radar station.

Raids against enemy infrastructure behind the Normandy front continued, and on 8 June Brothers detached Nos. 126 and 131 Squadrons to fly on separate Rodeos, shooting-up locos, rolling stock and military vehicles. Each raid contributed towards the overall plan of denying the enemy frontline troops supplies and reinforcements at a crucial time in the invasion.

Brothers led Nos. 131 and 616 Squadrons on a patrol just off the D-Day beaches between Trouville and Barfleur during the early evening of 9 June. No enemy aircraft were seen, but the pilots returned with 'stories of seeing the warships shelling enemy positions and having seen many fires along the coast.'

There could be no let-up and the sorties continued regardless of adverse weather, which normally might have warranted the order to abort. At 2129 hours, Brothers (flying NX – R) led the Wing (Nos. 131 and 616 Squadrons) on another beachhead patrol, noting in his logbook: 'Patrol Caen-Bayeaux, Carantin-Église 131 & 616. Weather on deck. Forced thro' and carried on ok. Some patrol. Weather clampers. Culmhead Wing the only people who "forced on"'. Brothers added later, 'Lost two in cloud. My radio failed'.

Brothers' daughter, Wendy, recalled her father talking about this mission, 'When ordered to take off, father said that the weather was too bad and was told that "100% losses were acceptable." He was proud of the fact that not only did they all get off, apart from the two aircraft that probably collided in the cloud, but he got them all back; without his radio and relying on his No. 2 to interpret his moves.' They flew back at low-level, down the valleys. Brothers led a further patrol before dusk, making a strafe of Le Mans and Laval airfields.

The Rhubarb and Rodeo operations continued through 10 and 11 June, while at 1300 hours on 12 June, Wing Commander Brothers (flying NX – U) led Nos. 131 and 616 Squadrons on No. 10 Group's Rodeo 169. Brothers took No. 131 Squadron down to make a strafe on Le Mans airfield, No. 616 Squadron providing close support. Warrant Officer Hannah damaged two unidentified single engine fighters on the ground, while hangars and ancillary buildings were also hit.

While making his pass Brothers fired his cannon at a number of ground targets, destroying one Fw 190, but his Spitfire was holed in his port elevator, tailplane, aileron and the leading edge of the port mainplane as he passed through heavy flak.

Flight Lieutenant Moody's Spitfire (NX – M) was also hit. He was seen going into a steep climb just after crossing the airfield and was heard to say he would have to bail out. Flight Lieutenant (J/15362) Vincent Kenneth Moody, DFC, RCAF, was the son of Fred and Louise Moody, of West Middle Sable, Clare Co., Nova Scotia, Canada. He was 22-years-old. Moody was buried in Yvre L'eveque Communal Cemetery. An American pilot, Moody had flown with both Nos. 131 and 610 Squadrons.

The two squadrons reformed and headed towards Laval airfield where the roles were reversed. The enemy had advanced warning of the raid and a number of aircraft were seen taxiing. Four Fw 190s were damaged on the ground following strafes by Squadron Leader Watts and Flying Officers Cooper, Hobson and McKenzie.

While orbiting the airfield, someone called out over the R/T, 'Huns about' and a Bf 109 was seen travelling south at zero feet about a mile to the west. Flying Officers Parry and Kelley (flying as his No. 2) half rolled down on it from the starboard side. The Bf 109 pilot dropped his jettison tank and turned towards Parry, who had no difficulty in getting astern, giving him a one second burst from 300 yards. Strikes were seen all over the cockpit and both wing roots, the starboard wing folded back and the port wing broke off before it crashed to the south-west. Flying Officer Kelley confirmed the 'kill'.

Meanwhile, No. 616 Squadron's pilots made a number of claims. Flying Officer Edwards damaged two Fw 190s on the ground, shooting-up a small factory, before landing, short of fuel, on one of the emergency beachhead landing strips at Sainte-Mère-Église.

Flight Lieutenant Harrison and Flying Officer Rogers attacked a Bf 109. Harrison's wing tip was torn off by the enemy's tail. The Bf 109 plunged to the ground moments later, Harrison's propeller suddenly stopped at 1,000ft while he was heard to say he was bailing out only moments before his aircraft plummeted into the ground. Flight Lieutenant (60102) Geoffrey Austin Harrison, RAFVR, was buried at La Pellerine Communal Cemetery.

Warrant Officer Hart claimed a Bf 109, while Flight Lieutenant Cleland shot down two Fw 190s, but his aircraft was hit by flak over the airfield and he was forced to bail out twelve miles from the English coast where he was picked up by an air-sea rescue launch. During the return leg Brothers led the fighters in strafing locos and military vehicles. Brothers summed up the raid, 'We were lucky enough to catch the Luftwaffe taking off and destroyed six Fw 190s, and damaged a further five for the loss of two Spitfires, much to our satisfaction and that of Air Marshal Sir Roderick Hill [CinC ADCS], our Commander-in-Chief, who wrote [on 16 June] to express his congratulations.'

Over the next few days Brothers detailed his squadrons to fly individually on a number of Rhubarb operations, making strafing attacks in support of the push inland from the D-Day beaches, but they encountered few targets of opportunity.

On 16 June, it was noted that there was a suspiciously high number of German vehicles marked with the Red Cross, indicating they were either breaking the Geneva Convention, or that with the Allies in total control of the air, only Red Cross vehicles risked moving in daylight.

Wing Commander Brothers led No. 616 Squadron on No. 10 Group's Roadstead 143, escorting Beaufighters against shipping in the Gulf of St Malo. Two days later, on 18 June, Brothers (flying NX – E) led Nos. 126 and 616 Squadrons on an escort to twenty Beaufighters on anti-shipping strikes on No. 10 Group's Roadstead 144. Brothers' logbook recorded, 'Saw only fires inland of Coutances-Carteret area. As a shipping strike it was a waste of time. Germans supposed to be evacuating Cherbourg. Good show.'

On 20 June, Brothers (flying NX – R) led No. 131 Squadron on Rhubarb 292, 'Our Spitfires carried the new ninety gallon drop-tanks for a very deep penetration into south-west France, allowing us to fly as far as Chateau Bougon.'

Brothers led Nos. 126 and 616 Squadrons on No. 11 Group's Ramrod 1032 on 22 June, acting as escort to twenty Lancaster bombers of No. 617 Squadron attacking V1 flying-bomb launching and V2 development sites at Wizernes. Hitler's first revenge weapon, the V1, had begun falling on Kent and the capital just over a week earlier, on 12 June 1944. Over the following days and weeks Brothers' squadrons would fly a number of operations escorting bombers striking at strategically important targets.

The following day saw Brothers detailing No. 126 Squadron on two raids directed at radar installations, while No. 131 Squadron flew a Rhubarb to the Loire valley and on a Roadstead to the Cherbourg peninsular.

The hit and run raids continued and on 24 June Brothers led No. 131 Squadron on a Roadstead to St Malo, as cover for Typhoons of No. 263 Squadron, while during the afternoon he detailed Nos. 131 and 616 Squadrons to fly as escort to Lancaster and Halifax bombers once again targeting V1 launch sites located by photo-reconnaissance. Their third mission of the day was on No. 10 Group's Rodeo 174 to 'Fecamp', Dreux and Evreux.

Nos. 131 and 616 Squadrons took part in Rodeo 175 during 27 June, No. 616 Squadron, also flying on Rhubarb 299. During the afternoon Brothers detailed Squadron Leader Plagis to lead his No. 126 Squadron on two attacks on a radar station at Cap Frehel, recording two direct hits. Squadron Leader John Argorastos Plagis had already won the DFC (*London Gazette*, 1 May 1942) and Bar (*London Gazette*, 7 July 1942) and would go on to be awarded the DSO (*London Gazette*, 3 November 1944):

'Since being awarded the Distinguished Flying Cross, this officer has participated in very many sorties, during which, much damage has been inflicted on the enemy. Shipping, radio stations, oil storage tanks, power plants and other installations have been amongst the targets attacked. On one occasion he led a small formation of aircraft against a much superior force of enemy fighters. In the engagement five enemy aircraft were shot down, two of them by Squadron Leader Plagis. This officer is a brave and resourceful leader whose example has proved a rare source of inspiration. He has destroyed sixteen hostile aircraft.'

On 30 June the Culmhead Wing took part in No. 10 Group's Rodeo 176. No. 126 Squadron damaged a locomotive along with its goods wagons, also later flying on a Rhubarb. This was No. 126 Squadron's last engagement with the Wing, transferring to the Harrowbeer Wing two days later.

Despite the lack of targets, Brothers' Wing had made a number of claims during June:

In the air:
Four enemy aircraft destroyed
One enemy aircraft probably destroyed

On the ground:
Four enemy aircraft destroyed
Five enemy aircraft damaged
Thirty-eight locomotives
Thirty-nine goods wagons
Thirty-three vehicles
Nine RDF stations
Two ships badly damaged

Brothers' Culmhead Wing was playing its part in a significant air campaign, not only keeping the Luftwaffe out of the air, but also severely disrupting the enemy's attempts to re-equip and support the Second Front.

On 2 July, No. 616 Squadron carried out two shipping reconnaissances off St Malo, also flying on Rhubarb 303. Meanwhile, Brothers ordered No. 131 Squadron to provided cover to No. 163 Squadron's rocket-carrying Typhoons flying on No. 10 Group's Ramrod 151, targeting the power station at Mur de Bretagne. Later they flew on Rhubarb 303, a sweep over the St Brieuc area. More Rhubarbs and Ramrod operations were flown on 3 and 4 July.

Brothers (flying his personalized Spitfire VII MD188 'PB') led No. 616 Squadron on the uneventful Rodeo 180 on 5 July. His squadrons began operations from first light on 6 and 7 July flying a number of Rhubarbs, adding to their tally of ground strikes. Brothers flew on two operations, commanding Nos. 131 and 616 Squadrons on Rodeos 181 and 182. On the following day he led No. 616 Squadron on another fighter sweep, 'We also hit a fair number of No Ball against V1 missile launch sites during this period, which were heavily defended by mobile AA batteries.'

Brothers was now on his fourth tour of operations and had convinced himself that the chances were he would not survive to see VE-Day, 'As a result of my state of mind, I would think nothing of handing over the lead of the Wing to my No. 2, and diving down on a flak battery that had opened up on us as we flashed past at low-level'.

Brothers was aware that the chances of knocking out the battery were minimal. He might kill the crew, but actually damaging the gun itself was unlikely. The possibilities of being shot down and not having sufficient altitude to bail out were, conversely, very high, 'I finally began to resist the temptation of strafing these targets after seeing colleagues lost to flak damage, but every now and then they would irritate me so much I just had to dive down and give them a squirt.'

Meanwhile, No. 131 Squadron was detailed to make a Rodeo to Mont Saint-Michel, also sweeping the Loire Valley, strafing two locomotives, four lorries and a petrol tanker.

With Brothers leading, twenty-two aircraft drawn from Nos. 131 and 616 Squadrons took off on No. 11 Group's Ramrod 1081 on 12 July, providing top cover to 153 Lancasters and six Mosquitos of Nos. 1, 3 and 8 Groups, targeting the Vaires-Sur-Marne marshalling yards.

During the day two Meteors (EE 213 G and EE 214 G) flew in from Farnborough. Nine days later No. 616 Squadron transferred to Manston. From 26 July their jets flew 'Anti-Diver' sorties against V1 flying-bombs, blowing the flying bombs up in mid-air, or tipping them into the ground.

For the Culmhead squadrons, the sorties continued apace and on 14 July, Squadron Leader MacDougall, DFC, was at the head of No. 131 Squadron when they flew on Rhubarb 316, damaging targets of opportunity including six rail trucks, a lorry and a staff car. Four days later Brothers detailed Nos. 131 and 616 Squadrons on No. 11 Groups Ramrod 1103, escorting Liberators carpet bombing enemy targets south-west of Caen. The raid was a prelude to General Montgomery's new push, code named Operation Goodwood.

On the following day Brothers led six pilots from Nos. 131 and 616 Squadrons on No. 10 Group's Rhubarb 319. While in the area of Mayenne, they encountered thirty enemy aircraft, who turned south with the Spitfires in pursuit. Overhauling a straggler between Le Mans and Paris, Brothers' No. 2, Flying Officer Edwards and No. 616 Squadron's Pilot Officer Wilson destroyed the Bf 109 over Alençon.

The pressure of the air campaign had to be maintained and more Rodeos were flown on 23, 24 and 30 July.

On 31 July, Wing Commander Brothers led Nos. 131 and 611 Squadrons on No. 11 Group's Ramrod 1146, acting as withdrawal cover to a force of 127 Lancasters and four Mosquitos of Nos. 1 and 5 Groups, bombing the marshalling yards at Joigny, La Roche. By now the Luftwaffe was defeated and it was rare to encounter them in the air. These missions were humdrum for Brothers and the more experienced pilots under his command: 'Darting up and down their lines like demented sheepdogs, no doubt good for their morale, but with little enemy fighter reaction, total boredom for us.'

Brothers was again at the helm when No. 131 Squadron took off on No. 11 Group's Ramrod 1148 on the following day. This was an attack by 385 Lancasters, 324 Halifaxes, sixty-seven Mosquitos and a Lightning, on V1 targets in the Pas de Calais.

On 4 August, Wing Commander Brothers (flying MD188 'PB') led Nos. 131 and 611 Squadrons on No.11 Group's Ramrod 1160, acting as return cover for a formation of 250 Lancasters of Nos. 1, 3 and 8 Groups, on their way back from their attack on Bec-d'Ambes and Pauillac oil stores. Brothers had trouble with his ASI and was forced to turn back, handing command over to Squadron Leader MacDougall.

With the Allies advance continuing, Wing Commander Brothers led Nos. 131 and 611 Squadrons on No.10 Group's Ramrod 163. The operation, made on 5 August, was as escort to a formation of 306 Lancasters of Nos. 1, 3 and 8 Groups, bombing oil storage targets on the River Gironde at Blaye, Bordeaux and Pauillac.

On 6 August, Squadron Leader MacDougall led No. 131 Squadron on Rodeo 193 which saw a rare encounter with the enemy in the air. Two aircraft had become detached from the rest of the formation and on their return leg sighted eight Fw 190s flying line abreast. Pilot Officer Parry attacked the aircraft at the centre of the formation, which was seen to explode. Warrant Officer Patten chased one Fw 190 as far as the Le Mans area, forcing its pilot to take to his parachute.

The Culmhead Wing's second mission of the day was flown out of Bolt Head, from where they flew on Ramrod 165, escorting No. 617 Squadron's Lancasters, which registered two direct hits on the U-boat pens at Lorient. These raids would greatly reduce the enemy's capability to attack Allied shipping in the Channel, thus materially assisting in the resupply of the invasion forces.

On the following day Brothers (flying MD188 'PB') led the Culmhead Wing on Rodeo 194 over Cherbourg, Chartres and Orleans, a flight path of some 760 miles, which meant they would carry a ninety gallon slipper tank.

Take-off was planned for 1400 hours. Squadron Leader 'Sammy' Sampson, who had flown under Brothers in No. 602 Squadron and was on leave from staff duties, acted as his No. 2.

While approaching Bourges, they spotted in the distance two Bf 109s. Brothers gave the signal for the Spitfires to drop their slipper tanks, but the Messerschmitts were pulling away. When it became apparent that they could not be overhauled, Brothers reluctantly called off the pursuit.

Now flying with reduced fuel levels, Brothers cut the corner on their planned route and headed instead along the Loire Valley, 'We got our reward though, as nearing Blois we ran into a dozen Fw 190s which dived away with us in hot pursuit.'

The enemy fighters half rolled as they dived to escape. Brothers called out the orders, 'Hack them down' and 'every man for themselves.' The tight formation broke and individual Spitfires dived after the enemy fighters, 'Sammy and I chased a pair which separated, mine to the left, his to the right.' As Brothers closed in to firing range the pursuit had gone down to ground level. 'I was surprised to see my 190 start a gentle climb and weave equally gently to left and right, offering a perfect target.'

Brothers' combat report read:

> 'W/Cdr Brothers was leading 131 Squadron on 10 Group Rodeo No. 194. On the return journey at approximately 1520 hours, when north of La Fleche at 7,000ft, twelve Fw 190s were sighted at 4,000ft. W/Cdr Brothers selected one and opened fire on it from the port quarter twenty degrees off from a range of 150 yards [firing seventy-six rounds 20mm, 120 rounds 0.303 armour piercing, 120 rounds 0.303 incendiary]. Strikes were seen on the cockpit and port aileron. The aircraft immediately rolled over to the right, the nose dropped and, as the aircraft dived down, it did the more complete rolls to starboard, going into the ground vertically and exploding, the position being about twenty miles north-west of La Fleche.'
> (signed) P.M. Brothers, W/Cdr.
> Wing Commander RAF Station, Culmhead.

When later asked about his thoughts regarding combat, it was this episode that came to the forefront of his mind, 'I think I am not alone in regarding air combat as tremendously stimulating fun as one shoots in an attempt to knock down an aircraft. There is nothing personal in it.'

Most combat took place at over 250 yards and pilots seldom saw the twisted, burnt-out wreckage of the aircraft they destroyed, or the remains of its crew: 'One is usually spared the thought or sight of bodily injury. It can be wholly impersonal, unless one had the misfortune to have suffered like the Poles, Czechs and others who had left loved ones behind in the hands of a brutal enemy.

'It was the last one I shot down. It nearly made me sick; he hadn't a clue. He was doing gentle turns, he was a sitting duck. I slapped the cannon shells right into the cockpit which would have killed him instantly. The aircraft flipped over and hit the ground. I thought, "Oh Christ, I didn't really mean that. I'd hoped you were going to jump out and parachute down." It was very unpleasant.'

Squadron Leader Sampson, DFC, claimed one Fw 190 destroyed at 1520 hours west of Le Mans, his combat report giving a more detailed account of the air battle:

'I was about 1,000 yds away when the two E/A on the extreme left broke to port and came towards me head-on. I climbed slightly to avoid a head-on attack and they rolled on their backs and went down. I half rolled after them. I had no difficulty in quickly closing the distance from 1,200 yds to 600 yds. We were now at zero feet. I gave a short burst at 600 yds to make them weave and they broke in opposite directions. I selected the starboard a/c. I gave a one and a half second burst of all armament at 450 yards. The E/A then broke starboard and I gave a two second burst at 300 yds one ring deflection. The Hun then started breaking both ways alternatively, and I was able to get in three more short bursts with small angles. I observed strikes on the cockpit and the E/A pulled up vertically to about 600ft, rolled over and went straight in, the pilot being killed.'

Meanwhile, Flight Lieutenant J.C.R. 'Closet' Waterhouse, one of No. 131 Squadron's flight commanders, sighted thirteen Fw 190s flying in two boxes, one above the other. He attacked one fighter in the lower box, saw strikes followed by an explosion near the cockpit; the enemy aircraft crashed near Le Mans.

With the combat over, Brothers gathered as many of the squadron as he could back into formation and set course for home.

While flying over the Argentan at 4,000ft, Sampson's Spitfire (NX – M) was hit in the port wing by flak. Brothers escorted the damaged aircraft home, going down to sea level to avoid the enemy. The Press got hold of the story and the *Evening News* wrote of Sampson's exploits:

'DAY OFF, SO HE GOT A 190
'Spits and 'Skitoes Range France.

'Squadron Leader R.W. Sampson, DFC, took a day off yesterday – and shot down an Fw 190. He comes from Cheam, Surrey, and is on the staff at his group HQ. When he can he flies a Spitfire.

'An 'on-duty' Spitfire man, Wing Commander P.M. Brothers, DFC & Bar, of Westerham, Kent, led the County of Kent Spitfires over France, and found them a bunch of 190s north of Alençon, 10,000ft above the allied tank columns racing for Le Mans.

'Sent scuttling, he personally shot down one – hitting the pilot – and led an attack which sent the others scuttling.'

While the press coverage was good for morale, it drew unwanted attention from Group HQ and Sampson was summoned by Air Marshal Cole-Hamilton, and was reminded that he was a staff officer and was not to fly.

Two days later, on 9 August, Brothers led No. 131 Squadron on Ramrod 167, providing cover for No. 617 Squadron hitting the U-boat pens at La Pallice. Thirty enemy fighters were successfully fended off. With Squadron Leader MacDougall commanding, the mission was repeated on 11 (Ramrod 171) and 12 August, causing severe damage to the pens.

No. 131 Squadron flew two operations during 13 August, with Wing Commander Brothers leading. The first was a dawn sweep to the Loire on Rodeo 199. During the afternoon they flew on Ramrod 174, a sweep down to Bordeaux where fifteen Lancasters of No. 5 Group were bombing oil targets.

At dawn on 15 August, Brothers led Nos. 131 and 611 Squadrons to target Le Clot Airfield. This operation was part of No. 11 Group's Ramrod 1203, a mass raid launched by 800 Lancasters and 1,100 Liberators and Fortresses, carpet-bombing nine airfields in Holland and Belgium in preparation for a renewed night offensive against Germany.

During the operation, Nos. 64 and 125 Squadrons of the Harrowbeer Wing, commanded by Bird-Wilson, provided cover for the front of the formation, while Brothers' Culmhead Wing protected the rear, Brothers and his wingman acting as Tail-end-Charlie to the whole formation. Radioing to Bird-Wilson he discovered that the aircraft were so spread that 'Birdy' was over the Channel Islands while he was just leaving the outskirts of Bordeaux!

In a new phase of the war the Allies invaded Southern France, the landings being only lightly opposed. Meanwhile the breakout from Normandy was growing in pace.

On the following day, 16 August, Brothers headed up Nos. 131 and 611 Squadrons on Rodeo 203. The operation, however, was aborted due to thick haze which was encountered soon after crossing the French coast. Brothers – many years later – noted in his logbook with some degree of satisfaction, 'Last operational trip. This completes 875 hours of operational flying.'

The front had by now advanced beyond the practical range of the Wing. On 27 August news came through that No. 131 Squadron was being transferred after three months at Culmhead, the Squadron's ORB read: 'We are moving to Friston in 11 Group and everybody, though sorry to say goodbye to Culmhead, is anxious to get nearer to the Hun.'

Before being posted away in October, Brothers was able to get in some recreational flying: 'I use to whip up to Manchester aerodrome where I'd learnt to fly and my father would collect me and take me home. I'd take a weekend off as wing leader, I'd got a Spit Mk XIV; a wonderful aeroplane, and I'd take it home and show it to my father.'

Brothers had made the journey north to spend time with his family whenever he could, usually getting permission to borrow a Spitfire under whatever pretence he could, 'I did that throughout the war'.

While this meant arriving in Manchester in style, flying home also maximized his time on leave – every moment at home was precious and with several tours under his belt, he never knew if his next leave would be his last.

Too young to have clear memories of her father's visits, Wendy recalled her grandparents' house, Pete's boyhood home:

'I have wonderful memories of Westfield. It was a large Victorian Gothic building, gloomy in its way, but I loved it. The lighting was by gas mantles and I loved lying in bed, reading to the sound of the shhhhhhh noise they made. We had stone water bottles to warm the beds in winter. Most magical of all were the attic rooms, stuffed with all sorts of forgotten 'treasures' (including many of my father's toys) and accessed by a beautiful, wrought-iron spiral staircase from the main landing. There were conventional back stairs too, but these were far less interesting! There were cellars as well – though I was forbidden to go down into these. I must have been taken down there as a baby, as everyone in the house, including our bull terrier, Merlin, would shelter there during the air raids on Manchester. Being forbidden, of course, they were the place I longed to go, and Aunty Matty, ever indulgent, took me down on the promise not to tell anyone else!'

Wendy remembers as a child seeing the hand-tinted photographs of Pete's sister, Iris, who had died tragically young: 'She looked like her mother. Most of all I was intrigued by the fact that one photo showed Iris with brown eyes and in another photo blue eyes.'

Wendy also recalls Pete's father with great fondness: 'My grandfather had a photographic memory – whether by chance or because his eyesight was so poor, I do not know. He would recite poems to Hilary and me, holding us spellbound whilst we marvelled at his ability to remember so much.'

The Culmhead Wing

Nominal roll of No. 126 Squadron pilots who flew operationally late May–30 June 1944:

Squadron Leader W.W. Swinden	Officer Commanding
Acting Squadron Leader J.A. Plagis, DFC and Bar	Officer Commanding, DSO, 3.11.44
Flight Lieutenant R.T.H. Collis	'A' Flight Commander
Flight Lieutenant J. Garden	
Flight Lieutenant Jones	
Flight Lieutenant Owen	
Flying Officer R.A. Caldwell	
Flying Officer Jan L. Flinterman	
Flying Officer Graham	
Flying Officer D. Kingsbury	
Flying Officer D. Owen	
Pilot Officer E. Cousins	
Pilot Officer F.K. Halcombe	
Warrant Officer Austin	
Warrant Officer Henderson	
Warrant Officer Hinten	
Warrant Officer Riseley	
Warrant Officer Smith	
Sergeant William Derek Webster	KIA 7.6.44

Nominal roll of No. 131 Squadron pilots who flew operationally 24 May–27 August 1944:

Wing Commander Crayford	
Squadron Leader MacDougall, DFC	
Squadron Leader O'Meara, DFC and Bar	DSO 27.10.44
Acting Squadron Leader C. Rudland, DFC	
Flight Lieutenant Cecil Ernest 'Pete' Bearman	D. air accident 25.8.44
Flight Lieutenant Richard Ulick Paget de Burgh	
Flight Lieutenant Stanley Aske Catarall	
Flight Lieutenant Dicky	
Flight Lieutenant King	
Flight Lieutenant Vincent Kenneth Moody, DFC	KIA 12.7.44
Flight Lieutenant Rudland	
Flight Lieutenant J. Sowery	
Flight Lieutenant J.C. Waterhouse	'A' Flight Commander
Flight Lieutenant Woolley	
Flying Officer Atkinson	

Flying Officer John Russell Baxter
Flying Officer Edwards
Flying Officer Hirst
Flying Officer Kelly
Flying Officer L. Lackhoff
Flying Officer Maingard
Flying Officer J. Morris   KIA 17.5.44
Flying Officer R.K. Parry
Flying Officer Patten
Flying Officer C.A. Smart
Flying Officer J.C.R. Waterhouse
Pilot Officer R.P. Cross
Pilot Officer Morris
Pilot Officer A.F. Tate
Pilot Officer J.R. Wilson
Lieutenant A Hartshorne (FAA)
Warrant Officer Clatworthy
Flight Sergeant E.J. Tanner
Sergeant Williams

Nominal roll of No. 610 Squadron pilots who flew operationally April–24 May 1944:

Squadron Leader R.A. 'Dicky' Newberry, DFC and Bar
Squadron Leader John Bean 'Shep' Shepherd   DFC 12.12.44
Flight Lieutenant Brian Minden Madden
Flight Lieutenant Hugh Harold Percy   KIA 22.5.44
Flight Lieutenant John Bean Shepherd, DFC
Flight Lieutenant Ronald 'Ronnie' West, DFC and Bar   KIA 23.5.44
Flying Officer Brian Thomas Colgan   PoW 28.5.44
Flying Officer Dodson (Australia)
Flying Officer 'Tex' Donohoo
Flying Officer Robert Hussey
Flying Officer Norman Frank 'Mac Mk III' McFarlane
Flying Officer George Mercer McKinlay   KIA July 1944 (V1)
Pilot Officer L.E. Finbow
Pilot Officer Benjamin R. Scaman
Flight Sergeant Inguar Fredrik Hakansson (Sweden)   KIA 9.7.44
Flight Sergeant Harding

Nominal roll of No. 616 Squadron pilots who flew operationally 22 May–21 July 1944:

Squadron Leader Watts, DFC	K. collision with Sgt B. Cartmel 29.4.45
Flight Lieutenant Dennis A. Barry	
Flight Lieutenant Jack Cleland	
Flight Lieutenant G.C. Endersby	
Flight Lieutenant M.A. Graves, DFC	
Flight Lieutenant Clive Gosling	
Flight Lieutenant G.A. Harrison	KIA 13.6.44
Flight Lieutenant H.G. Pennick	
Flight Lieutenant Pontsoron	
Flying Officer T.Gordon Clegg	
Flying Officer Mike H. Cooper (Kenya)	
Flying Officer T.D. Dean	
Flying Officer C.K. Doughton	
Flying Officer G.N. Hobson	
Flying Officer A.G. Jennings	
Flying Officer J.F. Kistruck	
Flying Officer J.N. McJay	
Flying Officer W.H. McKenzie	
Flying Officer Miller	
Flying Officer M. Moon	
Flying Officer Prule Mullenders (Belgium)	
Flying Officer J.R. Ritch	
Flying Officer J.K. Rodger	
Pilot Officer F. Clerc (France)	Croix de Guerre (France)
Pilot Officer G.E. Prouting	KIA 22.5.44
Pilot Officer K. Ridley	
Pilot Officer A. Stodhart	
Pilot Officer I.T. Wilson	
Warrant Officer R.S. George	
Warrant Officer R.A. Hart	
Warrant Officer 'Des' Kelly	
Warrant Officer G.M. Wilkes	
Warrant Officer T. Sidney Woodacre	
Flight Sergeant V.J.T. Allen	K. flying accident 29.6.44
Flight Sergeant E.W.J. Amor	
Flight Sergeant 'Sam' Easy	
Flight Sergeant 'Eddie' Epps	
Flight Sergeant D.A. Gregg	KIA (landing) 15.8.44
Flight Sergeant F.G. Packer	
Sergeant B. Cartmel	K. collision with S/L Watts 29.4.45
Sergeant J. Ost	

Chapter 15

Post War Service and Honours

rothers' next posting saw him crossing the Atlantic as a member of the RAF
Delegation which visited Washington between 8 and 28 October 1944. On 29
October he attended a course at the US Command and General Staff School,
Fort Leavenworth, Kansas. Meanwhile, Brothers had learnt that he was to be made
a member of the Distinguished Service Order, the award being promulgated in the
Supplement to the *London Gazette* of 31 October 1944, published on 3 November:

'Air Ministry, 3 November, 1944.

'The KING has been graciously pleased to approve the following award in
recognition of gallantry displayed in flying operations against the enemy: —

'Distinguished Service Order.

'Wing Commander Peter Malam BROTHERS, DFC (37668), RAFO.

'Wing Commander Brothers is a courageous and outstanding leader whose
splendid example has inspired all. He has led large formations of aircraft on
many missions far into enemy territory. Much of the success obtained can be
attributed to Wing Commander Brothers' brilliant leadership. He has destroyed
thirteen enemy aircraft.'

The Air Ministry's records were incomplete, as Brothers' tally was actually sixteen
confirmed destroyed, one unconfirmed, one probable and three claimed as damaged.
Meanwhile, Brothers had completed an almost unprecedented forty-four month
period on operations, during four tours (875 operational flying hours). And while he
had had to nurse a damaged aircraft back on more than one occasion, Brothers never
had to abandon an aircraft.

Looking back at his wartime career Brothers was characteristically modest when
he said, 'It was a great chance to try to live up to those characters [Ball, McCudden,
Mannock, et al]. I don't think I did.'

Of course, those who served under Brothers and who owed their survival to his
tactical abilities as a flight, squadron and wing leader, would have argued differently.
One such pilot was Wing Commander R.W.F. Sampson, OBE, DFC and Bar, who
flew under Brothers as a pilot officer in No. 602 Squadron and as a staff officer, when
he hitched a ride on one of the Culmhead Wing's operations.

While flying with No. 602 Squadron he had served under Brendan 'Paddy' Finucane, DSO, DFC and two Bars, Pete Brothers, DSO, DFC and Bar and James O'Meara, DSO, DFC and Bar, of these three outstanding commanders, he rated Pete as the best. In his autobiography *Spitfire Offensive* (1994), Sampson wrote:

> 'I was very fortune to serve under three brilliant squadron commanders. When it came to leading, first his squadron and then his wing, he had what can only be described as an instinctive feel for the battle. Pete invariably led us into an advantageous position before joining combat.'

Sampson was with the squadron during the Dieppe Raid, describing Brothers' leadership on 19 August as 'exceptional', adding that, 'he was an outstanding fighter pilot with well over twenty aerial combats in which he was invariably at the right end, with the Hun at the receiving end.'

Following a fortnight at Radfel, Washington, Brothers returned to the UK, where he was sent to No. 1 Personnel Despatch Centre on 24 January 1945. Having attended a month long No. 10 Senior Commanders Course at Cranwell, commencing on 7 February, Brothers was posted to the recently established Central Fighter Establishment, under his long-time friend, Air Commodore Richard Atcherley. Here he encountered Robin Olds. The legendary USAF pilot had arrived in a Lightning twin engine fighter and, after a cup of something in the mess, they swapped aircraft so that Olds could fly a Spitfire whilst Brothers leapt into the Lightning. Pete later joked that his learning curve on multi-engine taxiing was extremely steep and he, 'counted himself fortunate not to have wiped out most of the flight line.'

One of his first duties with his new unit was taking a leading role in the Battle of Britain commemorations. Sampson recalled that in September 1945 he had landed at RAF Tangmere. Stepping into the officer's mess he found Pete Brothers having tea with a number of recently freed PoWs, including Tuck and Bader, the pilots were discussing their roles in the flypast. It was fitting that Brothers and his fellow Battle of Britain aces were to lead the first major peacetime celebration.

Despite his impeccable war record and obvious leadership abilities, both in the air and on the ground, Brothers didn't initially settle back into his RAF career. The crunch came in 1947, 'The Air Force said they wanted me to go to the Staff College in Haifa for a one year course and I said, "Not bloody likely!"'

And so, following a period of extended leave, Brothers left the RAF on 28 March 1947, joining the Colonial Service as a District Officer in Meru, in the foothills of Mount Kenya, before moving to Kisumu, on Lake Victoria, a year later. He kept his hand in, however, piloting his own aircraft, an Auster, which proved extremely useful for patrolling outlying areas and frequently flying to Nairobi, 'I had a little plane in Meru; an expensive pastime, especially on Colonial Service pay. When you joined the Colonial Service, you were allowed to buy a car because that was the only way to get around, but it was on a seven year interest free loan that was deducted from your pay, which was a very good deal. But being awkward I said, "I want an aeroplane!"'

It is a testament to his flying skills that Brothers never had a mishap on either take-off or landing, as the strip had a gradient of about one in fifteen and looked, from photographs, to have been about the same length as a cricket pitch.

Brothers would fly when he could, giving lessons, 'to help pay for it and I had a thriving little flying club'.

'I only had one false landing, bringing my daughter [Wendy] back from school [The Beehive] in Nanyuki; the engine started coughing and spluttering and while I still had some control I put it down on a bit of scrub near Narok.' They and Brothers' other passenger, Ken Hunt, were taken to the local District Commissioner's house where they spent the night. The following morning Pete borrowed a tool kit and drove back out into the bush where he fixed the aeroplane. Having made a quick air test he returned with Wendy and Ken, 'and off we went home.' Communications being somewhat lacking, his wife, Annette, had no idea what had happened to her husband and daughter. She must have been very worried, but reassured Ken's wife that, 'Pete always turned up!'

Wendy, who was then only five, recalls the incident, writing of her father, 'He would have grass airstrips cleared in the bush as necessary and was known by the locals as "Bwana Ndege" – the rough translation being "Mr Birdman!"'

Pete was great with his two daughters, and could keep them entertained with stories he made up for them, the telling of which would always include his favourite phrase, 'Lo and behold'.

When the girls were young he had a fund of memorized poems and stories which he used to recite to his daughters and these stay with them still. Some of them probably would not have made it into the nursery rhyme books of today, but they still bring a smile to their lips.

Wendy recalled an early memory: 'I was a passionate reader [from the age of seven or eight] and was allowed to read in bed before my light was turned out. My father would come up to say good night and turn out the light, which I always resisted because I could never bear to put my book down. It became a game and he would stand between me and the light and declare, "beware the Hun in the sun!" He would then remove my book and when I struggled to regain it he would pin me down under the blankets, lean over me and say, "I have the advantage of height!" To me it was just a part of the game and, as he never referred to the war or talked about it to me or my sister until we had families of our own, it was only as a mature adult that I realized these were the basic rules of engagement of every pilot who flew during the war!'

In spite of the trials and tribulations of late 1940s Kenya, it was a happy time for Brothers and his family. He had to call on all his powers of diplomacy and persuasion in administering his patch. Whilst there Brothers met Dick Abrahams near Nairobi. Abrahams was commanding a squadron of Lancasters based at Eastleigh, but had been assigned to carry out an aerial survey of Kenya. The two talked at length, Abrahams hoping to persuade Pete to re-enlist.

Hilary, Pete's youngest daughter, recalls that: 'Dick and father were to remain great friends. He had done our father a great service in getting him back into the Royal Air Force that he so loved. Dick and Joyce's daughters, Linda and Jacqui, were of similar ages to Wendy and myself and so began our lifelong friendship.'

After two years in Kenya, Pete and Annette decided it was time to return to the UK. Here their children, Hilary and Wendy, would complete their education.

When Brothers sent in his letter of resignation he was informed that, 'no-one resigned without the permission of the Colonial Secretary, Mr Creech Jones.' Brothers duly wrote back saying, 'You'd better tell this Creech fellow that I'm leaving and since I am temperamentally unsuited to the administration, I do not intend to interfere with it further.'

The reply was equally as blunt, inviting Brothers to pay back £957, the cost of the family's passage and allowances. An indignant Brothers refused to pay. And then came a letter saying, 'In view of your service to-date, you are entitled to six month's leave on full pay and a passage home'.

Brothers said that he would pick up the pay in Nairobi. The 'passage home' turned out to be a voyage on a troopship, but Pete and Annette's send-off was first class, 'I threw a big party in Nairobi for all my chums.'

Brothers applied to rejoin the RAF on 2 June 1949 and was sent first to the Holding Unit at RAF Biggin Hill, his second home. He was commissioned as a squadron leader, but with seniority from 5 August 1946, 'they invited me back and said I'd be squadron leader. They were charging me five years seniority for my two years out, which meant that when I came back all my chums who'd been junior to me were now my bosses.'

Brothers took the ruling on the chin, adding wryly, 'I never had great ambitions to be Chief of the Air Staff or anything like that. All I wanted to be was a pilot who was paid the same salary as the Chief of the Air Staff!'

Attending No. 1 Pilot's Refresher Flying Unit, Finningley, between 21 July and 19 August, Pete transferred to No. 201 Advanced Flying School on 2 August, where he remained until 11 October. Following a month at the Air Ministry under Group Captain MacGregor, Brothers was sent to No. 230 Operational Conversion Unit, RAF Scampton.

During this period Annette and the girls lived at Pitts Cottage, in Westerham, where Annette's aunt still ran her restaurant. There were also visits to Pete's parents in Prestwich Park where Wendy and Hilary recall that:

'Aunty Matty did nearly all the cooking and was a wonderful cook. I particularly remember her teas – if we were going to stay we always seemed to arrive at teatime and the table would be properly laid, with perfect sandwiches, (the bread actually cut by my grandmother who could cut the thinnest slices of anyone I have ever known!) and a mouthwatering selection of cakes – everything from fruit cakes to brandy snaps, jam tarts to macaroons.

'Aunty Matty kept all her old ball gowns and shoes, in which we were allowed to dress up – a great treat. She was one of those souls who was always on the go. I boarded at a school near Westerham for a term and I can remember Aunty Matty sending me a huge tin of her home-made fudge – I was the most popular girl in the school while it lasted – which wasn't long!

'Aunty Matty was one of the many women of the First World War generation who never married. She doted on Pete and on us.'

Nearly three years into his commission, on 1 February 1950, Brothers was given command of No. 57 (B) Squadron, flying Avro Lincoln bombers, 'I was hauled up in front of the postings Air Commodore, who had been one of my bosses in Fighter Command and he said it was time I learnt other things and he was going to post me to Bomber Command.'

Brothers was none too keen and said, 'I can't go there Sir!'

He said, 'Why not?'

Brothers replied that his hands were, 'too small for four throttles! And I'm scared of the dark!'

In a rebuff Brothers was told, 'For God's sake stop wittering and for once go and do as you are told. You are lucky that you're getting command of a bomber squadron and there aren't many squadrons flying at the moment.'

On this occasion Brothers took the advice and reported to RAF Waddington, where he assumed command from Squadron Leader R.A.G. Ellen, MBE. 'So I had a Lincoln squadron which was a lot of fun actually.'

While it went against the grain to fly as a part of a crew, Brothers was determined to make the most of the posting. Quickly mastering the multi-engine bomber, he was keen to fly in action and soon saw an opportunity, calling in a favour:

'I heard a rumour that a squadron was wanted for the Far East and so I phoned up my postings chum, who was by then deputy commander of Bomber Command and asked if it was true. He said, "Yes" and I said, "Well write 57 Squadron down in your notes will you?" and he said, "Christ Pete, you shouldn't be talking to me. You should be talking to your AOC." I said, "I don't know him Sir, but I know you! Can you speak to him for me?" He said, "You are a bloody nuisance; you always have been. I'll do what I can."'

On 2 March, Brothers attended a Squadron Commander's Conference, where he learnt that his canvassing had paid off, and No. 57 Squadron would fly 'anti-bandit' operations in the Malaya Emergency. His would be the first Bomber Command unit to be deployed in Operation Firedog:

'We were to fly out on 15 March, which meant I had thirteen days to satisfy myself that my crews had sufficient training to perform under combat conditions. Meanwhile, the ground crews had to work around the clock; all the aircraft had to have 120 [flying] hours before they were due for a major inspection.'

The squadron's six Lincoln bombers were fitted with long-range fuel tanks, while two additional aircraft were transferred from No. 61 Squadron for the duration.

Brothers' daughter Hilary remembers, 'standing in the garden of our quarters in Waddington, with my mother waving a tea towel as the squadron flew overhead on its way to Singapore.'

The first of the squadron's aircraft arrived at Tengah on 20 March 1950. Six days later SASO AHQ Malaya, Group Captain Dunn, DFC, briefed the air crews in preparation for the squadron's first bombing operation. This was launched on the 27 March, a formation of six Avro Lincolns bombing enemy positions in tight formation.

On 1 April five aircraft took off, dropping sixty 1,000lb bombs on the target area: 'which from the air amounted to little more than a patch of jungle.' The bombers made three runs before positively identifying the target area. Two further missions were flown before the month was out.

With British ground forces often operating in close proximity to the target areas, it became regular practice for a lower flying Dakota to act as spotter, fluorescent markers being used to indicate 'friendly' troop locations.

The squadron flew only eight raids during May. The bombing campaign intensified in June with a total of eighteen missions, mainly flown towards the beginning of the month and tailing off as the squadron began winding down ready to hand over the baton to No. 100 Squadron.

Their tour nearing its conclusion, the first of No. 57 Squadron's Lincolns took off on the initial leg of the return journey to Waddington, via Negombo.

On 10 June, a formation of six Lincolns, three drawn from each squadron, took part in a bombing mission. In the absence of No. 100 Squadron's CO, Squadron Leader G.D. O'Brien, Brothers led the operation, but the Brigade was still in the target area and Brothers had to make a second run.

The squadron was addressed by C-in-C FEAF, Air Marshal Sir F.J. Fogarty, KBE, CB, DFC, AFC, on 27 June, congratulating them on their success in the campaign and the high standard of serviceability maintained during their time in the Far East.

Over the following days and weeks the squadron's aircraft and personnel were ferried back to the UK, the eight bombers between them clocking-up 239 hours and 54 minutes flying time during the return journey.

Back at Waddington a number of key personnel were granted leave during August. Those aircrew who had been attached to the squadron for the Malaya campaign returned to their own units. Meanwhile, the following communication had been received, commending Brothers and those under his command:

'From: HQ FEAF To: HQ Bomber Command. Dated: 30 June:

'For C-in-C from C-in-C
'No. 57 Squadron leave here within the next few days and I should like to take this opportunity of expressing my appreciation of the magnificent way in which they have carried out their task in this campaign.

'Since the first day of their arrival all ranks have shown the greatest enthusiasm and energy. This is in large measure due to the very able leadership of their commanding officer, Squadron Leader Brothers, DSO, DFC.

'The high rate of aircraft serviceability reflects the greatest credit on maintenance crews often working in extremely difficult climatic conditions. Similarly armament staffs as usual have worked like Trojans.

'No. 57 Squadron have indeed set a very high standard in squadron efficiency and, if I may say so, one which Bomber Command may well be proud.'

A provisional list of pilots and aircrew who flew operationally with No. 57 (B) Squadron (including aircrew who were attached to the squadron during the Malaya operations):

Pilots:
Squadron Leader P.M. Brothers DSO, DFC and Bar
Flight Lieutenant J.R. Cox
Flight Lieutenant Lang
Flight Lieutenant Scott
Flight Lieutenant Sinclair, AFC
Flight Lieutenant Viner
Flying Officer Gaywood

Flight Sergeant Warwick
Flight Sergeant Herbert
Sergeant Hedges
Sergeant Hudd
Sergeant Steed
Sergeant Whitaker
Sergeant Kidd (spare crew)

Flight Engineers:
Flight Lieutenant Cairns
Flight Lieutenant Cole
Flight Lieutenant Welsh
Flight Sergeant Buchanan
Flight Sergeant McEwan
Flight Sergeant Robinson
Flight Sergeant Rowe
Sergeant Arnold
Sergeant Lowery
Sergeant Oxenford
Sergeant Pountney
Sergeant Stalker

Navigator/Bomb-aimer:
Flight Lieutenant Ford
Flight Lieutenant Trotter
Flight Lieutenant Webb
Pilot Officer Webster
Sergeant Boyko
Sergeant Doyle
Sergeant Law
Sergeant Martin
Sergeant Walton

Navigators:
Flight Lieutenant Collard
Flight Lieutenant Garfit
Flight Lieutenant Mortimore
Flight Lieutenant Peasley
Flight Lieutenant Smythe
Flight Lieutenant Webb
Flight Lieutenant E.S. Welsh
Pilot Officer Iwachow
Flight Sergeant Collins

Sergeant Blicq
Sergeant Brown
Sergeant Buchan
Sergeant Cook
Sergeant Domican
Sergeant Holland
Sergeant Stevens
Sergeant Storey
Sergeant Walsh

Signallers:
Flight Lieutenant J. Carruthers
Flight Lieutenant Meeghan
Flight Lieutenant Thomson
Flight Lieutenant Williams

Mid-upper Gunners:
Flight Lieutenant Langston
Flight Lieutenant McDonald
Flight Lieutenant E.S. Roberts
Flight Sergeant Anderson

Flight Sergeant Evans

Flight Sergeant Hewitt

Flight Sergeant Judge

Flight Sergeant Walker

Sergeant Hoptroff

Sergeant Pringle

Flight Sergeant Law

Sergeant Dougherty

Sergeant Fenn

Sergeant Hough

Sergeant Stirk

Rear Gunners:

Flying Officer Thornley

Flight Sergeant Miles

Flight Sergeant Mantle

Sergeant Booth

Sergeant Cawkwell

Sergeant Edge

Sergeant Law

Sergeant Leeder

Air Gunners:

Flight Lieutenant Mitchell

Flight Sergeant Oram

Sergeant Erasmus

Sergeant Firth

Sergeant Holtham

Sergeant Ibbotson

Sergeant Powell

MG Tupper

Brothers recalled that, 'We came back from Malaya and re-equipped with B39 Washingtons; beautiful aeroplanes. [The] engines weren't much good though, but they flew happily on three or two so…'

Brothers had settled into the command, despite his initial reservations. However, nothing remained as it was for long in the Services and he soon found himself in a new role. Having been posted away from No. 57 Squadron to serve on the HQ Staff of No. 3 (Bomber) Group, Mildenhall, on 29 October, Brothers was promoted to the rank of Wing Commander on 2 July 1952. Between 11 January and 10 December 1954, he attended No. 44 Course, RAF Staff College, Bracknell, before joining the Air Staff at HQ Fighter Command, Bentley Priory the following year.

Pete's eldest daughter, Wendy, recalls that her paternal grandfather passed away suddenly while spending time with Pete, Annette and the family at Mildenhall in 1953:

'It came as a great shock for us all, especially my grandmother. The family suffered a further loss about a year later, with the death of Pete's Aunty Matty. Pete's Uncle Vince (his mother's brother) took over Westfield and my grandmother came to live with us at Stanmore.'

Wendy recalls her school holidays at about this time: 'Father always had time to read to us and play with us, even to the extent of rushing round the married quarters, joining in a game of Cowboys and Indians. He didn't care about what people thought; off duty he was a family man and not a wing commander with a string of medals to his name.'

On 10 June 1957 he was sent to RAF Coningsby, where he attended No. 232 Operational Conversion Unit, undertaking a course on Valiant bombers. Brothers returned to Bomber Command as Wing Commander (Flying) RAF Marham,

Norfolk, on 2 January 1958. Here he led the RAF's first 'V'-Bomber Wing, equipped with the Vickers Valiant, 'I went to Staff College from Bomber Command and then back to Fighter Command through Meteors, Hunters and then back to Bomber Command on the V-Force with Valiants, which was quite exciting.'

Also stationed at Marham were Wing Commander Ken Rees and his wife, Mary. Mary was Annette's cousin and, as they were both only children, they were very close. Ken served in Bomber Command during the war, was shot down and ended up in Stag Luft III in November 1942. He was one of the 'Great Escapers' and was fortunate in being still in the tunnel when the alarm was sounded. Had he escaped and subsequently been rounded up, he would most certainly have been shot. Ken's autobiography *'Lie in the Dark and Listen'* relates his experiences in Stalag Luft III, Sagan, and his role as a tunneller and the true story of the Great Escape.

As Group Captain, Brothers served on the staff of the Exercise Section Atomic at Supreme HQ Allied Powers Europe (SHAPE) in Paris from 15 May 1959. On 17 September the following year, Brothers joined the staff at Operations Branch, SHAPE. He later recalled arranging for his team, which included Americans and Germans, to fly by Dakota to Farnborough to take in the Air Show. During the flight a German colonel was acting as co-pilot, 'My deputy [a USAF officer] crept up behind him and shouted, "Achtung! Spitfire!" Which he took very well; took it on the chin.'

There was no animosity between fellow aviators, particularly the RAF and former Luftwaffe pilots, as Brothers recalled:

'When we were having drinks in the RAF Club, the bar was humming with people and the German Colonel turned to me and said, "Is zis ze club where only ze member can buy ze drinks?" I replied in the affirmative. He said, "Could you arrange for me to buy ze drinks for everybody?" I asked, "Why?" The former Luftwaffe pilot said, "Well, I can go home and say alone, I made it!" And so I approached the barman. "Don't report this! The Colonel is allowed to buy a drink." He bought a drink for everyone in the room, bless him. He was good value.'

Brothers' next posting, which came on 30 July 1962, was to the Air Ministry as Deputy Director of Operations (Air Defence and Overseas), Whitehall, while on 12 February he was given command of RAF Boulmer. On 11 October 1965, Brothers was appointed Air Officer Commanding, Military Air Traffic Operations, Uxbridge, being promoted to Air Commodore on 1 July the following year.

Brothers' continued faultless service during the post-war era was to earn him further recognition. He was appointed a Commander of the Order of the British Empire (CBE) in the 1964 Queen's Birthday Honours.

Meanwhile, Brothers was made a Freeman of the Guild of Air Pilots and Air Navigators in 1966 and was a member of its technical committee and of its court. He was elected Master of the Guild in 1973-74. It was a role he relished, and he threw himself into his year in office, which included a trip to Australia and the chance to meet former members of his RAAF Squadron.

In 1968, Brothers received his final posting, embarking on a five-year appointment as the RAF's Director of Public Relations, Ministry of Defence, Whitehall. With the world still in the grips of the Cold War, this job, which involved guiding and advising defence correspondents, was particularly demanding. His success in winning the respect of the media was due in part to his outstanding war record, but also to his skills as a communicator. This was helped in no small measure by his abilities as a raconteur, marked by his self-effacing humour.

On retiring from the RAF on 4 April 1973, Annette's birthday, Brothers established Brothers Consultants Ltd, of which he was Managing Director (1973-86).

It seemed only natural to Brothers that he should become an advocate for the pilots and ground crews who helped save the Free World at its darkest hour. Brothers was particularly mindful of those who never lived to see the final victory, and worked tirelessly to help keep their memory alive. Pete had remained close personal friends with many of the men who he served alongside, particularly those with whom he had shared the dangers of aerial combat. He gave great support to the Battle of Britain Fighter Association, being appointed its deputy chairman in 1993 and taking over as chairman ten years later. As with everything he gave it his all. Brothers brought to the post his enthusiasm, along with his endearing nature and great sense of fun. As ever, he led by shining example, becoming a great stalwart of reunions and commemorative events, ever mindful of the obligation he felt to his fellow members and those who had not survived the battle. Reunions were never a sombre affair with him at the helm. Ceremonial occasions brought Pete into the company of first, Her Majesty The Queen Mother and later Prince Charles, as Patrons of the Battle of Britain Fighter Association. A staunch Royalist and an admirer of the late King and his Queen during the war, particularly during the London Blitz, Pete was thrilled to be able to play host. He shared in the Royal Family's grief at the loss of Queen Elizabeth The Queen Mother, and he in turn was touched in later years by a personal letter from Prince Charles on the death of his beloved Annette.

A key supporter of the Battle of Britain Memorial Trust, Brothers campaigned for the monument on the Thames Embankment. Meanwhile, in recognition of his leadership of No. 457 (RAAF) Squadron, he was invited to become patron of the Spitfire Association of Australia. He also served as president of his local branch of the Air Crew Association at Hungerford, Berkshire.

When it was announced that RAF Bentley Priory, Fighter Command's headquarters during the Battle of Britain, was to close in 2008, he threw himself behind the campaign to save the historic building, going on record as saying: 'This is our [the RAF's] home, as HMS *Victory* is for the Navy.'

It is perhaps fitting that his last event as Chairman was at Bentley Priory, a venue that had a special place in his heart. Sadly, Pete passed away before the official opening of the museum he and his fellow Fighter Command veterans had championed, but he was ably represented by his daughters. Wendy commented: 'Hilary and I were immensely proud when Prince Charles quoted Peter, by name.' The Prince had earlier sent a letter of condolence on hearing the news of Pete's death, a kindness which greatly touched his daughters.

An inveterate cigar smoker and a connoisseur of malt whisky, Brothers was a keen golfer, sailor and fisherman, and of course, a popular raconteur who could hold an audience in the palm of his hand with anecdotes from a flying career which had spanned over thirty years, from 'string-bags' through to the 'V'- bombers.

In late 2003, Brothers was approached to take part in a four-part series made by RDF Media for Channel 4. '*Spitfire Ace: Flying the Battle of Britain*' saw four pilots, including members of the Armed Services, compete for selection to undergo nine hours flying time (the average time flown on type by the pilots who came through the OTU system in time for the latter phases of the Battle of Britain) on a Spitfire. It did not escape Brothers' notice that the pilot who eventually won the competition was from his own 'home' of Manchester.

The first programme of the series featured interviews with a number of former Battle of Britain pilots, including Brothers. Pete featured on the cover of the book which accompanied the series, and it was he who was chosen to fly with Carolyn Grace in her two-seater Spitfire (No. ML407).

Both Wendy and Hilary recall what a thrill it was for their father to be involved in the filming of the programme and to fly in ML407, the only surviving Spitfire to have flow on D-Day operations, recording the first 'kill' during the liberation of Europe. Brothers had, of course, led the Culmhead Wing over those same beaches. 'Pete and Carolyn got on famously.' Carolyn Grace later did Pete the great honour of performing a flypast in ML407 at his funeral, a fitting tribute and something for which his family will be forever grateful.

Brothers leapt at any opportunity to fly, even well into his late eighties, and demonstrated that he had lost none of his piloting skills. Brothers used to fly occasionally with his friend Robert 'Robs' Lamplough, who owned a Russian Yak 18. The pair had first met at the Battle of Britain 60th Anniversary Dinner held at Bentley Priory. The organizers had invited a number of owners and fliers of Spitfires and Hurricanes to the gathering. The modern day pilots were liberally dispersed amongst the Battle of Britain pilots and air crew seated for dinner. Sitting next to a bemedalled Brothers was Robs, 'I recall our first meeting very well for one very amusing coincidence. I happened to keep a Spitfire hangered and operating from my farm which was some 800 yards from the back door of Peter's new home. We were immediate neighbours, but this was not known by Peter or myself at the time.

'One of the first things I asked him was as to where was he now living? The reply, "We have just moved to a small village in West Berkshire." I asked him how did he find being there, his immediate reply was that it was ideal since there were big fields directly behind the house and that this was ideal for walking his dog each day. He had of course been using my fields for his morning exercise.'

Naturally Pete and Robs struck up a great friendship, sharing anecdotes, 'Over the years he told me many stories on flying including the last flights that he made in Griffon-engined Spitfires, circa 1955 in Malaya, from near Kuala Lumpa down to Singapore, in order that they could be serviced. At that time he was commanding a squadron of Lincoln bombers from the same base where the Spits were based.'

As ever though, Brothers was reticent when it came to saying anything about his combat years, preferring to extol the virtue of others, as Robs recalls, 'Pete had a fine recollection of all his years in the RAF. I particularly remember him telling me about the debriefing of the famous German fighter pilots at the time of the termination of hostilities in 1945. He had enormous respect for the likes of Adolf Galland. Hans Ulrich Rudel, the famous Stuka pilot and holder of the Knights Cross was, however, insistently arrogant according to Peter.'

Rudel had boasted to Brothers that if they gave him a fighter he could take on any number of Allied aces and shoot them all down in flames. Brothers did not take well to such comments, which belittled the achievements of others, especially given that they were made by a pilot of dive-bombers, Knights Cross or no Knights Cross!

Brothers kept his logbook up, adding details of his civilian flights. Wendy notes that against the Yak 18A (G-BMJY), he would comment in his logbook that it had 'very twitchy controls.' Once in flight Robs would hand over the controls to Brothers, who knew just how to get the most flying time out of any journey. When asked to 'take us home' by Robs, he managed to find the most scenic route, although he never failed to locate Robs' airstrip, no matter how long the detour.

Robs recalls their flights together, 'I flew several times with Pete, firstly in my Russian Yak 18A G-BMJY, he was very willing to take the controls and of course course flew impeccably. On one occasion we visited the former home of Ian Fleming of James Bond fame. Today the house is owned by Paddy McNally; he was giving a party on the eve of the British Grand Prix. We landed in the front garden.

'Paddy had asked me to give a flying display in my Spitfire the following day so I decided to have a practice in the Yak after we had had tea. I remember how game Pete was and I told him to let me know if he was uncomfortable at any time. Needless to say there was not the slightest squeak from Pete. He had gone through a complete Air Show routine and at that time he must have been about 90-years-old. We returned to my farm in West Berkshire with Peter piloting and navigating all the way without a map!'

It was Robs who pulled a few strings and had managed to arrange for Brothers to get some airtime with British Aerobatic Champion Nigel Lamb. It was on 13 August 2000 that Brothers took to the air in the Pitts Special. His logbook noted 'Self – Aerobatics. A perfect a/c looped and hit slipstream after all these years, roll left good, roll right abysmal. Flight was thirty minutes.'

Hilary recalls the events as though they were yesterday, 'His joy when he flew the aircraft and looped the loop and came back down into his own slipstream had to be seen! I think his feet were actually off the ground when he walked into his house to greet us with a, "Did you see me?" As if we would not have bothered to watch!'

While living in West Berkshire, Brothers was able to try his hand as a helicopter pilot, as Robs recalls, 'The only time I can remember Pete not being keen to take the controls was when Pete, as the President of the Battle of Britain Fighter Association, had to go to Bentley Priory and I decided to take him up there in the Gazelle helicopter. He found the power controls a little twitchy and soon handed back the stick.'

Brothers' last flight was in 2004 at the Brimpton Fly In, when he was offered a seat in a Messerschmitt Me 108 trainer, from a small airfield in Berkshire. Once airborne it very quickly became apparent that Brothers had lost none of his flying skills, even if his reactions might have slowed a little with the passage of time. Taking the controls, he put the trainer through its paces. Mid-flight, Pete's fighter-pilot instinct kicked in and he couldn't resist lining up in his sights the Piston Provost piloted by Alan House, which had Pete's son-in-law, Chas Cairns, in the second seat. Chas recalled that upon landing Pete climbed out and, fixing him with a steely eye said, 'I shot you down.' Chas later joked, 'I suppose that I was his last "kill". I didn't even know that hostilities had been declared!'

The pilot who had so generously agreed to take Brothers up was thrilled to have shared the flight with one of his life-long heroes. He was heard to comment to a friend afterwards that Brothers' signature in his logbook was worth more than the Me 108. Chas recalls, 'There was a wry humour all round when he was advised that he had better fly in another aircraft before he died.'

Sadly, it was not to be.

Another of Brothers' loves was driving. And like many former fighter pilots from the era of open cockpit flying, he enjoyed the feel of speed. Chas recalled, 'Ever the fighter pilot, Pete would drive with what one might call verve. On one memorable trip to Devon we were greeted on arrival by Annette, who pressed a large scotch into my hand with the words, "I know you need this." She was right; 120mph on the off ramp of the motorway had jarred my nerves a little. His favourite overtaking manoeuvre was to swoop to within gun harmonization range – about ten feet, then, having shot the blighter down, swing out and roar past. Fine on a motorway, but a little unnerving on a Devon country road!'

When he wanted to relax, however, Brothers took to the water. While living in retirement in Devon, Brothers purchased a boat. He would set off on adventures with a somewhat reluctant Annette as crew. Brothers' son-in-law, Mark Wallington, remembers sailing off round to Dartmouth, Brothers and his friend Roy Fuller, with pipes clamped in their teeth, each offering him advice on how best to steer to make the course. When the wind did not blow they would happily motor and trail a line and the bucket, which, it seemed, had held pink gin, and was now filled with mackerel. Those were happy days.

Another of Brothers' pastimes was golf and he became an avid player. He bought his son-in-law Chas his first set of golf clubs, 'Once I had acquired a reasonable level of skill, he took me out with his golfing friends for a round of golf. The oldest of the group was ninety and a bigger bunch of bandits you will never meet, which meant that I parted with money at every game! Pete's fund of stories and jokes meant that he was a great golfing companion and I enjoyed several rounds with him.'

Brothers always loved dogs. His first two were bull terriers, Merlin, who was acquired the year he married Annette and who finished his days in Kenya, and Kali, who arrived when Brothers was posted to Mildenhall. In his retirement he took on a waif and stray mongrel whom he christened Spindle. They became inseparable, which meant that he would take long walks along the canals of Devon, helping him keep fit. Moving up from Devon to Eastbury in West Berks, to be nearer their daughters Wendy and Hilary, Brothers and Spindle had extensive fields to the rear of the house in which to enjoy country walks. After the demise of Spindle, Brothers maintained his interest sponsoring two wolf cubs at the nearby Wolf Conservation Trust.

In 2005 Pete lost Annette, his wife, confidant and best friend of sixty-six years. The couple had always been extremely close. 'They', as Pete described it, 'were a team.' Annette was an accomplished hostess, imperturbable in most situations, even when during the Battle of Britain, Pete arrived back at their hiring, RAF pals in tow, and swung open the front door to find Annette having a bath in a tub in front of the fire. As Pete used to joke, 'I made the big decisions, like which fighter the Air Force should buy, whilst she chose where we lived, and where the girls were to be schooled.' Pete and Annette had four grandchildren and two great-grandchildren. They were immensely proud of them all and naturally their grandchildren adored them. Pete never really recovered from his loss. He adapted a couple of lines from a poem which somehow summed up his grief: 'She first deceas'd – he for a little try'd, to live without her, lik'd it not and dy'd.'

Deprived of his greatest love, Brothers threw himself into projects supporting his old RAF pals and keeping their memory alive in whatever way he could. Often interviewed on all matters relating to the battle, and a regular attendee at Battle of Britain commemorative events in his latter years, Pete astounded many journalists and aviation enthusiasts with his infectious enthusiasm and energy, 'People say to me, "You seem pretty fit, despite your age."'

Always quick-witted, he would reply, 'Yes; I've got the secret! Cigars, whisky and wild women, but I've run out of wild women so I need more cigars and whisky!'

Brothers was described by friend and fellow aviator 'Laddie' Lucas as 'one of those distinctive Fighter Command characters, full of bonhomie, humour and decorations, who made light of the serious things, no matter what his innermost thoughts.'

Pete Brothers died on 18 December 2008 following a lifetime of distinguished service to his country. As ever, he had planned ahead and left his own epitaph thus:

"A Lancashire man with an old-fashioned sense of right and wrong, an innocent belief that virtue will prevail, and truth will triumph in the end."

Bibliography

Arthur, Max, *Last of the Few: The Battle of Britain in the Words of the Pilots who won it*, Virgin Books, 2010

Bingham, Victor, *Blitzed: The Battle of France May – June 1940*, Air Research Publications, 1990

Bishop, Patrick, *Fighter Boys: Saving Britain 1940*, Harper Perennial, London, 2003

Bishop, Patrick, *Hurricane*, Airlife, 1986

Buckton, Henry, *Voices From the Battle of Britain: Surviving Veterans Tell their Story*, David & Charles, 2010

Cooksley, Peter G., *The Story of No. 11 Group, Fighter Command*, Robert Hale, London, 1983

Cull, Brian et al, *Twelve Days in May*, Grub Street, 1995

Dalton-Morgan, Group Captain Tom (with Clive Williams), *Tommy Leader: Group Captain Tom Dalton, DSO, OBE, DFC & Bar*, Griffon International, 2007

Deere, Group Captain Alan, DSO, OBE, DFC, *Nine Lives*, Cornet Books, London, 1959

Foreman, John, *Fighter Command War Diaries Volume One: September 1939 to September 1940*, Air Research Publications, 1996

Foreman, John, *Fighter Command War Diaries Volume Two: September 1940 to December 1941*, Air Research Publications, 1999

Franks, Norman L.R., *RAF Fighter Command Losses of the Second World War: Volume I 1939-1941*, Midland Publishing Ltd, 1997

Franks, Norman L.R., *RAF Fighter Command Losses of the Second World War: Volume 2 1942-1943*, Midland Publishing Ltd, 1998

Franks, Norman L.R., *RAF Fighter Command Losses of the Second World War: Volume 3 1944-1945*, Midland Publishing Ltd, 1997

Gelb, Norman, *Scramble: A Narrative History of the Battle of Britain*, Michael Joseph Ltd, London, 1986

Knight, Dennis, *Harvest of Messerschmitts; The Chronicle of a Village at War – 1940*, Frederick Warne (Publishers) Ltd, 1981

Ogley, Bob, *Biggin on the Bump*, Froglet Publications, 1990

Price, Alfred, *The Longest Day: 18 August 1940*, Macdonald and Jane's, London, 1979

Ramsey, Winston G., *The Battle of Britain Then and Now*, After the Battle Magazine, 1980

Sampson, R.W.F., *Spitfire Offensive*, 1994

Sarkar, Dilip, *Battle of Britain: Last Look Back*, Ramrod Publications, 2002

Sarkar, Dilip, *Last of the Few*, Amberley, 2010

Shores, Christopher, *Aces High*, Grub Street, London, 1994

Shores, Christopher, *Those Other Eagles*, Grub Street, London, 2004

Stewart, Adrian, *Hurricane: The War Exploits of the Fighter Aircraft*, William Kimber, London, 1982
Stokes, Doug, *Wings Aflame: The Biography of Group Captain Victor Beamish, DSO and Bar, DFC, AFC*, Crecy Publishing Ltd, 1985
Wallace, Graham, *RAF Biggin Hill*, Putnam & Co Ltd, 1969
Wynne, Kenneth G., *Men of the Battle of Britain*, Gliddon Books, Norwich, 1989

Original Documents
Operational Record Books (all in Air 27) and Combat Reports (all in Air 50) viewed in microfilm form at The Public Records Office, Kew: Nos. 32, 41, 57, 79, 111, 126, 131, 133, 145, 165, 222, 257, 263, 307, 401, 457, 485, 602, 603, 610, 611 and 616 Squadrons

Civilian and RAF Logbooks belonging to Air Commodore Pete Brothers, CBE, DSO, DFC and Bar

Correspondence with:
Air Commodore Pete Brothers, CBE, DSO, DFC and Bar
Wing Commander D. H. Grice, MBE, DFC
Wing Commander T. F. Neil, DFC and Bar, AFC
Squadron Leader T. G. Pickering, AE
Wing Commander J. Rose, CMG, MBE, DFC

Index